Oracle Press™

GW00370844

Oracle Application Server 10g Administration Handbook

ORACLE®

Oracle Press™

Oracle Application Server 10g Administration Handbook

John Garmany
Donald K. Burleson

McGraw-Hill/Osborne

New York   Chicago   San Francisco
Lisbon   London   Madrid   Mexico City   Milan
New Delhi   San Juan   Seoul   Singapore   Sydney   Toronto

The McGraw·Hill Companies

McGraw-Hill/Osborne
2100 Powell Street, 10th Floor
Emeryville, California 94608
U.S.A.

To arrange bulk purchase discounts for sales promotions, premiums, or fund-raisers, please contact
McGraw-Hill/Osborne at the above address. For information on translations or book distributors outside the
U.S.A., please see the International Contact Information page immediately following the index of this book.

Oracle Application Server 10g Administration Handbook

34567890 CUS CUS 0198765

ISBN 0-07-222958-6

Publisher
  Brandon A. Nordin

Vice President & Associate Publisher
  Scott Rogers

Acquisitions Editor
  Lisa McClain

Project Editor
  Emily Rader

Acquisitions Coordinator
  Athena Honore

Technical Editors
  Brian Conneen
  Peter Farkas

Copy Editor
  Judith Brown

Proofreader
  Linda Medoff

Indexer
  Jack Lewis

Composition
  Apollo Publishing Services
  Peter F. Hancik

Illustrators
  Kathleen Fay Edwards
  Melinda Moore Lytle

Series Design
  Jani Beckwith
  Peter F. Hancik

Cover Series Design
  Damore Johann Design, Inc.

This book was composed with Corel VENTURA™ Publisher.

To my parents, John and Carole Garmany
John Garmany

For Janet, the love of my life
Don Burleson

About the Authors

John Garmany is a graduate of West Point and a retired Lt. Colonel with more than 20 years of IT experience. John is an OCP-certified Oracle DBA with a Masters degree in Information Systems, a Graduate Certificate in Software Engineering, and a B.S. degree in electrical engineering from West Point. A Senior Consultant with Burleson Enterprise, Inc. and author of *Oracle Replication: Snapshot, Multi-master & Materialized Views Scripts* (Rampant TechPress, 2003), John can be reached at john.garmany@computer.org.

Don Burleson is one of the world's top Oracle Database experts, with more than 20 years of full-time DBA experience. He specializes in creating architectures for very large online databases, and he has worked with some of the world's most powerful and complex systems.

A former Adjunct Professor, Don Burleson has written 32 books, published more than 100 articles in national magazines, and serves as Editor-in-Chief of Oracle Internals, Senior Consulting Editor for DBAZine, and Series Editor for Rampant TechPress. Don is a popular lecturer and teacher and is a frequent speaker at OracleWorld and other international database conferences.

As a leading corporate database consultant, Don has worked with numerous Fortune 500 corporations, creating robust database architectures for mission-critical systems. Don is also a noted expert on e-commerce systems and has been instrumental in the development of numerous web-based systems that support thousands of concurrent users.

Don's professional web sites include www.dba-oracle.com and www.remote-dba.net.

Contents at a Glance

Contents

Acknowledgments

riting this book was a learning experience that allowed me to meet some of the real people that make the Oracle Application Server the great product that it is. Any time you work with beta software, you run into frustrating problems. I especially want to mention the help I received from Pete Farkas and Brian Conneen, who installed the original beta and were part of the team that provided the technical review of the chapters. I also want to thank Lisa Goldstein for her help during the entire process of writing the book. Oracle had members of the Application Server team on both coasts review the chapters of this book, and their comments and suggestions were invaluable. Most of the team I never got to meet, but they added immensely to the quality of this book. To the entire Oracle Application Server team, I thank you for your support and help, and for producing a great product.

Thanks also to the incredible McGraw-Hill/Osborne team. Special thanks to Lisa McClain and Athena Honore, who had to guide me through the production process and put up with all the missed deadlines. A special thanks to Emily Rader and Judith Brown, who did an incredible job editing my poor writing. You guys are great.

Finally, I want to thank the team at BEI who had to pick up the extra work and put up with me during the writing of this book. Thanks for all the support.

John Garmany

Introduction

he Oracle Application Server 10*g* is a large and complicated product that is hard to learn and sometimes confusing to use. With capability comes complexity. Many times we find clients that are improperly using their application server because they don't understand what each component does. More importantly, we find that the administration and support for the application server fall on the shoulders of the company DBA because it is an Oracle product. Many DBAs know what Java is because it goes in the database (somewhere, somehow), but that is the extent of their knowledge. The Application Server documentation is thousands of pages long and must cover every possible configuration of a component. As such, it is a bit overwhelming when trying to find specific information. The goal of this book is to provide the bases for anyone, from a Java developer to an Oracle DBA, to install and administer the Oracle Application Server 10*g*. Key to meeting this goal, we cover some critical tasks such as installation, performance tuning, and backup and recovery. We also explain the capability of each component of the Application Server and how it is used.

Even though the focus is on administration, some development topics are briefly introduced in the discussion of some of the Application Server components. However, this book does not cover either J2EE or Portal development. Those tasks are covered in detail in other Oracle Press books.

We tried to cover each component in a single chapter so that you could refer directly to that chapter for a needed component. Some chapters refer you to other chapters for additional information on specific topics. If you are new to Java and J2EE, you will need to read Chapter 6 to understand how the Application Server 10*g* supports J2EE components and APIs.

Lastly, one of the most annoying habits of computer books is to tell you what to do, without explaining how to do it. We have made every effort to detail the "how" in Oracle Application Server 10*g* administration.

CHAPTER
1

Oracle Application
Server 10g
Architecture and
Administration

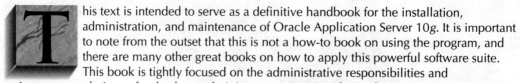his text is intended to serve as a definitive handbook for the installation, administration, and maintenance of Oracle Application Server 10*g*. It is important to note from the outset that this is not a how-to book on using the program, and there are many other great books on how to apply this powerful software suite. This book is tightly focused on the administrative responsibilities and maintenance techniques for database administrators using Oracle Application Server 10*g*.

Because Oracle has consolidated many software products under the umbrella of Application Server 10*g*, there has been widespread confusion about its scope and functionality. To a web developer, Application Server 10*g* is Oracle Portal and Oracle Web Cache, while to a developer, it is J2EE and OC4J. However, most users agree that the core functionality of the program is the support for Java development.

In order to properly administer Application Server 10*g*, you must first understand all of its components and how they fit together. Like any enterprise-wide solution, the components of the program are the result of an evolutionary process, with new subproducts being added as the software evolves. Because Application Server 10*g* is a broad offering of many tools, your particular functionality may be vastly different depending upon the way you have installed and configured the software. This chapter covers the following topics:

- Overview of the architecture

- Functional components

- Introduction to administration

Let's begin with a review of the Application Server 10*g* architecture and a look at each functional component.

Architectural Overview

Beginning with their WebServer product in the 1990s, Oracle has continuously improved and streamlined its products into a comprehensive solution for web-based applications.

Application Server 10*g* is the latest incarnation in a long evolution of application products. Starting in the mid-1990s with Oracle WebServer and Oracle Application Server, Oracle Application Server has evolved into an extremely sophisticated system of interrelated modules, all of which can be configured according to your specifications. There are two ways to view the architecture of Application Server 10*g*—from a design level and from a functional level. Both are based on a multitiered model.

The Multitiered Model

As Oracle products evolved into a multitiered architecture, we started to see Oracle products reside at several *tiers*, or layers, that represent hardware layers, with each tier made up of one or more servers (Figure 1-1). Because of the flexibility of Application Server 10*g*, Oracle shops can adopt a two-tiered, three-tiered, or four-tiered model. As a general rule, the larger the system, the more levels and more servers there will be at each level. Application Server 10*g* components reside at each of these layers in a four-tiered architecture.

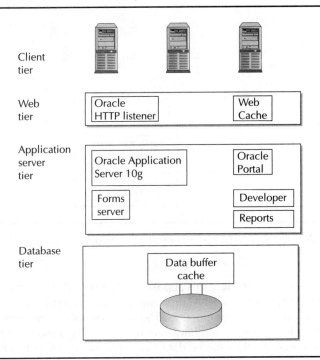

FIGURE 1-1. *Oracle application tiers and component products*

Application Server 10*g* components reside at each of these layers:

■ **Client tier**   Contains the web browsers for end users

■ **Web tier**   Contains the Oracle HTTP Server and the Web Cache

■ **Application server (app server) tier**   Contains the core Application Server 10*g*, plus ancillary products such as Oracle Application Server Portal 10*g*, Oracle Developer, Oracle Reports, and Oracle Forms Server

■ **Database tier**   Contains the core Oracle Database, which may be a single instance or many instances defined to a Real Application Cluster (RAC)

Not all shops will use all four tiers. Smaller shops commonly combine tiers into the same level. For example, in a three-tiered architecture, the web tier and app server tiers can be combined. Remember, most large four-tiered systems will have many servers at the web tier, dozens of application servers, and many Oracle instances (using Real Application Clusters) at each node. Also, one or many components may run on any number of servers, and small Oracle shops (or those with huge 16 CPU servers) may combine all three tiers onto a single server. The choice of the number of tiers is directly related to the size of the Oracle 10*g* implementation and the number of servers that are dedicated to the system.

For small shops, it is common to see a two-tiered data model. Figure 1-2 shows an example of the client tier consisting of all the external PC clients and a combination of the web server tier, the app server tier, and the database tier, all running on a large single server, usually with lots of

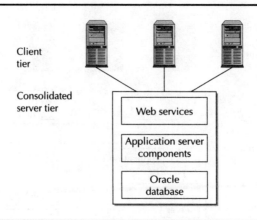

FIGURE 1-2. *Application Server 10g architecture for a two-tiered system*

RAM and multiple CPUs. The benefit of this approach is the shared server resources. The single server can supply additional CPU and RAM processing according to the specific demands of each of the Application Server 10*g* components. The downside of the two-tiered architecture is the limited flexibility. It is not easy to add hardware resources when you need them.

In medium-sized shops, the three-tiered data model predominates. In this model, shown in Figure 1-3, the client tier is followed by the web server tier and app server on separate servers.

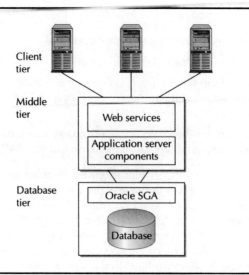

FIGURE 1-3. *Application Server 10g architecture for a three-tiered system*

The database tier is also separated onto a different server, thereby providing isolated data resources for the Oracle Database. The three-tiered data model has a few benefits over the two-tiered model. First, increases in processing demands either at the database or the app server level will not affect the performance of the other components within the Application Server 10*g* architecture. Another benefit is that additional Application Server 10*g* instances can be created, and additional Oracle System Global Area (SGA) regions can be easily added when processing demands warrant an increase.

Now that you've seen the components of each tier, let's examine how these tiers look when used in a large e-commerce system.

Hardware Architecture of Application Server 10*g*

Figure 1-4 shows that you can have multiple instances of the components at each tier. In this example, you see two sets of Oracle HTTP Servers (OHS), each listening on a different port for incoming database requests. As requests enter the system, OHS passes them to the least-loaded Application Server 10*g* instance on the app server tier.

At the app server tier, there may be multiple instances of Application Server 10*g* and multiple instances of the Oracle Forms Server, Oracle Developer, and Oracle Reports. These multiple instances are normally on separate servers, and this provides administrators with the ability to create an infinitely scalable architecture. Whenever any components at any tier become overwhelmed, administrators can create a new instance on a new server, add the instance into the Application Server 10*g* architecture using Oracle Universal Installer, and maintain it using the Enterprise Manager.

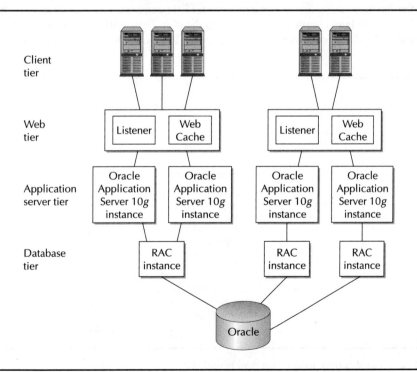

FIGURE 1-4.   *Application Server 10*g* tiers and instances*

The Application Server 10g instances will connect to the database tier. For very large systems, Real Application Clusters (RAC) provides the ability to have multiple instances of the database, all mapping to a single database. Using the same technique as the other tiers, whenever the existing instances become overloaded, another Application Server 10g instance can be created on a new server, and the server can be added to the architecture.

This ability to scale by adding new instances and servers is a critical aspect of Application Server 10g administration because it is the single most important tool for ensuring that the system always has adequate hardware resources.

Functional Architecture of Application Server 10g

Now let's look at the same architecture from a functional perspective. Figure 1-5 shows the functions of the instances at each level, and this should give you an idea about how the multitiered architecture is used to isolate the logical components of the application.

At the web tier, the main functions are the listener, which listens on a specific port for incoming requests; Web Cache components, which store web page components; and the load-balancing mechanism for ensuring optimal allocation of computing resources to the app server tier. The web tier is managed by the Oracle HTTP Server, which is based on the Apache web server.

The app server tier controls all of the business logic and content assembly. Components such as Oracle Portal are used to define web page components, Oracle Reports defines content specifications, and Oracle Single Sign-On (SSO) controls security for the app server layer. At the database tier are the standard Oracle data management functions for the storage and retrieval of application data. All the components running on the application tier can connect to and retrieve data from the database using any of the available J2EE database connection methods. These are discussed in detail in later chapters. However, Application Server 10g may have its own database if you install the Application Server 10g Infrastructure. With Infrastructure, an Oracle Database

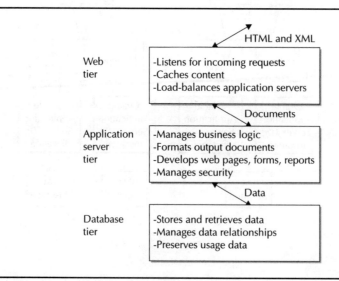

FIGURE 1-5. *Application Server 10g functional tiers*

instance called iasdb manages Application Server 10*g* components and security, and preserves its usage data.

Now that you understand the Application Server 10*g* architecture from a high level, let's take a closer look at each of these tiers and see how they interact with each other.

Client Tier

The client level consists of either a Java client application or a web browser. Using a web browser as the client allows the entire application to be located on the server. The client always gets the latest version when the application starts. Also, the client can use any web browser from any location, provided that the client can connect to the application server. The client tier can also consist of an application running on the client's desktop (usually presenting a rich user interface) and connecting directly or through HTTP to the application server. This requires that the client have the application installed on the desktop.

Web Tier

The web server layer contains two important components, the Oracle HTTP Server (OHS) and Web Cache component (Figure 1-6). This tier is responsible for managing incoming HTTP requests, caching web messages, and sending XML and HTML back to the client.

Let's take a closer look at the components inside the web tier.

Oracle HTTP Server (OHS)

All Oracle web systems must have enough listener processes so that a single port is not overwhelmed with incoming requests. The Oracle HTTP Server is a component of Application Server 10*g* that listens on a specific port and forwards J2EE incoming requests through mod_oc4j to the least-loaded OC4J container. It is imperative that the web servers have load-balancing intelligence so that a single OC4J container is not overloaded with work. Oracle has addressed

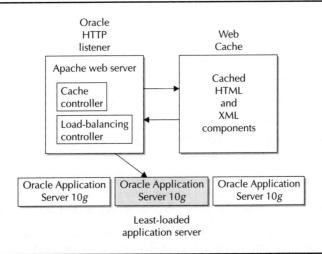

FIGURE 1-6.   *The Application Server 10*g *web tier*

this issue by incorporating the open source Apache product into the Oracle HTTP Server and providing the load-balancing capability to the mod_oc4j module. This makes customization quite easy.

Another huge benefit of the web listener load balancing is that you can customize the Web Cache to load-balance multiple Oracle HTTP Servers, thereby improving scalability. When the existing app servers become overwhelmed, more app servers can be easily added to the architecture.

It is the job of the web servers to manage the flow of the HTML and XML. On the incoming end, the web server validates and parses incoming XML strings. For outbound transactions, the web server takes data from the application server and creates the outbound HTML pages or XML strings. When an incoming transaction requests services, OHS either serves the HTML page or forwards the transaction to an OC4J container where the appropriate component (JSP engine, servlet, or Enterprise JavaBean) services the request.

Web Cache

The Application Server 10*g* Web Cache significantly enhances performance by reducing the need to regenerate dynamic or static information. The Web Cache is positioned in front of the HTTP server and stores both static and dynamic web content. It has a number of unique features, including partial-page caching, content-aware web server load balancing, the ability to cluster Web Caches so that multiple caches operate as a single logical cache, and the ability to cache content from third-party servers such as Sun, IBM, BEA, and others. Internal Oracle tests reveal that adding the Application Server 10*g* Web Cache to a three-tiered application (client, application server, and database tiers) can reduce the load on the database back end by 95 percent. The Web Cache feature has a dramatic impact on the ability of the application to scale to meet growing e-commerce demands.

Now, let's drill-down and examine the central tier, the app server tier.

App Server Tier

The core of Application Server 10*g*, along with a host of other tools and products, is in the app server tier. The central components are the Application Server 10*g* instances, and these instances support the Oracle Containers for Java (OC4J). The OC4J container hosts the application's Enterprise JavaBeans, providing security, naming, and connectivity support. In addition to the Application Server 10*g* instances, the app server tier contains separate components for the following functional areas:

- **Oracle Portal** This component allows for the fast definition and deployment of a dynamically created content-based web site.

- **Oracle Discoverer** This component allows for the easy end-user query implementation.

- **Oracle Forms Server** This component is used to format, deploy, and render end-user presentation pages, based on data in an Oracle Database.

- **Oracle Personalization** This component provides personalized URL referrer tracking and a facility for creating customized web pages, depending upon the user and his or her web page viewing history. The web page history is kept in Oracle Databases.

- **Oracle Wireless** This component allows for communications between Application Server 10*g* and wireless devices such as PDAs and cell phones. Wireless dynamically reformats information to display correctly on the limited screens of most wireless devices.

- **Oracle Reports Server**   This component allows for the fast deployment of reports, documents, and spreadsheets, all using data from the Oracle Database.

- **Single Sign-On (SSO)**   This is a complete authentication system for identifying users, managing roles and web services, as well as functionality for Java and portal security.

- **Oracle Internet Directory (OID)**   This LDAP-compliant directory service provides centralized storage of information about users, applications, and resources in your enterprise.

- **Metadata repository (Infrastructure)**   This critical component is sometimes referred to as the Infrastructure. It stores Application Server 10*g* metadata and allows for a common management interface between multiple instances of Application Server 10*g* and its other components.

- **Oracle Management Server (OMS)**   This component of the Enterprise Manager console allows for managing the Application Server 10*g* instances, databases, and other applications.

- **Oracle Application Server TopLink**   This component provides object persistence for Java information. TopLink contains the mapping interfaces to translate the Java structures into relational tables, thereby making Java persistent across independent executions.

These components are partitioned within the Application Server 10*g* app server layer, allowing administrators flexibility in the creation of multiple Application Server 10*g* instances.

Partitioning with Farms and Clusters
Application Server 10*g* provides several levels of collections within the App Server layer:

- **Instances**   An *instance* is defined as a collection of processes required to run a component within an application server instance. An instance is made up of one or more Java containers and the structure needed to support them. The Application Server 10*g* Infrastructure is an instance with a supporting database to store metadata.

- **Clusters**   A *cluster* is an arbitrary collection of instances that are part of the same farm and also share a common configuration and J2EE applications.

- **Farms**   A *farm* is a collection of instances and clusters that make up your Application Server 10*g* system and share a common repository infrastructure.

In sum, a farm is any related group of Application Server 10*g* instances sharing a repository, while a cluster must share a common definition and J2EE applications (Figure 1-7). Any Application Server 10*g* architecture may have many farms and many clusters defined within the system.

Application Server 10*g* Clusters   As just defined, a cluster is a collection of Application Server 10*g* instances that share identical configuration parameters, application deployment schemes, and J2EE applications. Clusters are used to enforce heterogeneity within the Application Server 10*g* instances. Hence, additions are commonly made to clusters when processing demands require additional Application Server 10*g* instances in order to manage an increased demand at the application server level. Instances in a cluster are managed by the Application Server 10*g* Infrastructure, which provides an easy method for creating and maintaining clusters.

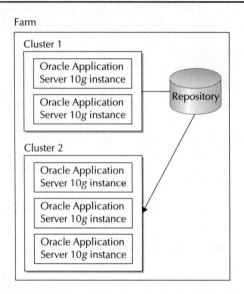

FIGURE 1-7. *Application Server 10g farms and clusters*

Clusters are used in conjunction with the Web Cache load-balancing algorithms, such that the load balancing at the Web Cache layer monitors all of the Application Server 10*g* instances in the clusters, and feeds work to the least-loaded Application Server 10*g* instance. Note that only J2EE and Web Cache components can be clustered, and that clusters must host a common set of J2EE applications.

Application Server 10*g* Farms   There is an important one-to-many relationship between an Application Server 10*g* instance and a metadata repository. Each Application Server 10*g* instance may have one, and only one, metadata repository, while each metadata repository may service many Application Server 10*g* instances.

From the Application Server 10*g* architecture point of view, a farm is a collection of Application Server 10*g* instances that all map to the same metadata repository. Because each Application Server 10*g* instance within a farm must contain the same metadata repository, all instances within the farm must share the same configuration and application membership information.

Database Tier

The standard Application Server 10*g* relational database (or any other database) resides in the database tier. The function of the database tier is to provide the application with persistent storage. The Application Server 10*g* also contains a special instance called the Infrastructure that uses a 10*g* database to store metadata. This database is more correctly in the application server tier since it does not provide persistent storage for the application. The application server provides a method to place the Infrastructure database schema into a database in the database tier; however, best practices will still recommend that the Infrastructure database support only the infrastructure and be separate from the customer database for performance reasons.

The following components have a tight integration with the Oracle Infrastructure database:

- **Oracle Application Server Portal**   Web screen component definitions are stored inside the Oracle Infrastructure database.

- **Oracle Reports**   Report specifications are stored inside the Infrastructure database.

- **Oracle Application Server Discoverer**   Discoverer metadata is stored inside the Infrastructure.

- **Oracle Application Server Personalization**   The Infrastructure database is used to store consumer group information and historical page viewing (referrer statistics) information.

Component Overview

Now that you have an overview of the architecture of Application Server 10*g*, let's continue our tour with a review of the components. Not all shops will have all of these components installed, but Application Server 10*g* allows for any or all of them to be created inside the architecture.

Application Server Portal

Like the non-Oracle tools such as Dreamweaver and Microsoft FrontPage, Portal allows developers to create and deploy web content. The important difference is that developers can include dynamically created, personalized web pages from multiple data sources using Portlets. The Portal product provides the following features:

- Portal page creation, management, and maintenance

- Assembly of web content from multiple sources using Portlets

- Web page content that contains data retrieved from a database

- Publishing facilities using easy wizards

- Advanced features such as text searching (via Oracle Text) and wireless support via XML and HTML interfaces

These components fit together into an architecture that allows developers to quickly create and deploy web page content. Figure 1-8 depicts a Portal administrator defining the Portlet content and the content for the basic web pages. At run time, Portal users access these definitions to create dynamic publishing content, using the Portlet definitions, the web page definitions, and data from the Oracle Database.

It is beyond the scope of this book to examine all of the content delivery features of Oracle Application Server Portal. For complete information on using Portal, see *Oracle9i Application Server Portal Handbook* by Vandiver and Cox (McGraw-Hill/Osborne, 2001).

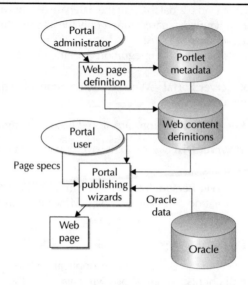

FIGURE 1-8. *The Application Server Portal 10*g *architecture*

Application Server Discoverer

This component allows for the easy end-user query implementation. In essence, Discoverer is an ad hoc query, reporting, analysis, and web publishing tool. Like Crystal Reports and Business Objects (commercial products that generate SQL queries from a graphical display, making database querying possible for those who do not understand SQL syntax), Discoverer provides a GUI metaphor for the specification of Oracle Database content and display format.

In addition, Discoverer is a business analysis intelligence tool, with interfaces with Oracle Clickstream and the Oracle Database. When using Discoverer, the end user develops workbooks. At a high level, a *workbook* is a bundle of metadata that includes the following components:

- Tables that participate in the query

- Report formatting for the result set

- Calculations to perform on the data

Once defined, these workbooks allow inexperienced end users to easily create ad hoc reports against the Oracle Database using the Discoverer End-User Layer (EUL) graphical user interface. In addition, Discoverer allows end users to view data at several levels, drilling down to more detail or rolling up to summary level.

As you see in Figure 1-9, there are two main phases in Discoverer usage. First, the Discoverer administrator creates the workbooks by specifying the tables, formatting, and computation rules for any given report. Second (the run-time phase), the end user accesses the EUL and creates customized reports using the Discoverer wizards.

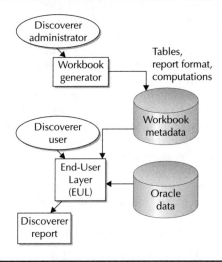

FIGURE 1-9. *Application Server Discoverer 10g architecture*

The core of administration for Oracle Discoverer is the development and maintenance of the workbooks and metadata objects. For example, each time an end user runs a report, Discoverer refers to the eul_qpp_statistics metadata table in the infrastructure to produce a time estimate for the report. For more details on the administration and use of Discoverer, see *Oracle Discoverer Handbook*, by Armstrong-Smith and Armstrong-Smith (McGraw-Hill/Osborne, 2000).

Oracle Forms Server

An evolution of the Oracle SQL*Forms application development tool, the Oracle Forms Server was originally used to render screen display from Oracle content. Enhanced to provide support for HTML, Oracle Forms Server is now used within Application Server 10*g* to render web pages that include Oracle Database content.

Because the Forms Server is the main engine for rendering web pages, tuning and administration of this component are critical aspects of overall Application Server 10*g* administration. We will discuss Oracle Forms Server administration and tuning in more detail in Chapter 10.

Application Server Personalization

Analyzing page viewing behavior and creating custom web page content on a busy e-commerce site constitute a formidable computing challenge. To address these issues, Oracle has developed the Oracle Application Server Personalization 10*g* and the Oracle Data Mining suite. Personalization is extremely sophisticated and relies on internal data about end-users' web page visits, web page clicks, and referrer statistics. Even more powerful, Personalization allows for the incorporation of external metadata such as customer demographics. It is worthwhile to note that Oracle has several competitors in the web personalization market, notably Blue Martini, Vignette, and Personify.

The goal of Personalization is to accurately identify classes of end users and correlate their behavior with the behavior of other known groups of end users. Using sophisticated multivariate correlation techniques, web page contact can be customized according to predictions about each end user's preference for web page content. The nature of this analysis is very resource intensive, and almost all large Application Server 10*g* shops devote large servers exclusively to developing these predictive recommendations.

IT marketing professionals know that it is critical to get the right products onto a custom web page. To be successful, Application Server 10*g* must be able to accurately predict a user's propensity to buy a product, based on prior buying and browsing patterns, and buying patterns of like-minded customers (customer profiling). The challenge in developing these predictive models is accurately placing visitors into consumer groups. A *consumer group* is a group of customers with similar demographics and buying patterns.

Figure 1-10 shows the process of analyzing demographic information to place visitors into consumer groups. A visitor can be placed into a consumer group in two ways:

■ Demographic category (collected from personal information)

■ Pattern of page views (collected from referrer URLs)

Once consumer groups have been defined in Personalization, you next start a data mining procedure to correlate the patterns of each consumer group with specific products. The customized HTML personalization is based on data from three sources:

■ **Known consumer group data** These groups consist of predetermined summaries of consumer group characteristics.

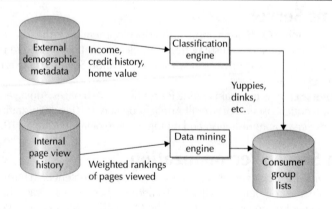

FIGURE 1-10. *Architecture of Personalization*

- **Weighted rankings of pages viewed**   This is a measure of the popularity of product pages according to each consumer group.

- **Historical data**   This is historical sales data, correlated by consumer group.

Personalization uses these sophisticated consumer group and data mining component mechanisms to create the web content (Figure 1-11). The administration of Personalization is simplified by using the Personalization GUI, and the Oracle documentation has an excellent discussion of Personalization administration.

Oracle Application Server Wireless

This component allows for wireless communications between remote wireless servers and the Application Server 10*g* architecture. The core of Oracle Application Server Wireless 10*g* is the use of XML communications. Wireless transforms XML data into whatever markup language is used by the wireless system, including standard HTML, Wireless Markup Language (WML), and other special wireless markups such as VoiceXML and HDML. This allows the application to generate one set of XML data that is reformatted for the presentation device, be it a cell phone, personal digital assistant (PDA), or pager.

Wireless communications with Oracle is becoming commonplace because of the ubiquitous nature of Internet service providers creating wireless infrastructures (mostly in major cities). Within these areas, Wireless can be used to establish direct communications with Application Server 10*g* using a standard J2EE and XML communications model. Wireless has the benefit of isolating the database communications from the complexity of the wireless protocol by encapsulating the communications into a separate, intermediate layer.

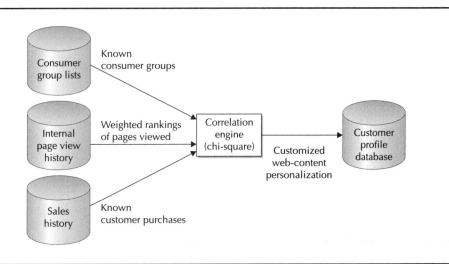

FIGURE 1-11.   *The Oracle Application Server Personalization 10*g *engine at run time*

This is one of the most exciting components of Application Server 10*g* because it holds the promise for wireless voice communications with Oracle Databases. This technology could bring millions of end users into far closer contact with their valuable data.

Oracle Reports Server

This component allows for fast deployment of reports, documents, and spreadsheets, all using data from the Oracle Database. To achieve this function, the Oracle Reports Server must interface with an Application Server 10*g* instance (and Portal) to manage the incoming report requests and send the completed reports back to the requesting user. To understand the Oracle Reports Server, let's take a simple example and follow the report steps (Figure 1-12).

■ **Invocation** The Reports Server is invoked via the end user entering a URL (or clicking a link on a web page).

■ **Routing** The Application Server 10*g* instance intercepts the HTML or XML request and directs the request to the Reports CGI (or Reports servlets).

■ **Request validation** Oracle Reports then parses the HTML or XML request and determines the report and the security rules for the report. If secure, Oracle Reports sends an HTML page back to the end user to accept a username and password.

■ **Execution** The verified request is then queued for execution in the Reports Server. Note that you can configure multiple run-time engines for each Reports Server.

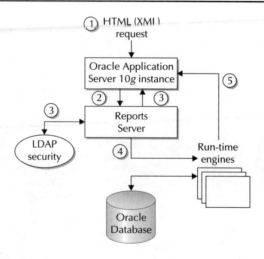

FIGURE 1-12. *The Application Server Reports Server 10*g *at run time*

- **Formatting**   Upon completion of the execution, the Reports Server formats the output as HTML and forwards the completed report to the Application Server 10*g* instance.

- **Delivery**   The Application Server 10*g* instance then completes the request by sending the completed report to the end user.

Single Sign-On (SSO)

With Single Sign-On, a client can sign onto the application once and be automatically authenticated for other components within the application server, as well as to external applications if properly set up. SSO provides a central authentication repository rather than having a separate authentication for each application on the server. SSO uses the Infrastructure instance to validate users as they move from application to application without forcing them to reauthenticate.

The SSO component interacts with the Oracle HTTP Server (OHS) and allows the formatting of Single Sign-On information as an open source Apache header. Note that SSO only functions within the domain of your Oracle system. Many distributed e-commerce systems communicate with third-party portals, and SSO cannot be extended to service these external clients. For example, an Oracle e-commerce site might need to process a payment request with Cybercash, and Cybercash would require its own independent SSO mechanism. Hence, many Application Server 10*g* administrators must develop XML Data Type Definition (DTD) protocols for communication with external third-party systems.

We will discuss SSO and other components of Application Server 10*g* security in great detail in Chapter 12.

Oracle Internet Directory

The Oracle Internet Directory (OID) is a Lightweight Directory Access Protocol (LDAP) directory service that provides centralized storage of information about users, applications, and resources in your enterprise. Coupled with SSO, OID allows end users to sign on one time and use their predefined OID credential (set up by the DBA). This credential defines those components of Application Server 10*g* with which the end user is allowed to interface.

Because it is LDAP-compliant, OID can be viewed as a simple lookup mechanism for web services. For example, LDAP entries can be used instead of entries in the traditional tnsnames.ora file, thereby allowing connectivity for clients anywhere on your network. This technique has replaced the obsolete Oracle*Names tool as a method for defining services for Oracle.

In sum, OID is an easy-to-configure tool for defining end-user access with Application Server 10*g*. Because it is tightly coupled with SSO and advanced security, OID is a critical component of Oracle security management. OID is managed with a GUI called Oracle Directory Manager (ODM). We will discuss this tool for managing data access rules in great detail in Chapter 12, along with other security topics.

Metadata Repository (Infrastructure)

The metadata repository is a critical component of Application Server 10*g* because it allows for a common management interface between multiple instances of Application Server 10*g* and the other components. The metadata repository is commonly referred to as the Infrastructure, which is common to all Application Server 10*g* farms and components that share a common definition. We will discuss the Infrastructure in great detail in Chapter 3.

Oracle Management Server (OMS)

With the Oracle Management Server, administrators can include the Application Server in a centrally managed configuration using Oracle Enterprise Manager (OEM--a separate product). OMS is a component of the Oracle Enterprise Manager console, used to manage Application Server 10*g* instances, databases, and other components. The foremost feature of OMS is its ability to store OEM data inside the metadata repository. This storage ability of OMS allows administrators to share server configuration information, scheduled events and jobs, and notifications of failures. To start OMS, you use the emctl command and issue the emctl start oms command to start the web servers and OMS processes.

Because OMS is the "glue" that binds all of the Application Server 10*g* components together, we will be visiting OMS functionality throughout this book. OMS provides the important functions of user administration, and manages the flow of information between the OEM console and all managed nodes. OEM allows for any server to become a managed node by installing an Oracle intelligent agent (OIA), thereby making it accessible with the central administrative GUI. An OIA is a daemon process that interfaces with the database and operating system on each server within each Application Server 10*g* farm. The intelligent agent performs localized execution of tasks as directed by the OMS, and for Oracle servers, the OIA performs time-based database monitoring. The concept of managed nodes adds power to OEM, allowing the Application Server 10*g* DBA to quickly apply configuration changes to many server components.

TopLink

For Java developers, TopLink provides a mechanism for making Java objects persistent across sessions. In object-oriented (OO) languages such as Java, C#, or C++, objects can be instantiated and destroyed according to the needs of the program.

The problem is that OO languages like Java create objects in the RAM heap, and upon termination of the program, all of the program's objects are destroyed. Oracle Application Server TopLink 10*g* is a persistence framework that enables object persistence by supplying routines that can be invoked to store Java objects in relational database tables (in any relational database that supports JDBC). In addition, TopLink provides a GUI tool, the Mapping Workbench, that greatly simplifies the task of mapping Java objects and their attributes to database tables. TopLink also provides powerful features like a query framework, object-level transaction support, relationship mappings, object caching, and much more. Prior to TopLink, the programmer would have to write custom JDBC code to store and retrieve the Java object's attributes to/from a relational table. This is not only extremely time consuming and error prone but also difficult to change. TopLink is built on top of JDBC but does not require developers to use JDBC (or even SQL!). TopLink supports all J2EE-compliant application servers, and can be used to store object data from standard Java objects, as well as entity beans. Please refer to the Oracle Application Server TopLink 10*g* documentation for more information.

Oracle Application Server 10*g* Administration

Unlike an Oracle Database, which has only a few administrative interfaces (OEM, SQL*Plus), Application Server 10*g* has many administrative utilities. To make matters even more challenging, these administrative tools are often tightly coupled, as in the case of the Application Server 10*g* Web Cache administration pages and the Oracle HTTP Server administration pages. Both of these administrative interfaces are separate, yet they are closely intertwined in the architecture.

Application Server 10*g* provides two methods for administration, the command-line interface and Oracle Enterprise Manager. This book will show both methods, and the choice of Application Server 10*g* administration methods is largely up to the individual.

We will start with a review of each administrative component and then look at using OEM and the command-line interfaces within each component.

Administrative Component Overview

As an Application Server 10*g* administrator, it is your job to become intimate with all of the management components. Of course, your shop may not have some of the optional components, such as Single Sign-On, but it is imperative that you understand the administrative components and how they fit together. This section will review the general administration tools, Web Cache administration tools, and application layer administration tools.

General Administration Components

Here are the main administrative interfaces for the Application Server 10*g* Infrastructure:

■ **LDAP Server (OID)**   This is the Oracle Internet Directory (OID) component of Application Server 10*g*. The LDAP server is the foundation of the automated provisioning methodology, and administrators must manage the LDAP repository (the directory) to maintain user-access privileges.

■ **Single Sign-On (SSO)**   The SSO component provides for centralized management among all of the Application Server 10*g* components. Large shops may have dozens of components, and SSO allows for easy password management and access control.

■ **Metadata repository (isadb)**   The isadb is an Oracle database that stores configuration information and metadata. This includes data used by LDAP, OMS, and SSO.

■ **Mod_osso module**   This provides communication between the SSO-enabled login server and the Oracle HTTP Server (OHS) listener. The mod_osso module is controlled by editing the mod_osso.conf file.

Web Administration Components

From the top down, the web server component (Web Cache and OHS) is one of the most important components of Application Server 10*g*, and one where tuning is vital. For details on Application Server 10*g* Web Cache and Oracle HTTP Servers, see Chapter 10.

■ **Oracle HTTP Server (OHS)**   This is the HTTP listener software that intercepts incoming requests and routs them to the appropriate Application Server 10*g* component. Upon completion of the transaction, the OHS sends the completed HTML or XML back to the originating IP address.

■ **Web Cache**   This component is associated with an OMS instance and server to provide RAM caching for images (GIFs and JPEGs), as well as page content. The Web Cache and the OHS are closely coupled, and tuning the Web Cache is addressed in Chapter 10.

Application Management Components

Moving down the Application Server 10*g* hierarchy, you next see the administrative tools for application development, primarily for Java applications. Administrators must use these interfaces to ensure optimal configuration of their systems.

- ■ **J2EE server (OC4J)**   This component allows you to deploy and manage Java-based applications. Administrators must configure the J2EE server to ensure proper communications between OC4J and other Application Server 10*g* components.

- ■ **Oracle Process Manager and Notification (OPMN)**   OC4J is started and managed with OPMN, which is also responsible for monitoring all Application Server 10*g* processes and propagating configuration changes across clusters.

- ■ **Distributed Configuration Manager (DCM)**   DCM is a handy command-line utility that can be used instead of the GUI for starting and stopping Application Server 10*g* services.

Command-Line Interfaces or OEM?

As we have already noted, administrators have two choices for managing Application Server 10*g*—the OEM console GUI or the command-line interfaces. Using the OEM console, the GUI will issue the appropriate commands without your having to memorize the syntax. On the other hand, many experienced Application Server 10*g* administrators find that the command-line interface offers a full range of administration commands.

Of course, some tasks must be done from the command-line interfaces. For example, you cannot use OEM until the OMS is started, so you must issue the emctl start oms command before you can use OEM. Internally, it makes no difference whether you use OEM or a command line utility to manage Application Server 10*g*. This is because the OEM console uses DCM (the dcmctl utility) to make configuration changes, and to propagate configuration changes and deployed applications across the cluster.

CAUTION
If you use the Infrastructure and you manually edit the configuration files, you may introduce corruption into the Infrastructure. This is true for both v9.0.2 and v9.0.3. Be sure to shut down the Enterprise Manager web site (emctl stop) before using dcmctl to change configuration. If/when both are used "at the same time," there is a strong possibility that the Infrastructure data may become corrupted, and you may have to reinstall Application Server 10g. The dcmctl-updateConfig command can be used to notify the environment that config files were updated so that the changes are properly picked up. This requirement will be referenced throughout the book.

Let's start with a quick tour of OEM for Application Server 10*g* and then review the command-line interfaces.

Managing Application Server 10*g* with Enterprise Manager

The Enterprise Manager console is the central management component for Application Server 10*g*. From a page of the EM central console, you can manage most of the areas of Application Server 10*g* on multiple servers.

If you have installed the Infrastructure component of Application Server 10*g* (iasdb database repository), then the default EM console page will be the EM Farm page. The Farm page is the highest level of the EM pages and is used to administer all instances within your Application Server 10*g* configuration. Let's quickly review the component hierarchy from the bottom up:

- ■ **Instances** Each J2EE app server or infrastructure is called an instance (not to be confused with an Oracle Database instance, which is quite different).

- ■ **Clusters** A cluster is an arbitrary collection of instances.

- ■ **Farms** A farm is a collection of instances and clusters that make up your Application Server 10*g* system and share a common repository database (iasdb).

Each farm may have many clusters, each cluster may have many instances, and each instance may have many Application Server 10*g* components. It is your job as the administrator to configure your components, instances, clusters, and farms according to the processing requirements of your application.

The purpose of the EM Farm page is to serve as the master console and display summary information about each instance and cluster within the farm (Figure 1-13).

Remember, each instance within the Farm page is an independent J2EE app server or an infrastructure, and the Farm page allows you to drill-down and see the details for each instance using the EM Instance Manager page. Using the EM Farm page, you can also define new clusters and assign instances to clusters. In Application Server 10*g* parlance, a "standalone" instance is a J2EE app server, belonging to a farm, which has not been assigned to a cluster. A cluster is two or more identically configured app server instances. To assign an instance to a cluster, you simply choose it and click the Join Cluster button.

Next, let's step down one level and look at what you see when you drill-down into an instance and see the EM Instance Manager page.

Instance Manager Home Page

Instance Manager is somewhat of a misnomer. To Oracle DBAs, an instance is a running Oracle Database, while to Application Server 10*g* administrators, an instance refers to a J2EE app server or an infrastructure within their Application Server 10*g* farm.

For each instance, the Instance Manager page allows you to manage all of the Application Server 10*g* components. When you select a server from the OEM Farm page, you get the Instance Manager page with details on all components on that server (Figure 1-14). The top of the page displays the host name and status of the server. You also see CPU and RAM memory usage for the server. The bottom half of the page shows all of the Application Server 10*g* components on that server.

For each component, you see the current status (up or down), the start time for the component, and the relative amount of CPU and RAM usage for each component. By selecting a component and clicking the management buttons, you can start, stop, enable, disable, and configure each component on the instance. Let's take a look at the links on this page.

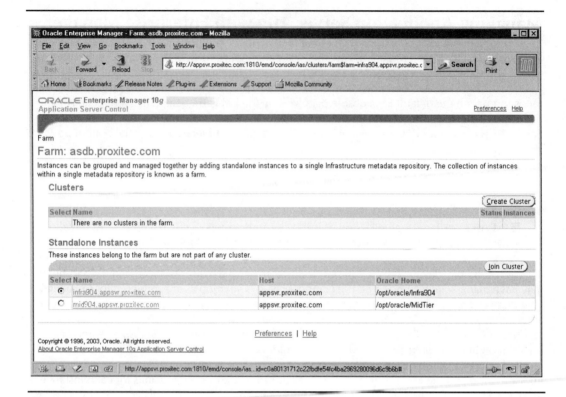

FIGURE 1-13. *The main Enterprise Manager console screen*

- **Infrastructure button** The Infrastructure link allows you to associate Application Server ("instances") components with database schemas. This includes associating a component to a schema in a database that is not in the farm's infrastructure. This allows you to share schemas across instances that do not belong to a particular farm.

- **Logs button** On the top right of this page, you can click the Logs link to see all of the log files for each component.

- **J2EE deployment button** In the Home tab, you can click J2EE Applications to see a list of all J2EE applications that are deployed on this server.

- **Ports button** This link displays the port numbers for each server component and allows you to change the port number for any component on the instance (server).

Managing Application Server 10*g* with Command-Line Interfaces

Many experienced Application Server 10*g* administrators prefer to use the command-line interfaces instead of EM. Remember, at the lowest level, EM generates the commands and

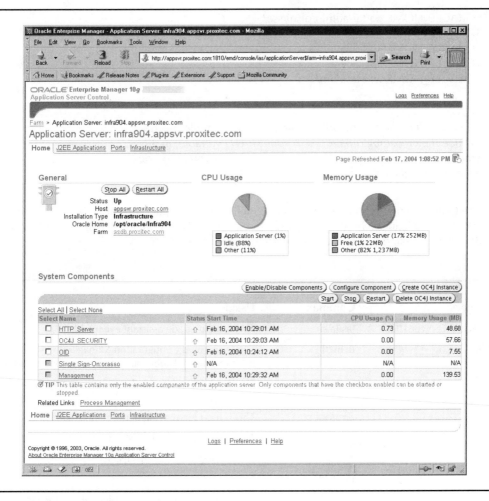

FIGURE 1-14.   *The EM console Instance screen*

parameters for Application Server 10g control files, and knowledgeable administrators already know the commands and parameters.

The command-line interfaces are spread across many file locations, and you will find Application Server 10g command-line programs in the following directories on your operating system:

$ORACLE_HOME/bin/
$ORACLE_HOME/dcm/bin/
$ORACLE_HOME/j2ee/home/
$ORACLE_HOME/ldap/bin/
$ORACLE_HOME/ldap/odi/admin/
$ORACLE_HOME/oca/bin/
$ORACLE_HOME/opmn/bin/

```
$ORACLE_HOME/portal/admin/plsql/sso/
$ORACLE_HOME/sso/lib/
$ORACᴵE_HOME/uddi/lib/
$ORACLE_HOME/upgrade/
$ORACLE_HOME/wireless/bin/
```

NOTE
To locate all of the command-line programs, you should always include the preceding directories in your $PATH variable. In UNIX, you can place in your .profile the ksh command (if you are using the Korn shell) or the csh command (if using the C shell).

The Oracle command-line utilities will be mentioned throughout this text, but let's just take a quick tour so you can see how they are used to manage Application Server 10*g*. Table 1-1 shows all 59 of the command-line executables with Application Server 10*g*.

Category	Command	Usage
Application Server 10*g*	iasua.sh	This is the upgrade assistant executable.
DCM	dcmctl	The Distributed Configuration Manager is for managing Application Server 10*g* components.
Discoverer	eulbuilder.jar	This is the Discoverer end-user layer Java command-line interface.
DMS	dmstool	This is used for viewing performance metrics.
Forms	fplsqlconv90	This is used to update PL/SQL for Forms6i.
Forms	ifbld90	This is used to start Forms Developer.
Forms	ifcmp90	This starts the Forms Compiler.
Forms	iff2xml90	This will traverse a module object hierarchy and produce an XML representation.
Forms	ifweb90	This allows you to preview a form in a web browser.
Forms	ifxml2f90	This will take a Forms XML format and convert it back into a module.
Forms	ifxmlv90	This is the XML validator to validate .xml files against the Forms XML Schema.
J2EE	ojspc	This is the JSP back precompiler.
J2EE	admin.jar	This tool is only used in the sample OC4J standalone installation. Do not use this command.

TABLE 1-1.   *Application Server 10g Command-Line Utilities*

Category	Command	Usage
J2EE	jazn.jar	This JAR file manages both XML-based and LDAP-based JAAS data.
LDAP	ldapadd	This is the OID add utility for adding entries, their object classes, and attributes.
LDAP	ldapaddmt	This is just like ldapadd, but with support for multiple threads for adding entries concurrently.
LDAP	ldapbind	This determines whether you can authenticate a client to a server.
LDAP	ldapcompare	This compares your attribute values with an OID entry.
LDAP	ldapdelete	This removes entries from OID.
LDAP	ldapmoddn	This modifies the DN or RDN of an Oracle Internet Directory entry.
LDAP	ldapmodify	This modifies OID attributes.
LDAP	ldapmodifymt	This modifies several OID entries concurrently.
LDAP	ldapsearch	This will search and retrieve specific OID entries.
LDAP	bulkdelete.sh	This deletes a whole OID subtree.
LDAP	bulkload.sh	This creates OID entries from data residing in or created by other applications.
LDAP	catalog.sh	This will add and delete OID catalog entries.
LDAP	hiqpurge.sh	This moves OID changes from the human intervention queue to the purge queue.
LDAP	hiqretry.sh	This moves OID changes from the human intervention queue to the retry queue.
LDAP	oidstats.sh	This analyzes Operational Data Store (ODS) schema objects to estimate statistics.
LDAP	remtool	This is used with an OID replication failure.
OCA	ocactl	This is the Certificate Authority administration tool.
OEM utility	emctl	This starts, stops, and manages security for OEM.
OID	bulkmodify	This will modify a large number OID entries.
OID	dipassistant	This is used with the Oracle Directory Integration and Provisioning platform.
OID	ldifmigrator	This is used to migrate data from application-specific repositories into OID.

TABLE 1-1.   *Application Server 10*g *Command-Line Utilities* (continued)

Category	Command	Usage
OID	ldifwrite	This converts OID data to LDIF and makes that information available for loading into a new node in a replicated directory or into another node for backup storage.
OID	oidctl	This will start and stop Oracle Internet Directory.
OID	oidmon	This manages OID processes.
OID	oidpasswd	This changes the OID database password.
OID	oidprovtool	This is used to administer provisioning profile entries in OID.
OID	oidreconcile	This synchronizes OID entries.
OID	resetiASpasswd.sh	This resets the internal password that instances use to authenticate themselves with OID. It resets the password to a randomly generated password.
OID	schemasync	This synchronizes schema elements between OID and third-party LDAP directories.
OID	stopodis.sh	This starts the directory integration and provisioning server without using the oidctl executable.
OPM	opmnctl	This will start, stop, and get status on OPMN-managed processes. This is the main tool for starting and stopping an instance.
OSSA	ossoca.jar	This configures additional languages for Application Server 10*g* Single Sign-On.
Reports	rwbuilder	This invokes the Reports Builder.
Reports	rwcgi	This translates and delivers information between HTTP and the Reports Server.
Reports	rwclient	This parses and transfers a command line to the specified (or default) Reports Server.
Reports	rwconverter	This converts report definitions or PL/SQL libraries from one storage format to another.
Reports	rwrun	This runs a report using the Application Server 10*g* Reports Services in-process server.
Reports	rwserver	This invokes the Reports Server.
SSO	ssocfg.sh	This updates host, port, and protocol of SSO URL.
SSO	ssooconf.sql	This points SSO to a different OID.
SSO	ossoreg.jar	This is the mod_osso registration tool.

TABLE 1-1. *Application Server 10*g* Command-Line Utilities* (continued)

Category	Command	Usage
Web Cache	webcachectl	This manages Web Cache processes, including the administration server process, cache server process, and auto-restart process.
Web services	uddiadmin.jar	This manages the UDDI registry.
Wireless	portalRegistrar.sh	This reregisters the mobile gateway parameter with Application Server Portal 10*g*.
Wireless	reRegisterSSO.sh	This reregisters the Wireless Single Sign-On partner application with the Single Sign-On server.

TABLE 1-1. *Application Server 10*g *Command-Line Utilities* (continued)

Knowing these commands and their parameters for Application Server 10*g* is very useful for automating administrative functions and creating batch scripts. These commands can easily be placed into scripts (shell scripts in Linux and UNIX) that can be executed to automate routine management tasks.

While each product with Application Server 10*g* has control files, there are three main command-line interfaces:

- **opmnctl** This is the control interface for the Process Management Notification (OPM) component. The opmnctl interface is located at $ORACLE_HOME/opmn/bin/opmnctl. The opmnctl interface provides a startall and stopall argument that will manage all of the Application Server 10*g* server processes.

- **dcmctl** This is the control interface for the Distributed Configuration Manager (DCM) component. The dcmctl interface is located at $ORACLE_HOME/dcm/bin/dcmctl.

- **emctl** This is the Enterprise Manager console utility. The emctl executable is located in $ORACLE_HOME/bin/emctl. It is used for managing the OEM agents, changing OEM passwords, starting the OEM console, and other miscellaneous tasks.

These command-line interfaces are critical for Application Server 10*g* administrative scripts. Let's take a look at how command-line interfaces are used as scripts.

Using Scripts to Manage Application Server 10*g*

You can automate many areas of Application Server 10*g* administration using scripts. Here is an example of a command list to start the iasdb database, the listener, the infrastructure instance, a midtier instance, and the Enterprise Manager web site on both instances.

echo Setting Env for Infrastructure

```
source envInfra.sh
echo Starting Listener
$ORACLE_HOME/bin/lsnrctl start
echo Starting Database
```

```
$ORACLE_HOME/bin/sqlplus /nolog<<EOF
connect / as sysdba
startup
EOF
echo Starting all opmnctl controlled processes
$ORACLE_HOME/opmn/bin/opmnctl startall
echo Starting the EM website
#$ORACLE_HOME/bin/emctl start em
echo Setting Env for MidTier Instance
source envMidtier.sh
echo Starting all opmnctl controlled processes
$ORACLE_HOME/opmn/bin/opmnctl startall
echo Starting the EM website
#$ORACLE_HOME/bin/emctl start em
echo Startup Completed
```

By themselves, the command list is not very useful, but it becomes very powerful when embedded into a shell script. The source envMidtier.sh statement changes the ORACLE_HOME environmental variable. Each instance of Application Server 10g must be installed in its own ORACLE_HOME. This is covered in the Chapter 2. Because the Application Server 10g command-line utilities exist in many locations, it is critical that you set up your OS environment so that your scripts can locate all of the utilities. Here are examples of the proper PATH commands for UNIX and Windows. These are normally placed in the startup shell script to be executed at sign-on time.

UNIX PATH Setup

```
ORACLE_HOME=/u01/app/oracle/product/9.2.0
export ORACLE_HOME
PATH=.:$PATH:.;$ORACLE_HOME/dcm/bin/:$ORACLE_HOME/j2ee/home/:$ORACLE_HOME/ldap/bin/:$ORACLE_
HOME/ldap/odi/admin/:$ORACLE_HOME/oca/bin/:$ORACLE_HOME/opmn/bin/:$ORACLE_HOME/portal/admin/
plsql/sso/:$ORACLE_HOME/sso/lib/:$ORACLE_HOME/uddi/lib/:$ORACLE_HOME/upgrade/:$ORACLE_HOME/
wireless/bin/
```

Windows PATH Setup

```
Set ORACLE_HOME=c:\oracle\ora92
SETPATH=.;$PATH;%ORACLE_HOME%\dcm\bin\;%ORACLE_HOME%\j2ee\home\;%ORACLE_HOME%\ldap\bin\
;%ORACLE_HOME%\ldap\odi\admin\;%ORACLE_HOME%\oca\bin\;%ORACLE_HOME%\opmn\bin\;%ORACLE_HOME%\
portal\admin\plsql\sso\;%ORACLE_HOME%\sso\lib\;%ORACLE_HOME%\uddi\lib\;%ORACLE_HOME%\upgrade\
;%ORACLE_HOME%\wireless\bin\
```

Once you have established the PATH variable, you can create shell scripts that can be submitted in batch mode (in UNIX with the nohup command) to automate Application Server 10g administrative tasks. For example, an Application Server 10g management shell script could be scheduled in the UNIX crontab to perform a scheduled shutdown of all services.

Of course, the PATH variable is only a part of an Application Server 10g script, and the complete environment, including ORACLE_BASE, ORACLE_HOME, and ORACLE_SID, must be enabled. The env.ksh script shows a common environmental setting for Application Server 10g command scripts. Note that $ORACLE_HOME is set to ORACLE_BASE/midtier for midtier command scripts and ORACLE_BASE/infra for infrastructure command scripts. Every Application Server 10g instance must be installed in a unique ORACLE_HOME, and startup/shutdown scripts must set the environment variables for that instance.

env.sh

```ksh
#!/bin/ksh
export ORACLE_BASE=/private/ias
# Use this ORACLE_HOME for midtier applications
#export ORACLE_HOME=$ORACLE_BASE/midtier
# Use this ORACLE_HOME for infra applications
export ORACLE_HOME=$ORACLE_BASE/infra
SETPATH=.;$PATH;%ORACLE_HOME%\dcm\bin\;%ORACLE_HOME%\j2ee\home\;%ORACLE_HOME%\ldap\bin\
;%ORACLE_HOME%\ldap\odi\admin\;%ORACLE_HOME%\oca\bin\;%ORACLE_HOME%\opmn\bin\;%ORACLE_HOME%\
portal\admin\plsql\sso\;%ORACLE_HOME%\sso\lib\;%ORACLE_HOME%\uddi\lib\;%ORACLE_HOME%\upgrade\
;%ORACLE_HOME%\wireless\bin\
export ORACLE_SID=iasdb
export LD_LIBRARY_PATH=$LD_LIBRARY_PATH:$ORACLE_HOME/lib
#export DISPLAY=tor:2.0

echo ORACLE_HOME : $ORACLE_HOME
echo ORACLE_SID  : $ORACLE_SID
echo DISPLAY     : $DISPLAY
echo Set PATH and LD_LIBRARY_PATH
```

Here is a script to submit when there is a problem with OHS and you need to restart it. Some Application Server 10*g* administrators place Apache user-exit code to automate the bouncing of the OHS. For example, if an external connection fails to attach to an OHS listener, after ten seconds, the following code could be automatically invoked to bounce OHS.

bounce_ohs.ksh

```ksh
#**********************************************************************
# Copyright (c) 2003 by Donald K. Burleson
#
#**********************************************************************
# Exit if no first parameter $1
if [ -z "$1" ]
then
    echo "ERROR: Please pass a valid ORACLE_SID to this script"
    exit 99
fi
# Validate Oracle
TEMP=`cat /etc/oratab|grep \^$1:|cut -f1 -d':'|wc -l`
tmp=`expr TEMP`          # Convert string to number
if [ $tmp -ne 1 ]
then
    echo
    echo "ERROR: Your input parameter $1 is invalid.  Please Retry"
    echo
    exit 99
fi

if [ `whoami` != 'oracle' ]
then
    echo "Error: You must be oracle to execute the script.  Exiting."
    exit
fi
```

```
# First, we must set the environment . . . .
export ORACLE_BASE=/private/ias
# Use this ORACLE_HOME for midtier applications
#export ORACLE_HOME=$ORACLE_BASE/midtier
# Use this ORACLE_HOME for infra applications
export ORACLE_HOME=$ORACLE_BASE/infra
SETPATH=.;$PATH;%ORACLE_HOME%\dcm\bin\;%ORACLE_HOME%\j2ee\home\;%ORACLE_HOME%\ldap\bin\
;%ORACLE_HOME%\ldap\odi\admin\;%ORACLE_HOME%\oca\bin\;%ORACLE_HOME%\opmn\bin\;%ORACLE_HOME%\
portal\admin\plsql\sso\;%ORACLE_HOME%\sso\lib\;%ORACLE_HOME%\uddi\lib\;%ORACLE_HOME%\upgrade\
;%ORACLE_HOME%\wireless\bin\
export ORACLE_SID=iasdb
export LD_LIBRARY_PATH=$LD_LIBRARY_PATH:$ORACLE_HOME/lib
#export DISPLAY=tor:2.0
#***********************************************************
#  Execute the DCM commands to bounce the OHS
#***********************************************************
$ORACLE_HOME/dcm/bin/dcmctl stop -ct ohs
$ORACLE_HOME/dcm/bin/dcmctl start -ct ohs
$ORACLE_HOME/dcm/bin/dcmctl start -co OC4J_Portal
```

As you can see, these shell scripts with embedded Application Server 10*g* commands are extremely useful for automatic administration. As each component is discussed in later chapters, detailed scripts will be introduced to assist with the administration of that component.

The next few sections give examples of commands that are used to perform frequent Application Server 10*g* administrative functions.

EM Commands with emctl

The emctl utility is used to manage all aspects of the Enterprise Manager console. While the EM console is greatly useful for managing components of Application Server 10*g*, the console itself must be managed. For example, all EM servers must have a running EM agent, and the emctl command-line utility can be used to start or stop OEM, OMS, or any OEM agent. As mentioned earlier in the chapter, OMS (Oracle Management Server) is used with Oracle Enterprise Manager for centralized management of all Oracle products installed.

EM Console Commands for Application Server 10*g*

```
emctl start em
emctl stop em
emctl status em
```

OEM Agent Commands

```
emctl start agent
emctl stop agent
emctl status agent
```

OMS Commands

```
emctl start oms
emctl stop oms
emctl status oms
```

Managing Application Server 10*g* with opmnctl

The Oracle Process Manager and Notification (OPMN) uses the opmnctl utility to manage all Oracle Application Server 10*g* server processes. The powerful startall and stopall commands will manage all server components. Unless a tier consists of a standalone component such as the Web Cache, opmnctl should be used rather than the separate component control program.

Start OPMN, DCM, and All Components

```
opmnctl startall
```

Stop OPMN, DCM, and All Components

```
opmnctl stopall
```

There may be times when you want to stop and restart all OPMN and DCM processes on your servers. The following shell script will perform this function:

```
#!/bin/ksh
#******************************************************************
#
# Copyright (c) 2003 by Donald K. Burleson
#
# Bounce all Oracle Application Server 10g server processes
#
#******************************************************************
# First, we must set the environment . . . .
export ORACLE_BASE=/private/ias
# Use this ORACLE_HOME for midtier applications
#export ORACLE_HOME=$ORACLE_BASE/midtier
# Use this ORACLE_HOME for infra applications
export ORACLE_HOME=$ORACLE_BASE/infra
SET PATH=.;$PATH;%ORACLE_HOME%\dcm\bin\;%ORACLE_HOME%\j2ee\home\;
%ORACLE_HOME%\dap\bin\;%ORACLE_HOME%\ldap\odi\admin\;%ORACLE_HOME%\oca\bin\;%ORACLE_HOME%opmn\
bin\;%ORACLE_HOME%\portal\admin\plsql\sso\;%ORACLE_HOME%\sso\lib\;%ORALE_HOME%\uddi\lib\
;%ORACLE_HOME%\upgrade\;%ORACLE_HOME%\wireless\bin\
export ORACLE_SID=iasdb
export LD_LIBRARY_PATH=$LD_LIBRARY_PATH:$ORACLE_HOME/lib
#export DISPLAY=tor:2.0
# Loop through each host name . . .
for host in `cat ~oracle/.rhosts|cut -d"." -f1|awk '{print $1}'|sort -u`
do
    # Get the ORACLE_HOME on each Oracle Application Server 10g server
    home=`rsh $host "cat /etc/oratab|egrep ':N|:Y'|grep -v \*|cut -f1 /
d':'"``

    # Execute opmnctl to bounce all Oracle Application Server 10g server processes:
    rsh $host "$home/opmn/bin/opmnctl stopall"
    rsh $host "$home/opmn/bin/opmnctl stopall"
done
```

Managing Application Server 10*g* with dcmctl

The Distributed Configuration Manager (DCM) is the master utility for Application Server 10*g*. The DCM is responsible for maintaining configuration by updating the configuration files on each server. DCM also stores the values of the parameters within each configuration file on each server within isadb. Note that if you choose not to implement the infrastructure (not recommended), the parameter files will exist as flat files on each server.

The dcmctl utility has two important argument settings, verbose (-v) and diagnostic (-d). These are important options because they provide additional diagnostic information about the state of your dcmctl commands. Starting in Application Server 10*g* release 9.0.4, you can use set commands to enable and disable these options:

```
dcmctl set -v on
dcmctl set -d on
```

Once you have established the settings, you can use dcmctl for a variety of Application Server 10*g* administrative functions. Here is an example of using dcmctl to start the HTTP server (OHS):

```
dcmctl start -ct ohs
http://diogenes:7777
http://diogenes:1080
```

You can also use the dcmctl command to deploy OC4J applications, and the dcmctl commands can be embedded into command lists for the purpose of deploying them on many servers. For example, let's create a list of dcmctl commands to deploy an OC4J application on multiple servers. Assume that we have saved this file as /home/oracle/dcm_dep.cmd on our main server:

dcm_dep.cmd

```
echo "creating testcluster"
createcluster testcluster
echo "joining testcluster"
joincluster testcluster
echo "creating component component1"
createcomponent -ct oc4j -co component1
echo "starting component to deploy application"
start -co component1
echo " deploying application"
deployapplication -f /stage/apps/app1.ear -a app1 -co component1
echo "starting the cluster"
start -cl testcluster
echo "verifying everything started "
getstate
exit
```

So, how can you execute this script on all 20 of your OC4J servers? You can create a shell script to loop through a list of all servers and deploy the J2EE application on each OC4J server. This script requires the remote shell (rsh) and remote copy (rcp) UNIX commands. The rsh command is enabled by placing server host names in your .rhosts file. The rsh facility should only be implemented if all Application Server 10*g* servers are safe behind a firewall, because rsh allows a hack who gains access to one server to access all other servers in the .rhosts file.

deploy_oc4j.ksh

```ksh
#!/bin/ksh
#******************************************************************
#
# Copyright (c) 2003 by Donald K. Burleson
#
# Deploy Oracle Application Server 10g application on multiple servers
#
#******************************************************************

# First, we must set the environment . . . .
export ORACLE_BASE=/private/ias
# Use this ORACLE_HOME for midtier applications
#export ORACLE_HOME=$ORACLE_BASE/midtier
# Use this ORACLE_HOME for infra applications
export ORACLE_HOME=$ORACLE_BASE/infra
SET PATH=.;$PATH;%ORACLE_HOME%\dcm\bin\;%ORACLE_HOME%\j2ee\home\;
%ORACLE_HOME%\ldap\bin\;%ORACLE_HOME%\ldap\odi\admin\;%ORACLE_HOME%\
oca\bin\;%ORACLE_HOME%\opmn\bin\;%ORACLE_HOME%\portal\admin\plsql\sso\;
%ORACLE_HOME%\sso\lib\;%ORALE_HOME%\uddi\lib\;%ORACLE_HOME%\upgrade\;
%ORACLE_HOME%\wireless\bin\
export ORACLE_SID=iasdb
export LD_LIBRARY_PATH=$LD_LIBRARY_PATH:$ORACLE_HOME/lib
#export DISPLAY=tor:2.0

# Loop through each host name . . .
for host in `cat ~oracle/.rhosts|cut -d"." -f1|awk '{print $1}'|sort -u`
do
   # Get the ORACLE_HOME on each Oracle Application Server 10g server
   home=`rsh $host "cat /etc/oratab|egrep ':N|:Y'|grep -v \*|cut -f1/
d':'"``

   # Copy the dcm command file and ear to the remote server
   rcp -p /home/oracle/dcm_dep.cmd ${host}:~oracle/dcm_dep.cmd
   rcp -p /stage/apps/app1.ear ${host}:/stage/apps/app1.ear

   # Set and check file permissions
   rsh $host "chmod 500 ~oracle/dcm_dep.cmd "
   rsh $host "ls -al ~oracle/dcm_dep.cmd"

   # Execute dcmctl to start the dcmctl shell:
   rsh $host "$home/dcm/bin/dcmctl shell -f ~oracle/dcm_dep.cmd"

done
```

As you can see, the dcmctl command is very useful when you must deploy applications across many J2EE instances.

Miscellaneous Application Server 10*g* Commands

While we will be exploring these commands in greater detail in later chapters, we want to introduce a few more common command-line utilities for Application Server 10*g* administration. Let's take a quick look at commands for managing the Web Cache (webcachectl) and the Oracle Internet Directory (oidctl and oidmon).

Shut Down the Application Server 10*g* Web Cache

```
webcachectl stop
```

Start the isadb Instance

```
oidmon connect=iasdb start
oidctl server=oidldapd instance=s flags="-port 4032 -host myhost" start
```

Summary

This chapter has given you an overview of Application Server 10*g* and all of its components. Application Server 10*g* is now the encapsulation of many application-related products, each with unique features and functionality. Remember, many of the components are optional, and few shops use all of them. The main points of this chapter can be summarized as follows:

- Oracle has implemented a flexible architecture for Application Server 10*g*, allowing administrators to define multiple servers to manage the application load.

- Application Server 10*g* architectures may be defined as two-tiered, three-tiered, or four-tiered, and there may be many independent servers at each tier.

- Multiple Application Server 10*g* instances can be grouped into farms, which are instances that share a common metadata repository.

- Common Application Server 10*g* instances can be grouped into clusters, which are instances that share a common definition and J2EE applications.

- The Oracle Management Server (OMS) helps with management and definition of farms, clusters, and instances, making it simpler to manage complex application environments.

- TopLink is an important component of Oracle Application Server 10*g* that allows Java objects to be stored for future reference by other Java tasks.

- For those who install the Application Server 10*g* Infrastructure, the Enterprise Manager is a fast and easy way to perform administrative functions.

- Application Server 10*g* defines a hierarchy of components, instances, clusters, and farms. Each farm has many clusters, each cluster has many instances, and each instance has many components.

- Application Server 10*g* also provides 59 command-line interfaces. The most popular command-line interfaces are emctl, dcmctl, and opmnctl.

Now that we have completed the high-level tour, we are ready to move on to examine the Application Server 10*g* Infrastructure in more detail. The Infrastructure includes SSO, LDAP, and the all-important metadata repository.

CHAPTER
2

The Oracle
Application Server 10g
Infrastructure

his chapter moves deeper into the administration and management of Oracle Application Server 10*g* as we start to look at management of the infrastructure. The Application Server 10*g* infrastructure is the heart of the Application Server 10*g* farm and is the central metadata repository for many critical application components. While many administrators limit their definition of the infrastructure to the metadata database (often referred to as the *iasdb instance*), the infrastructure consists of much more. In this chapter, we will examine the metadata repository (iasdb), the Single Sign-On (SSO) security framework, and the Oracle Application Server 10*g* Management Services:

- **Repository**   The Application Server 10*g* metadata repository (the iasdb database) contains important configuration and usage information for all Application Server 10*g* components. In addition to iasdb, the Oracle LDAP server (Oracle Internet Directory, OID) provides nondatabase information for use by Application Server 10*g* components.

- **Security**   Oracle SSO provides centralized security control across all Application Server 10*g* instances. This removes the need to manage each component independently and provides a simple, centralized security system.

- **Management Services**   The Application Server 10*g* OEM console screens provide complete administrative facilities for all farms, clusters, instances, and components. Virtually every management task can now be done using the OEM console.

In Application Server 10*g*, you can use the enhanced Oracle Enterprise Manager (OEM) tool to administer the infrastructure components. As an Application Server 10*g* administrator, it is your job to become familiar with all of these components. Of course, your shop may not have some of the optional components, such as Single Sign-On, but it is imperative that you understand how these infrastructure tools communicate with each other to provide the administrative framework for Application Server 10*g*.

Let's begin with an overview of the repository data structures.

The Infrastructure Repository

As the scope of Application Server 10*g* expanded, Oracle recognized that a centralized data repository was needed to handle all of the metadata required by Application Server 10*g*. This was achieved by creating an Oracle database on the Application Server 10*g* midtier called iasdb. The metadata repository is known by several names, including the Application Server 10*g* infrastructure repository, the infrastructure instance, and iasdb. The iasdb name is the default $ORACLE_SID for the Oracle 9*i* database that holds the data.

The metadata repository holds configurations for many of the Application Server 10*g* components, and is also extended for use by SSO. As of release 9.0.4, there are nearly 20 Application Server 10*g* components, and many of these use iasdb for centralized metadata storage. Also, starting in release 9.0.4, the infrastructure may be any supported release of Oracle 9*i* that is at the correct version and patch level.

Remember, not all Application Server 10*g* components make the same use of iasdb. For example, OID and SSO use iasdb to store security access data, while other components such as OHS and Web Cache only store configuration information in iasdb.

The iasdb database contains all of the metadata and internal information for all SSO components, Oracle Portal, Oracle Wireless, and some DCM components. The infrastructure repository holds data for all Application Server 10*g* components in a farm, and is critical to the proper operation of these components:

- ■ **OID**   Oracle Internet Directory (LDAP)

- ■ **DCM**   Distributed Configuration Manager

- ■ **Portal**   The web development component of Application Server 10*g*

- ■ **OEM**   The repository for many OEM components

- ■ **SSO**   Oracle Single Sign-On

- ■ **Wireless**   Oracle Wireless metadata

Let's take a quick tour of the various schemas within the iasdb database and see how each schema is used by the Application Server 10*g* components. Then we will examine the iasdb log files and look at queries that can be automated for easy viewing.

The iasdb database instance has many individual schemas. Each of these schemas has a special function to help control and manage each of the various Application Server 10*g* components. Table 2-1 lists the Application Server 10*g* schemas within iasdb. These schema components are always installed in the infrastructure database, even if you are not using a component.

Once you understand the schema owner's purpose, you can examine the complexity of each schema. As an Application Server 10*g* administrator, you must become intimate with these schemas and understand which schemas control what system functions. The iasdb instance has some schemas that must be locked, others whose passwords may be changed at will, and others that are registered with the OID and should only be changed using OEM.

Immutable iasdb Schemas

Some schemas are immutable, and the passwords and data structures must never be changed. This is especially true for this group of iasdb schemas:

Schema Name	Used By	Default Password
CTXSYS	Intermedia Text option	change_on_install
MDSYS	Spatial Data option	mdsys
OLAPDBA	OLAP Services option	olapdba
OLAPSVR	OLAP Services option	instance
OLAPSYS	OLAP Services option	manager
ORDPLUGINS	InterMedia Audio option	ordplugins
ORDSYS	InterMedia Audio option	ordsys
OUTLN	Stored Outlines	outln

Schema	Description
AURORAJISUTILITY$	Oracle Servlet Engine schema
AURORAORBUNAUTHENTICATED	Oracle Servlet Engine schema
DCM	Distributed Configuration Manager
DISCOVERER5	Oracle Application Server Discoverer 10*g*
DSGATEWAY	Oracle 9*i* Syndication Server
INTERNET_APPSERVER_REGISTRY	Contains the COMPONENTS table
IP	TCP/IP replication (advanced queuing) and Internet audit log tables
OCA	Oracle Application Server Certificate Authority 10*g*
ODS	Oracle Internet Directory metadata
ORAOCA_PUBLIC	Oracle Application Server Certificate Authority 10*g* synonyms
ORASSO	Oracle Application Server Single Sign-On 10*g*
ORDSYS	Oracle InterMedia Audio schema
ORDPLUGINS	Oracle InterMedia Audio schema
OSE$HTTP$ADMIN	Oracle Servlet Engine
OWA_MGR	Oracle Workflow
PORTAL	Oracle Application Server Portal 10*g*
PORTAL_APP	Oracle Application Server Portal 10*g*
PORTAL_DEMO	Oracle Application Server Portal 10*g* demonstration schema
PORTAL_PUBLIC	Oracle Application Server Portal 10*g* Public synonyms
UDDISYS	Oracle Application Server Web Services 10*g*
WFADMIN	Oracle Workflow
WIRELESS	Oracle Application Server Wireless 10*g*
WKSYS	Oracle Ultra Search
WK_PROXY	Oracle Ultra Search
WK_TEST	Oracle Ultra Search

TABLE 2-1. *iasdb Schema Components*

Workflow iasdb Schemas

The following iasdb schemas are used by the Oracle Workflow component, and the passwords may be changed as desired:

Schema Name	Used By	Default Password
BLEWIS	Workflow component	blewis
CDOUGLAS	Workflow component	cdouglas
KWALKER	Workflow component	kwalker
SPIERSON	Workflow component	spierson

Schemas Registered in the OID

The next group of iasdb schemas includes those that are registered in OID. Because the OID manages the passwords for these schemas, you should never attempt to alter any of these schema owner passwords with the alter user command. Instead, you should use the OEM facility for changing these passwords. When using OEM to alter these passwords, OEM will change the password inside the iasdb database and also update the appropriate OID system tables.

OID Schema Name	Used By
DISCOVERER5	Discoverer
DSGATEWAY	Syndication Server
DSSYS	Web Services
ODS	Internet Directory
ODSCOMMON	Internet Directory
ORASSO	Single Sign-On
ORASSO_DS	Single Sign-On
ORASSO_PA	Single Sign-On
ORASSO_PS	Single Sign-On
ORASSO_PUBLIC	Single Sign-On
PORTAL	Portal
PORTAL_APP	Portal
PORTAL_DEMO	Portal
PORTAL_PUBLIC	Portal
WIRELESS	Wireless

Now let's go deeper and explore SQL*Plus scripts that allow you to see the individual schema components in greater detail.

Viewing the Whole iasdb Instance

The entire iasdb instance contains more than 10,000 database objects and more than 1800 tables. You can run the following script to show the counts for each object type within iasdb.

iasdb_component_count.sql

```
set lines 60
set pages 999

ttitle 'OracleAS iasdb|Object Report'
```

```
spool obj_count.lst


col c1 heading 'Owner' format a30
col c2 heading 'Object|Type' format a15
col c3 heading 'Object|Count' format 99,999

break on c1 skip 2

compute sum of c3 on c1

select
   owner c1,
   object_type c2,
   count(*) c3
from
dba_objects
where
owner in (
'OSE$HTTP$ADMIN',
'DCM',
'DISCOVERER5',
'ORASSO_PS',
'ORASSO_PUBLIC',
'ORASSO',
'ODS',
'ORAOCA_PUBLIC',
'UDDISYS',
'WCRSYS',
'OCA',
'IP',
'OWF_MGR',
'WIRELESS',
'DSGATEWAY',
'PORTAL_APP',
'PORTAL_PUBLIC',
'PORTAL',
'ORASSO_PA',
'ORASSO_DS',
'WKPROXY',
'INTERNET_APPSERVER_REGISTRY',
'SPIERSON',
'SYSADMIN',
'WFADMIN',
'ORDPLUGINS'
)
group by
   owner,
   object_type
order by
  c1,
```

```
   c3 desc
 ;

 spool off
```

The output from this script is shown in the following listing. Even though there are more than 10,000 objects in the iasdb database, when you break them down into their components, you see that IP is the largest schema with 400+ tables, followed by PORTAL with 350+ tables, and WIRELESS and OWF_MGR with over 200 tables each.

```
                               OracleAS iasdb
                               Object Report


                                      Object              Object
Owner                                 Type                 Count
---------------------------- -----------------    -------
DCM                                   INDEX                    16
                                      TABLE                    11
                                      LOB                       1
                                      SEQUENCE                  1
* * * * * * * * * * * * * * * * * * * * * * * * * *        -------
sum                                                            29


DISCOVERER5                           INDEX                    34
                                      SEQUENCE                  8
                                      TABLE                     8
                                      LOB                       3
* * * * * * * * * * * * * * * * * * * * * * * * * *        -------
sum                                                            53


DSGATEWAY                             INDEX                    30
                                      TABLE                    30
                                      PACKAGE                  17
                                      PACKAGE BODY             16
                                      SEQUENCE                 12
                                      TYPE                     12
                                      LOB                       3
                                      VIEW                      1
* * * * * * * * * * * * * * * * * * * * * * * * * *        -------
sum                                                           121


INTERNET_APPSERVER_REGISTRY           INDEX                     2
                                      TABLE                     1
                                      VIEW                      1
* * * * * * * * * * * * * * * * * * * * * * * * * *        -------
sum                                                             4
```

```
IP                              TRIGGER          1,293
                                INDEX              762
                                TABLE              475
                                VIEW               437
                                LOB                223
                                PACKAGE              9
                                PROCEDURE            9
                                QUEUE                9
                                PACKAGE BODY         8
                                SYNONYM              7
                                SEQUENCE             4
                                TYPE                 4
                                FUNCTION             1
****************************                    -------
sum                                              3,241


OCA                             INDEX               11
                                TABLE               11
                                SEQUENCE             5
                                LOB                  2
                                PACKAGE              2
                                PACKAGE BODY         2
                                VIEW                 1
****************************                    -------
sum                                                 34


ODS                             INDEX              300
                                TABLE              156
                                TYPE                23
                                PACKAGE             20
                                PACKAGE BODY        20
                                SEQUENCE             7
                                LOB                  2
                                PROCEDURE            1
****************************                    -------
sum                                                529


ORASSO                          PACKAGE            176
                                PACKAGE BODY       162
                                INDEX              155
                                TABLE               91
                                TYPE                51
                                VIEW                43
                                SEQUENCE            39
                                TRIGGER             35
                                TYPE BODY           10
                                PROCEDURE            8
                                LOB                  7
```

```
                                  FUNCTION              4
                                  JAVA CLASS            2
                                  SYNONYM               2
                                  LIBRARY               1
*****************************                          -------
sum                                                     786


ORASSO_DS                         SYNONYM               4
*****************************                          -------
sum                                                     4


ORASSO_PA                         SYNONYM               1
*****************************                          -------
sum                                                     1


ORASSO_PS                         SYNONYM               5
*****************************                          -------
sum                                                     5


ORDPLUGINS                        PACKAGE              14
                                  PACKAGE BODY         14
*****************************                          -------
sum                                                     28


OSE$HTTP$ADMIN                    TABLE                 3
                                  SEQUENCE              2
*****************************                          -------
sum                                                     5


OWF_MGR                           INDEX               261
                                  TABLE               204
                                  PACKAGE             136
                                  PACKAGE BODY        132
                                  VIEW                 85
                                  SEQUENCE             49
                                  LOB                  36
                                  QUEUE                36
                                  TYPE                  9
                                  UNDEFINED             9
                                  SYNONYM               8
                                  TYPE BODY             3
                                  TABLE PARTITION       2
*****************************                          -------
sum                                                     970
```

```
PORTAL                          PACKAGE              729
                                PACKAGE BODY         704
                                INDEX                584
                                TABLE                379
                                JAVA CLASS           199
                                VIEW                 157
                                TRIGGER              130
                                TYPE                 114
                                SEQUENCE              89
                                LOB                   50
                                TYPE BODY             38
                                PROCEDURE             12
                                FUNCTION               5
                                SYNONYM                5
                                JAVA RESOURCE          4
                                JAVA SOURCE            1
*****************************                     -------
sum                                              3,200


PORTAL_APP                      SYNONYM                3
*****************************                     -------
sum                                                    3


UDDISYS                         INDEX                130
                                TABLE                 46
                                LOD                    4
                                PACKAGE                3
                                PACKAGE BODY           2
                                SEQUENCE               2
                                TYPE                   1
                                VIEW                   1
*****************************                     -------
sum                                                  189


WCRSYS                          TABLE                 10
                                INDEX                  9
                                SEQUENCE               2
                                PACKAGE                1
                                PACKAGE BODY           1
*****************************                     -------
sum                                                   23


WIRELESS                        INDEX                403
                                TABLE                236
                                TRIGGER               92
                                VIEW                  67
                                SEQUENCE              54
```

```
                         LOB                    46
                         TYPE                   43
                         QUEUE                  41
                         PACKAGE                33
                         PACKAGE BODY           32
                         PROCEDURE              16
                         FUNCTION                7
                         CLUSTER                 1
****************************                 -------
sum                                           1,071
```

It should come as no surprise that the iasdb database contains complex data structures and stored packages, but administrators must understand how these database components are used by the Application Server 10g application components. Of course, the iasdb schema components should never be altered or directly manipulated, but there are some important logging components within iasdb. Let's take a close look at some of the Application Server 10g infrastructure log tables.

The Infrastructure Log Tables

The Application Server 10g system contains numerous log files, some of which are stored in flat files while others are stored inside the iasdb instance. Remember that log files and audit trails may exist in many places, and you must become accustomed to looking for error messages and audits in the proper places.

In practice, administrators use shell scripts with SQL*Plus to automate this task, and filter out unwanted messages so they can see only those messages that are germane to their current needs. When the iasdb database is initially loaded, log files are created in the $ORACLE_HOME/config directory. These include the following files:

- **schemaload.log**   This file reports on the iasdb load process.

- **useinfratool.log**   This file reports on all tools whose definitions have been loaded into the iasdb instance.

- **infratool_instance_jazn.log**   This reports on the Java Authorization (JAZN) install using Oracle's Java Authentication and Authorization Service (JAAS).

- **infratool_mod_osso.log**   This file reports on the mod_osso load process.

After the iasdb initial load, it is a good idea to check these files for errors. Application Server 10g will report on all successful component installations in these logs, and you can easily check the status with a single command:

```
root> grep -i succeeded $ORACLE_HOME/config/*.log

infratool_instance_jazn.log:Configuration succeeded for IASProperty
infratool_instance_jazn.log:Configuration succeeded for IAS
infratool_instance_jazn.log:Configuration succeeded for LDAP
infratool_mod_osso.log:Configuration succeeded for JAZN
infratool_mod_osso.log:Configuration succeeded for HTTPD
```

```
infratool_mod_osso.log:Configuration succeeded for MODOSSO
schemaload.log:Configuration succeeded for SchemaLoad
```

Of course, there are many other flat files for logs within Application Server 10*g*, and they are fully discussed in later chapters. Next let's look at the OEM console interface for displaying Application Server 10*g* log messages.

Using the OEM Console to View Application Server 10*g* Logs

The Oracle Enterprise Manager console contains a graphical log viewer that can be used to display some of the log files, as shown in Figure 2-1. From this screen you can choose any Application Server 10*g* component and view some of the associated log files. In the example shown in Figure 2-2, we chose Wireless and selected the Search button. Here you see server-side error log messages associated with Oracle Portal. However, this screen can be misleading because the infrastructure database also contains repository logs.

FIGURE 2-1. *The OEM log file viewer*

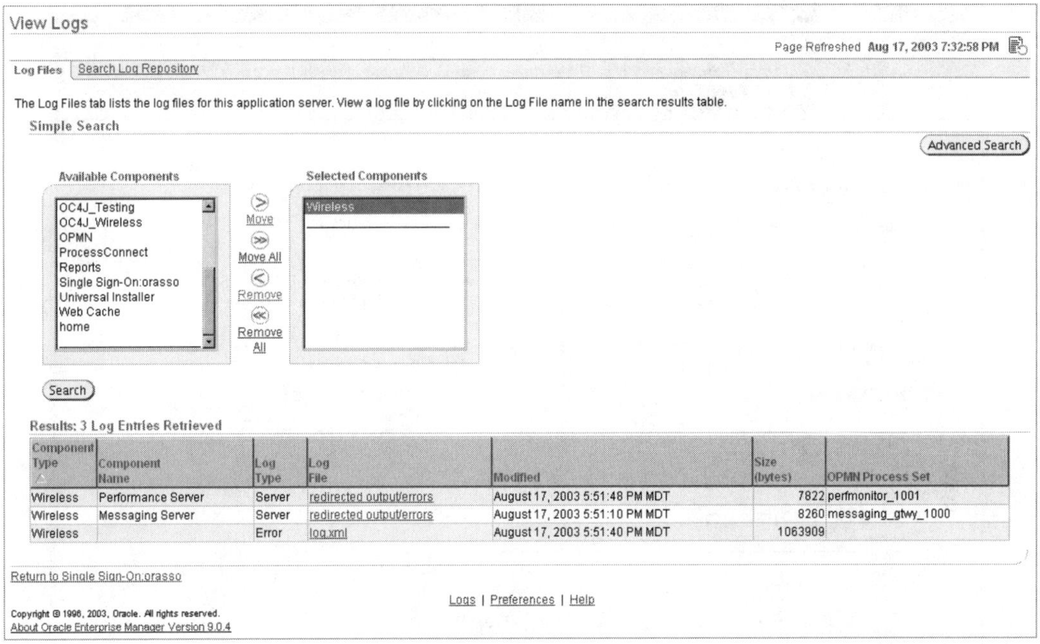

View Logs

Page Refreshed **Aug 17, 2003 7:32:58 PM**

Log Files | Search Log Repository

The Log Files tab lists the log files for this application server. View a log file by clicking on the Log File name in the search results table.

Simple Search

(Advanced Search)

Available Components

OC4J_Testing
OC4J_Wireless
OPMN
ProcessConnect
Reports
Single Sign-On:orasso
Universal Installer
Web Cache
home

Move
Move All
Remove
Remove All

Selected Components

Wireless

(Search)

Results: 3 Log Entries Retrieved

Component Type △	Component Name	Log Type	Log File	Modified	Size (bytes)	OPMN Process Set
Wireless	Performance Server	Server	redirected output/errors	August 17, 2003 5:51:48 PM MDT	7822	perfmonitor_1001
Wireless	Messaging Server	Server	redirected output/errors	August 17, 2003 5:51:10 PM MDT	8260	messaging_gtwy_1000
Wireless		Error	log.xml	August 17, 2003 5:51:40 PM MDT	1063909	

Return to Single Sign-On:orasso

Logs | Preferences | Help

Copyright © 1996, 2003, Oracle. All rights reserved.
About Oracle Enterprise Manager Version 9.0.4

FIGURE 2-2. *The OEM Wireless log file viewer*

Using the OEM Repository Log Viewer

The repository log viewer is easy to use, and you can select any Application Server 10*g* component and view the associated repository log messages (Figure 2-3). From this screen you can choose the repository components and specify filter conditions. This OEM screen then generates the SQL statements to query the native iasdb database log tables. In the example in Figure 2-3, we selected the OC4J wireless logs.

When you click the Search button, you see the error messages associated with the OC4J Wireless component displayed in HTML format. Although the OEM console GUI is great for ad hoc queries, administrators often supplement this GUI with custom scripts to extract and e-mail important error messages. Let's take a closer look at how this works.

Writing Your Own Infrastructure Repository Log Scripts

As we just noted, the OEM viewer is great for quick online queries, but most administrators write SQL*Plus scripts to directly extract the repository log message, often e-mailing it to the desktop.

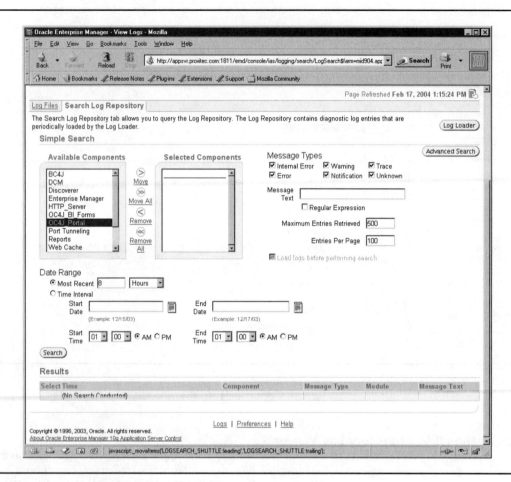

FIGURE 2-3. *The OEM infrastructure repository log viewer*

To see how this works, here is a sample Korn shell script that will extract the online repository logs for SSO and mail them to the Application Server 10*g* administrator:

mail_logs.ksh

```
#!/bin/ksh

# First, we must set the environment . . . .
ORACLE_SID=iasdb
export ORACLE_SID
ORACLE_HOME=`cat /etc/oratab|grep $ORACLE_SID:|cut -f2 -d':'`
export ORACLE_HOME
PATH=$ORACLE_HOME/bin:$PATH
export PATH
```

```
# Get the server name
host=`uname -a|awk '{ print $2 }'`

${ORACLE_HOME}/bin/sqlplus system/`cat password.txt`<<!
spool log_rpt_mgt.lst
@sso_audit_log.sql
spool off;
exit;
!
#**********************************
# Filter only error messages
#**********************************
grep -i error log_rpt_mgt.lst > errors_log.lst


#**********************************
# Mail the Object Statistics Reports
#**********************************
cat error_rpt_mgt.lst|mailx -s "Oracle AS 10g Repository SSO Messages" \
    larry_lizard@us.oracle.com \
    graham_cracker@oracle.com \
    bob_white@oracle.com
```

Note the password security in the SQL*Plus invocation line. You can save the SYSTEM password on your server in a file called password.txt and protect it by setting the file permissions such that only the Oracle user may view the password:

```
oracle> chmod 700 password.txt

oracle> ls -al *.txt
-rwx------    1 oracle    oracle          13 Aug 18 05:35 password.txt
```

Now that you've seen how easy it is to write SQL*Plus scripts against the iasdb instance, let's take a look at the log tables and see which are the most important to the Application Server 10g administrator.

Viewing the Repository Log Tables

Because Oracle has been very careful to use uniform table naming conventions, you can write a simple SQL*Plus query to see the Application Server 10g log tables. In the following listing, we select all iasdb tables that contain the string LOG.

```
    select owner, table_name
    from dba_tables
    where table_name like '%LOG%';


                        Log
Owner                   Table
-------------------- ----------------------------------
```

AURORAJISUTILITY$	JAVA$HTTP$LOG$
OSE$HTTP$ADMIN	HTTPLOG
	EVENT$LOG
	ERROR$LOG
ODS	PLG_DEBUG_LOG
	DS_LDAP_LOG
	ODS_CHG_LOG
	ASR_CHG_LOG
OCA	OCM_ERROR_LOG
WKSYS	WK$_TDS_LOG
ORASSO	WWSEC_SSO_LOG$
	WWLOG_ACTIVITY_LOG1$
	WWLOG_ACTIVITY_LOG2$
	WWLOG_EVENT$
	WWLOG_REGISTRY$
	WWSSO_LOG$
	WWSSO_AUDIT_LOG_TABLE_T
PORTAL	WWSEC_SSO_LOG$
	WWLOG_ACTIVITY_LOG1$
	WWLOG_ACTIVITY_LOG2$
	WWLOG_EVENT$
	WWLOG_REGISTRY$
	WWUTL_EXPORT_IMPORT_LOG$
	WWPTL_CONTENT_LOGS$
	WWPTL_CONTENT_LOG_HEADERS$
	WWCP_RENDER_LOG$
UDDISYS	SUBSCRIPTION_APP_LOG_LEVEL
WCRSYS	WWWCP_RENDER_LOG$
WIRELESS	PTG_LBS_LOG
	PTG_DEBUG_LOG
	PTG_SERVICE_LOG
	PTG_SESSION_LOG

```
                       TRANS_REQUEST_LOG
                       TRANS_HANDLE_LOG
                       TRANS_PROCESS_LOG
                       TRANS_ENQUEUE_LOG
                       TRANS_DEQUEUE_LOG
                       ASYNC_STATISTICS_LOG
                       MESSAGING_OUTGOING_LOG
                       LBEVENT_ENQUEUE_LOG
                       LBEVENT_DEQUEUE_LOG
                       LBEVENT_MSG_LOG
                       LBEVENT_ACTIVATION_LOG
                       STUDIO_LOG_MESSAGES
                       PROVISIONING_TRANSACTION_LOG
                       BILLING_SDR_LOG
                       SYS_LOGGER_TABLE
                       WWSEC_SSO_LOG$


OWF_MGR                ECX_OUTBOUND_LOGS
                       ECX_DOCLOGS
                       ECX_EXTERNAL_LOGS
                       ECX_OXTA_LOGMSG
                       ECX_INBOUND_LOGS
                       ECX_MSG_LOGS


IP                     TIP_ERRORLOGINSTANCE_T_AUD
                       TIP_ERRORLOGRECORDDATA_AUD
                       TIP_ERRORLOGINSTANCE_RT
                       TIP_ERRORLOGRECORDDATAINSTA_RT
                       TIP_RTLOG
                       B2BERROR_LOG
```

The output shows each of the iasdb schemas and their associated log tables. Remember, not all of the log tables are populated with meaningful information, so you must carefully examine each log file to see the contents.

Infrastructure Log Reports

The following script can be run to display all of the iasdb logs in your system. Next is a handy script called display_all_log_tables.ksh that can be embedded into a shell script to extract all log messages into a flat file.

display_all_log_tables.ksh

```ksh
#!/bin/ksh

# First, we must set the environment . . . .
ORACLE_SID=iasdb
export ORACLE_SID
```

```
ORACLE_HOME=`cat /etc/oratab|grep $ORACLE_SID:|cut -f2 -d':'`
export ORACLE_HOME
PATH=$ORACLE_HOME/bin:$PATH
export PATH

${ORACLE_HOME}/bin/sqlplus system/`cat password.txt`<<!
ttitle off
set heading off
set lines 200
set pages 999
set echo off
set feedback off
set long 4000;

spool runme.sql

select 'spool all_logs.lst' from dual;
select 'set echo on' from dual;

select
    'select * from '||owner||'.'||table_name||';'
from
    dba_tables
where
    table_name like '%LOG%'
and
    owner not in ('SYS','SYSTEM')
;

select 'spool off' from dual;
spool off;

@runme.sql
spool off;
exit;
!
#***********************************
# Filter only error messages
#***********************************
grep -i error   all_logs.lst > error_log.lst
grep -i warning all_logs.lst > warning_log.lst


#***********************************
# Mail the Object Statistics Reports
#***********************************
cat error_log.lst|mailx -s "Oracle AS 10g Repository Error Messages" \
    graham_cracker@oracle.com \
    tom_thumb@oracle.com
```

```
cat error_log.lst|mailx -s "Oracle AS 10g Repository Warning Messages" \
   graham_cracker@oracle.com \
   tom_thumb@oracle.com
```

Note that once you have run this script and off-loaded all repository log messages, you can then use the UNIX grep command to extract selected contents. Next, let's look at special types of iasdb repository log tables and see scripts to extract their messages.

Oracle Servlet Log Tables

The Application Server 10*g* servlet engine has several log tables in the repository that are used to track servlet errors:

- **ose$http$admin.error$log** This table contains the error message number and associated text.

- **ose$http$admin.event$log** This table contains servlet event numbers and their associated text messages.

- **ose$http$admin.httplog** This is the repository log table that contains specific log information about remote user servlet messages. The table contains the remote user ID, time of the servlet request, and the referrer URL. The referrer column is most useful because you can use it to track the source of servlet requests.

```
SQL> desc ose$http$admin.http$log$;
```

Name	Null?	Type
SERVER_NAME		VARCHAR2(80)
TIMESTAMP		DATE
REMOTE_HOST		RAW(4)
REMOTE_USER		VARCHAR2(80)
REQUEST_LINE		VARCHAR2(256)
STATUS		NUMBER(3)
RESPONSE_SIZE		NUMBER(38)
REQUEST_METHOD		RAW(1)
REFERER		VARCHAR2(80)
AGENT		VARCHAR2(80)

Portal Repository Log Audit Reports

Oracle Portal has several log tables in the iasdb repository, and these can be referenced with SQL to create developer activity reports for Portal. This produces a report similar to using the Oracle DDL system-level trigger, and tracks all Portal changes made by your development staff. The following report references the portal.wwlog_activity_log1$ and portal.wwlog_activity_log2$ tables and produces a useful report of all Portal development activity.

portal_summary_report.sql

```
set echo off
set feedback off
ttitle off
```

```
clear computes
set heading on
set pages 999
set lines 70
col c1 heading 'Date'    format a20
col c2 heading 'User'    format a10
col c3 heading 'Action'  format a12
col c4 heading 'URL'     format a15
col c5 heading 'Info'    format a20
col c6 heading 'Rows'    format 99,999

prompt **************************************************
prompt Portal Row Count Summary Report
prompt **************************************************

alter session set nls_date_format = 'YYYY MM DD';

break on c1 skip 2

select
    to_char(start_time,'yyyy-mm-dd') c1,
    sum(row_count)                   c6
from
    PORTAL.WWLOG_ACTIVITY_LOG1$
group by
    to_char(start_time,'yyyy-mm-dd')
UNION
select
    to_char(start_time,'yyyy-mm-dd') c1,
    sum(row_count)                   c6
from
    PORTAL.WWLOG_ACTIVITY_LOG2$
group by
    to_char(start_time,'yyyy-mm-dd')
;

prompt **************************************************
prompt Portal Action Summary Report
prompt **************************************************

select
    to_char(start_time,'yyyy-mm-dd') c1,
    action                           c3,
    sum(row_count)                   c6
from
    PORTAL.WWLOG_ACTIVITY_LOG1$
group by
    to_char(start_time,'yyyy-mm-dd'),
    action
```

```
UNION
select
    to_char(start_time,'yyyy-mm-dd') c1,
    action                           c3,
    sum(row_count)                   c6
from
    PORTAL.WWLOG_ACTIVITY_LOG2$
group by
    to_char(start_time,'yyyy-mm-dd'),
    action
;



prompt **************************************************
prompt Portal Detail Summary Report
prompt **************************************************

select
    to_char(start_time,'yyyy-mm-dd hh24:mi:ss') c1,
    userid         c2,
    action         c3,
    url            c4,
    row_count      c6
from
    PORTAL.WWLOG_ACTIVITY_LOG1$
UNION
select
    to_char(start_time,'yyyy-mm-dd hh24:mi:ss') c1,
    userid         c2,
    action         c3,
    url            c4,
    row_count      c6
from
    PORTAL.WWLOG_ACTIVITY_LOG2$
;
```

You can see the report output in the following listing. It shows the total number of rows processed by Portal developers, aggregated by date, and a summary of all Portal developer activity by date. This administration report is especially useful for change control tracking and quality control functions.

```
**************************************************
Portal Row Count Summary Report
**************************************************

Date                     Rows
-------------------      -------
2003-05-05                1,741
2003-06-03               44,321
2003-06-04                6,321
```

```
2003-06-05               83,301


****************************************************
Portal Action Summary Report
****************************************************
Date                  Action        Rows
-------------------   ------------  -------
2003-05-05            add_to_page       13
                      create           375
                      delete            99
                      edit              87
                      error          3,123
                      move               3
                      portlet          405
                      provider         948

2003-06-03            acl_event         77
                      add_to_page       54
                      create           377
                      delete            85
                      edit              42
                      portlet          923
                      process_back      37
                      ground_inval       9
                      provider          15
2003-06-04            create            53
                      edit             374
                      login            671
                      logout           102


****************************************************
Portal Detail Summary Report
****************************************************

Date                  User        Action        URL               Rows
-------------------   ----------  ------------  ---------------  -------
2003-05-05 17:50:26   PORTAL      create                              0


2003-05-05 17:51:59   PORTAL      create                              0


2003-05-05 17:53:50   PORTAL      create        URL/PAGE/SHARED       0
                                                /SAMPLE_BANNER1
                                                /?_mode=16

                      PORTAL      edit          URL/PAGE/SHARED       0
                                                /SAMPLE_BANNER1
                                                /?_mode=16
```

```
2003-05-05 17:53:51  PORTAL       add_to_page  URL/PAGE/SHARED       0
                                               /SAMPLE_BANNER1
                                               /?_mode=16

                     PORTAL       edit         URL/PAGE/SHARED       0
                                               /SAMPLE_BANNER1
                                               /?_mode=16

2003-06-03 18:39:11  PORTAL       process_back                      0
                                  ground_inval

2003-06-03 18:39:13  PORTAL       edit                              0
```

The iasdb repository also contains a wwlog_event$ table that provides total counts of Portal actions. This report is useful for Portal development auditing.

portal_actions_summary.sql

```
col c1 heading 'Action' format a20
col c2 heading 'Count'  format 999,999

select
   action     c1,
   count(*)   c2
from
   PORTAL.WWLOG_EVENT$
group by
   action
order by
   c2 desc
;
```

The following listing shows the output. Here you see all of the Portal activities and total counts for each activity.

```
Action                  Count
--------------------  --------
view                       18
create                     15
delete                     15
edit                       15
access_control             12
export                     12
copy                       12
execute                    12
generate                   12
insert                     12
update                     12
```

```
save                    12
rename                  12
query                   12
manage                  12
move                     2
add_to_page              1
search                   1
show                     1
delete_from_page         1
debug                    1
customize                1
hide                     1
checkin                  1
```

Now we're ready to look at the generic infrastructure management tools and components.

Repository Administration and Management

Because iasdb is an Oracle database, the Application Server 10*g* components rely on this database being available when they are started. After the components are started, the iasdb database can be stopped without adverse effects to OHS and Java. However, some Application Server 10*g* components, including SSO, Portal, and Wireless, will not be able to function without iasdb.

Hence, the iasdb database is a central point of failure for your Application Server 10*g* enterprise, and as the administrator, you should take steps to ensure continuous availability of the iasdb database. These steps may include the following:

- Using the Oracle9*i* standby database (Data Guard)
- Using Real Application Clusters (RAC)
- Using triple mirroring of disks

While the Oracle documentation does not specifically mention the use of RAC as an availability option for Application Server 10*g*, using RAC for the repository can protect you from lockups due to instance failure. Remember, when the infrastructure repository is not available, users cannot access the SSO login server, and the whole enterprise stops. Because the infrastructure is such a critical component of Application Server 10*g*, using a high-availability tool such as RAC guarantees continuous availability for the enterprise because the Oracle Transparent Application Failover (TAF) component will automatically continue processing any "in-flight" transactions if there is a failure on any iasdb instance.

Let's review the basic infrastructure administration tasks.

Starting and Stopping the Infrastructure

While performing general maintenance and backups, the Application Server 10*g* administrator must stop and restart the infrastructure instance. Because of its tight coupling to important Application Server 10*g* components, the infrastructure database must be started in a specific order. While the startup procedures for the infrastructure are the same as any other Oracle database, remember that iasdb must be running before other Application Server 10*g* components are started. Here is the order of iasdb startup steps:

1. Start the iasdb listener process (lsnrctl start).

2. Start the iasdb database.

3. Start the OID.

4. Start emctl.

5. Start the Oracle HTTP Server (OHS).

6. Start the OC4J_Das.

If you are using any optional Application Server 10*g* products, you may also include the following startup steps:

1. Start the Web Cache.

2. Start the OEM Intelligent Agent.

3. Start OMS.

With all these steps, it should come as no surprise that you use scripts to start and stop the Application Server 10*g* components. Application Server 10*g* uses a hierarchy of shell scripts to perform the start operations, with calls to Oracle executables at the lowest level (Figure 2-4).

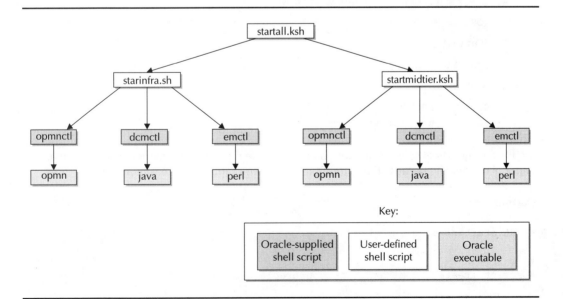

FIGURE 2-4. *The hierarchy of Application Server 10*g *scripts*

Here is the main driving script to start all the Application Server 10*g* infrastructure and midtier components:

startall.ksh

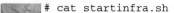

```
/bin/ksh
./startinfra.sh
sleep 10
./startmidtier.sh
sleep 10
```

Note that this script calls the start scripts for the infrastructure followed by calls to start the midtier application. Let's examine these scripts and their features. The start script for the infrastructure issues these Application Server 10*g* commands:

1. Start listener:

   ```
   $ORACLE_HOME/bin/lsnrctl start
   ```

2. Start the iasdb database:

   ```
   $ORACLE_HOME/bin/sqlplus /nolog<<EOF
   connect / as sysdba
   startup
   ```

3. Start all opmnctl controlled processes:

   ```
   $ORACLE_HOME/opmn/bin/opmnctl startall
   ```

4. Check status of infrastructure with DCM:

   ```
   $ORACLE_HOME/dcm/bin/dcmctl getState -v -i $INFRA
   ```

5. Start OMS:

   ```
   $ORACLE_HOME/bin/emctl start oms
   ```

6. Start OEM:

   ```
   $ORACLE_HOME/bin/emctl start agent
   $ORACLE_HOME/bin/emctl start em
   ```

Here is the whole script, ready for you to use. Note that the emctl commands are normally performed manually because they prompt for a password and are not easily scripted.

startinfra.sh

```
# cat startinfra.sh

#!/bin/bash
# script created by mikael.fransson@oracle.com

# Save the original path and restore it at the end of the script
```

```
export SAVED_PATH=$PATH

# Customize ORACLE_HOME and ORACLE_SID to your environment

export ORACLE_HOME=/home/oracle/infra904
export
PATH=$PATH:$ORACLE_HOME/bin:$ORACLE_HOME/dcm/bin:$ORACLE_HOME/webcache/
bin:$ORACL
_HOME/opmn/bin
export ORACLE_SID=iasdb
export LD_LIBRARY_PATH=$LD_LIBRARY_PATH:$ORACLE_HOME/lib
# Customize the following two to your environment
export DISPLAY=localhost:0.
export INFRA=infra_904.appvr.localdomain.com
echo
echo Starting Listener
echo ----------------
$ORACLE_HOME/bin/lsnrctl start
echo
echo Starting Database
echo ----------------
$ORACLE_HOME/bin/sqlplus /nolog<<EOF
connect / as sysdba
startup
EOF

echo
echo Starting all opmnctl controlled processes
echo ----------------------------------------
$ORACLE_HOME/opmn/bin/opmnctl startall


echo
echo Checking status of app server instances
echo ---------------------------------------
echo Getting status for $INFRA
$ORACLE_HOME/dcm/bin/dcmctl getState -v -i $INFRA

# If you want to automatically start the EM website
# uncomment the following lines.
# Remember stopping EM requires a password.
#
#echo Starting the EM website
#echo ---------------------
#$ORACLE_HOME/bin/emctl start oms
#$ORACLE_HOME/bin/emctl start agent
# Restore the original path
export PATH=$SAVED_PATH
```

Once the infrastructure is started, you invoke another script to start the midtier application. This script performs the following actions:

1. Start all OPM processes:

   ```
   $ORACLE_HOME/opmn/bin/opmnctl startall
   ```

2. Check midtier status:

   ```
   $ORACLE_HOME/dcm/bin/dcmctl getState -v -i $MIDTIER
   ```

3. Start Enterprise Manager:

   ```
   $ORACLE_HOME/bin/emctl start em
   ```

Here is the final script, ready to run.

startmidtier.sh

```
#!/bin/bash
# script maintained by mikael.fransson@oracle.com

# Save the original path and restore it at the end of the script
export SAVED_PATH=$PATH

# Customize ORACLE_HOME and ORACLE_SID to your environment
export ORACLE_HOME=/home/oracle/oraportal904
export
PATH=$PATH:$ORACLE_HOME/bin:$ORACLE_HOME/dcm/bin:$ORACLE_HOME/webcache/bin: \
$ORACLE_HOME/opmn/bin
export ORACLE_SID=iasdb
export LD_LIBRARY_PATH=$LD_LIBRARY_PATH:$ORACLE_HOME/lib

# Customize the following two to your environment
export DISPLAY=localhost:0.0
export MIDTIER=porta904.appsvr.localdomain.com

echo
echo Starting midtier instance with portal
echo Other components such as Forms, Reports and Discoverer
echo  should also be started here.
echo ----------------------------------
$ORACLE_HOME/opmn/bin/opmnctl startall

echo Sleeping 45 seconds
sleep 45

echo
echo Checking status of app server instances
echo ------------------------------------
echo Getting current stat of $MIDTIER
# $ORACLE_HOME/dcm/bin/dcmctl getState -v -i $MIDTIER
```

```
echo
echo Starting EM
echo -----------
$ORACLE_HOME/bin/emctl start em

# Restore the original path
export PATH=$SAVED_PATH
```

You also have scripts to stop the infrastructure. Note that the stopping process is the exact inverse of the start, shutting down all the Application Server 10*g* processes before stopping the infrastructure database.

stopinfra.sh

```
#!/bin/bash
# script maintained by mikael.fransson@oracle.com

# Save the original path and restore it at the end of the script
export SAVED_PATH=$PATH

# Customize ORACLE_HOME and ORACLE_SID to your environment
export ORACLE_HOME=/home/oracle/infra904
export
PATH=$PATH:$ORACLE_HOME/bin:$ORACLE_HOME/dcm/bin:$ORACLE_HOME/webcache/bin: \
$ORACLE_HOME/opmn/bin
export ORACLE_SID=iasdb
export LD_LIBRARY_PATH=$LD_LIBRARY_PATH:$ORACLE_HOME/lib

# Customize the following two to your environment
export DISPLAY=localhost:0.0
export INFRA=infra_904.appsvr.localdomain.com

echo
echo getting current state of $INFRA
$ORACLE_HOME/dcm/bin/dcmctl getState -v -i $INFRA
echo Stopping all opmn managed processes in $INFRA
$ORACLE_HOME/opmn/bin/opmnctl stopall
echo Sleeping 5
sleep 5

echo
echo Stopping Database Listener
echo ----------------
$ORACLE_HOME/bin/lsnrctl stop

echo
echo Stopping Database
echo -----------------
$ORACLE_HOME/bin/sqlplus /nolog<<EOF
```

```
connect / as sysdba
shutdown immediate
EOF

echo
echo Stopping Database Listener
echo ----------------
$ORACLE_HOME/bin/lsnrctl stop

echo
echo Stopping EM
$ORACLE_HOME/bin/emctl stop em<<EOF
<ias_admin_password>
EOF

# Restore the original path
export PATH=$SAVED_PATH

echo ----------------------------------------
echo
echo Listing processes owned by ias
ps -ef|grep ias
echo
echo Be Sure to kill any rogue processes
```

NOTE
The String <iasadmin_password> should be replaced with your password.

Now that we have reviewed the infrastructure administrative components, let's turn our attention to the most important infrastructure component, Oracle Single Sign-On, commonly called SSO.

Single Sign-On (SSO)

Before the introduction of Application Server SSO 10g, each component within Application Server 10g required separate password and authentication management. Besides the duplication of passwords, the lack of a unified security interface presented huge maintenance issues and also compromised the overall manageability of the application.

Without SSO, every user is required to maintain a distinct password for every application in the enterprise. As anyone who has dozens of passwords can tell you, this means that users must write down the passwords, which can cause a serious security breach. With SSO, each user has only one password for all applications within the Application Server 10g framework.

Unlike traditional Oracle applications, SSO is designed for web-based users. Any Oracle system can be web enabled, and end users can securely access their applications from the Internet, anywhere in the world. The central components of Application Server SSO 10g are the mod_osso module and the SSO login server, and these will be the focus of our SSO exploration. As an

Application Server 10*g* administrator, you are responsible for maintaining enterprise security, and knowledge of SSO administration is required.

Application Server 10*g* uses two techniques for end-user authentication, one for local "partner" applications (internal) and another for external applications. Because of the infinite possible authentication mechanisms of external applications, they cannot be integrated into SSO, and LDAP entries are used to manage security.

- **Local partner applications** Local application authentication is performed from a lookup table within the iasdb schema on the repository. The lookup table contains all of the data, including the user ID, password, and privileges for local users.

- **External applications** External SSO identification allows any third-party products to be incorporated in an Application Server 10*g* system. External applications use the Oracle Internet Directory, and Application Server 10*g* handles authentication using standard LDAP entries. At connect time, Application Server 10*g* binds to OID and looks up the remote user's credentials in the appropriate directory on the server.

This chapter focuses on SSO administration, and you can find details on user assignment and application management with SSO in Chapter 12. Let's get started by exploring the roles of the SSO administrator and SSO configuration and then look at the mod_osso utility to learn how it is used to administer Application Server 10*g* SSO security.

Roles of the SSO Administrator

The SSO administrator is responsible for all access controls and must manage all users who will connect to an application, all applications within the system, and the assignment of users to applications. There are three basic areas of SSO administration: server configuration, user management, and application management. We will focus on the server installation and configuration of SSO.

It's important to note that SSO should run seamlessly once it has been installed and configured. Afterward, the ongoing management of applications and users becomes trivial.

If you are using Oracle Portal or external applications, there are additional administrative interfaces to SSO. This is because Portal and any external applications must have customized authentication code. Because SSO controls the security for the entire Application Server 10*g* enterprise, it is critical that administrators ensure that proper security is maintained.

For more details on the daily operational use of SSO, see Chapter 12.

Configuring the SSO Server

The configuration of SSO involves the creation and management of the server-side components for the SSO login server. These configuration tasks include

- **Allocate SSO directories** These must be allocated with the proper OS permissions to maintain security.

- **Set up SSO configuration files** These must contain the correct values for your system.

- **Configure SSO programs** These must be configured properly.

- **Establish SSO library routines** These must have proper group permissions.

These are relatively trivial tasks, but crucial to the successful use of SSO. Let's start by looking at the SSO directory structures and understand the purpose and functions of the components within each directory.

SSO Directories

The SSO log-in server will have the following directories allocated at install time. Each of these directories serves a specific purpose to SSO and contains important scripts and executables.

- **$ORACLE_HOME/reports/conf** This directory has the configuration files for Oracle Reports.

- **$ORACLE_HOME/sso/bin** This directory contains SSO executables.

- **$ORACLE_HOME/dcm/bin** This is the directory for the DCM utility files.

- **$ORACLE_HOME/Apache/Apache/conf** This is the location of the mod_osso configuration file.

- **$ORACLE_HOME/sso/lib** This contains the ossoreg.jar file and other SSO library routines.

These are the main driving directories for SSO, and they contain important programs for SSO management. One of the most important is the SSO configuration utility. It is located in $ORACLE_HOME/sso/bin/ssocfg.sh, and ssocfg.sh is a shell script that invokes Java routines to manage the SSO layer. The ssocfg.sh script accepts the new_host_name and new_port name as arguments. For example, if you wanted to add server diogenes on port 1446, you would issue the following command:

```
ssocfg.sh diogenes 1446
```

Internally, the ssocfg.sh script issues the following Java invocation, calling the oracle.security.sso.SSOServerConfig Java program:

```
java oracle.security.sso.SSOServerConfig $*
```

Enabling SSO

Turning on SSO requires adjusting the SINGLESIGNON parameter in the rwservlet configuration file (rwservlet.properties). With singlesession=yes, you are telling Application Server 10*g* that you will use SSO to authenticate users. As we have noted, the rwservlet configuration file is usually found in the $ORACLE_HOME/reports/conf directory.

After you have completed configuring the SSO server, you must configure OHS to use SSO. This is done by making an entry in the mod_osso.conf file and enabling mod_osso in the OMS configuration file. The file osso.conf contains a partner registration record registered with the Single Sign-On server. Once the OHS is configured for SSO, you can use SSO to protect individual resources via the SSO server. There are several important directives in the file:

- **OSS idle timeout** If you set OssoIdleTimeout on, Application Server 10*g* will invoke a global inactivity timeout to disconnect idle sessions.

■   **OSS IP check**   If you set OssoIpCheck on, Application Server 10*g* SSO will invoke an IP address check to ensure that the authenticating browser is the same as the browser requesting access to protected facilities.

The SSO login server is the component of Application Server 10*g* that accepts the users' passwords and manages their access to all Application Server 10*g* applications. After a user enters an accepted password, Application Server 10*g* sends a message to all applications that this user has been authenticated and (optionally) stores a cookie on the browser. This cookie is used to avoid the need to reenter the password during subsequent visits.

TIP
Any web browser that uses SSO should be configured to accept cookies because the end user will become annoyed with the repeated login screens that are displayed without cookie support.

Because SSO governs security for the whole enterprise, you must have Full Administrator privileges on the login server to configure the SSO login server. If you want to access the SSO login server from Application Server Portal 10*g*, you must be an Authorized Application Server Portal 10*g* Administrator.

The Application Server 10*g* repository has some important SSO log tables that assist in tracking SSO interaction and errors. Let's take a look at these log tables.

Using the SSO Audit Log Tables

There is an important log table inside the iasdb instance in the orasso schema, called wsso_audit_log_table_t, that you can use to extract SSO interaction information. This table contains many detailed metrics about SSO interaction:

```
SQL> desc ORASSO.WWSSO_AUDIT_LOG_TABLE_T;
```

Name	Null?	Type
SUBSCRIBER_ID	NOT NULL	NUMBER
LOG_ID	NOT NULL	NUMBER
USER_NAME	NOT NULL	VARCHAR2(256)
AUDIT_TYPE	NOT NULL	VARCHAR2(32)
ACTION_CODE	NOT NULL	NUMBER
ACTION	NOT NULL	VARCHAR2(80)
IP_ADDRESS	NOT NULL	VARCHAR2(32)
APP_SITE	NOT NULL	VARCHAR2(80)
MESSAGE	NOT NULL	VARCHAR2(256)
LOG_DATE	NOT NULL	DATE
PROCESS_DATE		DATE
EMAIL		VARCHAR2(80)
MAINTAINER_ID		VARCHAR2(80)

You can take the data from this table and create an SSO summary report for execution in SQL*Plus. Here is a common SSO activity report:

sso_audit_log.sql

```
set echo off
set feedback off
ttitle off
set heading on
set pages 999
set lines 80

prompt ****************************************************
prompt SSO Activity summary Report
prompt ****************************************************

alter session set nls_date_format = 'YYYY MM DD';

col c0 heading 'date'    format a15
col c1 heading 'action' format a20
col c2 heading 'Count'  format 99,999

break on c0 skip 2

compute sum of c2 on c0

select
    to_char(log_date,'yyyy-mm-dd hh24') c0,
    action                              c1,
    count(*)                            c2
from
    ORASSO.WWSSO_AUDIT_LOG_TABLE_T
group by
    to_char(log_date,'yyyy-mm-dd hh24'),
    action;




prompt ****************************************************
prompt SSO Message summary Report
prompt ****************************************************

col c1 heading 'message' format a20

select
    to_char(log_date,'yyyy-mm-dd hh24') c0,
    message                             c1,
    count(*)                            c2
from
    ORASSO.WWSSO_AUDIT_LOG_TABLE_T
group by
    to_char(log_date,'yyyy-mm-dd hh24'),
    message;
```

```
set lines 80


prompt ****************************************************
prompt SSO Activity Detail Report
prompt ****************************************************


alter session set nls_date_format = 'YYYY-MM-DD HH24:MI:SS';

col c1 Heading 'Date'    format a20
col c2 heading 'User'    format a10
col c3 heading 'Action'  format a10
col c4 heading 'Message' format a20

select
    log_date       c1,
    user_name      c2,
    action         c3,
    message        c4
from
    ORASSO.WWSSO_AUDIT_LOG_TABLE_T
;
```

The following listing shows the output from this report. Here you see a summary of all login operations, summed by hour of the day. You also see counts of all SSO messages summed by hour of the day. The last report in this section shows all SSO details.

```
****************************************************
SSO Activity summary Report
****************************************************


date              action                  Count
---------------   --------------------   -------
2003-06-04 09     LOGIN                        4
**************                           -------
sum                                            4


2003-06-04 10     LOGIN                        1
**************                           -------
sum                                            1


2003-06-04 11     LOGIN                        2
**************                           -------
sum                                            2
```

```
2003-06-04 14   LOGIN                        1
***************                         -------
sum                                          1


2003-06-04 20   LOGIN                        2
***************                         -------
sum                                          2


2003-06-05 08   LOGIN                        1
***************                         -------
sum                                          1


2003-07-08 14   LOGIN                        3
***************                         -------
sum                                          3


2003-07-10 08   LOGIN                        4
***************                         -------
sum                                          4



*******************************************************
SSO Message summary Report
*******************************************************

date            message                 Count
---------------  --------------------   -------
2003-06-04 09   Login failed                 4
***************                         -------
sum                                          4


2003-06-04 10   Login Successful            11
                Login failed                 4
***************                         -------
sum                                         15


2003-06-04 11   Login Successful           334
***************                         -------
sum                                        334


2003-06-04 14   Login Successful           432
```

```
                 Login failed                14
***************                         -------
sum                                        446


2003-06-04 20   Login Successful            62
                Login failed                 3
***************                         -------
sum                                         65


2003-06-05 08   Login Successful           433
                Login failed                61
***************                         -------
sum                                        494


2003-07-08 14   Login failed                 3
***************                         -------
sum                                          3

2003-07-10 08   Login failed                 4
***************                         -------
sum                                          4



****************************************************
SSO Activity Detail Report
****************************************************
Date                 User       Action     Message
-------------------  ---------- ---------- --------------------

2003-06-04 09:45:42  GARMANYJ   LOGIN      Login failed
2003-06-04 11:46:27  GARMANYJ   LOGIN      Login Successful
2003-06-04 14:32:52  GARMANYJ   LOGIN      Login Successful
2003-06-04 20:58:44  GARMANYJ   LOGIN      Login Successful
2003-06-05 08:58:24  GARMANYJ   LOGIN      Login Successful
2003-07-08 14:28:20  GARMANYJ   LOGIN      Login failed
2003-07-08 14:28:26  GARMANYJ   LOGIN      Login failed
2003-07-08 14:28:37  GARMANYJ   LOGIN      Login failed
2003-07-10 08:29:49  GARMANYJ   LOGIN      Login failed
2003-07-10 08:29:53  GARMANYJ   LOGIN      Login failed
2003-07-10 08:30:00  GARMANYJ   LOGIN      Login failed
2003-07-10 08:30:05  GARMANYJ   LOGIN      Login failed
2003-06-04 09:42:24  IAS_ADMIN  LOGIN      Login failed
2003-06-04 09:42:12  ORACLADMIN LOGIN      Login failed
2003-06-04 09:42:44  ORACLADMIN LOGIN      Login failed
2003-06-04 10:22:18  ORCLADMIN  LOGIN      Login Successful
2003-06-04 11:39:45  ORCLADMIN  LOGIN      Login Successful
2003-06-04 20:53:24  ORCLADMIN  LOGIN      Login Successful
```

You can also write a script to check the availability of SSO. As noted earlier, if the infrastructure is down or SSO cannot accept connections, no users can access your system. Hence, frequently checking SSO connectivity is an important Application Server 10*g* administration task.

Here is a Perl script that you can use to check SSO availability. This script checks to see if the Single Sign-On (SSO) Server is accessible and is responding to HTTP requests.

check_sso.pl

```
PERL5LIB=$ORACLE_HOME/perl/lib/5.6.1:$ORACLE_HOME/perl/lib/site_perl/5.6.1 ;
export PERL5LIB ;
$ORACLE_HOME/perl/bin/perl -e '
$returncode = "NOK";
$oraclehome =  $ENV{'ORACLE_HOME'};
use IO::Socket;
 $url = $ARGV[0];
 $host = $ARGV[1];
$searchstring = $ARGV[2];
open FILE, "$oraclehome/install/portlist.ini" or die "File portlist.ini not
found";
while ($line = <FILE>) {
 $i = index $line, $searchstring;
 if ( $i == 0 ) {
        if ($line =~ /(=)([ ]*)(\S+)/) {
                $port =  $3;
        }
 }
}
close FILE;
 $this_socket = new IO::Socket::INET PeerAddr => $host, Timeout  => "9",
PeerPort => $port, Proto    => "tcp" ;
 if(!$this_socket){
   $returncode = "NOK";
 } else {
 $get_request = ("GET $url HTTP/1.0\r\n" );
 $this_socket->print ($get_request);
 $this_socket->print("Accept: text/plain\n");
 $this_socket->print("Accept: text/html\n");
 $this_socket->print("UserAgent: LoogBrowser/1.0\n\n");
 $returncode="POK";
 while ($line=($this_socket->getline()))
 {
   if ( $line =~ /(HTTP\/1.1 200 OK)/) {
     $returncode = "POK";
   }
   if ( $line =~ /(Access Partner Applications)/) {
     $returncode = "OK";
   }
 }
}
 print $returncode
' "/pls/orasso/orasso.home" "localhost"  "Oracle HTTP Server port"
```

If this script returns the standard output of "OK," then SSO can accept HTTP requests. Many Application Server 10g administrators place this script into a cron task and run it every five minutes. If there is a failure in SSO, a pager alert is immediately sent to the administrator. Now, let's look at using the mod_osso utility for SSO administration.

SSO Administration Using the mod_osso Utility

As SSO expanded into the Application Server 10*g* architecture, Oracle recognized that the Oracle HTTP Server (OHS) should be included in the SSO framework. Starting with Application Server 10*g* version 2, the mod_osso module was created to allow SSO to function within OHS.

Before mod_osso, specific logic would have to be embedded into the Java application if the application was to use SSO. The mod_osso module now makes it easy for incoming users to connect directly to SSO, become authorized, and get the required information to access their applications (Figure 2-5). The mod_osso utility also allows for a single security point, thereby relieving the tedious and cumbersome problem of maintaining multiple securities for each Application Server 10*g* component.

To see SSO in action, let's look at the steps that occur when an Application Server 10*g* client connects to his or her application:

1. The user requests a URL through a web browser. This URL is intercepted by the Oracle HTTP Server.

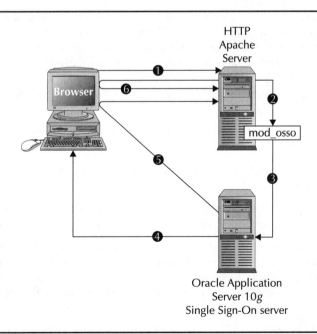

FIGURE 2-5. *Using SSO to connect to Application Server 10*g

2. The HTTP Server calls mod_osso to locate a cookie for the user on the HTTP Server. If the cookie exists, the web server extracts the user's information and uses it to log the user in to the requested application. At this point the connection is established.

3. If the cookie does not exist on the HTTP Server, mod_osso redirects the user to the Single Sign-On server.

4. The Single Sign-On server makes a request back to the user's browser to see if a local cookie exists on the user's PC. If it finds no remote cookie, SSO tries to authenticate the user with a username and password. If authentication is successful, the Single Sign-On server creates a cookie in the browser as a reminder that the user has been authenticated. If a cookie exists, the Single Sign-On server will authenticate using the cookie.

5. Upon successful sign-on, the SSO server then returns the user's encrypted information to mod_osso.

6. mod_osso creates a cookie for the user and sends it to the browser PC. It then redirects the user to his or her original URL page.

As you see, mod_osso is an alternative method for maintaining SSO, but it is not as powerful as server-side scripting for command interfaces.

Summary

The Oracle Application Server 10*g* infrastructure is a critical component of your enterprise because it serves as a centralized repository and management facility that controls the operation of several vital components. The focus of this chapter has been on the configuration and management of the infrastructure, and the main points are as follows:

- The Application Server 10*g* infrastructure is a database instance with an ORACLE_SID of iasdb.

- The iasdb instance contains separate schemas for each component within the Application Server 10*g* architecture.

- The infrastructure database contains more than 10,000 objects and over 1000 individual tables.

- The infrastructure contains log tables that monitor administration and usage activities for several Application Server 10*g* components, including Portal and SSO.

- Startup and shutdown of the infrastructure must be carefully coordinated with other system processes, such that the infrastructure is started before the Application Server 10*g* components. Upon shutdown, the Application Server 10*g* processes and services must be stopped before shutting down the infrastructure. Scripts are the recommended way of doing this!

- Because the infrastructure is a central point of failure for the entire enterprise, administrators commonly use tools such as Oracle9*i* and Oracle Data Guard or Oracle Real Application Clusters to ensure against instance failure. Many administrators also use multiple levels of RAID to ensure against unexpected disk failure.

■ The SSO component of the Application Server 10*g* repository is arguably one of the single most important components of the enterprise. All incoming connections to the Application Server 10*g* must pass through the infrastructure SSO login server; thus it is vital that the SSO login server be continuously available for servicing HTTP requests.

In the next chapter we will look at details of the initial installation and configuration of Application Server 10*g* and its components.

CHAPTER
3

Installing Oracle
Application Server 10g

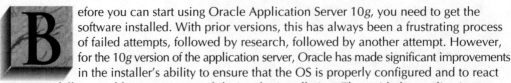efore you can start using Oracle Application Server 10*g*, you need to get the software installed. With prior versions, this has always been a frustrating process of failed attempts, followed by research, followed by another attempt. However, for the 10*g* version of the application server, Oracle has made significant improvements in the installer's ability to ensure that the OS is properly configured and to react more gracefully to problems encountered during the installation. That said, the application server is still a complicated set of interacting software components, and the installation still requires some planning.

This chapter will teach you how to install the Application Server 10*g* on a UNIX/Linux platform. At the time of this writing, the Windows version of the Application Server 10*g* was not yet available.

Planning for the Application Server Installation

As with installing any version of Oracle Application Server, some understanding of the components and their interaction is required. As discussed in Chapter 1, the application server is much more than the Apache web server. The application server is the marriage of the web server to the Oracle Containers for Java (OC4J). If your only requirement is to serve static web pages with servlets accessing a database, the Oracle Database installs with a fully functional web server that implements Apache's Jserv. On the other hand, if you need to configure and load-balance ten web servers connected to a back-end database, and your applications require a range of J2EE services, you will need the clustering capabilities and consolidated management that Application Server 10*g* provides.

Installation Types

Application Server 10*g* has four installation types. The smallest *midtier* installation is the J2EE and Web Cache installation type, the second type adds Oracle Application Server Portal and Wireless 10*g*, while the largest is the Business Intelligence and Forms installation. The fourth type of installation is the Oracle Application Server infrastructure. Installations that include more than J2EE also require the installation of an infrastructure instance, explained in Chapter 2.

J2EE and Web Cache
The J2EE and Web Cache installation includes the Oracle HTTP Server (OHS), the Oracle Containers for Java (OC4J), and the Web Cache. These are the base components and are included in all other installations. The J2EE and Web Cache installation can function in standalone mode or be included in an infrastructure instance's farm. When used in the standalone mode, the J2EE and Web Cache instance requires manual configuration and management. When installed as a member of a farm, the instance is configured within the Oracle Enterprise Manager Application Server Control.

Portal and Wireless
This installation includes the J2EE and Web Cache installation plus the Portal and Wireless components. Both components require access to Oracle's Identity Management and the metadata repository in the infrastructure instance.

Business Intelligence and Forms
To install all available components, you need to install the Business Intelligence and Forms. This installation type includes the Portal and Wireless components plus Oracle Application Server Discoverer, Personalization, Reports Services, and Oracle Forms. This middle tier also requires access to an infrastructure instance.

Even though the installation types build on each other, you are not required to configure and start all of the components. For instance, if your organization uses Oracle Forms, you can install the Business Intelligence and Forms installation type but choose not to configure Portal, Wireless, Discoverer, Personalization, and Reports Services. This will allow you to utilize your server resources properly by not starting components that are not needed. This will be discussed later when we walk through the installation.

Infrastructure

As discussed in Chapter 2, many of the application server's capabilities require the use of an infrastructure instance. The infrastructure instance provides access for the middle tiers to Oracle's Internet Directory, Identity Management, and the metadata repository. When a middle tier instance is installed, it is tied to an infrastructure instance, so the infrastructure instance must already be installed and running.

Server Configuration

Once you decide which installation type meets your needs, you must decide how you are going to configure your servers to support the installation. If all components of the application server are going to reside on one physical server, you need to ensure that the server contains enough memory and disk space. Since Application Server 10g runs very well on low-cost, commodity servers, most production deployments spread components/instances across multiple servers to increase scalability and availability. If you can afford the resources, deploy instances on separate servers and place Web Cache on a separate server, as shown in Figure 3-1.

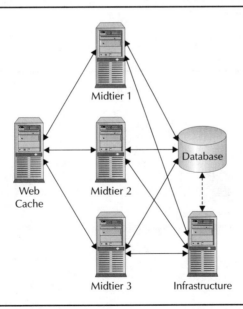

FIGURE 3-1. *Installing instances on separate servers*

By deploying Web Cache on a separate server, you can easily add midtier instances and load-balance them according to their capabilities. A new feature in Application Server 10*g* is the ability of the infrastructure instance to maintain the metadata repository in the infrastructure database or in a back-end database. This capability enhances manageability but could cause some performance degradation in a highly loaded back-end database. This is discussed in more detail in Chapter 9.

A common configuration (Figure 3-2) combines the infrastructure instance and a midtier instance on a single server and uses Web Cache to reduce the load on the midtier.

Finally, for smaller implementations, the entire Application Server 10*g* can be installed on a single server, from Web Cache to back-end database, provided the server has the capacity to handle the load. This configuration is recommended only for small implementations or development environments.

Server Requirements

At the time of this writing, Application Server 10*g* has been released on Solaris, HP-UX, and Linux operating systems. Table 3-1 lays out the minimum hardware requirements for each OS. Note that this includes installation of the infrastructure database on the same server as the midtier components. If you install the individual components on separate servers, the disk space requirements will be drastically lower.

The memory and disk space requirements are to install and run the application. As you continue through the book, you will find that you can increase performance by increasing the JVM HEAP size and having multiple JVMs for each of the OC4J instances. Unless you have multiple instances of one server, increasing server RAM beyond 4GB will probably not increase performance. The Application Server Control displays memory usage, and sizing memory requirements is discussed in detail in Chapter 10.

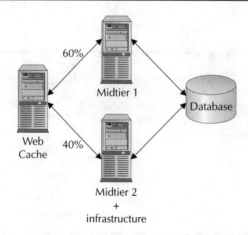

FIGURE 3-2. *Using Web Cache to load-balance multiple application server instances*

	Solaris 8, 9	HP-UX	Linux
Processor		64-bit PA-RISC 240 MHz	32-bit Pentium 450 MHz
Memory/Disk Space			
Infrastructure	1GB/2.6GB	1GB/3.6GB	1GB/2.5GB
J2EE and Web Cache	512MB/600MB	512MB/600MB	512MB/600MB
Portal/Wireless	1GB/975MB	1GB/1.6GB	1GB/1.1GB
Business Intelligence/Forms	1GB/1.6GB	1GB/2.3GB	1GB/1.65GB
TMP Space	3.5GB	3.5GB	3.5GB
Swap Space	1.5GB	1.5GB	1.5GB

TABLE 3-1.   *Minimum Server Requirements*

Other Planning Considerations

There are a number of requirements that you need to consider before starting the installation process. This section will explain these requirements.

Oracle Home

All Oracle DBAs are familiar with the environmental variable called Oracle Home— the directory where the installer places all the product-related files. Oracle Home must be unique for each instance installed on a server, including the back-end Oracle Database. In Table 3-1, the disk space requirements are for the Oracle Home directory, so ensure that you place it on a mount point with sufficient space. Throughout this book we will reference files using the $ORACLE_ HOME environmental variable to identify files, for example:

```
$ORACLE_HOME/opmn/bin/opmnctl startall
```

The specific file opmnctl is referenced under the $ORACLE_HOME of the instance that the command is starting. As you will see later, the installer will unset the ORACLE_HOME variable when it starts and ask you to define an ORACLE_HOME for each installation.

Ports

Each application server instance installed on the same server will be installed using unique ports. This includes all components that listen on ports, such as OHS or Web Cache. This could get complicated; however, the installer checks ports before assigning them and will assign unused ports as needed. When setting up the operating system, you will need to ensure that enough ports are available to the installer, and it will do the rest. Each installation will end with a page that displays the instance and Application Server Control port used. You should write this information down! You can find the ports used by an instance in the Enterprise Manager web site under the PORTS link or in the $ORACLE_HOME/install/portlist.ini file.

One port that must be available to install the infrastructure is port 1521, which is the Listener port for the database. That port can be shared with another Oracle database, but it must be available.

Documentation

This chapter will provide you with the information you need to install Application Server 10*g*. If you are planning to use the application server in a production environment, we recommend that you also review the Installation Guide and the Release Notes. These documents can be reviewed on the Oracle Technology Network (OTN) web site at otn.oracle.com or in the /docs directory on Disk1 of the installation disks.

Operating System Setup

In Application Server 10*g*, the installer has been greatly improved to include checking the OS to ensure that it is properly set up for the install. If the installer reports that the OS is not configured properly, cancel the install and fix the problem. You must install all OS patches that the installer identifies as missing. The following information is current as of this writing, but it is always best to consult the Installation Guide and README document for your operating system.

Solaris 8,9 Packages

- SUNWarc
- SUNWbtool
- SUNWhea
- SUNWlibm
- SUNWlibms
- SUNWsprot
- SUNWsprox
- SUNWtoo
- SUNWxwfnt
- SUNWi1cs
- SUNWi15cs

Solaris 8 Patches

- 108652-74 or higher: X11 6.4.1: Xsun patch
- 108921-17 or higher: CDE 1.4: Dtwm patch
- 108940-57 or higher: Motif 1.2.7 and 2.1.1: Run-time library patch

- 112003-03 or higher: Unable to load font set in 64-bit Solaris 8 iso-1 or iso-15
- 108773-18 or higher: IIIM and X input and output method patch
- 111310-01 or higher: /usr/lib/libdhcpagent.so.1 patch
- 109147-26 or higher: Linker patch
- 111308-04 or higher: /usr/lib/libmtmalloc.so.1 patch
- 112438-02 or higher: /kernel/drv/random patch
- 108434-13 or higher: 32-bit shared library patch for C++
- 111111-03 or higher: /usr/bin/nawk patch
- 112396-02 or higher: /usr/bin/fgrep patch
- 110386-03 or higher: RBAC feature patch
- 111023-02 or higher: /kernel/fs/mntfs and /kernel/fs/sparcv9/mntfs patch
- 108987-13 or higher: Patch for patchadd and patchrm
- 108528-24 or higher: Kernel update patch
- 108989-02 or higher: /usr/kernel/sys/acctctl and /usr/kernel/sys/exacctsys patch
- 108993-26 or higher: LDAP2 client, libc, libthread, and libnsl libraries patch
- 112138-01 or higher: usr/bin/domainname patch

Solaris 9 Patches

- 113096-03 or higher: X11 6.6.1: OWconfig patch
- 112785-26 or higher: X11 6.6.1: Xsun patch

HP-UX 11.0

- JDK 1.4.1.05 or higher, to include all patches from the HP JDK download site
- Sept 2002 Quality Pack (QPK1100 B.11.00.58.5) or higher
- Patches
    - PHKL_27813
    - PHSS_26559

HP-UX 11i

- JDK 1.4.1.05 or higher, to include all patches from the HP JDK download site
- Dec 2001 Consolidated Patches (Dec01GQPK11i_Aux_Patch B.03.02.06) or higher

- Patches
  - PHKL_25212
  - PHKL_25506
  - PHKL_27091
  - PHKL_28089
  - PHSS_24638
  - PHSS_26263
  - PHSS_26792
  - PHSS_26793

Linux RH 2.1 AS/ES

- Kernel 2.4.9-e.25 or greater
- Gcc-2.96-108.1 or greater
- Pdksh-5.2.14-13 or greater
- Openmotif-2.1.30
- Sysstat-4.0.1
- Compat-glibc-6.2-2.1.3.2
- Libstdc++-2.96-108.1 or greater

Linux RH 3.0 AS/ES

- Kernel 2.4.21-4-EL or greater
- glibc-2.3.2-95.3 or greater
- gcc-3.2.3-20 or greater
- setarch-1.3-1 or greater
- pdksh-5.2.14 or greater
- openmmotif21-2.1.30-8 or greater
- gnome-libs-1.4.1.2.90-34.1 or greater
- compat-glibc-7.x-2.2.4.32.5
- compat-gcc-7.3-2.96.122
- compat-libstdc++-7.3-2.96.122
- compat-gcc-c++-7.3-2.96.122
- sysstat-4.0.7

UnitedLinux 1.0

- SP2a
  - Kernel 2.4.19 or greater
  - Glibc-2.2.5-179 or greater
- SP3
  - Kernel 2.4.21
  - Glibc-2.2.5-213
- Gcc_old-2.95.3
- Pdksh-5.2.14
- Openmotif-2.1.30MLI4
- Sysstat-4.0.3
- Libstdc++-3.2.2-38

Now that your install plan is ready and you know your operating system requirements, it is time to install the application server.

Operating System Installation and Configuration

At this point, we are going to walk through the installation of the application server using RedHat AS 2.1. All installations follow the same methodology with some operating system–specific variations. As mentioned, you must ensure that the operating system is up-to-date and meets the minimum requirements before starting the installation. This step is the one most often skipped and the reason for most installation problems.

For this example we start with a fresh install. If you did not recently obtain your copy of RedHat 2.1 AS/ES, we recommend that you check the ISOs available for download from www.redhat.com, as they periodically update the disks.

Install RedHat 2.1 AS/ES

Start the installation and select your language. When you arrive at the disk partitioning screen, manually define your disk partitions using Disk Druid. You can implement RAID 0,1,5 at this time, but you must ensure that you meet the minimum disk space requirement on mount points that you will use for ORACLE_HOMEs according to Table 3-1. Also ensure that sufficient /tmp and swap space are defined.

When you get to the network configuration screen, it is recommended that you assign a static IP address instead of using DHCP. However, if you require the use of DHCP, you must configure the host to resolve the host name using the local loopback in the /etc/hosts file. We will discuss this later.

The next screen is the firewall configuration screen. If the server is behind a firewall, select No Firewall. If the server is not behind a firewall and you want to use the OS firewall, we recommend that you still select No Firewall and configure the firewall after the application server is installed.

If the firewall is active, you must ensure that the ports needed by the installer are open, or you will encounter problems with the installation. Once the installation is completed, you can get a list of used ports from the Application Server Control web site and then configure the firewall.

When you get to the root password screen, do not configure any other users. Continue with the installation until you get to the package group selection screen. Ensure that you include the following packages:

- Printing support
- Classic X Window System
- X Window System
- Gnome/KDE or both
- Sound and multimedia
- Network support
- Network managed workstation
- Utilities
- Software development
- Kernel development
- Windows compatibility/interoperability
- Advanced server

You should uncheck all other selections. At the bottom of the screen, choose the option Select Individual Packages and click Next. Locate the package compat-glibc-6.2-2.1.3.2 and select it. Also locate the Pdksh-5.2.14-13 package (don't worry if it is an earlier version at this time) and select it. Continue with the installation, selecting to have the server boot to your preferred desktop (Gnome or KDE).

Configure RedHat 2.1 AS/ES

When the OS reboots after the install, select the correct kernel for your system, and you're ready to configure the OS. The following sections walk you through this process.

Update Installed Packages

Log on as root and run the Red Hat update program. First run /usr/sbin/rhn_register. Next run the Update Agent located in the system or system-settings folder, depending on whether you are using Gnome or KDE. The Update Agent will check all the installed packages against the latest versions and update any needed packages. The Update Agent will also update the kernel to one optimized for the server processor. It is important that you select the kernel for update, as the default is to exclude the kernel. The first time you run the Update Agent, it may take quite a while to complete. Once the Update Agent has completed, reboot the server to begin using the updated packages.

Verify Minimum Requirements

The next step is to verify that all packages meet the minimum requirements to install Application Server 10*g*.

```
[root@appsvr root]# grep MemTotal /proc/meminfo
MemTotal:        1535772 kB
[root@appsvr root]# grep SwapTotal /proc/meminfo
SwapTotal:       2097136 kB
[root@appsvr root]# df -k
Filesystem           1k-blocks      Used Available Use% Mounted on
/dev/hda2            38362000   3449504  32963812  10% /
/dev/hda1             101089     22773     73097  24% /boot
none                 767884         0    767884   0% /dev/shm
/dev/hdb2           35445208   2729792  30914876   9% /u01
/dev/hdd1           38464340   1549752  34960684   5% /u02
```

As you can see from the example, this server has greater than the 1GB memory and greater than 1.5GB of swap space. There is also plenty of disk space for the installation of both the infrastructure and middle tiers. For performance reasons, you should install the infrastructure on a separate server, but for this example, both the infrastructure and the middle tier will be installed on a single server.

Next, verify that the kernel is greater than errata 25.

```
[root@appsvr root]# uname -r
2.4.9-e.34
```

At the time of this install, the current errata is 34. If your kernel is not greater than 25, rerun the Update Agent and select the kernel for update.

Now you need to verify the other packages. The easiest way to do this is to use the rpm utility. If you pass in the –qa parameters, rpm will list all packages installed on the server. If you only pass in the –q parameter, you must pass in the package name (without the version number). You can also use the grep utility to limit the return of the –qa parameters. Ensure that the packages are greater than the minimum required. If you ran the Update Agent, all packages should be greater than the minimum required.

```
[root@appsvr root]# rpm -q gcc
gcc-2.96-124.7.2
[root@appsvr root]# rpm -qa |grep gcc
gcc-2.96-124.7.2
gcc-c++-2.96-124.7.2
gcc-objc-2.96-124.7.2
gcc-g77-2.96-124.7.2
```

Check each of the required packages.

```
[root@appsvr root]# rpm -qa |grep openmotif
openmotif-2.1.30-11
openmotif-devel-2.1.30-11
[root@appsvr root]# rpm -qa |grep sysstat
```

```
sysstat-4.0.1-2
[root@appsvr root]# rpm -qa |grep libstdc
libstdc++-2.96-124.7.2
compat-libstdc++-6.2-2.9.0.16
libstdc++-devel-2.96-124.7.2
[root@appsvr root]# rpm -qa |grep pdkah
[root@appsvr root]# rpm -qa |grep pdksh
pdksh-5.2.14-22
[root@appsvr root]# rpm -qa |grep compat-glibc
compat-glibc-6.2-2.1.3.2
```

The last two packages must be installed. If rpm does not return anything for pdksh and compat-glibc, you must install them. Neither are installed by default, and both are found on the Red Hat installation disk 2 under the /RedHat/RPMS directory. To install a package from the CD-ROM, use the rpm utility.

```
rpm -i /mnt/cdrom/RedHat/RPMS/pdksh-5.2.14-13.i386.rpm
rpm -i /mnt/cdrom/RedHat/RPMS/compat-glibc-6.2-2.1.3.2.i386.rpm
```

After installing pdksh, you can run the Update Agent to update the package to the latest errata. Also, the errata number for these packages may be different in your distribution, so ensure that you use the rpm file name from your CD-ROM.

Modify Kernel Parameters

The next step is to modify the kernel parameters. Application Server 10*g* is highly multithreaded, and in Linux all threads are spawned as processes. As a result, the kernel must be configured to handle a large number of processes. If you are only going to install the J2EE and Web Cache, the default kernel parameters will work, otherwise you will need to make the modifications shown next. Since the kernel will need to maintain the configuration after rebooting, the modifications need to be implemented in the /etc/sysctl.conf file. Open the sysctl.conf file in your favorite editor and add the following lines:

```
#Oracle 9ias params
kernel.sem = 256 32000 100 142
kernel.shmmax = 4294967295
kernel.shmmni = 4096
kernel.shmall = 2097152
kernel.msgmax = 8192
kernel.msgmni = 2878
kernel.msgmnb = 65535
net.ipv4.ip_local_port_range = 1024 65000
fs.file-max = 131072
```

This configuration is the minimum except for

- shmmax = 2147483648

- shmmni = 142

If your current parameters are greater than those specified, use the current setting. Save the file and reboot the server to use the new settings. You can verify that the new parameters are being used after rebooting by listing them with this command:

```
[root@appsvr root]# /sbin/sysctl -a
```

The next step is to increase the shell limits. Edit the /etc/security/limits.conf file, adding the following lines at the end:

```
*               soft    nofile      2048
*               hard    nofile      16384
*               soft    nproc       2047
*               hard    nproc       16384
```

Each line follows this format:

```
*<Tab><Tab>soft<Tab>nofile<Tab><Tab>2048
```

Save the file. Next edit the /etc/pam.d/limits.conf file, adding the following line at the bottom if it does not exist:

```
session     required      /lib/security/pam_limits.so
```

Now verify that port 1521 is not being used:

```
[root@appsvr root]# netstat -an | grep 1521
```

You must verify that the port is not being used because it is required for the metadata repository database. This port can be shared with another Oracle database, but if it is being used by any other application, you must change the port used by the other application.

Create the *oracle* User and Groups

Like Oracle databases, the *oracle* operating system user usually installs the application server. The easiest way to create the *oracle* user and the install groups is from the command line as the root user. First create the install group to own all the product files:

```
[root@appsvr root]# groupadd oinstall
```

If you are installing the infrastructure instance, you will need the database groups to manage the metadata repository database:

```
[root@appsvr root]# groupadd dba
[root@appsvr root]# groupadd oper
```

Next create the *oracle* user and assign the oinstall as the primary group.

```
[root@appsvr root]# useradd -g oinstall oracle
```

If you are installing the infrastructure, the *oracle* user needs to be assigned to the dba and oper groups also:

```
[root@appsvr root]# useradd -g oinstall -G dba,oper oracle
```

Now set the *oracle* user's password:

```
[root@appsvr root]# passwd oracle
```

You will be asked for a password and then asked to verify the password.

Before you change to the *oracle* user, you need to set some environmental variables. As root, edit the /etc/profile file, adding the following code to increase the file number limit and process number limit for the *oracle* user.

```
if [ $USER = "oracle" ]; then
    if [ $SHELL = "/bin/ksh" ]; then
        ulimit -n 16384
        ulimit -p 16384
    else

        ulimit -u 16384 -n 16384
    fi
fi
```

Place the code before the export statement. At the end of the file before the "unset i" statement, define the TMP directory. You can also define a TMPDIR directory, but if you don't, the installer will just use the TMP directory.

```
TMP=/tmp; export TMP
TMPDIR=/tmp; export TMPDIR
```

Log out and log in as the *oracle* user. You can verify that the limits are set correctly with the following command:

```
[root@appsvr root]# su - oracle
[oracle@appsvr oracle]$ ulimit -aH
core file size        (blocks)    unlimited
data seg size         (kbytes)    unlimited
file size             (blocks)    unlimited
max locked memory     (kbytes)    unlimited
max memory size       (kbytes)    unlimited
open files                        16384
pipe size          (512 bytes)    8
stack size            (kbytes)    unlimited
cpu time             (seconds)    unlimited
max user processes                16384
virtual memory        (kbytes)    unlimited
```

NOTE
You must be the oracle *user when you execute the command because the limits are set only for the* oracle *user.*

Download the Software

You can get the Application Server 10g software from otn.oracle.com. Download the four files to a staging directory (whichever you choose, as long as it is owned by the *oracle* user). The four files are archived using a utility called cpio and then compressed using gzip. To extract the files, first unzip all four files using the gunzip utility:

```
[oracle@appsvr oracle]$ gunzip ias904_linux_disk1.cpio.gz
```

Next, use the cpio utility to extract the files from the archive. The cpio utility will create the files in the subdirectories from which they were archived, so after using cpio on the four files, you will be left with four subdirectories, Disk1 through Disk4:

```
cpio -idmv < ias904_linux_disk1.cpio
```

Notice that you pipe the file into the cpio utility.
   In the following example, we extracted the files in the /home/oracle/ias directory.

```
[oracle@appsvr ias]$ ls -l
drwxr-xr-x   7 oracle    oinstall    4096 Dec 15 18:21 Disk1
drwxr-xr-x   3 oracle    oinstall    4096 Dec 15 11:59 Disk2
drwxr-xr-x   3 oracle    oinstall    4096 Dec 15 12:00 Disk3
drwxr-xr-x   3 oracle    oinstall    4096 Dec 15 12:01 Disk4
```

You will find the installer in the Disk1 subdirectory.

Optional but Recommended Configuration

The next two changes are optional but recommended and were required in previous releases of Oracle's application server. The /etc/hosts file is used to resolve host names to IP addresses to include the local loopback. The installer should use the hosts file in its installed format, but it is recommended that you place it in the following format:

```
127.0.0.1         localhost.proxitec      localhost
192.168.1.49      appsvr.proxitec.com     appsvr
```

If you are not using a static IP address, you must add the local loopback address for the host name so that the different application server components can resolve the host IP.

```
127.0.0.1         localhost.proxitec      localhost
```

```
127.0.0.1         appsvr.proxitec.com     appsvr
```

Finally, it is recommended that you remove the Linux LDAP service and free the port for Oracle's LDAP implementation called Oracle Internet Directory. If you do not execute this step, the installer will assign a free port to OID without a problem. By executing this step, the installer can configure OID to use the standard LDAP ports. Unless you have applications using the Linux LDAP that you do not want to integrate into OID, you should execute this step. You need to edit the /etc/services file, removing all lines containing the port numbers 386 and 636. You should remove four lines, two for each port. Save the file and reboot the server.

Installation of Application Server 10*g*

At this point, you are ready to begin installing Application Server 10*g*. In reality, there are some other planning steps that should be accomplished first, such as determining how the system is to be deployed and on which set of machines, deciding where the infrastructure should be installed, how many midtier instances are required, and so on. These issues are discussed in later chapters, and there are numerous OTN articles, white papers, and product guides available on otn.oracle.com.

The following sections take you step-by-step through the installation process, starting with the installation of the infrastructure and then a midtier that contains Portal and Oracle Forms. Like the Oracle Database, Application Server 10*g* uses the Oracle Universal Installer (OUI), which will walk you through the installation. The OUI also supports silent and noninteractive installations.

If you have been making changes to operating system files and have not rebooted, do so now to ensure that all changes are in effect. Log onto the server as the *oracle* user. Change directory to the /home/oracle/stage/Disk1 directory (or to the directory to which you extracted the installation files).

Environmental Variables

Verify that at least the TMP environmental variable is set.

```
[oracle@appsvr Disk1]$ env |grep TMP
TMPDIR=/tmp
TMP=/tmp
```

Verify that no ORACLE environmental variables are set, such as ORACLE_HOME or ORACLE_SID. You should not try to preset the ORACLE_HOME variable, as it is unset by the installer. (Note that these environmental variables will not be present unless you have installed an Oracle product on your server before.)

```
[oracle@appsvr Disk1]$ env |grep -i oracle
USER=oracle
MAIL=/var/spool/mail/oracle
LOGNAME=oracle
HOME=/home/oracle
PATH=/bin:/usr/bin:/usr/local/bin:/usr/bin/X11:/usr/X11R6/bin
OLDPWD=/home/oracle
```

Ensure that the LD_LIBRARY_PATH, CLASSPATH environmental variables are not set and that there are no previous ORACLE_HOME variables in the PATH.

```
[oracle@appsvr Disk1]$ env | grep -i path
PATH=/bin:/usr/bin:/usr/local/bin:/usr/bin/X11:/usr/X11R6/bin
```

Next, ensure that TNS_ADMIN, ORA_NLS33 or LD_BIND_NOW environmental variables are not set.

```
[oracle@appsvr Disk1]$ env | grep -i tns
[oracle@appsvr Disk1]$ env | grep -i nls33
[oracle@appsvr Disk1]$ env | grep -i bind
[oracle@appsvr Disk1]$
```

The final environmental variable to set is DISPLAY. The Oracle Universal Installer is a Java-based graphical program, which requires that X Windows is available. To tell Java where to display the graphics, you use the DISPLAY variable. If the Display variable is not properly set, the installer will fail on startup.

If you are performing a local install, set DISPLAY to the server:

```
[oracle@appsvr Disk1]$ DISPLAY=appsvr.proxitec.com:0.0; export DISPLAY
```

If you are executing an install from another server, point the DISPLAY variable to the host you are on:

```
[oracle@appsvr Disk1]$ DISPLAY=192.168.1.109:0.0; export DISPLAY
```

Ensure that you run xhost + to allow your host to accept the X Windows data from the remote server. If you prefer, the DISPLAY variable can be set in the .bash_profile in the user's home directory.

To verify that the DISPLAY variable is properly set, run the following command:

```
[oracle@appsvr Disk1]$ xclock
```

You should see a graphic clock displaying the current server time on either the local system or the remote system, depending on how you set the DISPLAY variable.

Installing the Infrastructure

Application Server 10*g* uses the familiar Oracle Universal Installer (OUI). To start OUI, change to the Disk1 directory and execute the runInstaller command.

```
[oracle@appsvr Disk1]$ ./runInstaller
```

If you are installing from a CD-ROM, execute the runInstaller command using the fully qualified name.

CAUTION
Do not start OUI from the /mnt/cdrom directory, or you may not be able to unmount the CD-ROM to change disks. In this case, start OUI from another directory.

```
[oracle@appsvr oracle]$ /mnt/cdrom/runInstaller
```

The first action OUI takes is to verify the operating system prerequisites.

```
Starting Oracle Universal Installer ...

Checking requirements...

Checking operating system version: must be redhat-2.1, UnitedLinux-1.0 or
redhat-3                                        Passed

All requirements met.

Checking if CPU speed is above 450 MHz.
Actual 1532 MHz     Passed
Checking for Kernel version 2.4.9-e.25        Passed
Checking for glibc version glibc-2.2.4-32       Passed
Checking operating system packages: gcc-2.96,pdksh-5.2.14,openmotif-
2.1.30,sysstat-4.0.1,compat-glibc-6.2-2.1.3.2,libstdc++-2.96     Passed
Checking swap space: must be greater than 1536 MB.
Actual 1709MB     Passed
Preparing to launch Oracle Universal Installer from /tmp/OraInstall2003-12-29_
08-46-19PM. Please wait ...
```

If any of the prerequisites fail, OUI prints an error message and asks if you want to continue with the install. Once past the OS checks, the installer presents the Welcome page, as shown in Figure 3-3.

If this is the first installation on this server using OUI, clicking Next will bring you to the Inventory Directory screen. OUI tracks the products (and what components) are installed on a server in an inventory directory normally called oraInventory. Enter the fully qualified directory name for the inventory directory. For example:

```
/opt/oracle/oraInventory
```

Next, enter the UNIX group name that will own the installation. Earlier, we defined that group name as oinstall. Clicking Next will bring up a dialog box telling you to run the ?/oraInventory/orainstRoot.sh script as root. This script sets the UNIX permissions on the oraInventory directory. Open a new terminal, change to root, and run the script.

```
su - root
cd .../oraInventory (your oraInventory location)
./orainstRoot.sh
```

Once the script has completed, return to the dialog box and select Continue. This will bring you to the file locations screen, as shown in Figure 3-4.

The Source section specifies where the installer finds the product files. It is already set, and there is no need to edit it. The Destination section defines two items. The Name text box contains a name used by OUI to identify this installation. It is not the instance name. We chose to name this install orcl_infra. The Path is the ORACLE_HOME for this installation. In Figure 3-4, we are installing the infrastructure instance into /u01/oracle/infra904.

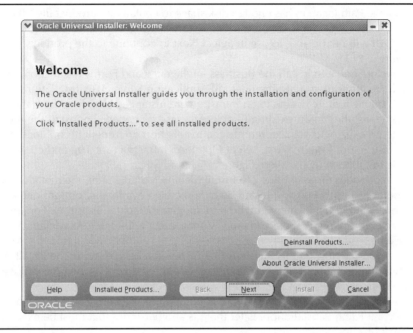

FIGURE 3-3. *Welcome page of the Oracle Universal Installer*

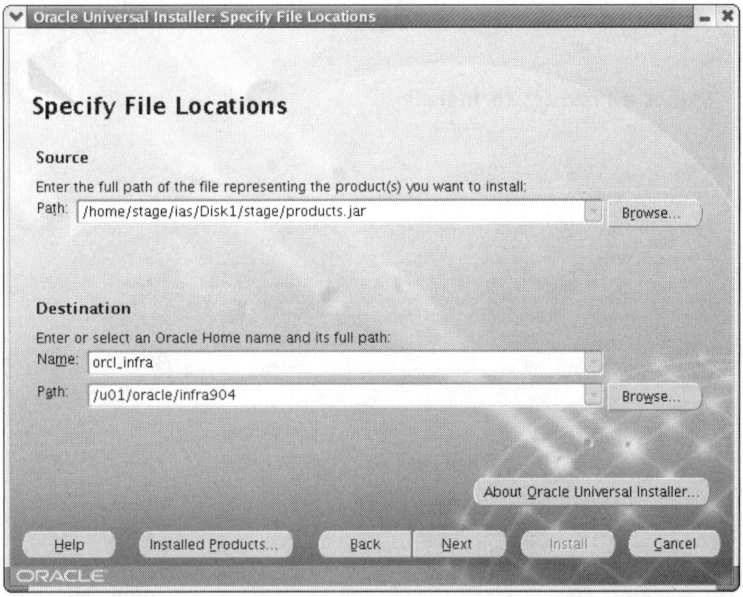

FIGURE 3-4. *Specify File Locations screen of the Oracle Universal Installer*

Ensure that the Path location has enough disk space to contain the product files. If the directory does not exist, OUI will create it. If you create it before starting OUI, ensure that the *oracle* user creates it, or OUI will not be able to use it. Select Next to continue to the products screen, as shown in Figure 3-5.

Because we are going to install the Business Intelligence and Forms installation, we will first need to install the infrastructure. Remember, all Application Server 10*g* installations except the J2EE and Web Cache require access to an infrastructure instance. Also, the metadata repository database can be installed in an existing Oracle database if needed. To install the metadata repository into an existing database, refer to the installation documentation. Since you must install the infrastructure instance first, select OracleAS Infrastructure 10*g* and click Next to proceed to the installation type screen (Figure 3-6).

This screen provides three options—to install Identity Management, the metadata repository, or to install both. Normally you will install both. Some high availability options allow you to install only the Identity Management and tie it to another metadata repository. For additional information, refer to Chapter 9. Select Identity Management and OracleAS Metadata Repository, and click Next.

The screen you see now details the steps that OUI will take to execute the install. You can read through this information, but there is no need to write it down, as the OUI will walk you through each step.

Select Next to proceed to the preinstallation requirements screen. You must be able to log on as root to complete the installation. Later there is another script that must be executed as root. Click the check box and select Next.

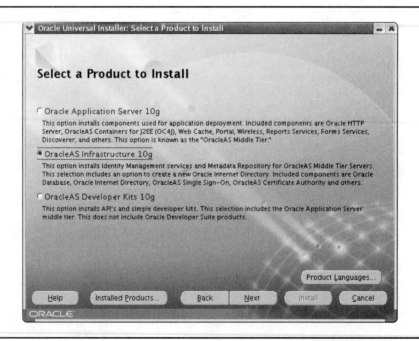

FIGURE 3-5. *Select a Product to Install screen of the Oracle Universal Installer*

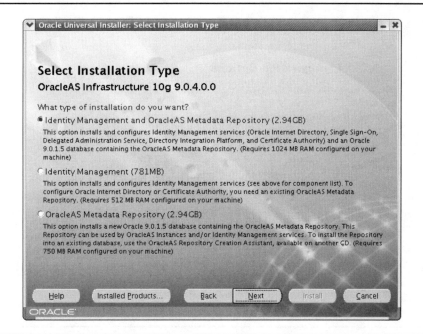

FIGURE 3-6. *Select Installation Type screen of the Oracle Universal Installer*

You are now at the configuration options screen, as shown in Figure 3-7. All of the grayed-out components are required, and you cannot select or deselect them. The other components can be added or dropped as required for your installation.

Since this example installation will include Portal, we want to maintain the default selection. If your application is not going to use OID or Single Sign-On, you can deselect all of the non-grayed-out options. If you are not sure, install the default selections. Select Next to continue to the Oracle Internet Directory namespace screen, shown in Figure 3-8.

The Oracle Internet Directory (OID) is an LDAP v3–compliant directory that is used to look up information. The Single Sign-On application uses OID to authenticate users, for example. OID places information into *realms*, and this screen is asking you to define a default realm for OID to store users, groups, and policies. We recommend that you accept the suggested namespace unless you wish to specify a namespace for your organization, such as dc=mycompany,dc=com. Click Next to proceed to the screen shown in Figure 3-9.

The Database Identification screen defines the SID and global database name for the Application Server 10*g* metadata repository database. The requirements for these items are the same as for any Oracle database. The SID is a unique name for the database. The default (which is used in the example) is asdb. In prior releases, it defaulted to iasdb. The global database name is normally the SID followed by the server's domain name. In the example, we use asdb.proxitec.com, but some of the examples in this book use iasdb.localdomain.com. The global database name is not an address but the full name of the database instance. It is used in connecting to the database and with database links. We recommend that you use asdb with your own domain name. Select Next to continue.

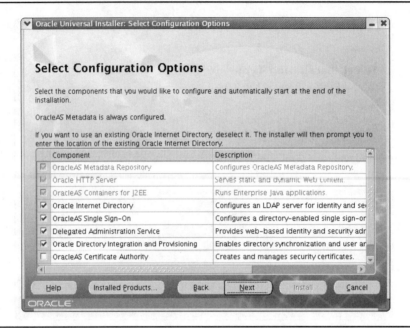

FIGURE 3-7. *Select Configuration Options screen of the Oracle Universal Installer*

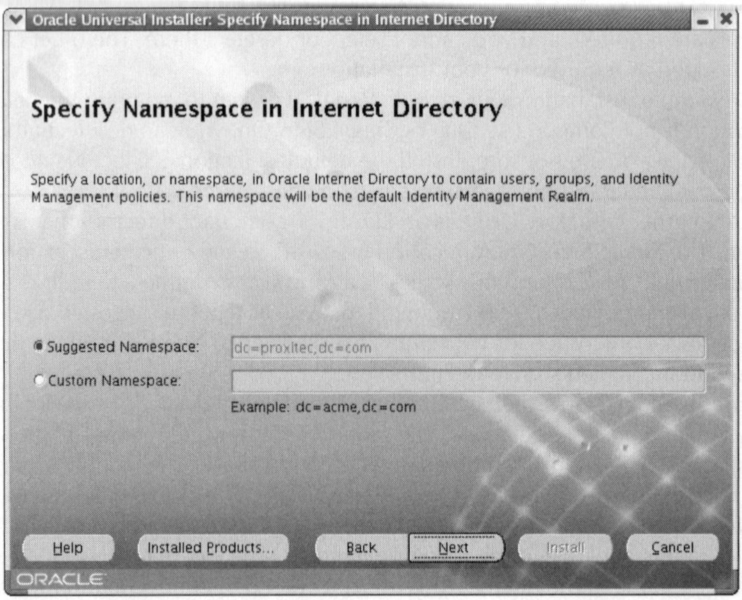

FIGURE 3-8. *Specify Namespace in Internet Directory screen of the Oracle Universal Installer*

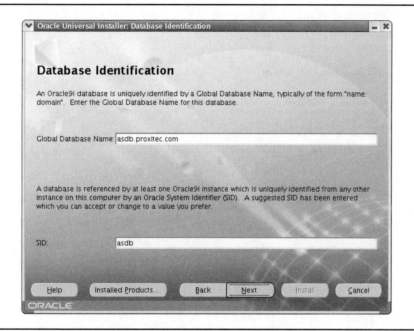

FIGURE 3-9. *Database Identification screen of the Oracle Universal Installer*

You will see a screen that allows you to set the SYS and SYSTEM passwords for the metadata repository database. Note that the passwords must meet minimum requirements, containing both letters and numbers. Write them down! There are a lot of passwords in Application Server 10*g*.

Click Next to see the screen shown in Figure 3-10. The default location for the database data files is the instance ORACLE_HOME/oradata directory, but you can locate them on any mount point that has enough disk space. All of the data files, log files, and control files are placed in this directory. Once you have entered the data file location, select Next to continue to the database character set screen.

The OUI sets a default character set based on the language setting of the operating system. If this is not correct, you can choose another character set. Normally, the default character set is correct. See the Oracle documentation for details on Oracle character sets. Select Next to proceed to the instance name and password screen, as shown in Figure 3-11.

The instance name is the unique identifier for this instance on this server. To uniquely identify the instance across multiple servers, the instance name is appended to the server name. In the example, we named this instance infra_904. The complete instance name will be infra_904.appsvr.proxitec.com. This is how Application Server Control uniquely identifies an instance from all other instances across the system architecture.

The Administrator Username is called ias_admin and cannot be changed. On the screen you set the password (letters and numbers required) for the ias_admin user. This password is unique to this instance. Multiple instances on the same server will each have an ias_admin user with its own password. You can make all the passwords the same, but it is no longer required. After entering an instance name and the ias_admin password, select Next to move to the Summary screen (Figure 3-12).

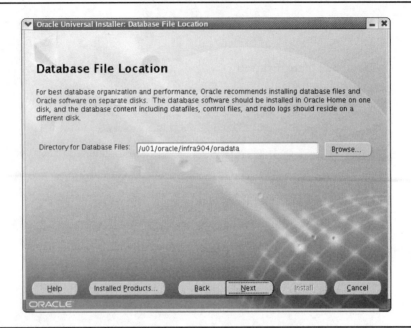

FIGURE 3-10. *Database File Location screen of the Oracle Universal Installer*

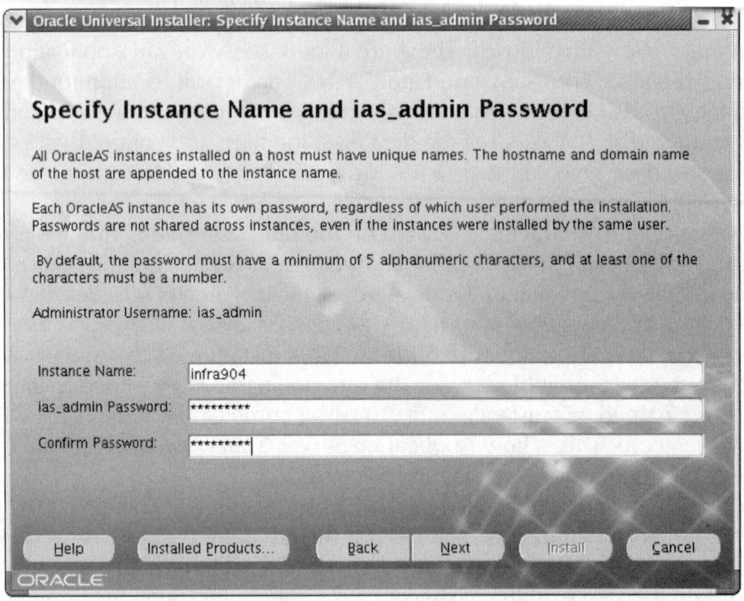

FIGURE 3-11. *Specify Instance Name and ias_admin Password screen of the Oracle Universal Installer*

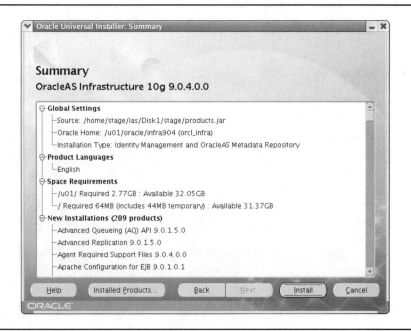

FIGURE 3-12.   *Summary screen of the Oracle Universal Installer*

As you can see, the Summary screen provides a list of all the selections you made in configuring this installation. Look through the summary to ensure you have not made any mistakes. Note that the space requirements list the mount point and the amount of space OUI will need during the installation. These figures may not be accurate, so at least in the early versions of Application Server 10g, do not trust the space requirements.

Once you have verified your selections, click Next to begin the installation. The OUI first copies the necessary files, links the required executables, sets up the applications, and then begins configuration. The installation screen, shown in Figure 3-13, has a progress bar to help you monitor the installation.

Depending on your system, this process can take quite a while (10–20 minutes), so be patient. If you are installing from the hard drive, OUI will complete this section without interaction. If you are installing from CD-ROM, you will be prompted when to change disks. If you are asked to switch disks but the drive will not open, go to the desktop, right-click on the CD-ROM icon, and select Unmount Volume.

As the progress bar nears the end, the installer will need you to run another script as root to set up privileges. The OUI will prompt you with the dialog box shown in Figure 3-14.

Open a new terminal window and change to the root user. Run the root.sh script, which is located in the instance ORACLE_HOME—in our example,

```
su - root
/u01/oracle/infra904/root.sh
```

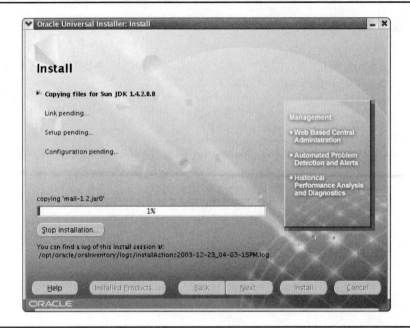

FIGURE 3-13. *Install screen of the Oracle Universal Installer*

The script will ask you where the /usr/local/bin directory is; press ENTER to select the default. The OUI will create three files in the /usr/local/bin directory that are used to set up the environment during configuration. The OUI will also execute a few other tasks. Once completed, close the terminal window and select OK on the dialog box to continue with the install.

Once the installation completes, OUI starts the configuration assistants that set up the application server, and deploy and configure components, as seen in Figure 3-15.

Each assistant is executed in order, and all need to succeed for the application server to install successfully. One new feature of the configuration assistants is that if one fails, it will stop, allowing you to retry the failed assistant. This is a nice feature since if one assistant fails, other assistants behind it will also fail or be improperly configured.

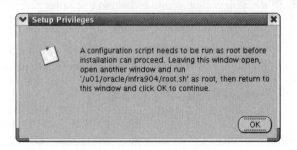

FIGURE 3-14. *Setup Privileges dialog box*

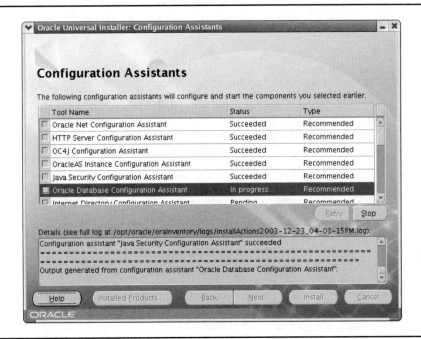

FIGURE 3-15. *Configuration Assistants screen of the Oracle Universal Installer*

Once all the configuration assistants have succeeded, OUI will display the End of Installation screen, as shown in Figure 3-16. Make a note of the server ports to connect to the instance and its Application Server Control. To log onto the instance, point your browser to the address shown. This information is also stored in the instance's ORACLE_HOME/Apache/Apache/setupinfo.txt file.

At this point, select Exit to exit the OUI. The installer is not capable of installing multiple instances without exiting.

Before proceeding to the midtier install, you should check the infrastructure to ensure that all components are up and running. Enter the Enterprise Manager Application Server Control URL into your browser. When prompted, enter the username as ias_admin and the password that you selected during the installation. This should take you to the Farm page. Select the instance link to move to the instance page, as shown in Figure 3-17.

At the end of the installation, all components should be up and running (green arrows in the Status column). If not, select the down component (red downward-pointing arrow) and click the Start button. With the infrastructure instance running, you are ready to install the middle tier.

Installing the Portal and Forms Middle Tier
If you are going to install the midtier on the same server as the infrastructure, there is no configuration change required. Unlike previous versions that required you to shut down the Enterprise Manager web site, Application Server 10*g* installs over the fully running infrastructure. In fact, provided that the infrastructure installation was successful, you can exit the installer and immediately restart it for the next installation.

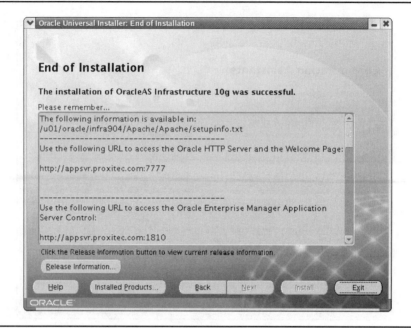

FIGURE 3-16. *End of Installation screen of the Oracle Universal Installer*

If you are installing the midtier on a separate server (recommended), you must ensure that the OS is configured and is able to communicate with the intrastructure server. Any midtier installation that includes components above the J2EE and Web Cache must be able to communicate with an infrastructure tier, or the installation will fail.

Before starting the midtier installation, open a browser and navigate to the instance status page shown in Figure 3-17. Notice the link at the top of the page labeled Ports. Select the Ports link to get a list of the ports used by the infrastructure (Figure 3-17).

Note the Oracle Internet Directory non-SSL port number—in this case, 389. The installer tries to use the standard LDAP port 389 (non-SSL) and 636 (SSL). If you did not remove those ports from the /etc/services file, OUI will have installed OID to another open port. The ports are also listed in the $ORACLE_HOME/install/portlist.ini file. You will need to know the OID ports during the midtier installation.

Start the Oracle Universal Installer in the same manner discussed under "Installing the Infrastructure." If this is the first OUI install on this server, you will have to identify the inventory location and OS installation group name (oinstall in the example). Continue to the Specify File Locations screen shown in Figure 3-18.

Remember that the Name text box contains the name of this installation, not the instance name. The Path is the ORACLE_HOME for this instance. Click Next to continue to the select products screen. Select the Oracle Application Server 10*g* to install any of the midtier options, and select Next to proceed to the installation type screen (Figure 3-19).

Notice that this screen lets you select the installation options that your system requires. In this example, we are installing both Portal and Forms, so we select the Business Intelligence and

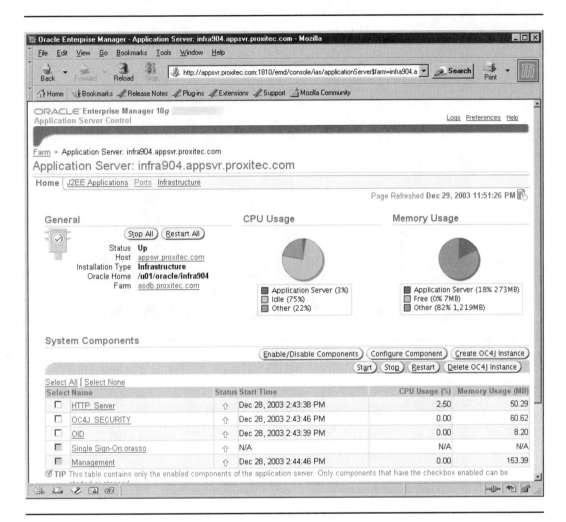

FIGURE 3-17. *Application Server Control instance status page*

Forms because it includes BI and Forms, plus Portal and Wireless, all running on the J2EE with Web Cache. Since we do not need BI and Wireless, we will not configure those components.

NOTE
If you choose the J2EE and Web Cache installation, the new instance will not be added to an infrastructure. To take advantage of the security, manageability, and high availability features of the infrastructure (farms, clusters, and so on), you must add the J2EE instance to an infrastructure. Another easy way to achieve this is to select the Portal and Wireless installation and then choose not to configure Portal or Wireless. This will cause the OUI to configure the new instance as part of an infrastructure.

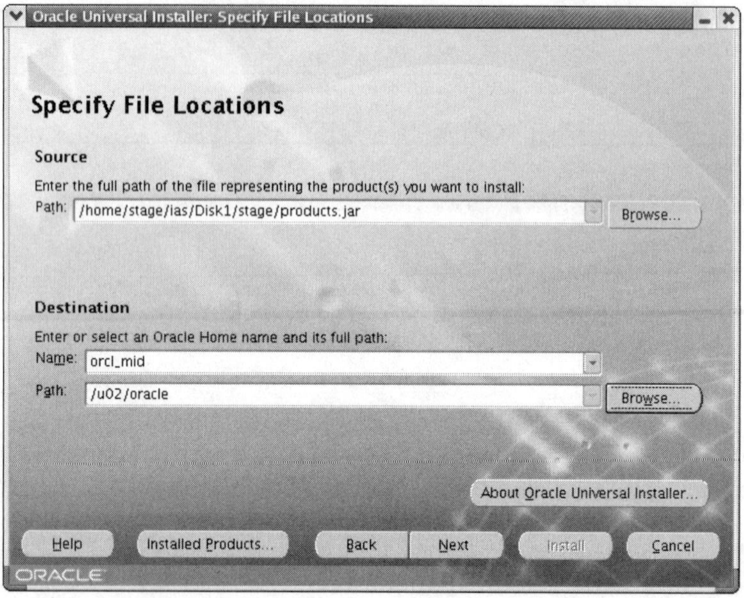

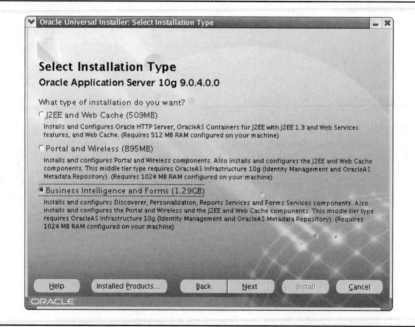

FIGURE 3-18. *Specify File Locations screen of the Oracle Universal Installer*

FIGURE 3-19. *Select Installation Type screen of the Oracle Universal Installer*

After making your selection, click Next to proceed to the Steps for Middle Tier Installation screen. Read through this screen and click Next to move to the Pre-Installation Requirements screen. You will need to have root privileges to run the script near the end of the install. Continue to the configuration options screen shown in Figure 3-20.

This is the point where you determine which components are to be configured. The component will be installed, but will not be configured and will not start. If needed, you can configure the deselected components manually at a later time. In the example, we chose not to configure the BI components—Discoverer, Personalization, and Reports Services. After making your configuration choices, select Next to proceed to the registration screen shown in Figure 3-21.

Here you are identifying which Oracle Internet Directory this new instance will use. Host is the server host name where the infrastructure is installed. The Port parameter is the port on the host where OID is listening for requests. If you select the Use Only SSL check box, you need to enter the OID SSL port; if not, use the non-SSL port. Normally, the non-SSL port is used because Secure Sockets Layer provides encryption of the communication, which is normally behind a firewall and encryption is unnecessary. Continue to the Oracle Internet Directory logon screen shown in Figure 3-22.

In this page, you enter the username and password for connecting to OID. The default is cn= orcladmin, and the password is the ias_admin password for the infrastructure instance supporting the OID. For additional information on OID, refer to Chapter 12.

The next screen identifies which metadata repository this instance will use. Select the database connection string from the drop-down list and click Next to move to the Specify Instance Name

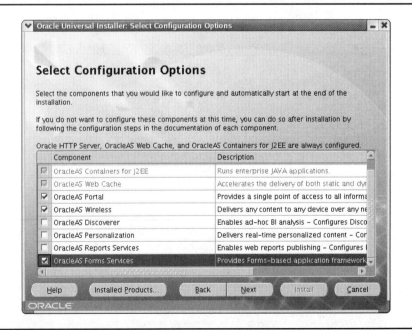

FIGURE 3-20. *Select Configuration Options screen of the Oracle Universal Installer*

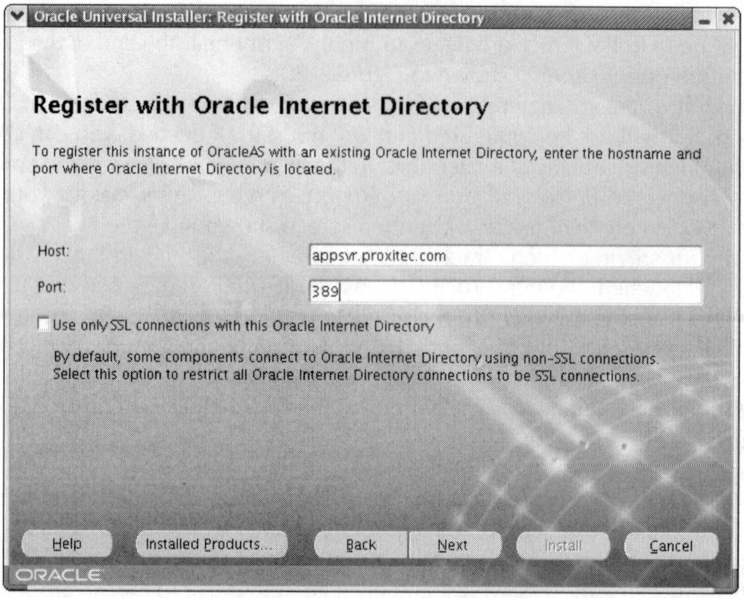

FIGURE 3-21. *Register with Oracle Internet Directory screen of the Oracle Universal Installer*

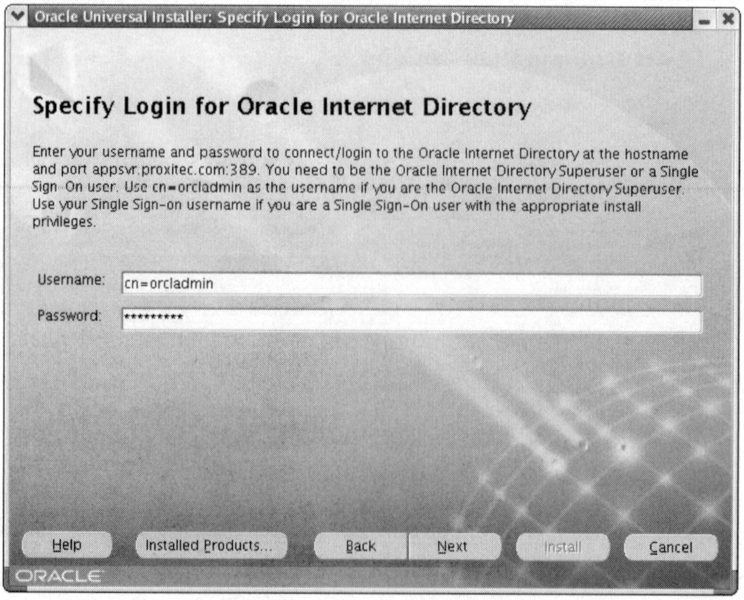

FIGURE 3-22. *Specify Login for Oracle Internet Directory screen of the Oracle Universal Installer*

and ias_admin Password screen. As with the installation of the infrastructure, the instance name must be unique to each server. The administrator for the instance is called ias_admin and cannot be changed. Enter a password for the ias_admin user. The password must contain both numbers and letters and be at least five characters long. The password is unique to the ias_admin user for this instance.

The OUI will now display the Summary screen. Remember, do not trust the disk space requirements on this screen. Select Install to begin the copying, linking, and configuration process. You will again be asked to run the root.sh script as the root user. After installing the components, the OUI will start the configuration assistants. Finally, the OUI will display the End of Installation screen, shown in Figure 3-23.

After taking note of the ports for this instance, select Exit to leave the OUI. Log onto the mid904 instance (or whatever you named your instance) by pointing your browser to the Welcome page URL listed on the End of Installation screen. Figure 3-24 shows the Welcome page.

Although the End of Installation screen said that the URL was to the Oracle HTTP Server, in fact, the URL points to the Web Cache, which in turn requests uncached pages from the HTTP Server. You will learn more about this in upcoming chapters. The Welcome page has a number of useful links, and you might want to spend some time looking at them. Select the link on the right side of the page to log onto the Oracle Enterprise Manager Application Control. This link takes you to the Farm page of the infrastructure that supports the instance. Select the instance link to go to the Instance Status page shown in Figure 3-25. Here you can see the status of all the components belonging to this instance.

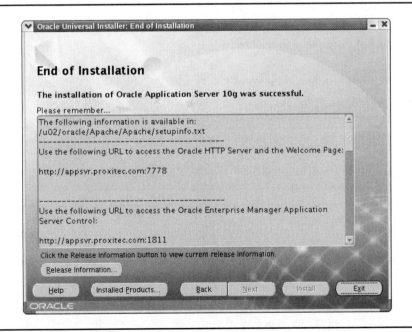

FIGURE 3-23. *End of Installation screen for midtier installation*

FIGURE 3-24. *Mid904 instance Welcome page*

At this point, we have installed the infrastructure and a midtier instance, and both are up and running. A couple of quick review points:

■ Ensure that the server has enough resources to support the installation according to Table 3-1 at the beginning of this chapter. You cannot trust the Summary page space-requirement numbers.

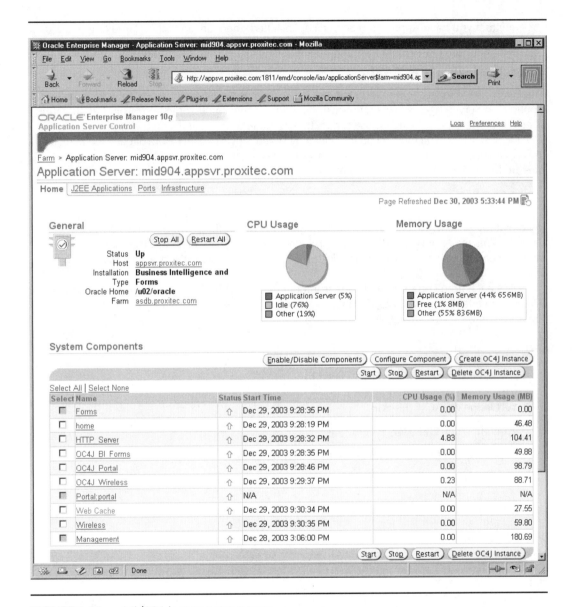

FIGURE 3-25. *Mid904 instance status page*

- Ensure that the OS is configured. If you are installing more than the J2EE and Web Cache, you must modify the kernel parameters. Follow the Install Guide located at DISK1/docs/index.html.

- Midtier installations of more than J2EE and Web Cache require a running infrastructure instance.

Now that you have Application Server 10*g* installed, there are some post-installation tasks that need to be performed.

Post-Installation Tasks

The Enterprise Manager Application Server Control is a powerful web-based tool for managing Application Server 10*g*. However, you will want to execute some commands from the operating system prompt, especially if you use scripts to automatically start and stop the application server with the host server. You must set up the operating system environment before directly manipulating the application server components. Each instance has its own ORACLE_HOME where its data files are located. If you issue the command

```
[oracle@appsvr oracle]$ opmnctl stopall
```

the operating system will execute the first opmnctl file that it finds while traversing the PATH variable. This may not be the file you are trying to execute. Since each instance has its own environment, the easiest way to do this is to make an environment file for each instance on the server.

Since each time you execute the environment file the PATH is set, we capture the current PATH in a variable called ORG_PATH at login by adding the following line to the .bash_profile file of the *oracle* user:

```
ORG_PATH=$PATH; export ORG_PATH
```

For each instance on a server you need to

1. Define ORACLE_HOME.

2. Define LD_LIBRARY_PATH.

3. Define the ORACLE_SID of the metadata repository.

4. Update the PATH variable.

Here is the environment file for an infrastructure instance called infenv:

```
# Environment for infra904
ORACLE_HOME=/u01/oracle/infra904; export ORACLE_HOME
LD_LIBRARY_PATH=$ORACLE_HOME/lib:/lib:/usr/local/bin;
export LD_LIBRARY_PATH
ORACLE_SID=asdb; export ORACLE_SID
PATH=/usr/bin:$ORACLE_HOME/bin:$ORACLE_HOME/opmn/bin:$ORG_PATH
export PATH
```

NOTE
A notice in the Release Notes states that after installation you need to place /usr/bin as the first element of your PATH.

The file is easily modified to support the middle tier.

```
# Environment for mid904
ORACLE_HOME=/u02/oracle; export ORACLE_HOME
LD_LIBRARY_PATH=$ORACLE_HOME/lib:/lib:/usr/local/bin;
export LD_LIBRARY_PATH
ORACLE_SID=asdb; export ORACLE_SID
PATH=/usr/bin:$ORACLE_HOME/bin:$ORACLE_HOME/opmn/bin:$ORG_PATH
export PATH
```

Each instance on a server should have its own environment file. To use the file, invoke it with the source command:

```
[oracle@appsvr oracle]$ source mid904
```

or in scripts, use the . command

```
[oracle@appsvr oracle]$ . /home/oracle/mid904
```

Once you source the environment you can be sure which opmnctl file is being executed. So now it is time to *bounce* the server.

Starting and Stopping Application Server 10*g*

Even a UNIX/Linux server will eventually need to be rebooted (no Windows jokes please). You need a method to stop and restart all the application server parts together. Following is a simple script to start the two tiers you just installed. Since executing commands from the OS while the EM site is running can potentially lead to problems, you should first shut down the EM site.

```
#!/usr/bin/ksh
# Source Infra904
. /home/oracle/infenv
# Shutdown Application Server Control
$ORACLE_HOME/bin/emctl stop em
# Source Mid904
. /home/oracle/midenv
# Shutdown Application Server Control
$ORACLE_HOME/bin/emctl stop em
# Stop the Mid904 Instance
$ORACLE_HOME/opmn/bin/opmnctl stopall
# Source Infra904
. /home/oracle/infenv
# Stop the Infra904 Instance
$ORACLE_HOME/opmn/bin/opmnctl stopall
# Stop the Metadata Repository DB
$ORACLE_HOME/bin/sqlplus "/ as sysdba" << EOF
shutdown immediate;
exit;
EOF
# Stop the database Listener
$ORACLE_HOME/bin/lsnrctl stop
```

This script is named stopall.ksh. The opposite script is logically named startall.ksh and is used to start the application server.

```ksh
#!/usr/bin/ksh
# Source Infra904
. /home/oracle/infenv
# Start the Listener
$ORACLE_HOME/bin/lsnrctl start
# Stop the Metadata Repository DB
$ORACLE_HOME/bin/sqlplus "/ as sysdba" << EOF
startup
exit;
EOF
# Wait 30 seconds to let the database settle.
sleep 30
# Start the Infra904 Instance
$ORACLE_HOME/opmn/bin/opmnctl startall
# Wait 15 seconds to let the OID settle.
sleep 15
# Source Mid904
. /home/oracle/midenv
# Start the Mid904 Instance
$ORACLE_HOME/opmn/bin/opmnctl startall
# Wait 15 seconds to let the Everything settle.
sleep 15
# Source Infra904
. /home/oracle/infenv
# Start Application Server Control
$ORACLE_HOME/bin/emctl start em
# Source Mid904
. /home/oracle/midenv
# Start Application Server Control
$ORACLE_HOME/bin/emctl start em
echo Startup Completed
```

All of these commands are discussed in detail in the appropriate chapters.

Summary

This chapter contains a lot of information. Although we have focused on installing Oracle Application Server 10g on Linux, installing on another UNIX/Linux is very similar. The key difference is how you prepare the operating system before you start the installer. The main points in this chapter are as follows:

- Plan your installation topology. Determine how many small servers or how many instances to install on larger servers will be required. If you are using multiple servers, what components need to be installed on each server?

- Verify that your host server has the necessary memory, disk, and swap space.

■ Configure your operating system to support the Application Server.

■ Install the infrastructure instance first (if needed).

■ Have a plan for passwords. Once you are running multiple instances on multiple servers, password control becomes important. Most of the systems we have worked with have opted to use one password for all ias_admin users.

■ Create an environment file for each instance to avoid confusion when working with the operating system command line.

Now that you have Application Server 10*g* installed and running, it is time to dig deeper into each of the components. The next chapter details the Oracle HTTP Server (OHS). Built on the famous Apache web server, OHS does the heavy lifting, acting as the interface between the user and Application Server 10*g*.

CHAPTER
4

Using the Oracle
HTTP Server (OHS)

he Oracle HTTP Server (OHS), built on Apache version 1.3, is a reliable, secure, and capable web server. OHS (and Apache) can handle multiple simultaneous requests in multiple languages and formats. The Apache base that OHS is built upon has earned a solid reputation throughout the world for its capabilities and performance.

For the most part, this chapter refers to the Oracle HTTP Server as OHS; however, many of the actual files refer to the server as Apache. Because OHS is designed to be the front end to the application server, there are a number of additions to the base Apache server and a few features that are not implemented. An example of this is starting and stopping OHS. While the Apache server can be started from the command prompt and can be passed parameters at startup, OHS is normally started and monitored by the opmnclt script as part of the 10*g* Application Server, and the opmn must pass startup parameters to OHS.

This chapter focuses on how to administer and maintain the Oracle HTTP Server. The best place for additional information is the *Oracle HTTP Server Administration Guide*. And since OHS is built on the Apache 1.3 server, you can also find information in the online documentation at www.apache.org.

Managing the Oracle HTTP Server

In Oracle 9*i*AS, OHS (with a standard Apache server) was started and stopped using the httpd command located in the $ORACLE_HOME/Apache/Apache/bin directory. Applicaton Server 10*g* (9.0.4) uses the apachectl script (located in the same directory). However, when used, it returns a warning not to use apachectl, but instead to use the $ORACLE_HOME/dcm/dcmctl script. The best way to ensure that the Application Server starts up all parts, including OHS, is to use the $ORACLE_HOME/opmn/bin/opmnctl script, passing it the startall or stopall parameters. This is because OHS is an integral part of the Application Server—stopping just OHS will cause problems in the instance. Also, opmn monitors the processes and may restart OHS if it detects that it is down. Thus, it is recommended that the instance be brought down using opmn if you need to bring down or restart OHS from the command line. Once running, OHS is easily configured, started, or stopped using the Enterprise Manager web site. Using Enterprise Manager is discussed later in this chapter.

When OHS starts, it begins as a single parent process that writes its operating system pid in the file httpd.pid. The parent process spawns a number of child processes that are used to handle client requests. As the server runs, the parent process checks the number of idle child processes and either adds processes (if there are too few) or destroys processes (if there are too many) to ensure that the server is ready to respond instantly to a request and is not wasting server resources with too many idle processes.

When OHS starts, the configuration information is obtained from a file called httpd.conf, which is located in the $ORACLE_HOME/Apache/Apache/conf directory. On an Apache server, this file can be moved and the new location passed into the server as a startup parameter. Since OHS is started and monitored by the opmn program, the configuration file should remain where it was installed.

The httpd.conf file is discussed in detail later in this chapter. The Apache server that OHS is built on provides a basic framework and then expands its capabilities by utilizing modules. This modular structure allows the administrator to add or remove capabilities to the base server as needed.

NOTE
*The Distributed Configuration Management utility maintains
a repository of configuration data. If you manually update the
configuration files, you must update the repository. To execute this
update, use the command dcmctl –updateConfig –ct ohs. If you
update the configuration using Enterprise Manager, the repository
is automatically updated for you.*

Oracle HTTP Server Modules

Some of the modules that OHS uses to add capabilities to the base server are self-contained, while others rely on separate modules, and some call external programs. Each module adds features to implement a specific function. There are nearly 50 core modules in a basic Apache server, while OHS adds even more modules to support specific Application Server 10*g* features.

Each module may add new directives that need to be defined in the httpd.conf file. The httpd.conf file contains a number of directives, enclosed within IfModules, that load parameters only if that module is loaded. Modules are not actually loaded at startup. OHS scans the module's file and loads headers that will call the module if its functionality is required.

Table 4-1 provides a brief list of some of the main modules and the functions they add to the basic server. Many will be discussed in greater detail in the sections that follow. Because the function of an application server is to support enterprise applications using J2EE, mod_jserv and mod_oc4j are discussed in detail in Chapters 6 and 7.

In this chapter and throughout the book, some modules will be discussed in detail. For detailed information on each module, refer to the Oracle HTTP Server Administration Guide.

Type	Name	Function
Security	mod_access	Provides access control based on client host name or IP
	mod_auth	Provides authentication using text files
	mod_auth_anon	Provides anonymous user authentication
	mod_ssl	Supports SSL certificates
	mod_osso	Provides integration with Single Sign-On
Configuration	mod_actions	Executes CGI scripts
	mod_alias	Maps directories into the document tree and supports URL redirecting
	mos_setenvif	Sets environmental variables based on the request
	mod_dir	Supports trailing slash redirects and directory index files
	mod_headers	Supports customization of HTTP response headers

TABLE 4-1.   *Common Oracle HTTP Server Modules*

Type	Name	Function
Debug	mod_log_config	Supports logging of requests
	mod_status	Presents current server performance statistics
Response	mod_mime	Determines file types from filename
	mod_negotiation	Supports selecting the best from multiple documents that support user's capabilities
URL_Changes	mod_rewrite	Provides rule-based rewriting engine to rewrite requests on the fly
	mod_userdir	Supports user-specific directories
Language	mod_perl	Forwards Perl scripts to the Perl interpreter
	mod_jserv	Forwards servlet request and handles response (not used in Application Server 10*g*)
	mod_oc4j	Routes request to OC4J instances and supports load balancing
	mod_plsql	Forwards plsql requests to the Oracle database engine for execution of stored procedures
	mod_include	Supports server-parsed HTML
	mod_CGI	Executes CGI scripts
Session	mod_unique_id	Supports unique identifiers for certain requests
	mod_usertrack	Supports user tracking using cookies
Performance	mod_proxy	Supports caching proxy server

TABLE 4-1. *Common Oracle HTTP Server Modules* (continued)

Configuring OHS and Using Server Logs

The OHS is configured using one main configuration file called httpd.conf and a supplemental file called oracle_apache.conf. Both files are located in the $ORACLE_HOME/Apache/Apache/conf/ subdirectory. Each Application Server 10*g* instance installs an Oracle HTTP Server and has a unique httpd.conf file.

When OHS starts, it reads three files: httpd.conf, access.conf, and srm.conf. The oracle_apache.conf file is used to load and configure specific Oracle modules and is an INCLUDED file at the end of httpd.conf. It is common practice to place all configuration data in the httpd.conf file and leave the access.conf and srm.conf files empty. In the following sections, we will walk through a sample httpd.conf file and discuss the important configuration parameters.

Like the familiar init.ora of Oracle databases, the httpd.conf file starts with heading data and uses the # character for comments. When the Oracle Universal Installer creates the httpd.conf file, it sets the parameters necessary to get the application server up and running. Most settings are appropriate and should only be changed when specific situations warrant. Be sure to read the comments before making changes. The parameters are grouped into three sections: global parameters, default server parameters, and virtual host parameters. At the very end are the Oracle-specific configuration files.

Global Parameters

ServerRoot in the OHS is analogous to the database ORACLE_HOME. When OHS is looking for configuration or log files, it will use the ServerRoot as the base directory.

```
ServerRoot "/home/oracle/oraportal904/Apache/Apache"
```

When defining a file location, placing the backslash (/, or X:\ in Windows) defines a path/file in httpd.conf and tells OHS to use only that path/file. If the path/file is defined without a leading /, then OHS will consider it a relative path/file and append the ServerRoot to the front. Thus, if the ServerRoot is set to "/opt/oracle/mydir" and ErrorLog is set to "logs/error_log", OHS will log errors to "/opt/oracle/mydir/logs/error_log".

```
PidFile /home/oracle/oraportal904/Apache/Apache/logs/httpd.pid
```

As you saw earlier, OHS prespawns server processes (or threads in Windows) to speed the handling of requests. The UNIX OS pid of the parent server process is stored in the PidFile location. To reset log files or kill OHS from the operating system, you need to use the pid located in the PidFile. Other parts of the application server may also need this information, so it is not recommended to change the file name or location once installed.

```
MinSpareServers 5
MaxSpareServers 10
StartServers 5
```

The Server Pool Size parameters configure the number of child server processes created when starting, and dictate when to add or remove processes. In this case, the OHS spawns five child server processes on startup and checks periodically to ensure that there are five spare processes waiting to handle new requests. If the processes are fewer than specified in MinSpareServer, the parent process will spawn additional processes. If there are more than specified in MaxSpareServers, the parent process will kill some of the idle child processes. This allows OHS to dynamically adjust to changing load levels. Set StartServers to a number between Max and Min SpareServers, or OHS will simply adjust the number on its first check.

```
MaxClients 150
```

MaxClients is similar to the database processes parameter. It is used to limit the number of child server processes that OHS can create. When it reaches this limit, all new requests are rejected. It should be set higher than the expected high-water mark of users connected to the system. It can be used to limit resource use on a restricted system. However, refusing connections from clients is rarely a good idea. Normally, it is better to run slowly than to refuse the client. The main value of this parameter is to stop the runaway creation of child processes in case of an error.

```
# LoadModule foo_module libexec/mod_foo.so
LoadModule mmap_static_module libexec/mod_mmap_static.so
LoadModule vhost_alias_module libexec/mod_vhost_alias.so
```

The next important task is the loading of module directives. Here, OHS reads the directives from each module file so that it can dynamically load and use the module when needed. One important note: some modules rely on other modules; therefore, the order that OHS reads each set of directives is important. Do not change the order of the module listings unless you are sure you will not break another module.

All the modules available to OHS are listed under ServerRoot/libexec and end with ".so." To list the modules currently loaded, use ServerRoot/bin/httpd –1.

Default Server Parameters

Here, we transition to the default or main server parameters. These parameters are used by the child processes and, as you will see later, establish the default parameters used by a virtual host, unless overridden. The default parameters start with the ports that OHS will listen on.

```
Port 7778
Listen 7779
```

The port is where OHS waits for a request. Normally, HTTP requests are sent to port 80 by default. Oracle has set the port to 7777 for the application server. If you install multiple instances on one physical server, the first instance will be assigned port 7777. As each successive instance is installed, the OUI will detect that 7777 is used and will increment the port number by 1 until it finds an unused port. Thus, the second instance installed will be on port 7778, and the third on 7779, and so forth.

The Listen parameter allows you to have OHS listen on additional ports or even for other IPs. It can be used either with the Port parameter or in place of it. If your server is on multiple networks, you can use the Listen parameter to limit the networks that OHS accepts requests from. For example, Listen 192.168.3.124:80 will direct OHS to service requests that arrive at that address. Listen replaces the BindAddress directive that performed the same function. However, you can have multiple Listen parameters, but you can only have one BindAddress parameter. A second BindAddress will overwrite the first. BindAddress is no longer available starting with Apache 2.

```
User oracle
Group oracle
```

Apache normally uses port 80 and is started as root. Apache must be started as root to use ports below 1024. However, for security reasons, you do not want Apache responding to requests as root. By setting the User and Group parameters, you are telling the primary server process (which is running as root) to spawn child processes running under the user and group specified. However, since OHS uses ports above 1024, it is started under the user and group that it was installed under, and the User/Group parameters are not required. If you decide that all or some of your OHSs will listen on port 80, you will have to start those OHSs as root and use the User/Group parameters to reprivilege the child processes.

```
ServerName appsvr.localdomain.com
```

The ServerName is a misunderstood parameter. It defines the response name and is used in redirecting URLs (which will be discussed later in the chapter). It can be either a fully qualified domain name or an IP address. If you are using virtual hosting (described later in this chapter), you can override this parameter in the virtual host.

Be careful changing the ServerName. If you create a name that happens to be an actual domain name, you might confuse your clients or cause redirection to fail.

```
ServerAdmin jwg@oracle10gas.com
```

The ServerAdmin parameter is an e-mail address that is included on most server-generated documents, such as error messages. This will give your clients an address to contact if necessary.

```
DocumentRoot "/home/oracle/oraportal904/Apache/Apache/htdocs"
```

The DocumentRoot parameter defines the directory that OHS will serve static content files from. It can be defined explicitly, as in the example, or as a directory off the ServerRoot. The preceding example can also be defined as DocumentRoot/htdocs, since our ServerRoot is /home/oracle/oraportal904/Apache/Apache. The directory defined in DocumentRoot can be any directory that the User/Group of the child processes has permission to read, including a Network File System (NFS). Static files are normally separated into subdirectories located off the DocumentRoot, such as

- **htdocs**   Opening page
- **htdocs/resume**   Resume for company employees
- **htdocs/consulting**   Company consulting services
- **htdocs/consulting/database/oracle**   Oracle database consulting pages

Many administrators are starting to change the DocumentRoot to /var/www. This is fine as long as the User/Group has the necessary permissions to access the files.

Once the document directories have been defined, you need to tell OHS what actions it can perform in each directory. To do this, you will need to understand container directives.

Container Directives

Container or block directives change the configuration within the area defined by the container. They use the familiar HTML notation, with some restrictions. Directives must be on their own line. Container directives have limited scope, and if included directives are outside the scope of the container, they will be ignored. The following code sample demonstrates the basic structure of a container directive.

```
<ContainerType objects>
    list of directives
</ContainerType>
```

The following example container is a Directory container for our DocumentRoot directory.

```
<Directory />
    Options All
    AllowOverride All
</Directory>
```

Before going into detail about how directory containers are defined, let's discuss the different types of container directives and their functions.

Directory Container Directives   Directory container directives apply only to the named directory and all subdirectories under the named directory. For this reason, an administrator normally starts by defining a Directory container for the root directory to set up default directives for all directories that are not explicitly defined. For example:

```
<Directory />
     Options FollowSymLinks MultiViews
     AllowOverride None
</Directory>
```

One alternative to control access to directories is to place a .htaccess file in each subdirectory containing specific directives. If the AllowOverride is not set to None, OHS will read the .htaccess file and override the directives in the httpd.conf file with the directives in the .htaccess file. To preclude this, set AllowOverride to None. Note that we have set AllowOverride to None in the container for the root directory. This will not preclude us from specifying other Directory containers in the httpd.conf file.

AllowOverride only applies to the .htaccess file. The Options parameter can be set to None, All, a combination of Indexes, FollowSymLinks, ExecCGI, or MultiViews.

None is self-explanatory, as is All, except that All does not include MultiViews. If you use MultiViews, you can't use All and must list each option.

MultiViews is a nice capability that allows OHS to do an implicit file name search and pick from the results. For example, if you request the file pictures.html and it does not exist, OHS will look for pictures.html.* and may find pictures.html.en, pictures.html.fr, and so on. OHS will check the mapping for languages and select pictures.html.en, if that is the first language on the language mapping priority. OHS could also find pictures.html.gz (a compressed file), and either uncompress the file before serving it, or serve it compressed and let the client uncompress it.

ExecCGI allows the execution of CGI scripts located in that directory. FollowSymLinks allows OHS to follow symbolic links to another directory or file. This does not change the directory directives that it is executing under. If the symbolic link leads to a directory with different defined options, OHS will continue to execute under the directives of the directory that it came from. The SymLinksIfOwnerMatch option is the same, except that the target directory or file must be owned by the same user ID as the link.

The Indexes option will cause OHS to return a formatted listing of the directory if it fails to find the Index.html file; otherwise, it returns an error message. The Includes option allows Server Side Includes. If not set, the Options directive defaults to all (excluding MultiViews).

Normally, an administrator will define all options explicitly; however, to avoid confusion, you can add a + or – to an option. If the option uses a +, as in option +Indexes, the Indexes option is added to the options of the directories' parent options. Likewise, the –, as in –FollowSymLinks, will exclude that option from the options of the directories' parent options. For example:

```
<Directory /www/docs>
     Options FollowSymLinks MultiViews
     AllowOverride None
</Directory>
<Directory /www/docs/time>
```

```
      Options -FollowSymLinks +Indexes
</Directory>
```

The directory /www/docs/time has the Indexes and MultiViews options.

Defining Directory Containers   Now let's return to the httpd.conf file and look at how the Directory containers are defined. The first step is to define the directives for the root directory, since all other directories are subdirectories of root. By defining the root directives, you establish default directives for any directories that are not explicitly defined.

```
<Directory />
      Options FollowSymLinks MultiViews
      AllowOverride None
</Directory>
```

Next, the httpd.conf file defines directives for the DocumentRoot directory.

```
<Directory "/home/oracle/oraportal904/Apache/Apache/htdocs">
      Options Indexes FollowSymLinks MultiViews
      AllowOverride None
      Order allow,deny
      Allow from all
</Directory>
```

This container contains a couple of new clauses used to limit access to the directory. Since the container can both limit and grant access, it uses the Order clause to direct the order in which grants and limits are evaluated. In this case, execute the Allow clause or clauses, then the Deny clauses.

```
Order Deny,Allow
Deny from all
Allow from oracle.com
```

Here, we first deny access to all users, and then allow access to those users from the oracle.com domain. If the order clause was Order Allow, Deny, the result would be to deny access to everyone, including those from oracle.com. At this point, you need to understand the Limit and LimitExcept containers.

Limit and LimitExcept Containers   The Limit and LimitExcept containers define directives on HTTP methods. Limit defines directives on named HTTP methods, while LimitExcept defines directives on all HTTP methods, except those named.

```
<Limit POST PUT DELETE>
Require valid-user
</Limit>

<LimitExcept POST GET>
Require valid-user
<LimitExcept>
```

The first example limits the POST, PUT, and DELETE methods to a valid user. The second example limits all methods to a valid user, except for the POST and GET methods. The Limit and LimitExcept containers should rarely be used.

As we continue through the httpd.conf file, we find a block directive.

Block Directives   Block directives are used to test for an item during the processing of the configuration file. The directives that they contain are only executed if the test returns true. If the test returns false, the directives between the block start and end are ignored. The two types of block directives are <IfModule> and <IfDefined>.

```
<IfModule mod_userdir.c>
    UserDir public_html
</IfModule>

<IfDefine ReverseProxy>
   LoadModule rewrite_module libexec/mod_rewrite.so
   LoadModule proxy_module    libexec/libproxy.so
</IfDefine>
```

If module mod_userdir.c is loaded in the first example, the variable UserDir is defined as public_html. If the module is not loaded, the block is skipped, and UserDir either remains with its current definition or is undefined. In the second example, if ReverseProxy is defined, the directed module headers are loaded.

Note that block directives can be nested, and they do not limit the scope of the contained directives, which execute within the scope of the container in which they were called, as well as globally.

Files and FilesMatch Containers   The Files and FilesMatch containers allow for file-level access control. The difference between the Files container and the FilesMatch container is that the FilesMatch container uses regular expressions to identify affected files. The Files containers are placed after the Directories container in the httpd.conf file; however, they can also be nested inside a Directory container. The following Files container is located in the httpd.conf file of the OHS.

```
<Files ~ "^\.ht">
    Order allow,deny
    Deny from all
</Files>
```

This Files container denies all access to any file that starts with .ht. Since directories may contain a .htaccess file that contains access information, this Files container ensures that no user can request that file. If the Files container is nested inside a Directories container, the scope of the Files container directive is limited to the scope of the Directories container.

The use of the ~ character in the file name allows Files to use regular expressions. Starting with Apache 1.3, it is preferred to use FilesMatch when regular expressions are needed. Many directives have a *Match companion. It is preferred to use the *Match version rather than the ~ option when using regular expressions. Last, the Files and FilesMatch containers can be used in the .htaccess file.

Location Containers   The OHS httpd.conf file contains a number of Location containers spread through the file, so we will briefly explain them here. Location containers limit access by URL.

They are normally located after the Files section of the httpd.conf file. For all origin (nonproxy) requests, the URL to be matched is of the form */path /*, and you should not include any http:// servername prefix. For proxy requests, the URL to be matched is of the form *scheme://servername/ path*, and you must include the prefix.

```
<Location /status>
    Order Deny,Allow
    Deny from all
    Allow from .oracle.com
</Location>
```

Here, access to the /status path is limited only to those requests originating from oracle.com. For more information on the Location container, see the Apache documentation.

Languages and File Types

The next section of the httpd.conf file deals with file types or mime support. Again, this section is inside a block directive and will only be read if the test returns true. Mime support provides metadata about files so that OHS can service requests correctly or, if necessary, pass that information to the client so that the client can handle the file correctly. You saw this in action with the MultiViews option earlier. A good example is language support.

OHS uses the module mod_negotiation to select the correct file using file mappings, or by executing a file name pattern match and choosing from the results. Files used by OHS to service requests can have multiple extensions. The order of the extension does not matter unless OHS cannot identify an extension. In that case, OHS uses the extensions to the right of the unidentified extension only. For example:

```
filename.jwg.html.en
filename.jwg.en.html
filename.en.jwg.html
```

The preceding three files define types for html and en, but not for jwg. The first two files are identified as HTML files associated with the language English. The last file is only identified as an HTML file, and no language information can be determined. So, the order of file extensions added is irrelevant, as long as the undefined extensions are to the left of the defined extensions. Also, extensions are case sensitive (.z and .Z are two different extensions). Let's return to our httpd.conf file and walk through this section.

```
<IfModule mod_mime.c>
    TypesConfig /home/oracle/oraportal904/Apache/Apache/conf/mime.types
    AddEncoding x-compress Z
    AddEncoding x-gzip gz tgz
```

The first step is to read a file that is used to define a long list of file types called mime.types. Next, it defines additional extensions for compressed files. This mapping is added to existing mappings and will override any mappings that already exist for these extensions. The preceding example marks a file with the .Z extension as encoded using x-compress, and any file with the .gz or .tgz as encoded using x-gzip.

Now let's look at the language types and character sets. When a client browser initiates a request, it supplies a heading that also identifies the preferred language. The preferred language is used to determine which file to serve that browser if there are a number of files to select from. Taking another section from the httpd.conf file:

```
AddLanguage da .da
AddLanguage nl .nl
AddLanguage en .en
AddLanguage et .ee
AddLanguage fr .fr
AddLanguage de .de
AddLanguage el .el
AddLanguage es .es_ES
AddLanguage he .he
AddCharset ISO-8859-8 .iso8859-8
AddLanguage it .it
AddLanguage ja .ja
AddCharset ISO-2022-JP .jis
AddLanguage ko .ko
AddLanguage kr .kr
AddCharset ISO-2022-KR .iso-kr
AddLanguage no .no
AddLanguage pl .po
AddCharset ISO-8859-2 .iso-pl
AddLanguage pt .pt
AddLanguage pt-br .pt-br
AddLanguage pt-BR .pt_BR
```

This section defines file extensions that support different languages. Using the AddLanguage directive allows you to map an extension to a language code. Normally, the extension is the same as the language code, but some will differ. For example, the language code for Poland is pl, but the .pl extension usually denotes a Perl script. Thus, you can map .po to the language code pl and use the .po extension on the Polish documents.

Another thing to note is that documents in some languages need a specific character set to display properly. This can be defined using the AddCharset directive. For example, the Korean language code is kr. You can see in the preceding code that it maps to the .kr extension. However, for the browser to properly display this document, it also needs to know which character set to use. The character set ISO-2022-KR is mapped to the extension .iso-kr. Thus, a document in the format filename.html.iso-kr.kr is an HTML document that requires the ISO-2022-KR character set and is in Korean.

It is important to note that an extension can only be mapped to one language. In the following code segment, .en is mapped only to kr, while both .po and .pl are mapped to Polish.

```
AddLanguage en .en
AddLanguage pl .pl
AddLanguage pl .po
AddLanguage kr .en
```

If more than one mapping is present for a single extension, the last occurrence is used. The final step in defining language support is to provide a priority list, so that if two files tie, OHS will know which to use.

```
<IfModule mod_negotiation.c>
     LanguagePriority en da nl et de el it ja kr no pl pt pt-br ru
</IfModule>
```

This nested block directive establishes a priority list in descending order to be used by the module mod_negotiation to break a tie. Note that it is a language list, not an extensions list.

The final directive dealing with file types is the location of the magic file. This file is used by the module mod_mime_magic and is normally located in the ServerRoot/conf directory. This module will look into an unknown file and use the definitions in the magic file to try and determine the file type.

Log Files

The next section of the httpd.conf file defines log locations, logging levels, and formats. Logging levels determine how much information is logged. The greater the level, the more information and the faster the logs grow.

```
HostnameLookups Off
ErrorLog /home/oracle/oraportal904/Apache/Apache/logs/error_log
LogLevel warn
```

You can have OHS log the host name instead of the IP address, but that is not recommended since OHS must hit the DNS to resolve the IP address. The default is HostnameLookups Off, which logs the IP address instead of the host name. The ErrorLog directive establishes where the error log is located, and the LogLevel determines how much information is logged. The levels of logging in descending order of verbosity are as follows:

Level	Description	Example
emerg	Emergencies—system is unusable	"Child cannot open lock file. Exiting"
alert	Action must be taken immediately	"getpwuid: couldn't determine user …"
crit	Critical conditions	"socket: Failed to get a socket, exiting child"
error	Error conditions	"Premature end of script headers"
warn	Warning conditions	"child process 1234 did not exit "
notice	Normal but significant condition	"httpd: caught SIGBUS, attempting to …"
info	Informational	"Server seems busy"
debug	Debug-level messages	"Opening config file …"

The selected level will log those items and all items above the selected level.

Another important log is the access_log file. OHS uses the module mod_log_config to log each request in the access_log file, normally located in ServerRoot/logs/access_log.

The first step is to define one or more LogFormats. The LogFormat directive can take one or two arguments. If there is only one argument (the formatting variables), it will be used in all subsequent TransferLog directives. If there are two arguments (the formatting variables and an alias), subsequent TransferLog and CustomLog directives can use the alias to define the format to use.

In the httpd.conf file, Oracle has defined four formats with the LogFormat directive aliased by combined, common, referrer, and agent. Next, the CustomLog directive is used to assign the "common" format to the access_log file.

```
LogFormat "%h %l %u %t \"%r\" %>s %b \"%{Referer}i\" \"%{User-Agent}i\"" combined
LogFormat "%h %l %u %t \"%r\" %>s %b" common
LogFormat "%{Referer}i -> %U" referrer
LogFormat "%{User-agent}i" agent
CustomLog /home/oracle/oraportal904/Apache/Apache/logs/access_log common
```

The CustomLog directive establishes the log location and format. In the preceding example, CustomLog defines the location of the access_log file and its use of the format aliased by "custom." It could also directly define the format rather than use the format alias.

TransferLog functions like CustomLog, except that TransferLog takes the format of the last defined LogFormat without an alias, or if no LogFormat exists without an alias, it uses the Common Log Format (the default format). You will see an example of TransferLog in the "Virtual Host" section, later in the chapter.

There can be multiple CustomLog/TransferLog directives, but OHS will only use the last one found, except in the case of a virtual host, which can have its own log file, format, and location.

There is one last important note about the access_log file. This file constantly grows, because every request received by the server is logged. To speed this logging, OHS maintains the file offset for the next write. If you delete the file, OHS will open a new file and write to the stored offset, which means that the new file will start as large as the deleted file but will be totally empty. To fix this, you must "reset" the log file by removing it, and then signal OHS using the SIGHUP (–1) signal.

```
mv access_log access_log.bak
kill -1 `cat httpd.pid`
```

This will move and rename the old access_log file and cause OHS to create a new file when it logs a new request. The file httpd.pid contains the operating system process ID for the parent OHS process.

Aliases
The next section of the httpd.conf file deals with aliases. OHS uses the module mod_alias to allow the use of directories not under DocumentRoot. One important note about using aliases is that if they end in a /, the subdirectory itself is not aliased. For example, you can see in the following code that /icons/ is aliased, so a request for //myserver/icons/oracle/OracleWorld.gif will work, but //myserver/icons/OracleWorld.gif will not because of the trailing /.

```
<IfModule mod_alias.c>
    Alias /icons/ "/home/oracle/oraportal904/Apache/Apache/icons/"
    Alias /jservdocs/ "/home/oracle/oraportal904/Apache/Jserv/docs/"
    Alias /javacachedocs/ "/home/oracle/oraportal904/javacache/javadoc/"
    <IfModule mod_perl.c>
        Alias /perl/ "/home/oracle/oraportal904/Apache/Apache/cgi-bin/"
    </IfModule>
    <Directory "/home/oracle/oraportal904/Apache/Apache/icons">
        Options Indexes MultiViews
        AllowOverride None
        Order allow,deny
```

```
     Allow from all
   </Directory>
   ScriptAlias /cgi-bin/ "/home/oracle/oraportal904/Apache/
                      Apache/cgi-bin/"
```

Another important point is that using aliases opens additional subdirectories for use and thus may require Directory containers to define access. If no Directory containers are given for the new locations, the access will default to the access granted the root / directory.

ScriptAlias (at the bottom of the example) works in the same manner as Alias, except that OHS will execute the script/application instead of sending it as a page to the requester.

The AliasMatch directive is not shown in the example but is another powerful tool. It allows the use of regular expressions instead of just prefix matching.

```
AliasMatch ^/icons(.*) /usr/local/apache/icons$1
```

OHS substitutes the parenthesized matches into the string $1 and uses it to identify file names.

The Redirect directive will take a matching request and send the client a new URL, causing the client to re-request from the new location.

```
Redirect /joke http://fun.house.com/jokes
```

Here, a client requesting http://myserver/jokes/good_one.txt would be redirected to http://fun.house.com/jokes/good_one.txt. To include regular expressions, use the RedirectMatch directive. The Redirect directive can also contain a status, such as Permanent or 301, Temporary or 302, See Other or 303, or Gone or 410. In the cases where a document is permanently removed, you would want to use "gone" and leave off the URL.

```
Redirect permanent /joke http://fun.house.com/jokes
Redirect 301 /joke http://fun.house.com/jokes
Redirect gone /joke
```

Indexing and FancyIndexing

The next section of the httpd.conf file deals with indexing. Indexing in OHS has nothing to do with indexing in an Oracle database.

When OHS gets a request for a directory, it looks for a file called index.html. If it is present, OHS uses it; if it is not present, OHS creates an index or catalog of the directory and serves that. To create this index, OHS uses the module mod_autoindex. OHS will not create an index if the Options directive for that directory does not include +Indexes. The httpd.conf file contains a DirectoryIndex directive that establishes what OHS should do if a request resolves to a directory instead of a file.

```
<IfModule mod_dir.c>
    DirectoryIndex index.html
</IfModule>
```

Following this directive, OHS will look for a file called index.html. If it is not present, OHS will check the directory for Options +Indexes and, if present, will use mod_autoindex to create a listing of the directory and serve that listing.

The DirectoryIndex directive can have a list of space-separated files, and OHS will attempt to locate each of the files in order before creating its own listing. If you do not want a server-created listing of the file, you can place an error file at the end of the DirectoryIndex list that will be served if the previous file is not found.

```
DirectoryIndex index.html welcome.html goodby.html standard/error.html
```

Once OHS has exhausted the options defined in DirectoryIndex and the directory Options +Indexes is valid, it must create the index or file list.

One important directive is IndexIgnore. The IndexIgnore directive allows you to stop mod_autoindex from including certain files, such as backup files or files that begin with a "dot," such as the .htaccess file. Multiple IndexIgnores add files to the exclude list and do not overwrite each other.

```
IndexIgnore .htaccess README* *.bak
```

The httpd.conf file contains a detailed listing for FancyIndexing that creates a format for the OHS-generated index listing. If you wish to modify this listing, please refer to the Apache documentation (Google "Apache mod_autoindex").

Browser/Environment Variables

OHS can modify the way it talks to different browser types. Each browser has different implementations, and some have bugs that require special attention. OHS uses the module mod_setenvif to add this functionality. OHS gets this information from the request's header. The directive BrowserMatch is used to set variables based on the requester's browser.

```
BrowserMatch "Mozilla/2" nokeepalive
BrowserMatch "MSIE 4\.0b2;" nokeepalive downgrade-1.0 force-response-1.0
```

Here, OHS will inactivate the keepalive feature because Mozilla does not support it. This version of Internet Explorer has a faulty implementation of HTTP 1.1, so OHS downgrades its responses to HTTP 1.0. The directive BrowserMatchNoCase is functionally equivalent to BrowserMatch but is case insensitive. Mod_setenvif also contains the SetEnvIf and SetEnvIfNoCase directives. The SetEnvIf directive is used to check current variables and, if they match, set a custom variable.

```
SetEnvIf User-Agent ".*MSIE.*" nokeepalive ssl-unclean-shutdown
```

If the user-agent from the request header contains MSIE, the variables nokeepalive and ssl_unclean_shutdown are set to true.

Proxy Server

Apache implements a proxy server and caching with mod_proxy. Application Server 10*g* and OHS use Web Cache and so do not implement mod_proxy. If you need to implement this feature, please refer to the Apache documentation (Google "Apache mod_proxy").

Virtual Host

One of the most powerful capabilities of the Apache web server, and hence OHS, is the ability to host more than one complete web site with its own domain name, as if it were on a standalone machine. The ability to support multiple web sites from one server is called *virtual hosting*. Virtual hosts are easy to set up in the httpd.conf file, and OHS uses a virtual host to support the Secure HTTP connection.

```
Listen 4446
SSLPassPhraseDialog builtin
SSLSessionCache shmcb:/home/oracle/oraportal904/Apache/Apache/
                    logs/ssl_scache(512000)
SSLSessionCacheTimeout 300
SSLMutex file:/home/oracle/oraportal904/Apache/Apache/logs/ssl_mutex
SSLLog /home/oracle/oraportal904/Apache/Apache/logs/ssl_engine_log
SSLLogLevel warn
<VirtualHost _default_:4446>
        DocumentRoot "/home/oracle/oraportal904/Apache/Apache/htdocs"
        ServerName appsvr.localdomain.com
        ServerAdmin you@your.address
        ErrorLog /home/oracle/oraportal904/Apache/Apache/
                  logs/error_log
        TransferLog /home/oracle/oraportal904/Apache/Apache/
                    logs/access_log
        Port 4445
        SSLEngine on
        SSLCipherSuite SSL_RSA_WITH_RC4_128_MD5:SSL_RSA_WITH_RC4_128_SHA:SSL_
RSA_WITH_3DES_EDE_CBC_SHA:SSL_RSA_WITH_DES_CBC_SHA:SSL_RSA_EXPORT_WITH_RC4_40_
MD5:SSL_RSA_EXPORT_WITH_DES40_CBC_SHA
        SSLWallet file:/home/oracle/oraportal904/Apache/Apache/
                    conf/ssl.wlt/default
        <Files ~ "\.(cgi|shtml)$">
            SSLOptions +StdEnvVars
        </Files>
        <Directory "/home/oracle/oraportal904/Apache/Apache/cgi-bin">
            SSLOptions +StdEnvVars
        </Directory>
        SetEnvIf User-Agent ".*MSIE.*" nokeepalive ssl-unclean-
                    shutdown
        CustomLog /home/oracle/oraportal904/Apache/Apache/
                  logs/ssl_request_log "%t %h %{SSL_PROTOCOL}x
                  %{SSL_CIPHER}x \"%r\" %b"
    </VirtualHost>
```

This looks like a lot, but most of it has already been covered. So let's walk through the code.

First come the server-level directives. OHS is directed to listen on port 4446. Secure Sockets Layer (SSL) will be covered in detail in Chapter 12, but from what has already been covered, you can see that there are a number of log files identified, and the SSLLOGLEVEL is set to "warn."

Once the server-level directives are through, you are ready to define the virtual host. Virtual hosts can have separate host names, IP addresses, or ports. Anything not defined within the virtual host block directives will be inherited from the default server parameters. The first five parameters are explicitly defined. They actually point to the same files as the default server because the virtual host is designed to replicate the default server, using SSL for security.

One important directive is the ServerName. The ServerName is used to redirect links to other files, and if it is not defined, the OHS will have to hit the DNS to determine the server name for the virtual host's IP.

Through the remaining code, you can see examples of Directory container directives, Files container directives, TransferLog, and CustomLog. Almost every default server parameter can be redefined for a virtual host. Directives that establish the overall OHS server, such as MinSpareServers, MaxSpareServers, StartServers, and so on, cannot be changed in a virtual host.

The example virtual host is IP based, using the default IP. Another option is to use a *name-based virtual host*, which allows you to operate multiple hosts on the same IP address. This must be supported by your DNS. When the browser submits a request, it contains the server name that it is requesting the document from. OHS will accept the request and pass it to the named virtual host for servicing. To use this feature, you must add the NameVirtualHost directive that identifies the communal IP, before any virtual host directives.

```
NameVirtualHost 192.168.2.101
<VirtualHost 192.168.2.101>
    ServerName bigdata.oracle.com
    ServerAlias bigdata
</VirtualHost>
```

This example introduces another directive, ServerAlias. ServerAlias is used when the server needs to be accessible using more than one name. This directive identifies multiple names for the same virtual host. Local users can access the host simply by using bigdata as the server name. More commonly, ServerAlias is used to direct multiple host names to the same virtual host.

Dynamic Content

Since you are using Application Server 10*g*, you will be using OHS to connect to your application to generate dynamic content. The Oracle HPPT Server can generate dynamic content within the server using CGI and SSIs.

CGI (Common Gateway Interface) defines a method of communication used between the web server and various programs and scripts that generate the dynamic content. Called CGI programs, they are in fact written in any language from Perl to C, or even a Korn script. The only requirement for OHS to execute the program is that the OHS user must have execute rights on the program. OHS uses the mod_cgi module to handle CGI scripts, including loading and executing operating system programs.

You have already seen the use of the ScriptAlias directive to identify locations of CGI programs. If the CGI program is located in a directory other than those pointed to by ScriptAlias, that directory must have the ExecCGI enabled in either the .htaccess file or in the Directory directives for the directory in the httpd.conf file.

The second method of including dynamic content is SSIs (Server Side Includes). SSIs are directives in the HTML page that are parsed as the page is served to the client. Instead of having a CGI program serve the entire page, SSIs can be used to embed dynamic content from other documents. Content can include other documents, CGI program scripts, or server environment variables (such as the current time) as the page is being served. Since SSI requires that the pages be parsed as they are served, you must tell OHS which files to parse. You do this by adding directives to the httpd.conf file.

```
AddType text/html   .shtml
AddHandler server-parsed .shtml
```

OHS will now parse all .shtml files as they are served, provided that the Directory directives for the location of the .shtml file have Includes enabled. This option can also be set in the .htaccess file.

This is a brief introduction to CGI and SSI to set the stage for later chapters.

Oracle HTTP Server Performance Tuning

Since OHS is built on the proven capabilities of the Apache web server, there are not many things you can do to tune the actual server. OHS must be tuned as part of the total Application Server. This is discussed in Chapter 9. That said, there are a number of things you can do to improve OHS performance:

- **Paging** Any time the operating system has to page memory to swap, there is performance degradation. Virtual memory allows an OS to overallocate physical memory, but it comes at a price. Constant swapping of memory pages is a significant overhead. The only way to stop excessive swapping is to reduce the memory footprint of the application or increase the memory on the server.

- **Logging** The more that must be written in logs, the more time is spent writing to files. One way to reduce the load on OHS is to reduce the logging level. Once the system is functioning properly, you may be able to reduce the logging level.

- **Using .htaccess** Directory containers are used in the httpd.conf file so that all configuration is in one place. A disadvantage is that each directory accessed requires that its access privileges be determined along with the access privileges of all directories above it. If each directory contains a .htaccess file and all access privileges are stored there, then OHS only needs to read that one file. The trade-off is maintaining a .htaccess file in each subdirectory versus the overhead of determining access privileges from Directory containers in the httpd.conf file. The more directories the system uses, the more overhead from determining access privileges if .htaccess files are not used.

- **KeepAlive** *Always* set this to on! This parameter allows multiple requests to be serviced on a single connection. This reduces the overhead of creating and dropping network connections. This can have a significant impact on OHS performance.

- **OHS load** The Enterprise Manager web console provides a large range of performance/load metrics. Monitoring these metrics can help you determine the load your application places on OHS. You must remember to monitor during appropriate times to ensure that you are gathering appropriate statistics. Web server usage fluctuates continuously, depending on work schedules, time of day, or day of the week. Gathering statistics will help you account for these variances.

Also remember that some metrics reported are for the entire application server. Throughput and response time will include actions performed by other parts of the application server and possibly an interaction with a database.

Monitoring the Oracle HTTP Server with Enterprise Manager

Oracle provides a web-based interface to monitor all parts of the Application Server, including OHS. To access this interface, ensure that Enterprise Manager (EM) is running, and if not, you will need to start it.

```
$ORACLE_HOME/bin/emctl status em
$ORACLE_HOME/bin/emctl start em
```

Open a web browser, connect to the Application Server (http://server_domain_name:port), log onto Enterprise Manager, and navigate to the instance page shown in Figure 4-1. The OHS is designated HTTP_Server in the System Components list.

If you need to start, stop, or restart OHS, select the check box next to HTTP_Server, and select the appropriate button, and EM will execute the command. When you make changes to the HTTP_Server, EM will write the change to the httpd.conf file and restart the OHS. To get OHS details, select the HTTP_Server link for the HTTP_Server page shown in Figure 4-2.

The data on this page is a snapshot of OHS performance at the time the page was loaded. The data is not updated unless you refresh the page. Many of the directives set in httpd.conf can be verified and changed from this and subsequent pages, to include creating virtual hosts and

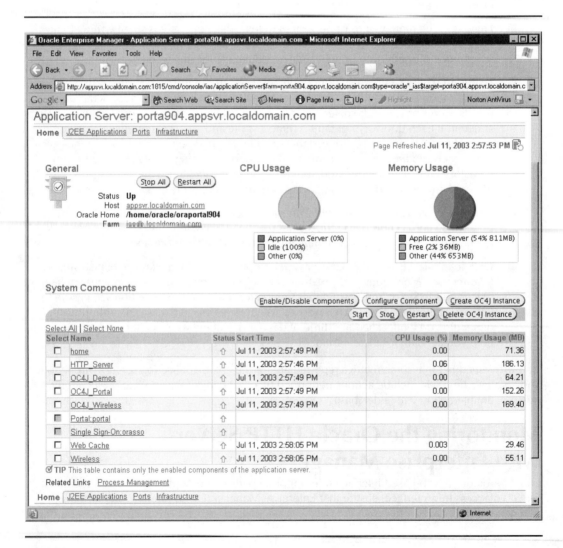

FIGURE 4-1. *Enterprise Manager instance page*

FIGURE 4-2. *Enterprise Manager HTTP_Server page*

looking at logs. Selecting Create in the Virtual Host section will walk you through a setup wizard (detailed at the end of this section).

The Administration section contains all the directives from httpd.conf. Selecting Server Properties in the Administration section will take you to the directives in the first section of httpd.conf, as shown in Figure 4-3.

All changes made in EM are written back to the httpd.conf file, and OHS is restarted to load the new parameters. All of the directives in httpd.conf can be found in the Administration section of the HTTP_Server page.

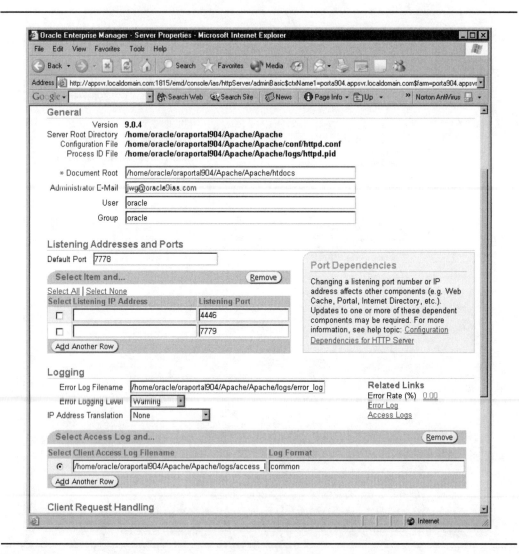

FIGURE 4-3. *Enterprise Manager Server Properties page*

Let's look at some of the metrics that you can use to monitor OHS's performance. Start at the HTTP_Server page (shown in Figure 4-2) and select the Status Metrics link to get to the Status Metrics page shown in Figure 4-4.

Here you see three sections, System Usage Metrics, Error Metrics, and Connection Metrics.

OHS System Usage Metrics

The System Usage Metrics page shows CPU and RAM memory usage for the HTTP Server. Note that the RAM is displayed in a pie chart, with HTTP Server RAM, Free RAM, and Other. On an active Application Server, there is normally little free RAM, as many components will expand to use the available RAM.

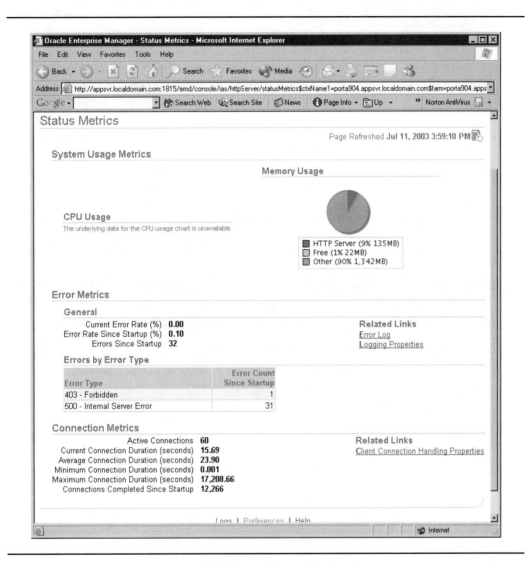

FIGURE 4-4. *Enterprise Manager HTTP_Server Status Metrics page*

OHS Error Metrics

The Error Metrics page shows the error rate as a percentage of total transactions, error rate since startup, and total errors since startup. You also see a listing of all error types and a count of the types. From this section you can click the Error Log and Logging Properties links for further details.

Clicking the Error Log link displays EM's log page, with the HTTP_Server in the right-hand box. At the bottom of the page is a list of error logs from the HTTP_Server. Select the error_log link to see the details (Figure 4-5). To add logs from other components, simply select the component in the left box and move it to the right box. EM will add its logs to the available log list.

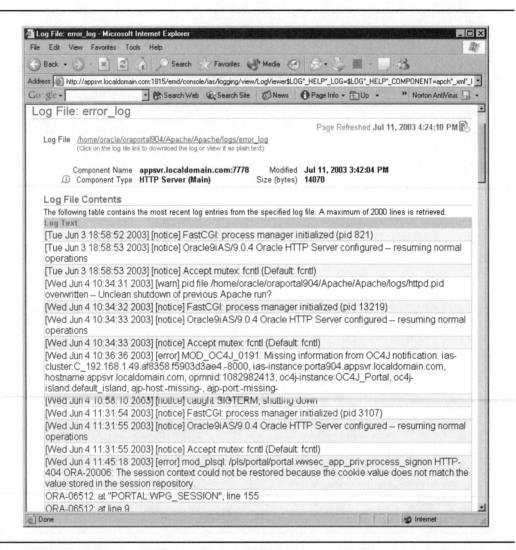

FIGURE 4-5. *Enterprise Manager HTTP_Server error_log page*

HTTP Server Response and Load Metrics

Now let's return to the HTTP_Server page (Figure 4-2) and click the Response and Load Metrics link. The page shown in Figure 4-6 appears. This page provides a snapshot of the current load on OHS, including request throughput and processing time. It also gives a snapshot of the number of active and idle processes on the server.

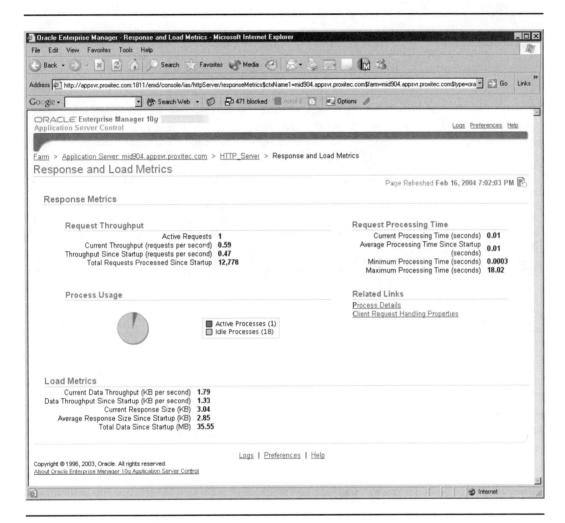

FIGURE 4-6. *Enterprise Manager HTTP_Server Response and Load Metrics page*

Finding a performance problem in the Application Server is difficult, due to the number of components interacting within the server. This is a good place to look for performance problems. Slow response time and large numbers of active processes on OHS may indicate a need to add an instance to the cluster. If one user appears to be experiencing a problem, you can drill-down and get process information, as shown in Figure 4-7, by selecting the Process Details link.

A processor that is gaining time may indicate a problem within the application server and assist you in tracking it down.

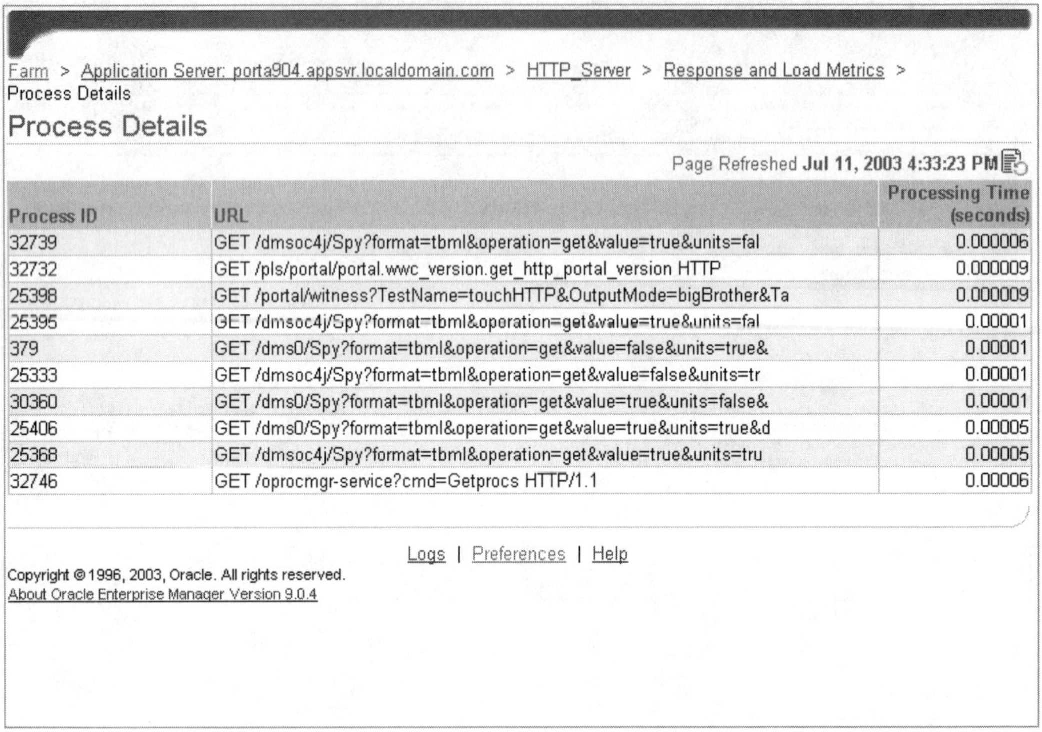

Farm > Application Server: porta904.appsvr.localdomain.com > HTTP_Server > Response and Load Metrics > Process Details

Process Details

Page Refreshed **Jul 11, 2003 4:33:23 PM**

Process ID	URL	Processing Time (seconds)
32739	GET /dmsoc4j/Spy?format=tbml&operation=get&value=true&units=fal	0.000006
32732	GET /pls/portal/portal.wwc_version.get_http_portal_version HTTP	0.000009
25398	GET /portal/witness?TestName=touchHTTP&OutputMode=bigBrother&Ta	0.000009
25395	GET /dmsoc4j/Spy?format=tbml&operation=get&value=true&units=fal	0.00001
379	GET /dms0/Spy?format=tbml&operation=get&value=false&units=true&	0.00001
25333	GET /dmsoc4j/Spy?format=tbml&operation=get&value=false&units=tr	0.00001
30360	GET /dms0/Spy?format=tbml&operation=get&value=true&units=false&	0.00001
25406	GET /dms0/Spy?format=tbml&operation=get&value=true&units=true&d	0.00005
25368	GET /dmsoc4j/Spy?format=tbml&operation=get&value=true&units=tru	0.00005
32746	GET /oprocmgr-service?cmd=Getprocs HTTP/1.1	0.00006

Logs | Preferences | Help

Copyright © 1996, 2003, Oracle. All rights reserved.
About Oracle Enterprise Manager Version 9.0.4

FIGURE 4-7. *Enterprise Manager HTTP_Server Process Details page*

HTTP Server Module Metrics

Returning to the HTTP_Server page (Figure 4-2), select the Module Metrics link to get to the page shown in Figure 4-8. This page lists all modules that have had at least one request since OHS was started. This can also be helpful in tracking down a performance issue. Request-processing time that is abnormally high could indicate a problem in the module or in a program called by the module.

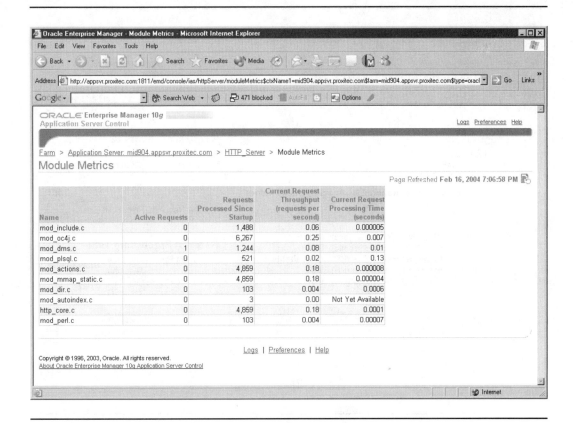

FIGURE 4-8. *Enterprise Manager HTTP_Server Module Metrics page*

HTTP Server Virtual Host Page

Returning to the HTTP_Server page (Figure 4-2) again, let's look at the Virtual Host section. Currently, OHS only has one virtual host defined, and it supports SSL connections to the default server. By selecting the virtual host's server name, you get the virtual host's page shown in Figure 4-9.

Farm > Application Server: porta904.appsvr.localdomain.com > HTTP_Server > Virtual Host: appsvr.localdomain.com

Virtual Host: appsvr.localdomain.com

Page Refreshed **Jul 11, 2003 4:56:00 PM**

Configuration

Type	**default**
Port	**4446**
Protocol	**https (SSL)**
Document Root	**/home/oracle/oraportal904/Apache/Apache/htdocs**

Load

Current Data Throughput (KB per second)	**0.00**
Data Throughput Since Startup (KB per second)	**0.003**
Current Response Size (KB)	**Unavailable**
Average Response Size Since Startup (KB)	**2.83**
Total Data Since Startup (MB)	**0.07**

Request Throughput

Active Requests	**0**
Current Throughput (requests per second)	**0.00**
Throughput Since Startup (requests per second)	**0.001**
Total Requests Processed Since Startup	**26**

Request Processing Time

Current Processing Time (seconds)	**Unavailable**
Average Processing Time Since Startup (seconds)	**0.002**

Administration

Virtual Host Properties

Virtual Host MIME Encodings

Virtual Host MIME **L**anguages

Virtual Host MIME **T**ypes

Logs | Preferences | Help

FIGURE 4-9. *Enterprise Manager HTTP_Server Virtual Host page*

This page provides a snapshot of the load and performance statistics for that virtual host. The Administration section allows you to update all the host parameters defined in the httpd.conf file for this virtual host.

You can also create or delete a virtual host using Enterprise Manager. Returning to the HTTP_Server page (Figure 4-2), notice that the Virtual Host section contains Create, Delete, and Create Like buttons. At the far left of the Virtual Host section is a radio button that is on for our single virtual host. That button is used with the Create Like button to create a new virtual host like the one selected. Let's create a new virtual host using the wizard. Selecting the Create button starts the wizard.

The Introduction, shown in Figure 4-10, lists the type of information you will need to successfully create the new virtual host. This information was covered in the "Virtual Host" section earlier in the chapter. Selecting the Next button takes you to the General page shown in Figure 4-11.

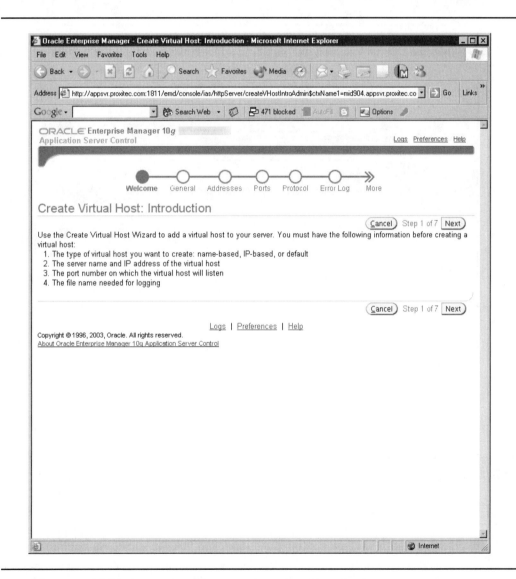

FIGURE 4-10. *HTTP_Server virtual host creation wizard Introduction page*

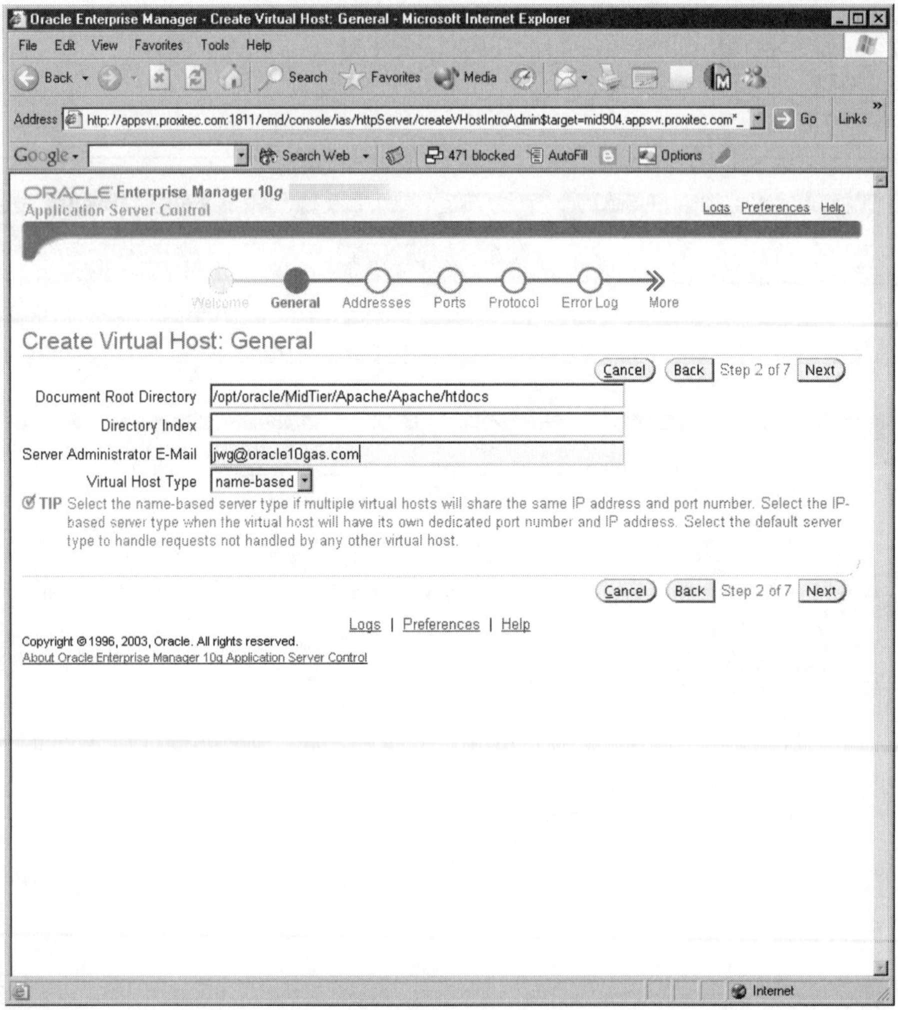

FIGURE 4-11. *HTTP_Server virtual host creation wizard General page*

The General page allows you to set a DocumentRoot directive for the new virtual host. It also allows you to select which type of virtual host you will create—IP, named, or default. It defaults to the default type and the default DocumentRoot. In this example, we are creating a name-based virtual host, which, as discussed earlier, allows hosts with different names to use the same IP address. The defaults are fine for the remaining items. Selecting the Next button takes you to the Addresses page shown in Figure 4-12.

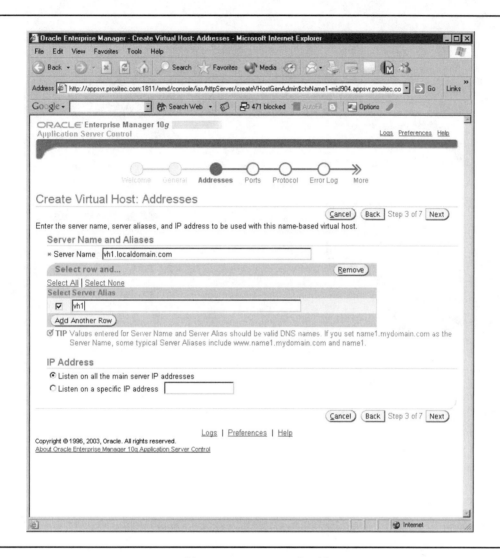

FIGURE 4-12. *HTTP_Server virtual host creation wizard Addresses page*

Here, we entered the DNS name for our new virtual host. Since we are sharing the same IP as the default host, we did not enter a new IP address. Selecting the Next button takes you to the Ports page shown in Figure 4-13.

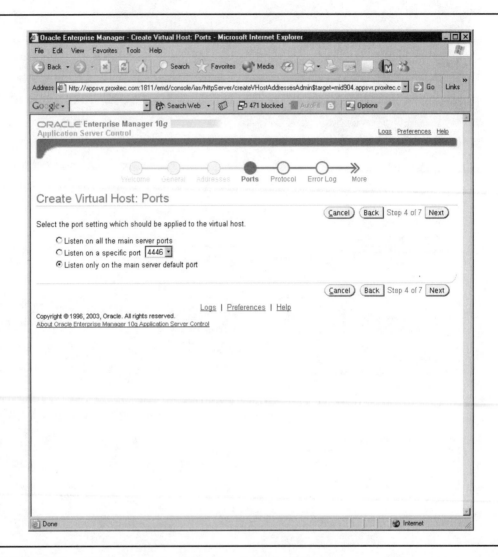

FIGURE 4-13. *HTTP_Server virtual host creation wizard Ports page*

For this example, we will just listen on the default port for the main server and continue to the Error Log page shown in Figure 4-14. Notice that we skipped the Protocol page. Since we are using the default server's IP and ports, we can't change the protocol.

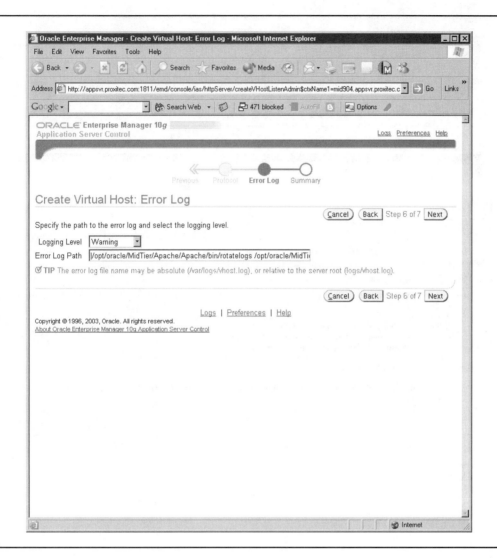

FIGURE 4-14. *HTTP_Server virtual host creation wizard Error Log page*

Here we define a new error_log for our virtual host and leave the logging level at Warning. The next page, shown in Figure 4-15, is the Summary page. This page lists all of our selections for the new virtual host. Select Finish, and Enterprise Manager updates the httpd.conf file, provides a confirmation (as shown in Figure 4-16), and then restarts OHS (as shown in Figure 4-17).

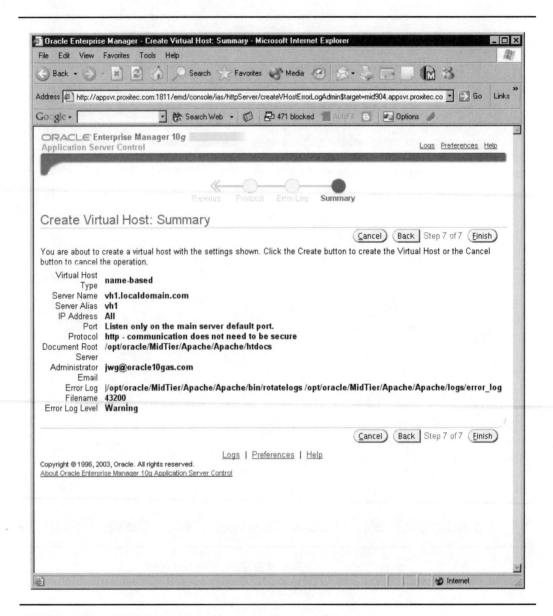

FIGURE 4-15. *HTTP_Server virtual host creation wizard Summary page*

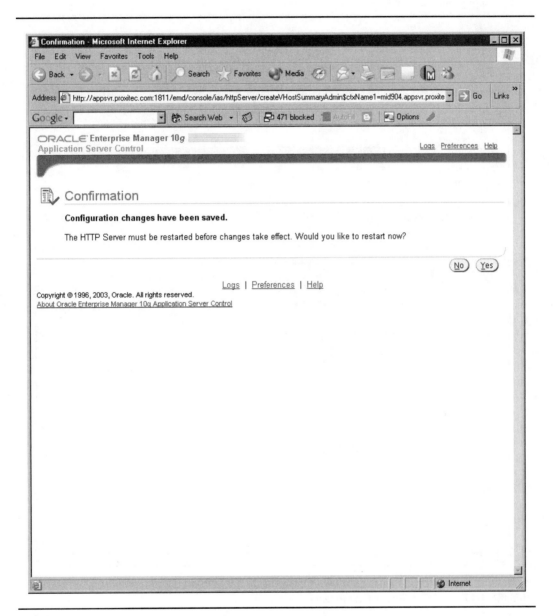

FIGURE 4-16.   *HTTP_Server virtual host creation wizard Confirmation page*

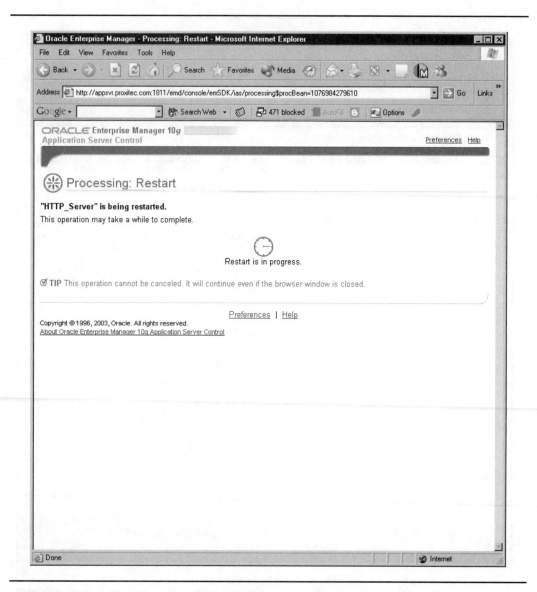

FIGURE 4-17. *HTTP_Server Restart page*

Once OHS has restarted, the new virtual host is now up and running. You can see the additional code created by the wizard in the httpd.conf file.

```
NameVirtualHost *
<VirtualHost *>
    ServerName vh1.localdomain.com
    ErrorLog /home/oracle/oraportal904/Apache/Apache/logs/vh1_error_log
</VirtualHost>
```

Very little additional code is needed since our new virtual host mainly uses the default server's settings. When we return to the HTTP_Server page, our new virtual host is now listed, as shown in Figure 4-18.

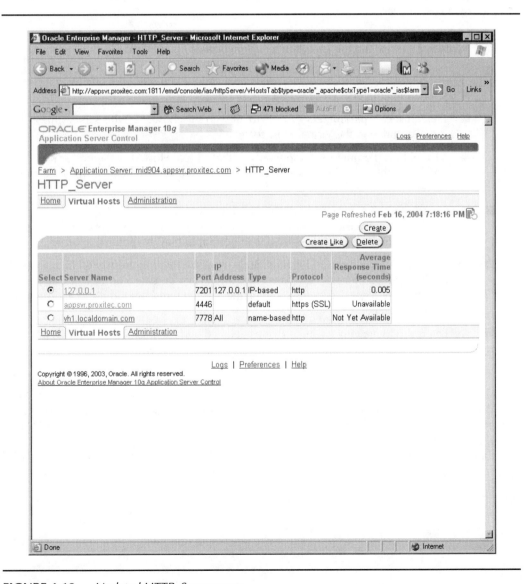

FIGURE 4-18.   *Updated HTTP_Server page*

Summary

In this chapter, we covered the Oracle HTTP Server. Built on the Apache 1.3 HTTP server, OHS provides a high performance, reliable interface to the Oracle Application Server 10*g*. OHS is responsible for serving static content and passing Servlet, JSP, and application requests back to the OC4J container for processing. The main points are as follows:

- OHS obtains its configuration information from the $ORACLE_HOME/Apache/Apache/ conf/httpd.conf file. OHS configuration changes should be made using the Enterprise Manager web site.

- OHS uses modules to add functionality to the main server. Modules are identified in the httpd.conf file and are loaded when their functionality is required.

- The httpd.conf file is divided into three sections:

  - **Global parameters**   Apply to the entire OHS.

  - **Default server parameters**   Apply to all web sites hosted on this server unless they are overridden in the Virtual Host section.

  - **Virtual host parameters**   Apply only to that Virtual Host. Any parameter not defined in the Virtual Host section will default to the value defined in the default server parameters.

- Container directives are used to define parameters for a particular area or function. A Directory container is used to allow or deny access to a particular directory. The order in which container directives are listed is important as they are applied in order.

- OHS logs access and errors to log files. Because of the method used by OHS to write to the log files, you cannot just delete the files, or OHS will create a new file the same size as the deleted (or moved) file. Also, setting the logging threshold too high can impact overall performance.

- The Enterprise Manager web site provides detailed performance statistics for OHS. However, many of the statistics apply to the entire application server and can be used to determine the total response time of your application.

As you have seen in this chapter, the Oracle HTTP Server is the gateway between your clients and all other components of the application server. Later chapters will detail areas such as dynamic content and security, as well as adding capabilities to the OHS and the application server. The next chapter will introduce Oracle's Web Cache, which provides the capability to cache both static and dynamic content. Web Cache enhances the ability of OHS to manage high user loads.

CHAPTER
5

Web Cache
Administration

omeone once said that the World Wide Web is nothing more than a giant system for distributing copies of things. When you log onto a web site, your browser downloads a copy of a page contained on or generated by that web site. If your company has an intranet web site that contains employee notices, as each employee logs in to check the site, a copy is sent across the network to that employee's browser. If this is a static page and the company has thousands of employees, the web server will send (or create and send) the same page for each request. As the company continues to grow, the web server will become overloaded, sending the same page over and over again.

To take the example further, each page on the company's web site has a copy of the company logo at the top. If a thousand employees start each day by browsing five pages of the company's web site, the web server has sent 5,000 copies of the company logo across the net.

The problem is twofold. First, the web server is overworked and provides poor response time while sending the same five pages over and over again. Second, the network is filled with copies of the same data being sent over and over again.

Now, imagine this example at a much larger scale with company web sites like Amazon.com or AOL. Reducing the constant sending of the same data is the job of a cache.

Caching: Basic Concepts

A cache stores objects that are used frequently. Caches reduce the amount of redundant data sent back and forth between web servers and browsers and are used all over the Internet. Web content is placed on a page (for example, an HTTP page) that defines how objects are displayed on the browser page.

Returning to the company logo example, the picture (.jpg, .gif, and so on) and each HTTP page instruct the browser to retrieve the logo from the server and display it at the top of the page. In reality, all browsers implement a local cache, so the browser only retrieves the logo picture once (Figure 5-1). For every subsequent page displayed, the browser simply uses the logo from the local cache and does not have to retrieve a new copy. Because the browser does not have to retrieve the logo across the network, the local cache reduces the network load and displays the page faster.

Caches come in many forms, but their basic function is to hold frequently used objects in order to speed up access. There are caches used throughout a computer (such as a processor cache, or a cache on a serial port), but we are interested in caches that improve the performance of our application, both from a user perspective and a server/network load perspective. Before jumping into the types and locations of caches, we need to talk about some of the advantages and disadvantages of using caches.

Advantages and Disadvantages of Using Caches

The main advantage of using caches is improved performance, for both the user and the server infrastructure. How much of an improvement? One Oracle test showed that adding the Oracle Web Cache in front of the Oracle Application Server reduced database load by over 85 percent. Caches work best on static data. An object like the company logo will not change, so it can safely be cached. If the company changes the logo, it needs to rename the new logo object, or the browser/proxy caches will continue to serve the old object. All caches use some type of LRU (least recently used) algorithm to age unused objects out of the cache.

There are also some disadvantages in using caches. The major disadvantage is the chance that someone will be served old or stale data, like the old company logo. As web pages have become

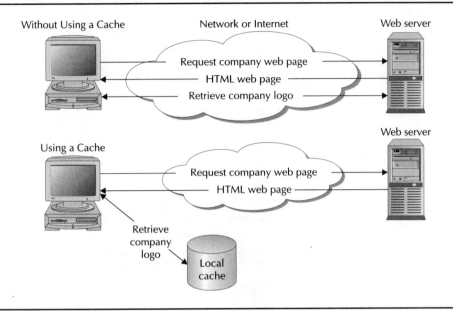

FIGURE 5-1.   *Using the web browser's cache vs. not using a cache*

more dynamic, techniques have been developed to inform a cache when a page is stale. We will discuss these techniques a little later in the chapter.

Other problems arise if the cache maintains sensitive data. When you buy a book from your favorite web site and it displays your receipt, that information could be saved in any number of caches between you and the web site. Again, we will talk about methods to prevent caches from preserving a document later in the chapter.

Types of Caches

There are caches all over the Internet aimed at reducing redundant network traffic. Starting with the user, the first cache we find is the cache built into the browser. This cache is used to store objects, so that the browser can quickly display the page. Many web sites are built to take advantage of the browser cache. Web sites that use common headers and a table of contents for each page allow the browser to build most of the web pages from the cache, reducing the amount of time it takes to retrieve each page. The slower the Internet connection, the more advantageous the cache becomes, if users tend to surf the same locations.

The next cache we find is usually a proxy server. A proxy server is normally placed at some common connection to the Internet—at the edge of your company network or at the local ISP. A proxy server is a cache for a large group of users. If there is a major news event and 100 users log onto the local news site, the proxy server could cache the web page when the first user requests it and serve the 99 other users the same page without burdening the web server or sending all that network traffic out of the company. The web page you read may have passed through a number of proxy servers as it traveled from the web server to you (Figure 5-2).

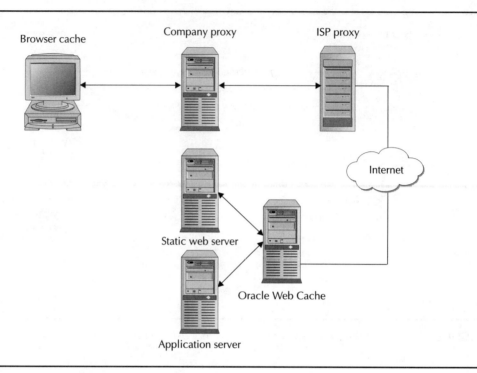

FIGURE 5-2. *Caching of web objects*

Last, the web site itself may have a cache to reduce the load on the web server and back-end database. This cache is the one we are going to focus on with the Oracle Application Server 10g Web Cache.

Most web server cache products are designed to cache static content and pages that rarely change. Web pages can contain information in the HTTP header that tells a cache that the page expires after so much time or not to cache it at all. This is useful for pages and objects that rarely change. Also, when a browser requests a page that it has already cached, it checks the time of the cache, and if the page has not changed, the web server will simply tell the browser to serve the page in its cache.

We will cover this in more detail later in this chapter. This system of including data in the header information works very well in situations where the information is relatively static. The problem for web cache designers is that the web is becoming more dynamic all the time. Web sites are personalizing their web pages to provide customized information for each user. If the cache simply stored the page and served it to the next user, the second user would get the page created for the first user.

There is another change going on in the software development area. Developers are finding it advantageous to locate all the application code (including the user interface) on an application server and utilize the browser to present the data. As you can imagine, a company finance or human resources application will serve many dynamically generated web pages that change constantly. In this situation, the normal cache in front of the application server is of little use, since the data is constantly changing. The old solution is to have the web/application server handle each request.

As the load on the server increases, additional web/application servers are added. This becomes a costly, high-maintenance option. By placing a cache that is capable of caching dynamic data in front of the application server, server load and the need for multiple servers are reduced. This is where the Application Server 10g Web Cache comes in.

The Oracle Application Server 10g Web Cache

The Oracle Application Server 10g Web Cache is designed to support not only a basic web server but also an application server creating dynamic data. For clarity, we will refer to the Application Server 10g Web Cache as the Web Cache. We will refer to the Web Cache's internal cache as the cache. Web Cache integrates with any manufacturer's application server and can be used to load-balance a group of application servers. The Web Cache sits between the user and the application server. When a user requests a page, the Web Cache verifies that the page is still valid and, if so, returns the page from the cache. If the page has expired or is marked stale, the Web Cache will request the page from the application server, send the page back to the user, and store it in the cache for future use.

Pages that consist of multiple objects that become stale at different times can be stored in the cache, and the Web Cache will request the stale objects from the application server and serve the valid object from its cache. This ability to mix static and dynamic content can significantly reduce the load on the application server. Before covering how the Web Cache knows when a document is stale, we need to discuss where Oracle's Web Cache fits into the web infrastructure.

Locating the Web Cache

Because Oracle's Web Cache not only caches static and dynamic content, but also load-balances across multiple application servers, there are many configurations available to meet individual needs.

Single Server

A surprising number of companies deploy the entire Application Server 10g on one server, including the infrastructure, the customer database, the application server, and the Web Cache. This method is useful as long as the server is capable of handling the user load. In this configuration, the Web Cache may be used mainly to cache dynamic content and let the OHS server handle the static content. In these configurations, memory is normally at a premium, and so there is a trade-off between memory used by the Web Cache and the memory requirements of all the other application server/database components.

Separate Server for Web Cache

If possible, you will want to place the Oracle Web Cache on a separate server. Because of Web Cache's relatively small footprint, it can be hosted on inexpensive commodity servers with 2GB of RAM and still provide a significant performance boost.

Remote Web Cache Servers

The Web Cache does not have to be directly in front of the OHS/application server. As depicted in Figure 5-3, a company with dispersed offices can set up a local Web Cache that will support only that office. If the separate offices use the application in different ways, the Web Cache will only be caching their pages. This improves efficiency, because as pages become stale, they will only need to be refreshed in the cache that is serving that page. The application server supports all the company's offices, but each office has a Web Cache supporting only its operation.

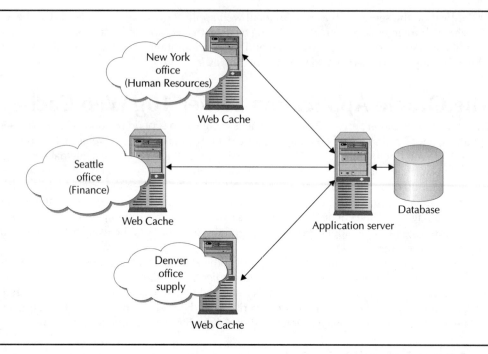

FIGURE 5-3. *Using remote Web Cache servers*

Load Balancing

Another key feature of Oracle's Web Cache is its ability to load-balance across multiple application servers. As the application server load behind the Web Cache grows, additional application servers can be added, and the Web Cache will load-balance the requests across the available servers. You can also use multiple Web Caches to create an infrastructure without a single point of failure.

Single Web Cache

A single Web Cache can support multiple application servers. Each application server can have a unique application, or they can all be running the same application and sharing the load. The Web Cache will distribute requests across all available application servers. If the application servers run on servers with different capabilities, a weighting can be used to cause the Web Cache to "favor" some application servers over others.

For example, if a company creates an application on a large multi-CPU server, but adds single CPU commodity servers as the load exceeds the capability of the large server, Web Cache can be configured to send most of its requests to the large server and less to the smaller commodity servers. Figure 5-4 illustrates this setup.

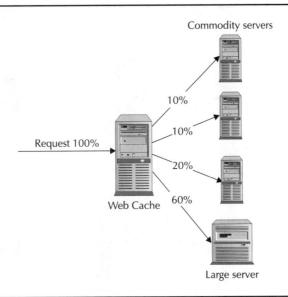

FIGURE 5-4.   *Single Web Cache, multiple application servers*

Multiple Web Caches

The problem with a single Web Cache is that it is a single point of failure. To build redundancy in, Oracle's Web Caches can be used in parallel, as shown in Figure 5-5. When coupled to multiple entry points from the Internet/company network, you can create an infrastructure that has complete redundancy. The Web Cache instances can function as independent entities or can be clustered to act as one logical cache.

When multiple Web Caches are clustered, they will request cached content from each other before sending the request back to the application server (Figure 5-6). The Web Caches in a cluster will also monitor each other to ensure that none of the caches in the cluster have failed. The cluster will normally only store one copy of a document, thereby making all caches into one large virtual cache. However, documents with high request rates can be stored on each cache in the cluster to improve response time. The large virtual cache results in more content being cached and further reduces the load on the application servers. Also, all Web Cache instances in a cluster use the same configuration and invalidation rules, resulting in better cache consistency.

Now that you know where to place the Oracle Web Cache within your application server infrastructure, you need to make sure it is caching the right documents and invalidating documents that have gone stale. If the Web Cache believes that content is valid, it will continue to serve the content to users. The method of informing a cache that a document is stale is called cache invalidation.

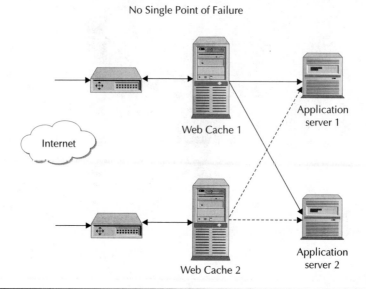

FIGURE 5-5. *Multiple Web Caches supporting multiple application servers*

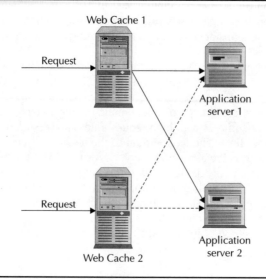

FIGURE 5-6. *Clustered Web Caches*

Cache Invalidation

With the Internet containing helpful caches throughout its infrastructure, from the browser to the web site, there must be a way to ensure that caches are not serving old content. Basic caching information is actually sent with the document when it is served.

Are Static Pages Really Static?

When you request a web page, your browser will first look for that page in its own cache. If it finds it in the cache, it will include the Last-Modified time stamp in the HTTP 1.1 Request Header If-Modified-Since. If the page has not been modified, the server will return a 304 code (Not Modified), and the browser can serve the page from the cache.

Oracle's Web Cache will check the Last-Modified timestamp on the page in the cache and either send the fresh page or reply with the Not-Modified code. So how does Oracle's Web Cache know if the page in its cache is fresh? It uses a number of different methods, from monitoring headers like all caches, to being told by the application or database that content has changed. There are a number of HTTP headers in HTTP 1.1 to control caching of web pages. The two main headers are the Expires and Cache-Control.

Expires The Expires header contains a timestamp for when the page is no longer valid. For example, a web page that displays sports scores may be updated every 30 minutes. As each page is served, the Expires header will contain the timestamp for the next update. If a cache services a request, it will know if the page contained in the cache is valid or if it should retrieve an updated version by the information in the Expires timestamp.

Cache-Control The Cache-Control header defines in more detail which caches can cache the page. If the Cache-Control is set to "public," any cache can cache the page. If Cache-Control is set to "private," only the local cache should cache the page. A setting of "no-cache" means that the server must verify that the page is current before the browser can display it. A setting of "no-store" tells all caches not to cache the page. This would be used for a page that contains sensitive information that you don't want sitting around in caches. Other Cache-Control parameters determine how long a page is fresh, such as "max-age" in seconds.

HTTP header information is necessary to define how caches maintain and serve you web pages, but they are not capable of supporting dynamically generated web pages.

Caching Dynamic Content

The Application Server 10g Web Cache is designed to cache dynamically generated content. When the Oracle HTTP Server (OHS) receives a request for nonstatic data, it passes that request to an application to create and serve the content. This may be a Java servlet that queries a database and formats the results, or a J2EE application.

Once the result is formatted, it is sent back to the requester. The results are cached in the Web Cache. The browser does not know that the page was created on the fly. The Web Cache, however, must have a mechanism to ensure that the page is still valid before re-serving the page to another request. The Web Cache must also ensure that the page is only served to the correct requester. If a brokerage firm has a web site that displays your current holdings, the site must ensure that it serves your page only to you and not the next requester, which may be your neighbor. The Web Cache has this same problem of what page to serve for which request.

HTTP Invalidation Messages

One problem with the invalidation methods just discussed is that they require that you know how long the page will remain fresh at the time it is served. For example, if a web site is used by a parts supplier to show stock on hand, it will contain fresh data until the stock levels change. How will the cache know that the stock level of widget #5634 changed when 20 were shipped to Florida?

One method is to use HTTP invalidation messages. An HTTP invalidation message is nothing more than an HTTP POST request sent to the Web Cache that tells it what URLs are now invalid. These messages can be sent by the application server, the database, or manually from a terminal (Figure 5-7). The database can contain triggers on key tables that fire during UPDATE, INSERT, and DELETE operations to invalidate content based on those tables. Likewise, the application may contain a method that will create and send an invalidation message to invalidate content in the Web Cache.

Invalidation from Within the Application

Oracle provides a toolkit located in the $ORACLE_HOME/webcache/toolkit directory that contains a Java JAR file and a couple of PL/SQL procedures that allow you to integrate Web Cache invalidation of content into your application or database. In this way, when the database or the application changes data, it can send a notice to the Web Cache to invalidate content based on that data. Oracle provides the complete Javadocs for the Web Cache Invalidation API in the Oracle Application Server 10*g* documentation. Please refer to the documentation for additional information.

Caching Multiple Versions of the Same Document

Consider the earlier example of the brokerage web site that produces a document containing information about your stock portfolio. As each separate user requests the basic template portfolio

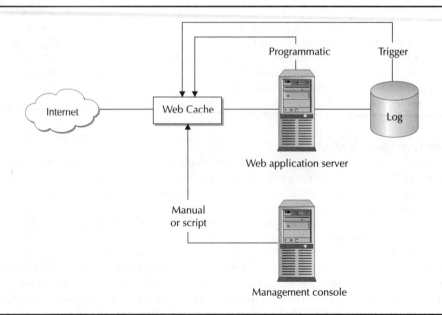

FIGURE 5-7.   *Using HTTP invalidation messages*

page, the Web Cache will contain multiple copies of basically the same page. Oracle's Web Cache uses one of two methods to ensure that it serves the correct page to the correct requester: cookies and embedded URL parameters.

When the Web Cache receives a request for the portfolio document, it either checks the cookie returned with the request, or it will look for a parameter in the request URL to determine whether the page is present in the cache. If not, it passes the request back to the application server to retrieve the data and create the document. When the document is returned, it is returned with the cookie or URL parameter, and the Web Cache will cache a copy of the document with the cookie or URL parameter in its cache. If the same user requests the portfolio page again and the page is valid, the Web Cache will serve the page directly from its cache. If the page is stale or invalid, it will pass the request to the application server. If the requester does not accept cookies, the second request for the portfolio page will not contain the cookie, and the Web Cache will have to pass the request back to the application server, even if the page is present and valid in its cache.

Partial Page Caching

To understand how partial page caching works, you need to understand how a web page is served. The web server will return an HTML (or JSP, etc.) document to the browser telling it how the page is to be displayed. Items like pictures, icons, and so on, are defined in the document but must be retrieved in a separate request, many times from a different web server. Thus, a web page that contains your local weather, sports scores, and stock quotes may be made up of separate requests to different servers that the browser displays as one web page.

Oracle's Web Cache is capable of caching these page parts and serving them as required. For example, a request is received for the company's home page that contains a cookie (defined previously) identifying the requester as employee #9843. The application server generates the home page containing general data plus data personalized for this employee. For instance, if the employee works in the supply section, the application server includes a news bulletin for all supply personnel. The employee is also participating in the employee stock program, so a section is generated showing the current stock value and his current holdings. The employee also works in the Denver office, so the current weather in Denver is included on the page.

Each of these customized elements is a separate web object that is retrieved either by the browser in a separate request, or by the Web Cache using Edge Side Includes. Each separate element will have its own caching rules. The weather information may be valid for only 4 hours, while the stock values are updated every 15 minutes, and current stock holdings may not be cacheable. In this way, Oracle's Web Cache supports caching parts of the page and allowing each part to have separate caching rules and invalidations.

Now that we have covered some of the capabilities of Oracle's Web Cache, let's look at how you can put all this power to work relieving the load on your application server.

Managing the Oracle Web Cache

When you start Application Server 10*g* using the opmnctl startall command, the Web Cache is also started.

```
$ORACLE_HOME/opmn/bin/opmnctl startall
```

You can work with Web Cache using the webcachectl utility, but the recommended way to work with Web Cache is to use the Web Cache Manager web site. We are going to discuss the

Web Cache Manager web site first and then cover the webcachectl utility. To log onto the Web Cache Manager web site, direct your browser to port 4000 on the server hosting Web Cache.

```
http://web_cache_host_name:4000
```

This is the default port for the first instance installed on the machine. In my case, I open my browser and log onto

```
http://appsrv.localdomain.com:4000/
```

This places you at the welcome page. Select the Log on to Web Cache Manager link on the right side of the page, and enter the administrator username and password. The default user is administrator, and the password is the ias_admin password defined during installation. You need to change the administrator's password, especially if the Web Cache is located in front of a firewall and is open to the Internet. You can skip the welcome page by logging directly to

```
http://appsrv.localdomain.com:4000/webcacheadmin
```

As you can see in Figure 5-8, in the upper-right corner are the buttons to apply or discard configuration changes. Along the left side of the page is a list of links to separate configuration pages. These are divided into the following categories:

Operations
Monitoring
Properties
Logging and Diagnostics
Ports
Origin Servers, Sites, and Load Balancing
Rules for Caching, Personalization, and Compression
Rule Association

Selecting any of the links will display the configuration web page for that topic.

Operations

When you start the Web Cache Manager, you are placed at the Cache Operations page. This page lists the Web Cache name, how long it has been up, and what actions need to be performed. As you make changes to the configuration, this page will remind you if the cache needs to be restarted. On the right is the page refresh button and a drop-down box to define a refresh interval. This refreshes the page, but it has no impact on the cache. If this configuration supported a cluster of caches, each Web Cache in the cluster would be listed along with its statistics.

To start, stop, or restart a cache, select the cache name from the list and click one of the buttons to execute the command. In a cluster configuration, you also have the option of selecting all the caches at once. Note that to use the Start button the cache must have been running and then stopped. To start and initialize a cache, use the webcachectl utility covered later in this chapter. The Restart button is used to stop the Web Cache (if running) and then to restart it. This will allow static

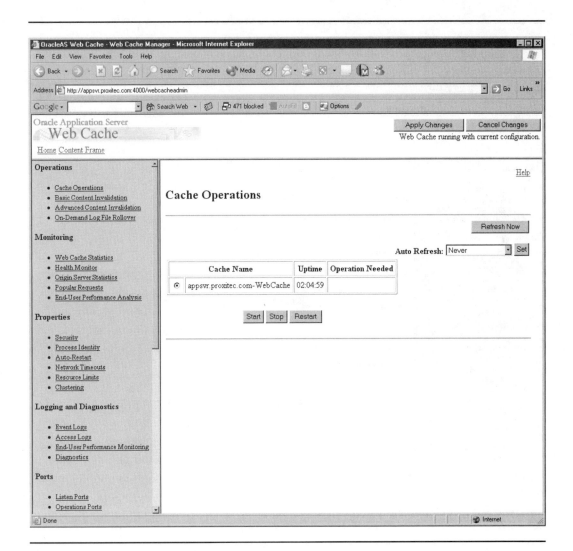

FIGURE 5-8. *Web Cache Manager web site*

configuration changes to be applied. If you make security or port changes, you cannot use the Restart (Stop and Start) buttons to implement those changes. You must shut down and restart the cache using the webcachectl utility.

Selecting the Basic Content Invalidation link brings up the page shown in Figure 5-9. Here, you can define a URL for all documents to be marked invalid, or invalidate the entire cache.

If you are using a cluster, the documents will be invalidated for all caches in the cluster. To see the contents of the cache, select the Remove All Cached Documents option and Preview List

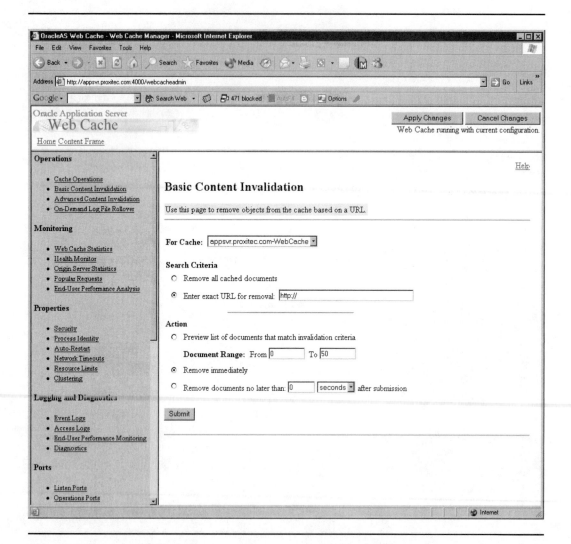

FIGURE 5-9. *Web Cache Manager, Basic Content Invalidation page*

of Documents, and select Submit (Figure 5-10). In the following partial list, you can see that the Web Cache is caching images from our Pet Store application:

```
/appsvr.localdomain.com:7778/estore/images/button_more.gif
/appsvr.localdomain.com:7778/estore/images/button_submit.gif
/appsvr.localdomain.com:7778/estore/images/fish2.gif
```

If you decide that the fish2.gif is no longer valid, you can place it in the URL field and preview it; then select Remove Immediately, and the fish2.gif image will be removed from the cache (Figure 5-11).

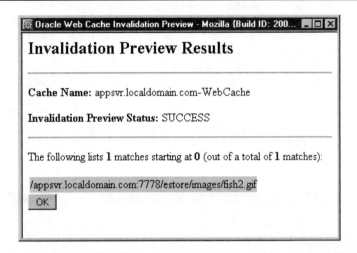

FIGURE 5-10.   *Web Cache Manager, Invalidation Preview*

Returning to the Basic Content Invalidation page, the Document Range defines the number of items displayed in the Preview window. The Remove Immediately option marks the objects as invalid and removes them from the cache. When the item is next requested, the cache will pass the request to the application server. If you select the Remove Documents No Later Than option, the document is marked invalid but will continue to be served until the application server load allows

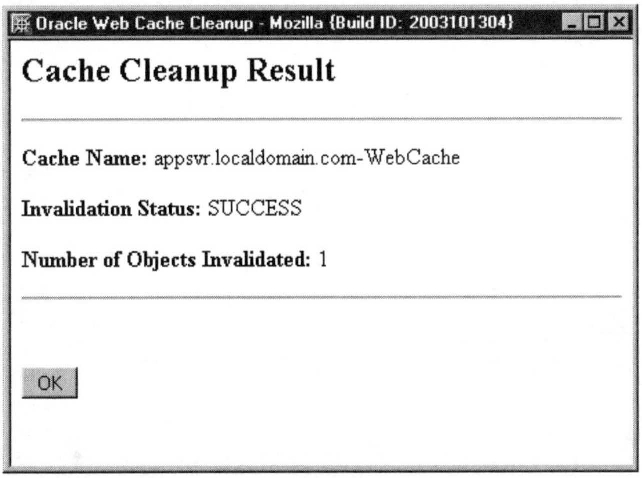

FIGURE 5-11.   *Web Cache Manager, invalidation success notification*

the documents to be refreshed. This feature keeps the application server from returning "Server Busy" errors back to the client. The client will possibly be served a stale document rather than get an error.

You may want to choose the Advanced Content Invalidation page, shown in Figure 5-12, to invalidate documents using more defined methods to identify the specific pages to invalidate.

The top section provides advanced search capabilities to locate content cached using URLs. The Cookies/Header Information section allows you to locate and invalidate items cached using cookies or header information. To invalidate all content associated with a particular cookie, select Cookie in the combo box and enter the cookie's name and value. To invalidate based on a header value, select Header in the combo box and enter the header's name and value. If you scroll down, you find the URL Parameters section and the Search Keys section, shown in Figure 5-13.

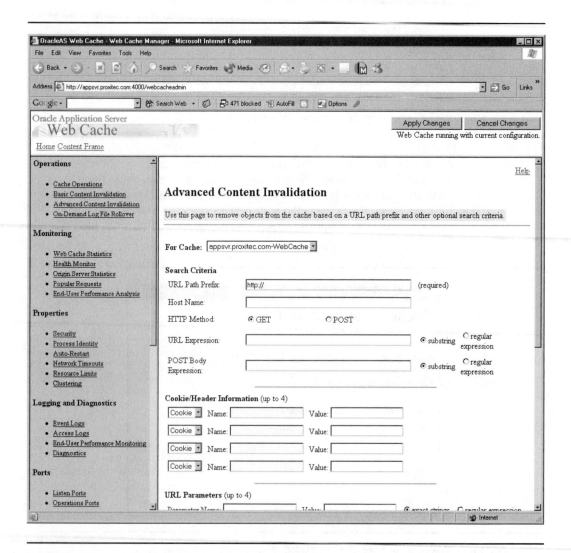

FIGURE 5-12. *Web Cache Manager, Advanced Content Invalidation page*

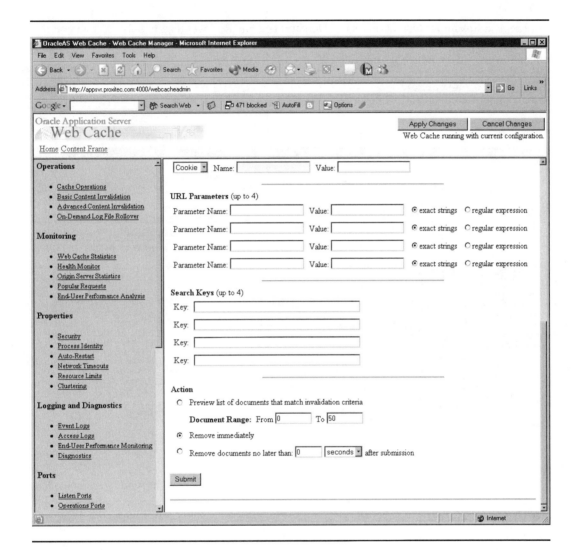

FIGURE 5-13. *Web Cache Manager, Advanced Content Invalidation page, continued*

To invalidate all documents being cached based on parameters passed in the URL, enter the parameter's name and value. The Search Keys section allows you to invalidate content based on the Surrogate-Key response-header field.

Once you have identified the content to be invalidated, it is a good idea to preview the results before actually invalidating them. When you are sure you have identified the correct content, select the method of invalidation and click Submit. Again, the Remove Documents selection will refresh the content based on server load, while the Remove Immediately option will force the content to be refreshed at the next request.

The next link under Operations is On-Demand Log File Rollover (Figure 5-14). When you roll over a log file, Web Cache will rename the current log file to log_file.yyyymmdd and start a new one. The Web Cache log files are located at

```
$ORACLE_HOME/webcache/logs
```

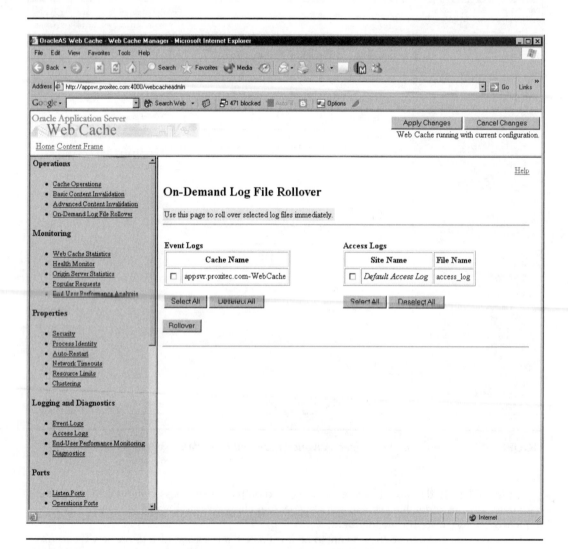

FIGURE 5-14. *Web Cache Manager, On-Demand Log File Rollover page*

The following listing shows my logs before and after rolling over:

```
[oracle@appsvr oracle]$ cd $ORACLE_HOME/webcache/logs/
[oracle@appsvr logs]$ ls -l
20241975 Nov  2 16:50 access_log
  616866 Nov  2 16:50 event_log
[oracle@appsvr logs]$ ls -l
       0 Nov  2 21:12 access_log
20241975 Nov  2 16:50 access_log.20031102_1650
       0 Nov  2 21:12 event_log
  616904 Nov  2 21:12 event_log.20031102_1650
```

My demonstration system is inactive. A Web Cache under normal load will produce quite a large log file, and you should set up a script to routinely copy old logs off the system or delete them.

Monitoring

At this point, we'll move to the Monitoring category of the Web Cache Manager. This section focuses on Web Cache performance statistics. Most of the performance statistics are self-explanatory. Using the combo boxes at the top of the Web Cache Statistics screen, shown in Figure 5-15, you can identify the Web Cache instance, or all caches. The For Site combo box allows you to identify a particular origin OHS server or all the servers supported by that cache instance. Once you make your selections, click the View button to display the statistics for your selection.

The page is divided into five parts. This first table shows cache start and reset information. The Cache Overview table provides the current stats of the cache. The Requests Served table (Figure 5-16) provides performance data on how well the cache is serving the request demand to include fresh and stale hits and cache misses. On a heavily loaded Web Cache and application server, the number of stale hits will go up as pages expire or are invalidated, but should drop, allowing the application server to refresh the content. If you invalidate content with Remove Immediately, stale hits will not increase, but cacheable misses (and possibly Site Busy Errors) will increase.

The final two tables on the Web Cache Statistics page are Errors Served and Invalidations. The Errors Served table shows the number of error (or apology) messages returned. The Invalidations table details the number of invalidation request processes, as shown in Figure 5-17. The one invalidation shown is from our exercise earlier.

The next section in the Monitoring category is the Health Monitor, which provides a look at what the Web Cache is currently executing. One of the interesting bits of information is that in the example, Web Cache is communicating with the OHS server on port 7779, as you can see in Figure 5-18. OHS is listening on port 7778 and 7779. If Web Cache fails, the OHS server will directly service the request on port 7778. Otherwise, Web Cache will service 7778 and pass back requests to OHS on 7779.

The page provides information on the origin servers (the application servers) that Web Cache is communicating with (Figure 5-19). If a server is up and available, Web Cache will forward requests

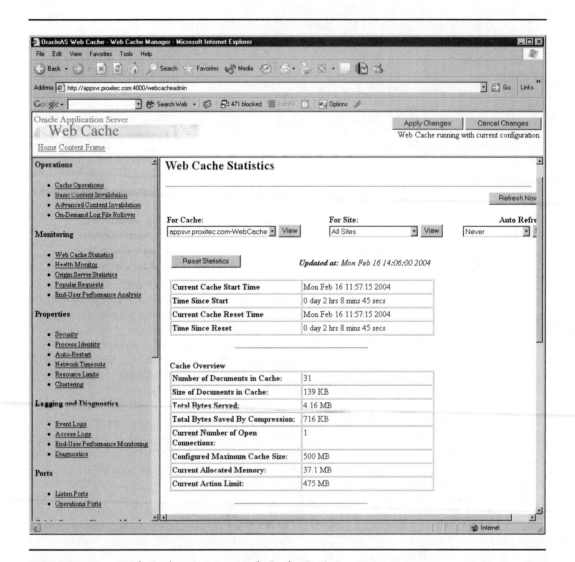

FIGURE 5-15. *Web Cache Manager, Web Cache Statistics page*

to it as necessary. If it is down, Web Cache will forward requests to another server if available and continue to ping the down server until it comes back up. If the unavailable server is the only one, then Web Cache will continue to forward requests to it even when it is down.

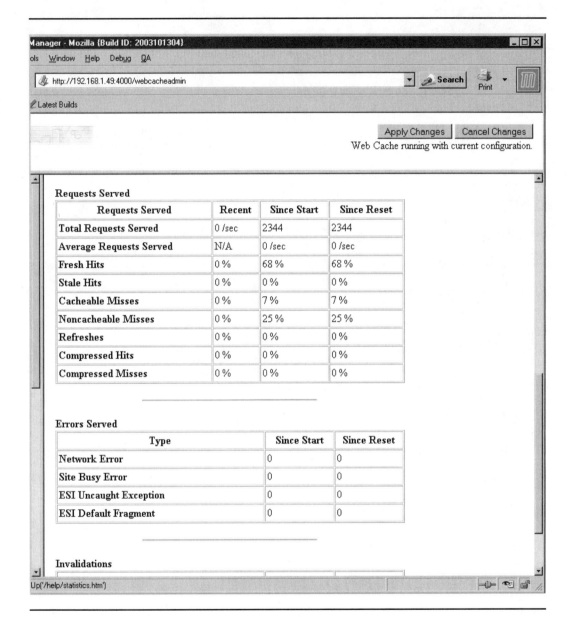

FIGURE 5-16. *Web Cache Manager, Web Cache Statistics, Requests Served*

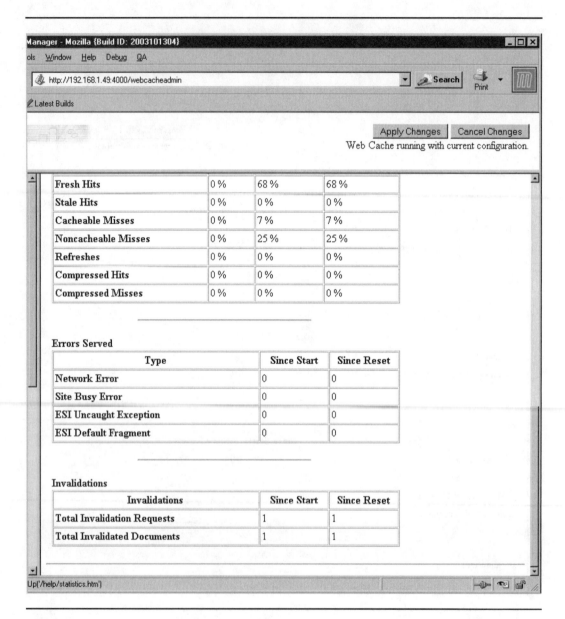

FIGURE 5-17. *Web Cache Manager, Web Cache Statistics, Errors Served, and Invalidations*

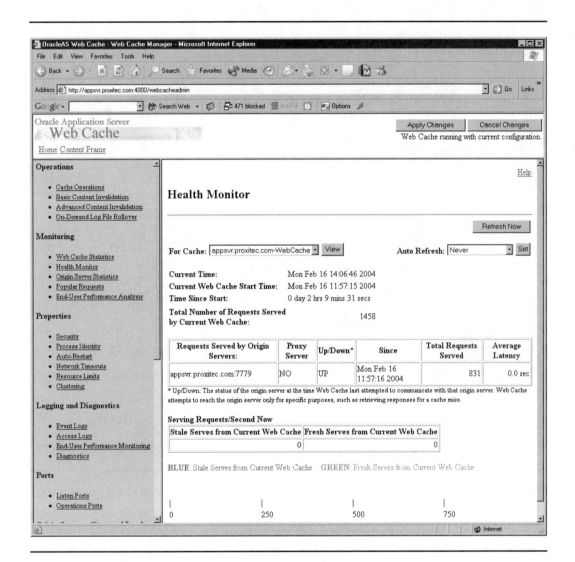

FIGURE 5-18. *Web Cache Manager, Health Monitor page*

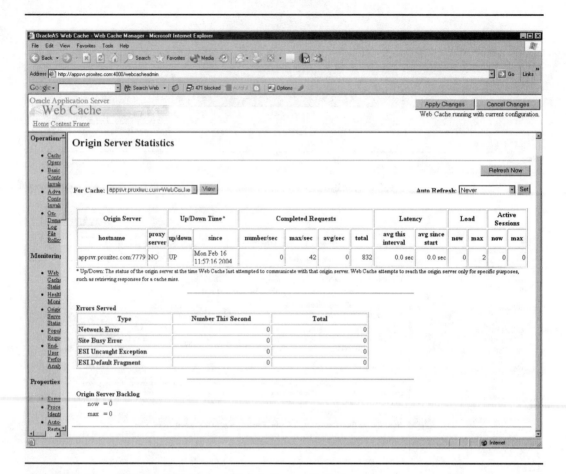

FIGURE 5-19. *Web Cache Manager, Origin Server Statistics page*

The next page, shown in Figure 5-20, simply ranks the content in the cache by the number of requests. Selecting the Export to File button will open a File dialog box to identify the file name and location.

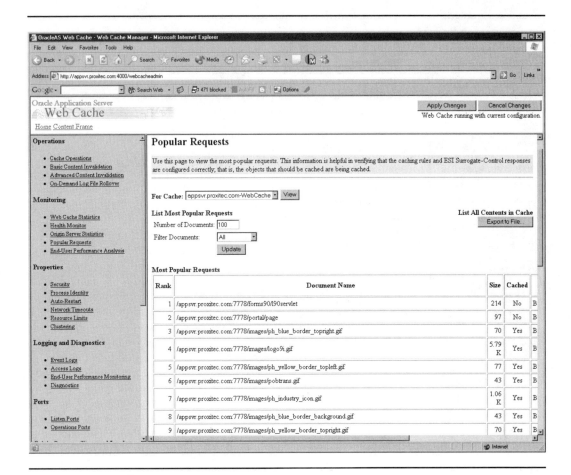

FIGURE 5-20. *Web Cache Manager, Popular Request page*

Properties

Next we move into the Properties category. The Security page allows you to change the administrator and invalidator users and passwords. It also allows you to define trusted subnets or IP addresses used to define valid computers that users can use to connect to the Web Cache. The default is All, as shown in Figure 5-21, which allows you to connect to the Web Cache from any IP. Limiting

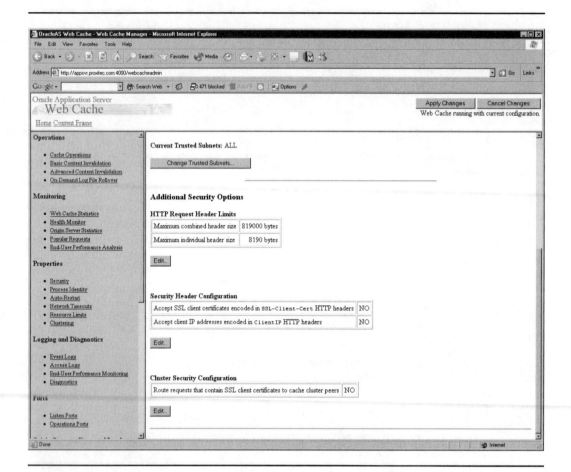

FIGURE 5-21. *Web Cache Manager, Security page*

this to local computers enhances security. Remember that when you change a password or trusted subnet on this page, the Web Cache must be restarted using opmn before the change becomes effective.

The Process Identity page displays the UNIX user and group that Web Cache processes are running under. You can use the Change ID button to modify these values.

The Auto-restart page determines the method used to restart Web Cache if it fails. This determines how opmn or webcachemon (depending on how the cache was started) monitors the status of the Web Cache.

The Network Timeouts page allows you to adjust the amount of time Web Cache maintains connections. The first value, Keep-Alive Timeout, determines how long the Web Cache will keep open a connection to the browser after sending a response. The default allows five seconds from the time a response is sent for the browser to send another request. Remember that web pages define the layout and usually require the browser to retrieve additional content, such as pictures or icons. It is much more efficient for the browser to respond with those requests while the connection is still open than to go through the overhead of opening a new connection. If your users are connecting over dial-in modems, this value may need to be increased.

The next parameter, Origin Server Timeout, defines how long Web Cache will wait for the origin server (the application server) to respond to a request before sending an error/apology page.

Next is the Resource Limits page. The parameters on this page define the resources that Web Cache can use, such as the maximum number of connections and the maximum size. Unlike the database cache, Web Cache will not grab its total memory allocation on startup but will grow as cached content grows.

The final page in the Properties category is the Clustering page. This page shows Web Caches that are in the cluster and allows you to add Web Caches to a cluster. When adding a cluster, you assign a capacity rating based on the capacity of all Web Caches in the cluster. This allows the cluster to balance the cluster cache across all the available Web Caches in the cluster based on the individual Web Cache's capabilities.

Logging and Diagnostics

The first page in the Logging and Diagnostics category defines parameters for the event log, such as the location, name, buffering options, and the logging level. Each Web Cache has an event log. The log location and logging level are edited by selecting the log in the Cache Specific Event Log Configuration section. By selecting the Edit button in the Global Event Log Configuration section, you can set the automatic rollover option for the selected cache log, as shown in Figure 5-22.

The Access Logs page allows you to configure the access logs produced by Web Cache. Each web site supported by Web Cache will get its own access log. Here again, you can define automatic rollover. You can use the User Defined Access Format section to modify the information included in the access logs.

End-user performance monitoring allows you to gather statistics on performance of all or part of your application. You can monitor users as they enter the site until they exit, or only specific application servers or specific application sections. This is helpful in determining which sections of the application are not performing as required.

Finally, the Diagnostics page is where you can cause the Web Cache to display diagnostic information in the response page body. By default, diagnostics information is sent in the server header.

Ports

The Ports category contains two pages. First, the Listening Ports page defines which ports Web Cache is listening on for incoming requests. When Application Server 10g is installed, it points a number of components at the installed ports. Before changing the listening ports, you need to ensure that you will not invalidate parts of the application server that are set to redirect pages. Normally, you will want to set the listening port to 80, the default web server port. Another option is to leave the Web Cache listening to the default port and forward port 80 through the firewall to the Web Cache port. Also note that changing the listening port to 80 will cause you to start Web Cache as UNIX root because non-root users do not have access to the lower range of ports on UNIX/Linux systems. The Operational Ports page shows the ports that Web Cache is listening on for connections by the Web Cache Manager, the administrator, and the invalidator.

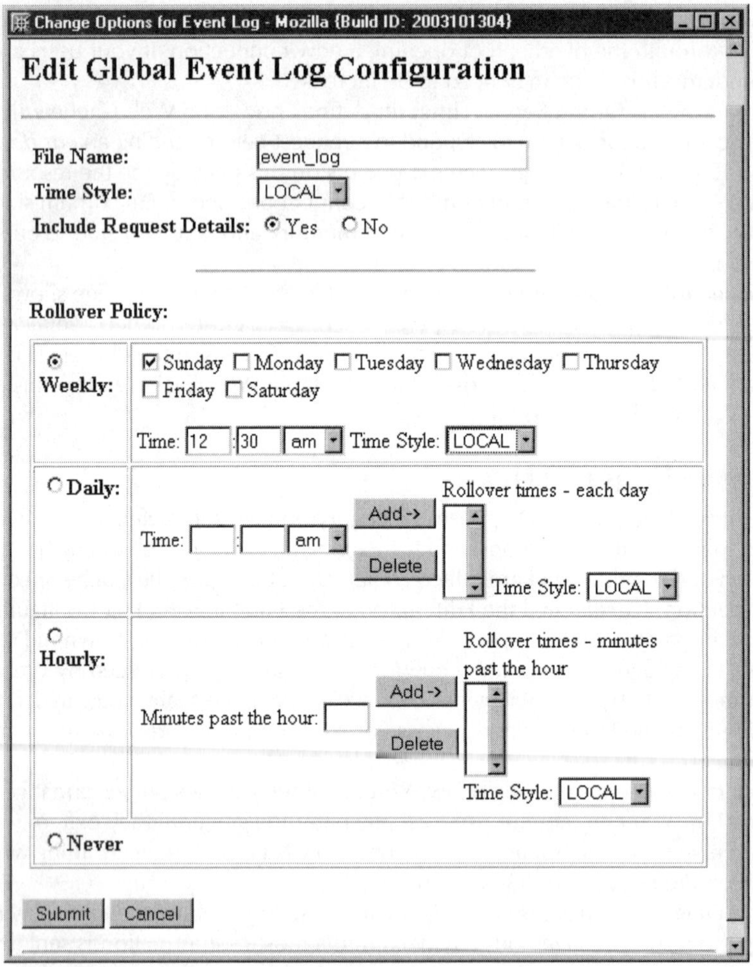

FIGURE 5-22. *Web Cache Manager, Event Logs Automatic Rollover*

Origin Servers, Sites, and Load Balancing

The Origin Servers page (Figure 5-23) maps Web Cache to all supported origin servers. This is also where you define the server's capacity to assist Web Cache in load balancing. Note that the port defined on this page tells Web Cache where to look for the server, and the server must be separately configured to listen on that port. Proxy servers supporting web servers and application servers behind firewalls are also defined on this page. This page only maps to the server; before a server is used, a web site must be mapped to the server on the Site-to-Server Mapping page (Figure 5-24).

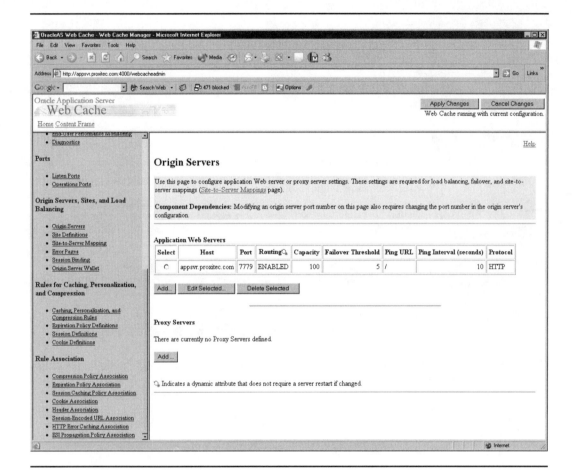

FIGURE 5-23. *Web Cache Manager, Origin Servers, Sites, and Load Balancing, Origin Servers page*

The Site Definitions page defines actual web sites (or application sites) to include sites that are being virtual hosted by a server. One origin server may host many web sites, and this page allows you to identify each web site. At this point, we are just defining the site.

Now that we have a list of sites and a list of origin servers, let's map the site to the servers. All sites listed in the Site Definitions page should be mapped to a server defined in the Origin Servers page. Web Cache prioritizes requests in accordance with the priority defined on this page. To add a new site, select the site with the priority you want the new site to be, and select the Insert Above button. This opens the Edit/Add window shown in Figure 5-25.

Either manually enter a site name or select a site already defined from the Host Name combo box. Check all the application web servers that support this site, and select the Submit button. You can use the wildcard character to include multiple sites in one mapping, such as *.appsvr.localdomain.com, which will map requests from site1.appsvr.localdomain.com and site5.appsvr.localdomain.com to the same origin server.

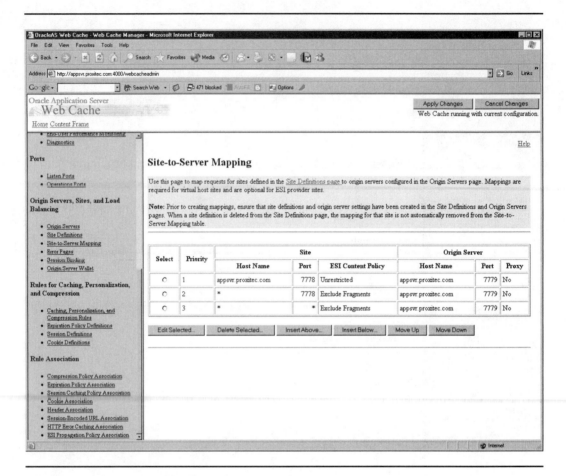

FIGURE 5-24. *Web Cache Manager, Origin Servers, Sites, and Load Balancing, Site-to-Server Mapping page*

The Error Pages page defines error pages that are sent by Web Cache when errors are encountered. Generic pages are provided with Web Cache, but these pages should be edited to match the style of the web site.

The Session Binding page enables/disables session binding. Session binding is used to keep a session interacting with the same application server, based on the idea that the server generated the first response and will be more efficient in processing future responses. Session binding is required if the server is maintaining some state for the session in the server that will not be available to other servers. Before enabling session binding, understand that the origin server must produce and maintain the session binding information (cookie or URL parameters). The Web Cache ensures that the session requests are routed to the correct server.

The Origin Server Wallet page defines the location of the Oracle SSL Certificate Wallet.

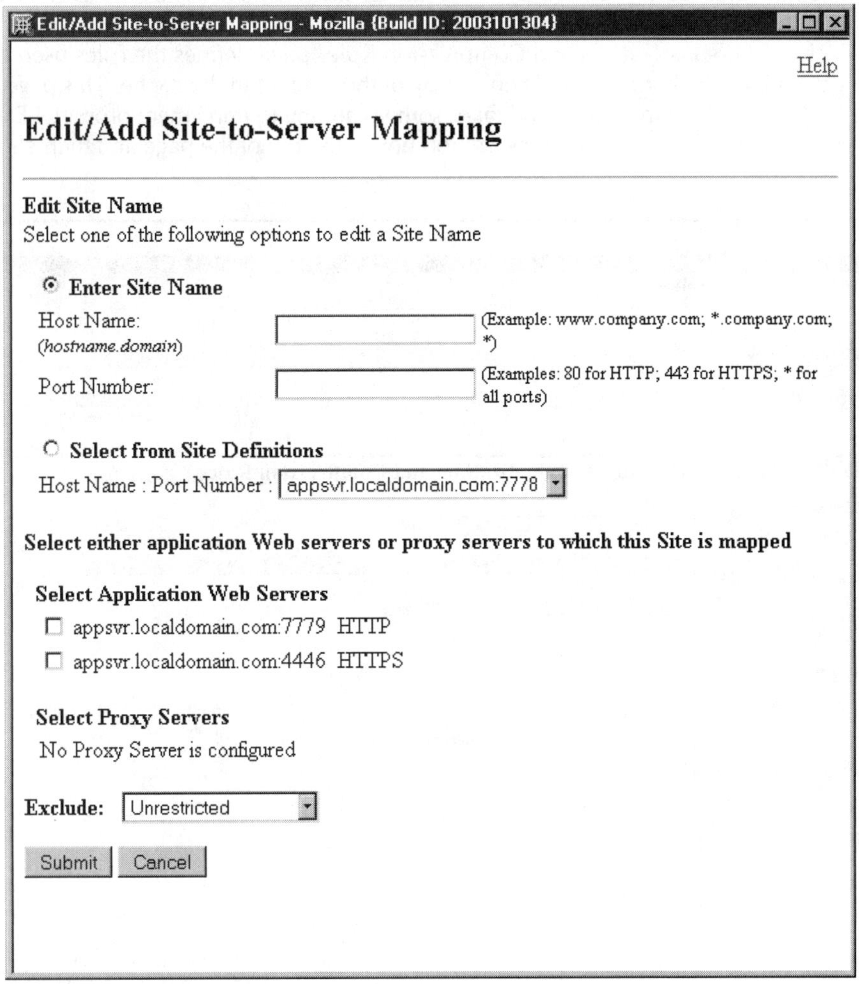

FIGURE 5-25. *Edit/Add window for adding a site*

Rules for Caching, Personalization, and Compression

The next category in the Web Cache Manager is used for defining caching rules. These caching rules tell Web Cache what content to cache and what not to cache. The defined caching rules override the caching directives embedded in the HTTP heading. This is an important area of Web

Cache configuration because you want to ensure that as much content as possible is cached while also ensuring that stale content is not served.

The Caching, Personalization, and Compression Rules page defines the rules used by Web Cache to determine whether or not to keep a copy of the content in the cache. This page, shown in Figure 5-26, is a little complicated and takes some planning to implement properly. Each site can have its own rules. Select a site in the combo box at the top of the page and then click View.

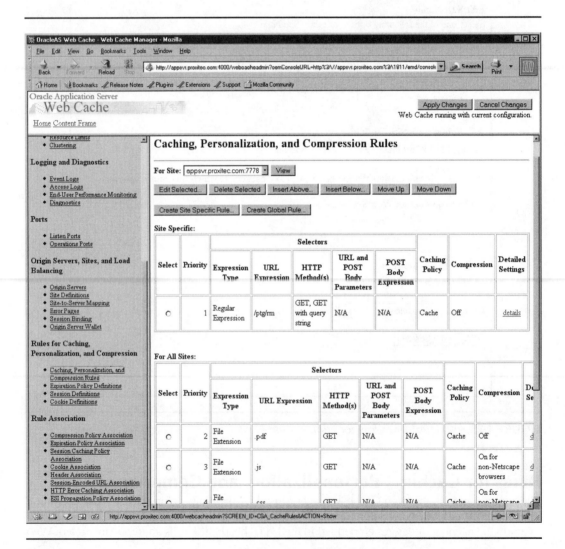

FIGURE 5-26. *Web Cache Manager, Caching, Personalization, and Compression Rules page*

The Web Cache Manager displays the current caching rules defined for that site. Each rule has a priority and is applied in that order. So, if you have a document tree that contains some documents that will be cached and some that should not be cached, first determine which caching rule applies to most of the documents. If most of the documents are cached except two, for example, then define the rule not to cache the two documents (it may take two rules), and then define the rule to cache all the other documents.

Let's say that all documents in the /Big_News directory are to be cached except /Big_News/ Layoffs.html. First define a rule not to cache Layoffs.html. Then define a rule to cache all documents in /Big_News. The first rule will have a higher priority than the second, so all documents in /Big_ News will be cached except Layoffs.html.

To define a new rule, select the priority for the new rule and select the Insert Above button, or just select the Create Global Rule or Create Site Specific Rule button. In the example in Figure 5-27, we are creating a global rule to cache Java Server Pages (.jsp).

For the Expression Type, we have selected File Extension and entered **\.jsp** for the expression. We selected the Cache option and "Expires:300" seconds, "remove immediately" for the Expiration Policy. After clicking Submit, the rule is created. Since we created the rule using the Create Global Rule button, the new rule is created at the bottom of the list. If you wanted to change the priority, you could select the rule and then select the Move Up or Move Down button to raise or lower the priority. To remove a rule, select it and press the Delete Selected button.

The next page, Expiration Policy Definitions, is used to define expiration policies used by the caching rules. Three policies are predefined, but you can create your own by selecting the Add button, which brings up the Create Expiration Policy page shown in Figure 5-28. Once you define the policy, it will be available to the rules defined on the Caching, Personalization, and Compression Rules page.

In the Session Definition page, you tell Web Cache how to identify session information, either by a cookie or by a URL parameter, or both. If session binding is turned on, Web Cache will use the session definition to track content based on the session.

The final page in this category is the Cookie Definition page. This tells Web Cache either to cache or not to cache pages that contain the defined cookie. To add a cookie definition, select the Add button, name the cookie, and tell Web Cache whether or not to cache the document (Figure 5-29).

Rule Association

The final category in the Web Cache Manager is the Rule Association category. This category covers the association of rules to their definitions. Most of this information has already been seen. The Compression Policy Association reviews the compression information applied in the Caching, Personalization, and Compression Rules page. The Expiration Policy Association page rolls up the expiration policies defined earlier. These pages are important when you are looking for a specific policy and don't want to search through the individual rules.

The Web Cache Manager is a powerful configuration tool that can be used to define specific instructions on how and for how long Web Cache maintains content in its cache. It is important to

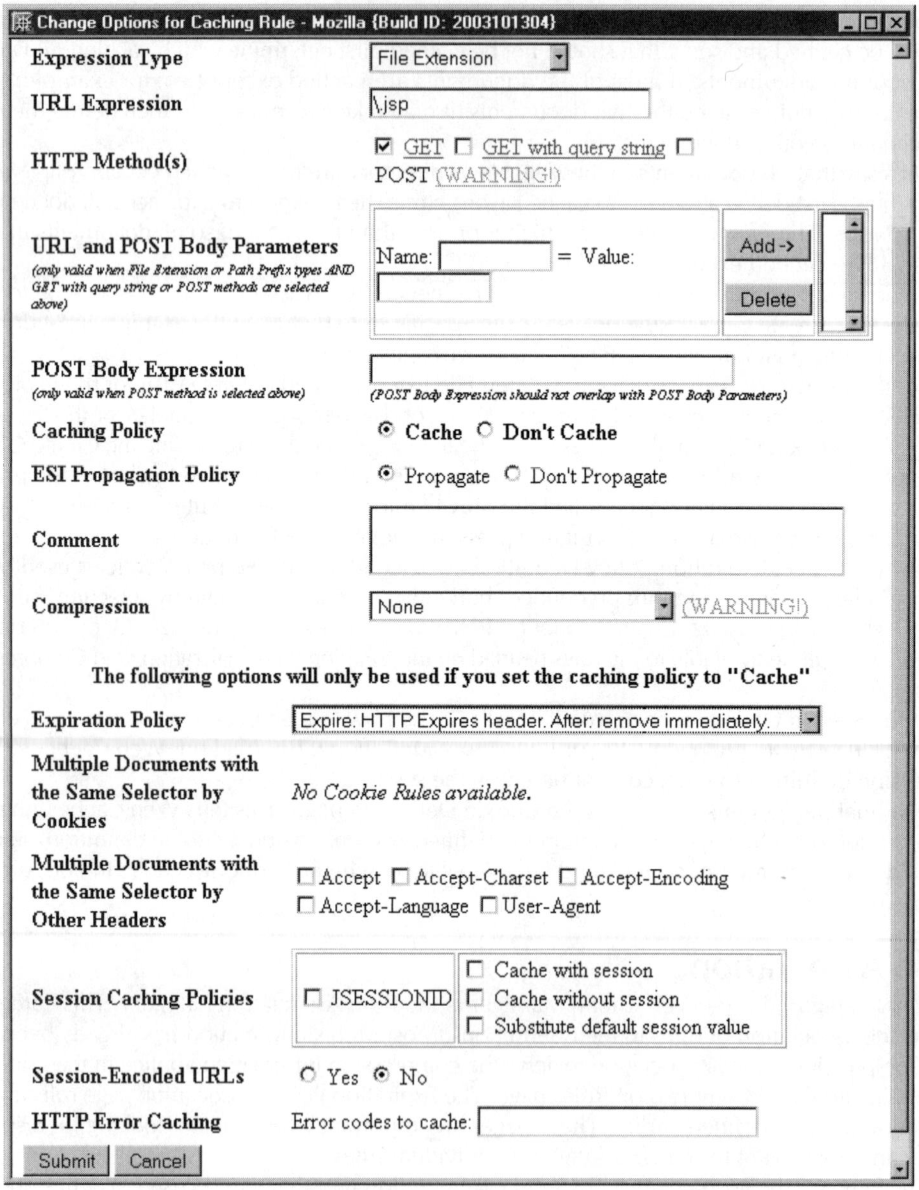

FIGURE 5-27. *Adding a rule in Caching, Personalization, and Compression Rules*

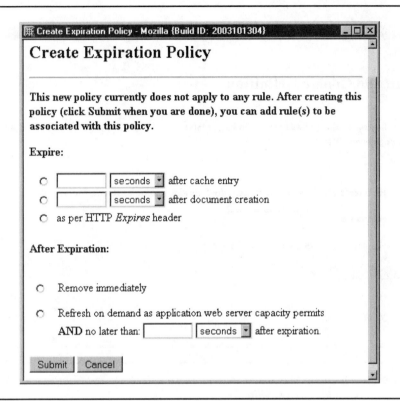

FIGURE 5-28. *Web Cache Manager, Caching, Personalization, and Compression Rules, Create Expiration Policy page*

remember to apply your changes and to recheck the Cache Operations page to determine whether you need to restart the Web Cache. Also, changing the administrator or invalidator password will require that Web Cache be restarted by opmn or webcachectl. The Web Cache Manager is an invaluable tool for configuring the Web Cache, but, to maintain Web Cache using scripts, you need to use the webcachectl utility or opmn.

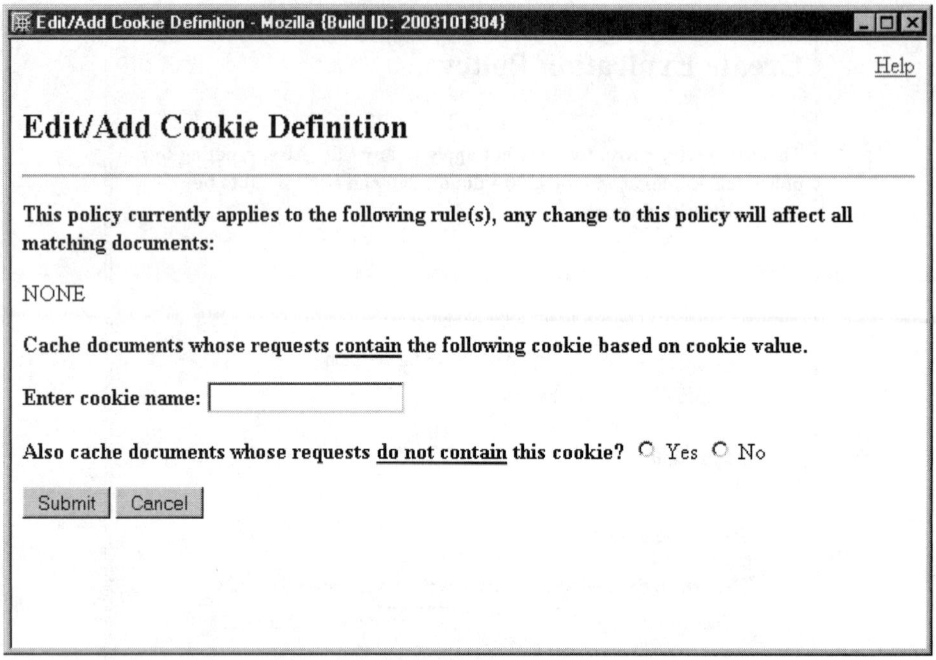

FIGURE 5-29. *Web Cache Manager, Caching, Personalization, and Compression Rules, Edit/Add Cookie Definition*

Webcachectl Utility

The webcachectl utility is used to control the three processes that make up the Web Cache. For the most part, you will not necessarily use webcachectl directly unless Web Cache is installed on a separate server. When co-located with the application server, you will use opmnctl.

```
opmnctl startproc ias-component=WebCache
opmnctl startall
```

However, if Web Cache is installed on a separate server, you will need to use webcachectl to start and stop the Web Cache processes. Web Cache consists of the admin server process, which is the interface for Web Cache Manager, the cache server processes that manage the cache, and the autostart process that restarts Web Cache if it crashes. The autorestart process is directly tied to the cache process and as such, starts and stops with it. When Web Cache is installed on a separate server, it is normally set to listen on port 80 and in UNIX/Linux, must be started as root. Only programs run as root can access ports below 1024.

On Windows, the Web Cache processes are started as Windows services and will start and stop with the server. On UNIX/Linux, you must create a script to start and stop Web Cache. These scripts are discussed in detail in Chapter 2.

The webcachectl utility's basic commands are start, stop, and restart:

```
webcachectl start
webcachectl stop
webcachectl restart
```

In addition, each of these commands has an admin or cache variant:

```
webcachectl startadm
webcachectl stopadm
webcachectl restartadm

webcachectl startcache
webcachectl stopcache
webcachectl restartcache
```

Each of the admin commands affects only the admin process, while each of the cache commands affects both the cache and the autostart processes. The utility also has a status command:

```
[oracle@appsvr bin]$ export ORACLE_HOME=/home/oracle/oraportal904
[oracle@appsvr bin]$ ./webcachectl status
**************************************************************************
WARNING! With the exception of standalone OracleAS Web Cache
installations, direct use of webcachectl within Oracle Application Server is
deprecated.
Using webcachectl in conjunction with Oracle Process Management
and Notification (OPMN) may lead to unexpected behavior (such as OPMN
automatically restarting OracleAS Web Cache after it has been shutdown
using webcachectl).

Please use opmnctl (located at $ORACLE_HOME/opmn/bin/opmnctl) instead.
webcachectl may not be shipped with future versions of Oracle Application
Server.
**************************************************************************
Web Cache admin server is running as process 31044.
Web Cache auto-restart monitor is not running.
Web Cache cache server is running as process 31053.
*****************************Web Cache is being monitored by opmn and so
```
does not have the autorestart monitor running. Lastly, webcachectl has a reset
command that returns the configuration to the last configuration saved with
the Apply button in Web Cache Manager. After using the reset command, you must
restart Web Cache.

Summary

As you have seen, the Oracle Application Server 10*g* Web Cache is a powerful tool that can significantly reduce the load on the application server and back-end database. On the Internet, caching happens at multiple levels and at multiple sites. However, unless your cache is tied to the application, you can only cache static content. The ability to cache static and dynamic content, along with powerful caching rules and dynamic content invalidation, will allow you to better utilize the resources you have instead of adding more servers. The main points of this chapter are as follows:

- Web Cache can significantly reduce your application server/database load by serving content directly from its cache.

- Multiple Web Cache instances can be clustered to create a large logical cache and remove the Web Cache as a single point of failure.

- To support the caching of dynamically created content, Web Cache must know when content becomes stale. This is accomplished by defining expiration rules or caching rules, or by having the application server or database invalidate content as needed.

- All Web Cache configuration is performed by the Web Cache Administration web site.

By integrating Web Cache capabilities into your application/web site development, you can better take advantage of dynamic caching. This will allow Web Cache to serve the maximum number of requests while ensuring against serving stale content. With powerful features like load balancing and cache clustering, Oracle's Web Cache is an integral component in creating a fault-tolerant, redundant infrastructure for your J2EE applications.

The next chapter introduces some of the concepts needed to understand J2EE applications and how the Oracle Application Server 10*g* supports them.

CHAPTER
6

Using J2EE in the
Application Server 10g

his chapter and the next revolve around supporting Java and J2EE applications with Oracle Application Server 10*g*. Providing access to J2EE Enterprise JavaBeans along with connectivity to the web and customer databases is the basis of any application server. As such, this chapter introduces the components needed to understand and support J2EE within the Oracle Application Server. Many DBAs are tasked to administer the application server without a basic understanding of J2EE components and their interaction with the application server.

The Java language and the Enterprise Edition extensions are beyond the scope of this book. Indeed, a trip to the local bookstore will reveal shelves of books covering this subject. If you wish to dig deeper into developing J2EE applications, it is covered in detail in the excellent Oracle Press books *Oracle9iAS Building J2EE Applications*, by Morisseau-Leroy (McGraw-Hill/Osborne, 2002) or *Oracle9i Web Development*, by Brown (McGraw-Hill/Osborne, 2001). Because Oracle's Application Server and Oracle's JDeveloper are very tightly integrated, another important reference is the *Oracle9i JDeveloper Handbook*, by Koletzke, Dorsey, and Faderman (McGraw-Hill/Osborne, 2003). Here we will only discuss J2EE application components and how to administer them within the Oracle Application Server and leave the application development to others.

J2EE Introduction

Java is both a compiled and an interpreted language. Java source code is compiled into a file containing byte-code. The Java Virtual Machine (JVM) interprets the byte-code into machine code and executes it. It is because of this intermediate step that the Java code is portable to many different operating systems. Any operating system that implements a JVM can run the Java class file. Java also implements a number of technologies that allow it to communicate easily across a network or the Internet. As Java matured, more and more developers were using it to produce large, complex, distributed transaction programs. To assist this development, Sun produced the Java 2 Platform, Enterprise Edition (J2EE), which consists of a component-based approach to designing, developing, assembling, and deploying an enterprise application. J2EE uses a multitiered set of technologies that allow developers to focus attention on each tier during development. Developers implementing Enterprise JavaBeans may not know how to program Java Server Pages, but because the J2EE specification defines methods for Enterprise JavaBeans (EJBs) to communicate, they can be developed separately and still seamlessly mesh within the application. The J2EE specification divides its technologies into three tiers: the client tier, the web tier, and the business tier, as shown in Figure 6-1.

The client tier consists of either an application (possibly using JavaBeans) or the user's browser with static or dynamic pages and Java applets. The client tier runs on the user's desktop. Utilizing the user's browser to serve the application interface allows the flexibility of having the entire application located on the server. Clients are always working on the latest version because their application is served from the application server each time it starts. Having a client application running on the user's desktop that communicates with the server portion of the application can allow for extensive processing locally and reduced server loads; however, updating the client application involves reinstalling on each client.

The web tier consists of an HTTP server providing static and dynamic HTML pages, Java Server Pages, and servlets.

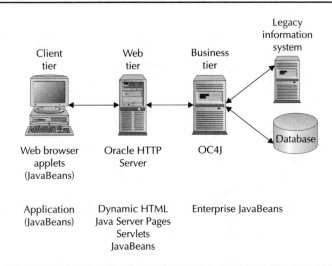

FIGURE 6-1. *J2EE component tiers*

Behind the web tier is the business tier. Here is where the business logic is executed within EJBs. This tier may be located on one server or spread across a number of possibly geographically dispersed servers. Co-locating the business logic in one tier allows for easier maintenance. The business tier may communicate with a back-end database or a legacy information system.

Now that you have an idea of how J2EE divides an enterprise application into tiers, we need to define some J2EE terms.

Applets

Applets are usually small Java programs that are downloaded to the browser and run locally inside the browser's Java Virtual Machine. Applets can be small programs like banner ads or large applications that run a GUI. A request for an applet is embedded into an HTML page, and when the browser renders the page, it will find the tag and request the applet. Once the applet is downloaded to the client machine, the browser executes the applet. All applets require that the browser have a JVM installed, and more complicated applets may require a security policy file in order to execute successfully. Applets are a powerful component that can provide a rich user interface, but they must be downloaded from the server, which can take a considerable amount of time.

Client Applications

Client applications are Java programs that run on the client system and communicate with an application server. They are usually rich clients, meaning that they can perform extensive user interaction through a GUI. Client applications are normally implemented using JavaBeans, which will be discussed later in this section. They can also access EJBs on the application server or access a servlet through an HTTP connection. In multitiered systems, client applications normally execute the user interface, leaving all the business logic to the application server.

Servlets

Servlets are Java web components that execute on the HTTP server side (the web tier). Called in an HTTP or Java Server Page (JSP) document, or directly from an application, servlets are used to produce dynamic data. Since they operate on the server side of the communication, they have full access to the server's Java APIs. They also remain active on the server and can be used to maintain persistent data. Servlets are called as the document is being served and normally produce HTML that is served to the client browser for displaying. Servlets can access JavaBeans and/or Enterprise JavaBeans during execution.

Java Server Pages

Java Server Pages are Java web components used to embed Java into an HTML coded page. JSPs can place Java code directly into the HTML code so that it is compiled and executed when served. Java Server Pages allow for easy interaction between the user and the server application. JSPs are not served directly by the HTTP server, but are instead served by the JSP container through the HTTP server. You'll learn more about this later in the chapter.

JavaBeans

A JavaBean is a reusable software component that implements Sun's JavaBean specification. Beans are normally implemented in some type of integrated development environment (IDE) used to create applications and build user interfaces, such as Oracle's JDeveloper. Think of a bean as a black box that implements some needed functionality and can be dropped into a Java program and used. JavaBeans are part of the Java programming language and are not really part of the J2EE specification. However, since JavaBeans are just reusable "chunks" of Java code, they can be found on all three tiers.

Enterprise JavaBeans

Enterprise JavaBeans (EJB) are server-side, reusable components that are used to implement business logic. EJBs run inside containers that implement all of the required support infrastructure, such as system resource security, locating, and connecting to other EJBs and clients. EJBs will be discussed in greater detail later in this chapter. There is a significant difference between a JavaBean and an Enterprise JavaBean. A bean is a chunk of reusable code that is integrated into an application. An enterprise bean must run in a container and can be thought of as an independent subapplication that waits for requests and then answers them. Thus, a J2EE application can be thought of as a series of subapplications, all running to support the main application.

J2EE Containers

A container provides the infrastructure for running EJBs. An EJB must be deployed into a container before it can be used. The container starts the EJB when it is accessed and provides all required services the EJB needs. If EJBs are the heart of a J2EE application, the container is the heart of the application server. Oracle's container, OC4J, is covered in detail in Chapter 7.

JAR Files, WAR Files, and EAR Files

To deploy EJBs and other components in the J2EE application, you must package them. In keeping with J2EE modular programming methodology, all parts of a module are packaged together. This includes JSP files, images, utility classes, and whatever is required to make that component a self-contained package. JAR files, or Java Archives, are really just zipped archives of files ending in the .jar extension. In fact, you can pack and unpack a JAR file with any zip utility. Java provides a utility for creating archives, called jar, that has the advantage of creating a Manifest automatically. By creating an archive of the required class file and other supporting files (like images, bitmaps, and so on), you package everything into one neat file. An entire application can be packaged into a JAR file that the Java Virtual Machine will execute. This allows you to deploy applications in one file. The JAR file maintains the file's subdirectories there by maintaining Java package integrity. Standard JavaBeans and Enterprise JavaBeans, mentioned earlier, are packaged into JAR files.

WAR files are Web Application Archives. WAR files are JAR files that end in .war and are used to package and deploy web components into web containers. They can contain HTML documents, servlets, JSPs, or even applet class files. WAR archives also contain an XML file called a deployment descriptor that describes the components. This file is normally called web.xml.

An EAR file is an Enterprise Archive and is used to package modules of a J2EE application. An EAR file is a JAR file that ends in .ear and can contain JAR and WAR files in addition to any other file required by the module. EAR archives also contain a file describing their contents—called an application descriptor, typically, application.xml.

As with all zip files, Java archives maintain subdirectories and thus package scope. To create these files manually, you use the Java packager tool called jar.

```
jar -cfv archive_name.jar
jar -cvf archive_name.war
```

Almost all IDEs, such as JDeveloper, automate the creation of these archives and their deployment into containers.

J2EE Components

As we've established, J2EE is a set of Java technologies designed to assist in the implementation of large, distributed, multitiered applications from the client back to the database connection—in other words, enterprise applications. J2EE includes a wide range of components that support security, messaging, transactional integrity, sending e-mail, processing XML, and more. The Java 2 Platform, Standard Edition Software Development Kit (J2SE SDK) is the basic Java language and is required to run J2EE. The J2EE SDK provides the specifications and APIs (Application Programming Interface) to build J2EE applications. In addition to defining the EJB specification, J2EE provides APIs to support a number of technologies, discussed next.

Java Database Connectivity

The Java Database Connectivity (JDBC) API defines methods for connecting and accessing a database within the Java language. Most major databases, such as Oracle's, come with JDBC drivers. The JDBC API allows complete access to the database, including data definition and data manipulation. The JDBC also supports bulk inserts, bind variables, and prepare statements. Entity EJBs (discussed later in the chapter) have built-in connectivity with the database provided by the container; however, if you override the container-maintained persistence, you must use the JDBC API. Also, any bean that is not an entity EJB must use the JDBC API to connect to a database.

Java Message Service

The Java Message Service (JMS) allows J2EE components to create, send, receive, and read messages. By implementing JMS, a distributed component can process messages asynchronously, thereby improving the reliability of the distributed action. JMS allows for loose coupling of components. JMS is used by message-driver EJBs and provides a publish and subscribe (topic-based) model and also a point-to-point (queue-based) model for messaging flexibility.

Java Naming and Directory Interface

The Java Naming and Directory Interface (JNDI) provides methods for finding objects by using attributes. This is how EJBs and other registered objects are located inside a container. A container can list the EJBs that it holds with JNDI so that other components can locate them. When you deploy an archive into a container, you may need to identify what JNDI resource it uses. The JNDI can be used to interface with other naming directories such as LDAP (Lightweight Directory Access Protocol). Using JNDI, a J2EE application can coexist with legacy systems.

Java Transaction API

Database administrators understand transactions, but many developers do not. When the application accesses the database, it will return only committed data. For simple updates, inserts, or deletes, committing or rolling back data can be handled easily by the application either manually or using autocommit. If the application conducts multiple database operations that are interdependent, you will need to use the Java Transaction API (JTA) to demarcate the transaction limits so that the entire transaction is committed or rolled back together.

JavaMail API

Implementing the JavaMail API allows the application to send e-mail notifications. Using JavaMail, an application can notify an administrator when problems or errors are encountered. JavaMail can also be used to provide standard performance statistics at periodic intervals and to integrate e-mail into an application.

Java API for XML Processing

XML (Extensible Markup Language) is an effective way to write out data in a structured hierarchy. Almost all of the configuration files used by the Application Server are XML documents. (Some components that were brought into the Application Server do not use XML, such as the http.conf file for OHS, which came from the Apache web server.) An example of an XML configuration file is the web.xml deployment descriptor stored in a WAR file. As you work with XML parameter files, you need to understand two important requirements of XML: it is case sensitive, and it must have an ending tag.

Here is an example of an XML file that defines three servlets—intro, timer, and recTime:

```
<servlet>
  <servlet-name>intro</servlet-name>
  <servlet-class>com.localdomain.appsvr.servlet.Intro</servlet-class>
</servlet>

<servlet>
  <servlet-name>timer</servlet-name>
  <servlet-class>com.localdomain.appsvr.servlet.Timer</servlet-class>
  <init-param>
    <param-name>time</param-name>
    <param-value>/tmp/timer.properties</param-value>
  </init-param>
  <init-param>
    <param-name>tickCount</param-name>
    <param-value>60000</param-value>        <!-- every minute -->
  </init-param>
</servlet>

<servlet>
  <servlet-name>recTime</servlet-name>
  <servlet-class>com.localdomain.appsvr.servlet.RecordTime</servlet-class>
</servlet>
```

Each servlet has a servlet-name tag and a servlet-class tag defining the name and class file for each servlet. The timer servlet also has a few parameters defined. The time parameter defines a temp file to store information as /tmp/timer.properties. The other parameter defines the number of Timer ticks to count—in this case, 60,000, or every minute. Notice that each tag has a closing tag.

Because XML produces "well-formed" text documents, it is a great way to pass information between different platforms or systems. J2EE provides native support to both create and read XML documents. Both J2EE and Application Server 10*g* use XML extensively, so as an administrator, you will need to have a basic understanding of XML.

Java Authentication and Authorization Service

The Java Authentication and Authorization Service (JAAS) API supports user (or groups of users) authorization and privileges. JAAS implements a standard pluggable authentication module (PAM) in Java that extends Java's security framework in order to support user authorizations using standard authentication providers such a LDAP, JNDI, or the operating system. Security is discussed in detail in Chapter 12.

That's a lot of information, but you will run into these terms throughout the remainder of this book and need to have a basic understanding of their meaning.

Java Virtual Machines

A Java Virtual Machine is needed to execute compiled Java code or class files. When Java code is compiled, it creates a file of byte-code that ends in .class. The JVM interprets the byte-code when the application is run. This provides Java's portability. Once Java code is compiled, it will operate on any platform that has a compatible JVM. It is the job of the JVM to take the byte-code in the class file, convert it into the local computer's machine code, and execute it (Figure 6-2).

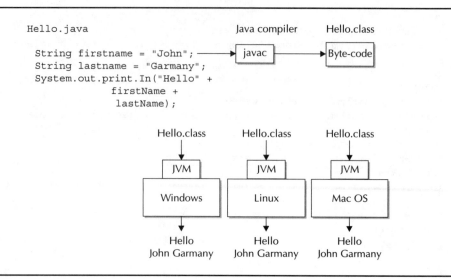

FIGURE 6-2. *Executing Java on the Java Virtual Machine*

Hence, a Java application written on a Windows box will execute in the same way on a Solaris or Linux server. Java Virtual Machines also allow you to have nonhomogenous systems, with a powerful Solaris server hosting the database, two servers (one Linux and one Windows) hosting the application server, and clients using Netscape, Mozilla, and IE, all accessing the same Java application. Most Java tools (such as JDeveloper) are written in Java, and so the same program can run on multiple operating systems with pretty much the same appearance.

JVMs do much more than just execute class files. The JVM is responsible for security, allowing the application access only to those parts of the server allowed. This is why some applications have problems running in a browser. For example, the JVM that supports a browser "assumes" an applet is untrustworthy and will not allow it to interface directly with operating system resources.

Enterprise JavaBeans

Enterprise JavaBeans often constitute the heart of an application running on Application Server 10*g* because EJBs contain the business logic of the application. They require a J2EE container to run, and they support distributed objects within the application. EJBs are constructed following a strict specification that ensures EJBs work together within a large application. Applications find EJBs by using the JNDI service and interact with them through the container. By encapsulating business logic inside EJBs, you can distribute the application across different servers or have multiple copies of an EJB on different servers to load-balance the application. Although the discussion of writing EJBs is beyond the scope of this book, an introduction to the types of EJBs is needed. For additional information on creating EJBs, refer to the books identified at the beginning of this chapter.

There are three types of Enterprise JavaBeans: session, entity, and message-driven.

- **Session EJBs** These support a single client in the execution of a task. A session EJB exists only as long as that single client exists. It is not shared. A session EJB can be used to interact with a customer database to include executing dynamic or static SQL, or stored Java, or PL/SQL procedures or functions. Session EJBs are either stateless or stateful. The state of a bean is defined as the variable values it holds. A stateless session EJB implements business logic and does not maintain a state between calls. A stateful session EJB maintains a state (a set of variable definitions) between method calls. Methods can be used to change its state, and the new state will be maintained until it is changed again or it is removed from the container. Hence a stateful bean can support only one client, while a stateless bean can support multiple clients (one at a time).

- **Entity EJBs** These represent business data rather than business logic. An entity EJB represents data in a database, such as a customer order. Like data in a database, an entity bean can be shared by many clients and has a unique identifier called a primary key. Because an entity EJB's state is based on some external persistent storage, its state does not change unless the data in the persistent storage changes. Entity beans normally connect to a database through the container. The container implements all the database connectivity. As with session EJBs, entity EJBs also come in two flavors—container managed or bean managed. Container managed persistence (CMP) is more popular because this type of EJB forces the container to handle the task of reading and writing object attributes back and forth to the database. The developer is normally not required to write any JDBC or SQL code. Bean managed EJBs, on the other hand, require that the developer handle the task of persisting object attributes to the database and then loading them back into the EJB when it is instantiated. This means writing all the SQL required via JDBC. This offers a great deal of flexibility, but it can be quite complex. It is easy to see why container managed persistence is the more popular choice today among Java developers. This will be discussed in detail in Chapter 8.

- **Message-Driven EJBs** These process JMS (Java Message Service) messages asynchronously. This differs from session EJBs, which will block while sending a request to another bean. Unlike session or entity EJBs, message-driven EJBs have no interfaces that clients can call directly.

Introduction to Oracle Containers for J2EE

Enterprise JavaBeans are J2EE software components that exist and operate in a container. The container provides all the services an EJB needs to interact with other EJBs, the client application, and the server resources. It is through the container that the client application accesses the EJB. The container lists the EJBs it holds in a Java Naming and Directory Interface. When an EJB is accessed, the container is responsible for starting the EJB and managing the execution of the request. The request could require that a new copy of the bean be instantiated; select one from a pool of instantiated beans, or use an EJB already running. The container is responsible for supporting the operation of the EJB, and this includes maintaining transactions, security, and persistence. The container may handle the database connectivity of an entity bean, or the entity bean may connect to the database using a JDBC connection. OC4J is Application Server 10*g*'s container for J2EE.

Servlets, JSPs, and Apache Jserv

OC4J is Oracle's container for EJBs, servlets, and JSP processing. OC4J implements a servlet container to execute servlets. The module mod_oc4j (on the Oracle HTTP server) is the default method for communicating with OC4J to handle servlets and JSPs. Mod_oc4j communicates with the servlet container using AJP (Apache Jserv Protocol) or by a direct HTTP request. Using a direct HTTP request allows OHS to communicate through a firewall to the servlet container. However, communications using AJP between mod_oc4j and the OC4J container are not secure, so it is recommended that both OHS and OC4J be located behind a firewall. Although Application Server 10*g* embeds the OC4J containers in the application server, you can implement a standalone OC4J container. OC4J containers and their administration are covered in more detail in the next chapter.

Executing Servlets in OC4J

The OC4J servlet container implements the Servlet 2.3 specification. It is also 100 percent code compatible with Apache's Tomcat. All servlets are normally deployed into the servlet container as WAR files, but they can also be manually placed in a subdirectory where the servlet container will look for them when needed. When deployed as a WAR file, the servlet container is responsible for executing the servlets contained in the WAR file, which includes uncompressing the file and installing the servlet. The servlet container also provides for high availability through automatic restart if the JVM fails. A servlet running inside the OC4J servlet container has access to the full array of J2EE APIs, including database connectivity and EJBs running in the OC4J container (Figure 2-3). The servlet container also provides the servlet access to properties included in the HTTP request.

Again, coding a servlet is beyond the scope of this book, but you do need to understand how servlets are maintained in the Application Server. The OC4J servlet container looks in the $ORACLE_HOME/j2ee/home/default-web-apps/WEB-INF/classes directory for servlet class files. During development, using this directory will speed the testing process because the servlet container can detect changed code and automatically recompile the servlet before executing it.

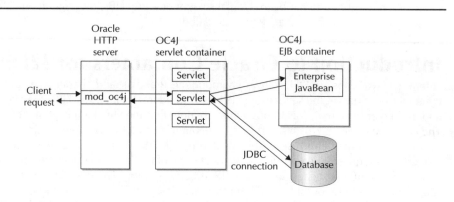

FIGURE 6-3. *Servlet running in the OC4J servlet container*

To activate this feature, edit the global-web-application.xml configuration file located in the $ORACLE_HOME/j2ee/home/config directory and set development="true" as shown here:

```
<orion-web-app
          jsp-cache-directory="./persistence"
          servlet-webdir="/servlet"
          development="true"
          jsp-timeout="0"
>
```

Now when the servlet container executes the servlet, it will first check the source file (.java), and if it has changes, the servlet container will recompile the servlet with the new source code before executing it. The global-web-application.xml file sets default parameters for applications and will be discussed in detail in the next chapter. While it is effective to call the servlet's class file directly during development, it is not recommended for a production environment for security reasons. In a production environment, servlets should be deployed in a WAR file, normally inside an EAR file.

When a web component is deployed, the WAR file contains a deployment descriptor called web.xml. This XML file is read when the servlet is started and can be used to pass initial parameters if needed. Many times, the web.xml file declares a name for the servlet that is different from the servlet's class file. In the next example, the servlet snoop is defined using the SnoopServlet class file.

```
<web-app>
   <servlet>
     <servlet-name>snoop</servlet-name>
     <servlet-class>SnoopServlet</servlet-class>
   </servlet>
</web-app>
```

If the servlet's web.xml file declares the tag <load-on-startup>, the servlet container loads it when the container starts. Otherwise, the servlet is loaded when a client requests it.

Deployment of web components (servlet/JSPs) is discussed later in this chapter as part of deploying an application.

Java Server Pages (JSPs) and OC4J

Java Server Pages are another web component handled by mod_oc4j. JSPs are HTTP pages that contain Java code or calls to servlets or both. JSPs are passed to the JSP container for processing. JSP code is compiled into class files for execution like a servlet. In fact, the JSP container is itself a servlet running in the servlet container. The JSP container complies with the JSP 1.2 specification. A JSP can contain anything an HTTP page can contain.

```
<HTML>
<HEAD><TITLE>John's Neat Web Site</TITLE></HEAD>
<BODY>
<H3>H1 Welcome to my web site!!!</H3>
<P>Current time on my server is <%= new java.util.Date() %>.</P>
</BODY>
</HTML>
```

This small JSP appears to be mostly standard HTTP tags, and it is. The only Java on the page is defined by the <% %> brackets—in this case, a call to the Java Date class that returns the current server date. This is a simple example of embedding Java code directly into a JSP.

JSPs are typically used in the application presentation layer and are an effective way to separate the presentation code from the application code. However, JSPs are powerful enough to contain a lot of the application code, thereby violating this separation of layers. Oracle has provided an extensive array of added JSP features that include custom tag libraries, monitoring capabilities, and caching technology. Again, a discussion of developing and coding Java Server Pages is beyond the scope of this book, so we will focus on managing and administering JSPs in the Oracle Application Server. Development of JSPs is covered extensively in the references named at the beginning of this chapter.

Normally, the JSP container runs Java Server Pages on demand. When OHS receives a request for a JSP, it passes the request to the JSP servlet that finds the file, translates and compiles it (if necessary), and executes it, resulting in the JSP being served to the client. If the JSP servlet finds a compiled version with a timestamp after the source version, it will execute the compiled version without recompiling. There are cases where you will want to precompile your JSPs. The most common is deploying an application when you do not want to include the source files. In this case, Oracle provides a tool called ojspc that compiles the JSPs into the appropriate directories. The ojspc program, located in $ORACLE_HOME/bin, takes a JSP file (ending in .jsp) and normally produces two class files, one for the page and the other containing the Java code. There are a number of limits on the use of ojspc to precompile JSPs, so you will need to refer to the documentation before using it.

The JSP container is preconfigured when installed. The global-web-application.xml file defines the files that are mapped to the JSP container for serving and contains the Jspservlet configuration parameters.

```xml
<servlet>
  <servlet-name>jsp</servlet-name>
  <servletclass>oracle.jsp.runtimev2.JspServlet</servlet-class>
  <load-on-startup>0</load-on-startup>
  <init-param>
    <param-name>check_page_scope</param-name>
    <param-value>true</param-value>
  </init-param>
  <init-param>
    <param-name>main_mode</param-name>
    <param-value>justrun</param-value>
  </init-param>
```

The preceding code snippet from the global-web-application.xml file defines the Servlet used to execute JSP pages as oracle.jsp.runtimev2.JspServlet. It then sets a parameter called main_mode with a parameter value of justrun. A number of parameters can be used to configure the JSP servlet. To use the default parameter settings, simply do not define the parameter in the file. The following are the parameters specific to the JSP servlet:

```xml
<init-param>
  <param-name>debug_mode</param-name>
```

```
    <param-value>true</param-value>
</init-param>
```

The debug_mode parameter defaults to true and will cause a stack trace to be printed for a run-time exception.

```
<init-param>
    <param-name>emit_debuginfo</param-name>
    <param-value>false</param-value>
</init-param>
```

The emit_debuginfo parameter defaults to false. In the default mode, an error will generate a map to the .java files. If true, it will generate a map to the .jsp file. Set this parameter to true during development to enable JSP debugging.

```
<init-param>
    <param-name>external_resource</param-name>
    <param-value>false</param-value>
</init-param>
```

The external_resource parameter defaults to false. If set to true, static page content is placed in a separate resource file during translation. This will speed translation and may speed execution of JSPs with a large amount of static content.

```
<init-param>
    <param-name>javaccmd</param-name>
    <param-value>javac -verbose</param-value>
</init-param>
```

The javaccmd parameter can be used to specify command-line compile options, a different compiler, or both. By specifying a Java compiler to use, you will cause the compiler to execute in a separate JVM. The new compiler must be in the CLASSPATH. The preceding example uses the default compiler but forces it to execute in a separate JVM with the verbose argument added to the command line.

```
<init-param>
    <param-name>main_mode</param-name>
    <param-value>recompile</param-value>
</init-param>
```

The main_mode parameters tell the JSP container whether to use automatic recompilation. The default is recompile, which will cause the JSP servlet to check the timestamp on the .jsp file to determine whether it must automatically retranslate and recompile it before executing. This will also cause it to check any other resource used by the JSP, including JavaBeans, and recompile them if needed. The reload option will verify all required class files and recompile as needed. The justrun option will run the compiled code without checking the source.

During development, it is recommended that you maintain the default setting. However, once your application is deployed and source files no longer change, it is more efficient to change to the justrun option.

```
<init-param>
    <param-name>old_include_from_top</param-name>
    <param-value>false</param-value>
</init-param>
```

The old_include_from_top parameter is used for compatibility with pre-Oracle9*i*AS Release 2 versions. It defaults to false where page locations relate to the parent page. Setting it to true will cause page locations in nested includes to relate to the top-level page.

```
<init-param>
    <param-name>precompile_check</param-name>
    <param-value>false</param-value>
</init-param>
```

The precompile_check parameter defaults to false, which causes the JSP servlet to ignore the HTTP jsp_precompile parameter. Setting it to true will cause the servlet to check the jsp_precompile setting and if present, translate and compile the JSP without executing it.

```
<init-param>
    <param-name>reduce_tag_code</param-name>
    <param-value>false</param-value>
</init-param>
```

The reduce_tag_code parameter defaults to false. If set to true, the JSP servlet will produce smaller code for custom tags; however, tag reuse (pooling) may be reduced, affecting performance.

```
<init-param>
    <param-name>req_time_introspect</param-name>
    <param-value>false</param-value>
</init-param>
```

The req_time_introspect parameter defaults to false. When set to true, the JSP container will perform JavaBean introspection at run time if it was unable to at compile time. JavaBean introspection is the process of examining a bean to determine which properties, methods, and events it supports. In some cases, a compile-time introspection will not be able to determine this information, and therefore it may be necessary to conduct introspection at run time.

```
<init-param>
    <param-name>sqljcmd</param-name>
    <param-value>sqlj -user=scott/tiger</param-value>
</init-param>
```

Like the javaccmd parameter, the sqljcmd command can identify a different sqlj processor to use, set command-line options, or both. It defaults to null. If it is set, the sqlj processor will run in a separate JVM, and all necessary libraries must be in the CLASSPATH.

```
<init-param>
   <param-name>static_text_in_chars</param-name>
   <param-value>false</param-value>
</init-param>
```

The static_text_in_chars parameter defaults to false. This parameter must be set to true if you need to change the character encoding at run time. Setting the parameter to true will reduce performance.

```
<init-param>
   <param-name>tags_reuse_default</param-name>
   <param-value>true</param-value>
</init-param>
```

The parameter defaults to true and establishes a default setting for tag reuse. Each page can contain this parameter and will change the behavior for only that page. An example of a JSP page setting the tag reuse behavior for that page is shown here:

```
pageContext.setAttribute("oracle.jsp.tags.reuse", new Boolean(false));
```

The preceding parameter will change the default behavior for that JSP to false.

```
<init-param>
   <param-name>xml_validate</param-name>
   <param-value>false</param-value>
</init-param>
```

The xml_validate parameter specifies whether the web.xml file and the tag library description files are validated before use. The default is false.

Apache Jserv

Apache's Jserv module (mod_jserv) is still shipped with Application Server 10*g*, even though it is not the default method for supporting Java servlets. Before Apache had access to an application server, it needed a method to reliably and efficiently execute servlets. Since adding a Java Virtual Machine to the Apache code was prohibitive, mod_jserv was created to pass servlets to an external servlet engine called Jserv. Once loaded, mod_jserv was passed all servlet requests, which it then passed to Jserv. The communication between the two programs used the AJP (Apache Jserv Protocol), which is the same protocol used by mod_oc4j. Mod_jserv was also responsible for starting, stopping, and monitoring Jserv.

To install mod_jserv, uncomment the line in the OHS configuration file http.conf.

```
# Include the configuration files needed for jserv
include "/home/oracle/oraportal904/Apache/Jserv/etc/jserv.conf"
```

A look in the $ORACLE_HOME/Apache/Jserv/etc/ directory will display the Jserv configuration files.

```
jserv.conf
jserv.properties
zone.properties
```

Jserv.conf loads the mod_jserv module and configures the AJP version used for communication. At the end is a location directive that when uncommented, will allow you to check Jserv's status from the identified URL. The jserv.properties file is the main configuration file for the servlet engine. Zone.properties identifies file repositories from which classes are loaded. Because mod_jserv has been deprecated, we are not going to go any deeper into its configuration. If you need additional information, refer to the Oracle HTTP Server Administration Guide. Application Server 10*g* can also be configured to use mod_jserv and mod-oc4j together. You need to designate which programs run under which engine. Although it is possible to use these two programs together, it is recommended that you use mod_oc4j unless there is a compelling reason to activate mod_jserv. Also note that with the release of the Apache 2.0 web server, Tomcat is the preferred servlet engine and mod_jserv is no longer supported.

> **NOTE**
> *You will still find OHS using Jserv with the Oracle Database because it does not ship with the OC4J container.*

Deploying Applications Using Enterprise Manager

As already discussed, components are packaged into archives for deployment onto the application server. However, a number of files must be updated before the application server can provide support for a component. Web components are packaged into WAR files that contain all the files needed to support that component. These may include HTML pages, Java Server Pages, servlets, or image files. Enterprise JavaBeans are packaged into JAR files with all their supporting class files. When deploying groups of packages together, they are placed in an EAR (Enterprise Archive) that contains all of the JAR, WAR, and other files needed for that package. An entire application can be packaged into one EAR archive that is deployed to the application server.

Deploying an application to Application Server 10*g* requires that a number of support files be updated. For this reason, Oracle recommends that you use Oracle Enterprise Manager to deploy your application. Alternatively, your developers can deploy components to the application server directly from JDeveloper. You can also deploy your application using the Java admin.jar tool. And, finally, you can manually deploy your application and modify the appropriate files, but this is not recommended. Because this book focuses on administration of the Application Server and not on J2EE development, we are not going to discuss the mechanics of packaging a component for deployment. You should receive the application properly packaged from the developers.

Since you have Enterprise Manager (if you are running Application Server 10*g*), we will discuss using EM to deploy an application. For the purpose of this exercise, we are going to deploy an EAR file from the administrator's computer (running the browser) to the application server using Enterprise Manager. The file we are going to deploy is called petstore.ear, and it was sent to us by the developer ready to deploy. The application is going to be deployed into the OC4J container called OC4J_Demos, which was created when we installed the Application Server. Once you start Enterprise Manager, navigate to the instance where the application will be deployed. If EM is not running, you need to start it.

```
ORACLE_HOME/bin/emctl start em
```

At the top of the status page shown in Figure 6-4, is a link to J2EE Applications. Selecting this link will display a list of current applications installed on all OC4J instances, as shown in Figure 6-5.

Return to the instance status page. For this exercise, we are going to use the OC4J_Demos container. Selecting the OC4J_Demos link displays the OC4J Status page, where you can configure, start, or stop the OC4J container (covered in the next chapter). It also lists the current EAR files deployed inside this container. In Figure 6-6, Enterprise Manager lists two deployed EAR files: FAQApp and transtrace. To deploy the petstore.ear file, select the Deploy Ear File button located in the Applications section.

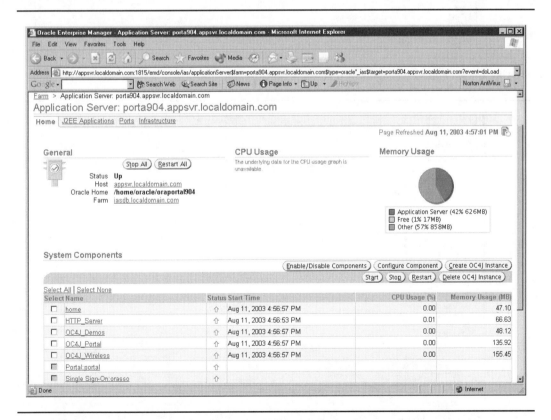

FIGURE 6-4. *Enterprise Manager instance status page*

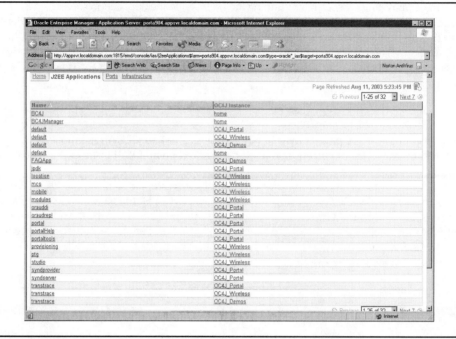

FIGURE 6-5. *Enterprise Manager J2EE Applications page*

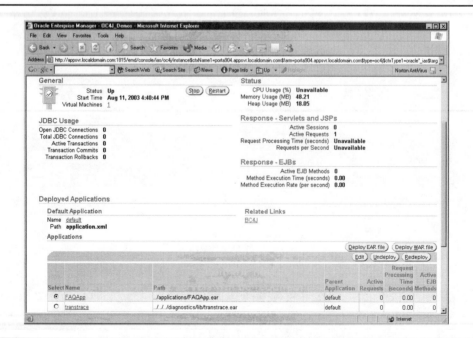

FIGURE 6-6. *Enterprise Manager's OC4J Status page*

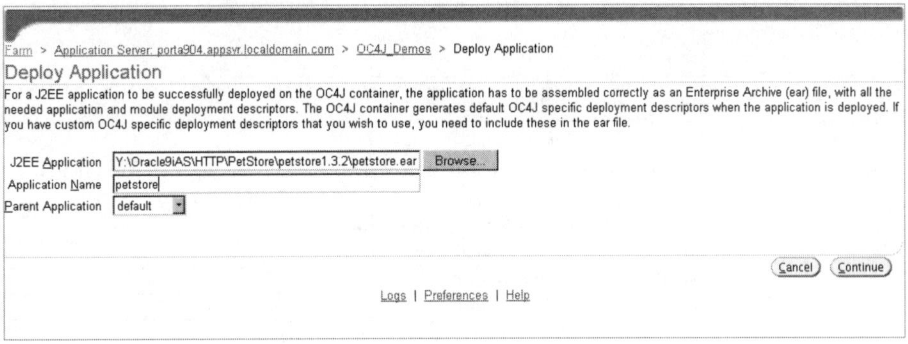

FIGURE 6-7.   *Enterprise Manager's Deploy Application Wizard*

The Deploy Application Wizard (Figure 6-7) starts by requesting the location of the EAR file and the application's name. Using the Browse button, locate the petstore.ear file. The application name is petstore. Since this is a new application, it does not have a parent, so leave the Parent Application combo box set to Default. Select the Continue button.

The web component (PetStoreWAR) contained in the petstore.ear file must be mapped to a URL so that browsers can access it from OHS. Enter the URL beginning with a /, such as /petstore. This will map the application to http://<host>:<port>/petstore, as shown in Figure 6-8.

Select the Next button to continue to the Resource Reference Mappings page, shown in Figure 6-9. Here you map a resource reference to an entity such as a data source. To map to a resource, you must have already deployed that resource to the container. Selecting Next again will take you to the Review page, shown in Figure 6-10. Selecting the Deploy button will begin the process of deploying the EAR file to the container (Figure 6-11).

Depending on the size of the application being deployed, the actual deployment process can take quite a while. If the EAR file contains web components (as this one does), the wizard will

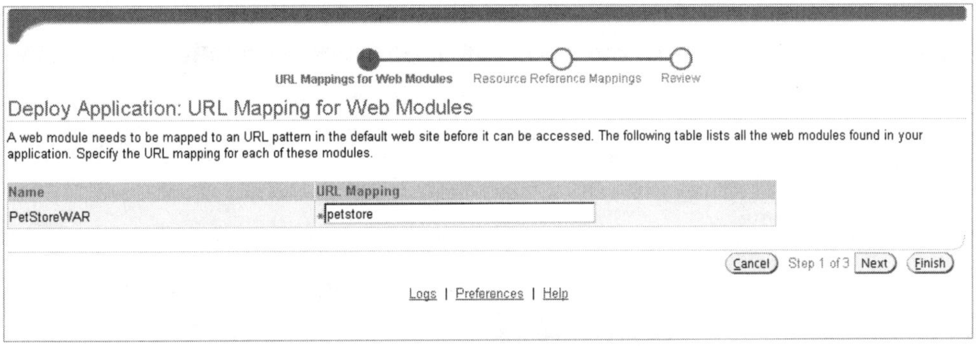

FIGURE 6-8.   *Enterprise Manager's Deploy Application: URL Mapping*

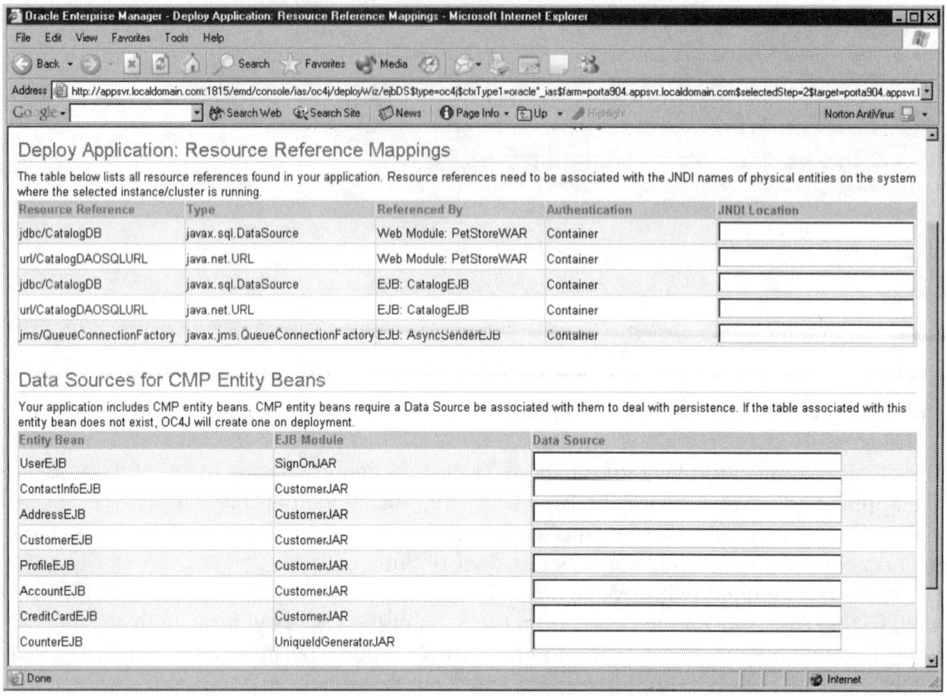

FIGURE 6-9. *Enterprise Manager's Deploy Application: Resource Reference Mappings page*

automatically restart OHS after completing the deployment. Once completed, Enterprise Manager will display the Confirmation page (Figure 6-12).

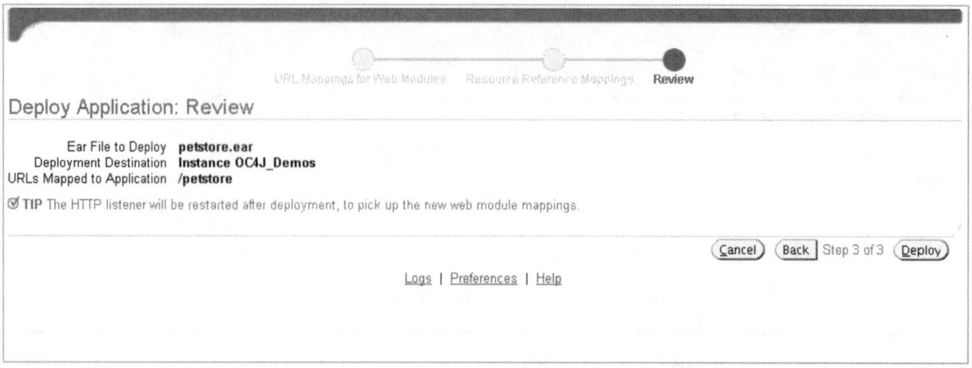

FIGURE 6-10. *Enterprise Manager's Deploy Application: Review page*

FIGURE 6-11. *Enterprise Manager's Deploy Application: Deploy page*

Selecting the OK button will return you to the OC4J Status page, displaying the new petstore application in the application section (Figure 6-13). If this new application is dependent on other components, they must also be deployed in order for petstore to function.

Summary

This chapter has been a brief introduction to J2EE components and how the Oracle Application Server 10*g* supports those components. Many applications have been built using only HTTP, JSPs, and servlets to implement both the presentation layer and the program logic. However, as programs become larger and more complicated, the benefits of using Enterprise JavaBeans

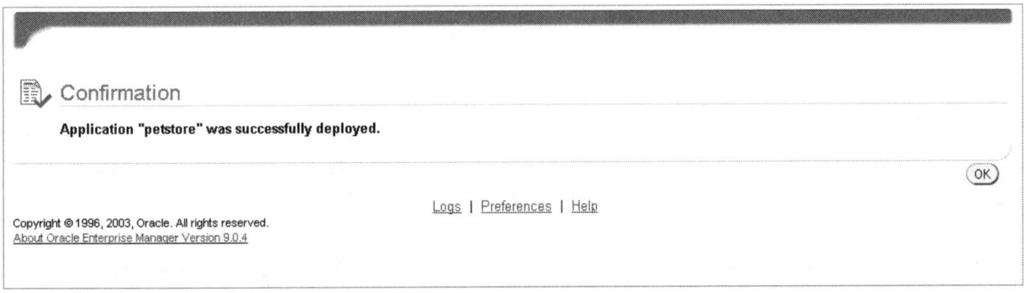

FIGURE 6-12. *Enterprise Manager's Deploy Application Wizard Confirmation page*

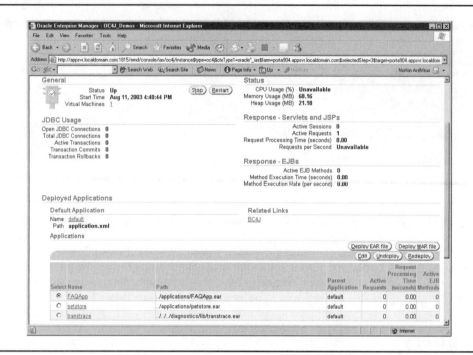

FIGURE 6-13. *Enterprise Manager's OC4J Status page with our example file deployed*

to implement business rules and to maintain persistence data become apparent. The main points are as follows:

- The primary function of any application server is to run enterprise Java applications. The Application Server 10*g* uses the Oracle Container for Java to run Enterprise JavaBeans, Servlets, and Java Server Pages.

- Enterprise Java applications use the Java 2 Platform, Enterprise Edition (J2EE) APIs to support component-based design, implementation, and deployment.

- Entity Enterprise JavaBeans (EJBs) provide data persistence to the enterprise Java application. The OC4J supports both container managed persistence and direct database connection using the JDBC API.

- Enterprise Java applications are packaged into EAR files and deployed into the Application Server. The J2EE specification defines the makeup of the EAR file, and the Application Server 10*g* uses the files in the EAR file to configure the application during deployment.

Now that you have a basic understanding of J2EE, its components, and how they work, we need to delve deeper into the details of supporting those components within the Application Server. Starting with the OC4J container in the next chapter, we will discuss the details of how it supports the application and what the Deploy Application Wizard actually accomplished when it deployed the EAR file to the container.

CHAPTER
7

Oracle Containers
for J2EE

he heart of Oracle Application Server 10*g* is the Oracle Container for Java (OC4J). This container runs on Java version 1.3.1 or later, thereby leveraging the features and performance enhancements that this release provides. OC4J performs the heavy lifting for the application server. The pure Java J2EE container not only hosts customer-developed enterprise applications but also runs Portal, Delegated Administration Services (DAS), and other components like those in Business Intelligence (BI). In addition to this, OC4J is the basis for how clustering is achieved to handle application loading. Each Oracle Application Server instance, including the infrastructure instance, will contain a number of OC4J containers to support its applications.

As we discussed in the previous chapter, OC4J provides a servlet container and a JSP translator. OC4J is also J2EE certified and provides all the required J2EE standard interfaces. Of course, OC4J provides support for Enterprise JavaBeans, including standard deployment of EAR and WAR archives. The OC4J container provides EJB services, including database access, transaction support, security, caching, and concurrency. Entity EJBs can use OC4J container managed persistence (CMP) to access persistent storage (databases) through the container without directly coding the JDBC API. OC4J's ability to transparently map an entity EJB to the database relieves the programmer from creating this connection. OC4J provides support for both simple and complex object–relational mapping, including objects like BLOBs, CLOBs, and collections (nested tables and VARRAYs). Database connectivity, including the use of TopLink, is discussed in Chapter 8.

Management of OC4J

You will need a number of configuration files to manage the OC4J container. Some, like application.xml and web.xml, are J2EE standard packaging files and are used to establish default values that may be overwritten by the files deployed in an EAR or WEB file. Some are application configuration files, while the rest configure OC4J itself. Many are updated automatically when EAR and WAR files are deployed, which is why most development programs use an automated method to deploy the application (such as Enterprise Manager, used in the previous chapter). Table 7-1 lists some of the standard XML configuration files used by OC4J.

You do not need to know what each of these files does or the data it contains because you should not be directly editing any of these files. Your development environment should automate the creation and maintenance of deployment descriptor files within the EAR and WAR archives, and you should always use Enterprise Manager or the dcmctl utility to configure OC4J parameters. Because the OC4J instance configuration parameters are stored in the infrastructure repository, manually changing these XML files can corrupt the repository, possibly requiring a reinstall of the application server. If you do manually update OC4J configuration files, execute the following command:

```
dcmctl -updateConfig -ct oc4j
```

This will update the configuration stored in the infrastructure repository. Or, use EM's advanced properties pages to edit the files internal to EM, allowing EM to automatically update the repository. Editing configuration files directly or inside EM could also cause the instance to be unable to start because of a typo or a missing XML tag. For developmental purposes, you can obtain a standalone version of OC4J; however, we do not cover the standalone version except to mention that it is available.

Type of File	File Name	Description
Server configuration files	server.xml	Used to configure OC4J, and identify other configuration files and application names.
	default-web-site.xml http-web-site.xml	Used to define web site properties. http-web-site.xml is used when OC4J is not part of the application server.
	application.xml	Defines web and EJB default parameters for components within a J2EE application.
J2EE package files	application.xml	Same as server configuration files, except deployed in an EAR file. During the deployment, the file is updated to contain default values that it does not overwrite.
	web.xml	Deployment descriptors for JSPs and servlets.
	ejb-jar.xml	Deployment descriptors for EJBs within a JAR.
	application-client.xml	Contains JNDI information.
OC4J deployment files	orion-application.xml	Configures default application parameters such as data sources, security role mappings, and JNDI access rules.
	orion-web.xml	Deployment descriptor for mapping web settings.
	orion-ejb-web.xml	OC4J-specific deployment descriptor for EJBs in a JAR.

TABLE 7-1. *OC4J Configuration Files*

Managing OC4J Using the dcmctl/opmnctl Utilities

There are times when you will want to maintain OC4J from the command line. An example of this is the creation of scripts that start Application Server 10*g* when the server starts, or bringing instances down for backup or maintenance. Many administrators are just more comfortable using the command line. That is where the dcmctl and opmnctl utilities are useful.

opmnctl

The easiest and recommended way to start and stop instances is with the opmnctl utility:

```
export ORACLE_HOME=/home/oracle/oraportal904
export PATH=$PATH:$ORACLE_HOME/bin:$ORACLE_HOME/dcm/bin: \
    $ORACLE_HOME/webcache/bin:$ORACLE_HOME/opmn/bin
```

```
export ORACLE_SID=iasdb
export LD_LIBRARY_PATH=$LD_LIBRARY_PATH:$ORACLE_HOME/lib
$ORACLE_HOME/opmn/bin/opmnctl startall
```

After setting the environment, you execute opmnctl startall. The opmn script will start the instance, in this case oraportal904, which will automatically start the OC4J containers within oraportal904. Once this command completes, you can start the Enterprise Manager web site and connect to EM for maintenance:

```
$ORACLE_HOME/bin/emctl start em
```

Use of the command-line utilities was covered in greater detail in Chapter 1. One issue with emctl is that to stop Enterprise Manager, you must provide a password. This can be accomplished in one of two ways. You can pass the ias_admin password within your script:

```
$ORACLE_HOME/bin/emctl stop em <<eof
<ias_admin_passwd>
eof
```

An alternative method is to set the environmental variable EM_ADMIN_PWD:

```
EM_ADMIN_PWD=<ias_admin_passwd>; export EM_ADMIN_PWD
$ORACLE_HOME/bin/emctl stop em
```

Either way, ensure that Enterprise Manager is stopped before shutting down the server.

Distributed Configuration Management

The Distributed Configuration Management utility can be used instead of EM for some management activities, but not all. The dcmctl utility only manages the OHS/OC4J portion of the instance. It can be used within scripts to automate maintenance functions. If you are working with one instance, you will either need to pass dcmctl, the instance's ORACLE_HOME variable, or set it before executing the command. To avoid confusion, we recommend that you always set environmental variables in the script before executing either opmnctl or dcmctl. In a cluster environment, failure to set the appropriate ORACLE_HOME could result in making changes to the wrong instance. You can also use the environment variable ORACLE_DCM_JVM_ARGS to pass arguments to the Java Virtual Machine.

The dcmctl utility can be started so that commands can be directly entered using the command shell:

```
$ dcmctl shell
dcmctl> createcomponent -ct oc4j -co OC4J_T2
dcmctl> exit
$
```

The dcmctl utility also has an extensive help listing obtained with the help argument:

```
$ dcmctl help
```

Arguments are made up of a one-word command and a set of options, all of which are case insensitive. Options start with a dash, followed by the option in short or long format, followed by the option's arguments. In the previous example, the command is createcomponent, and the options are -ct and -co. First, let's discuss the options available and then introduce the commands. Options have a long and short format:

Short Format	Long Format	Description
-a	-application	Application name
-cl	-cluster	Cluster name
-co	-component	Component name
-ct	-componenttype	Component type
-i	-instance	Instance name (Application Server 10g instance)
-d	-debug	Print stack trace on exception
-l	-logdir	Location for the error log log.xml
-o	-oraclehome	ORACLE_HOME for that command
-t	-timeout	Max time to complete command (default: 45sec)
-v	-verbose	Verbose listing of state and error messages

Now that we have defined the options, you can begin using the commands. Since dcmctl is used mostly within scripts, you need to be able to start and stop the instances/components. The following command starts the porta904 instance. Notice that we use the fully qualified instance name.

```
$ dcmctl start -i porta904.appsvr.localdomain.com
Current State for Instance:porta904.appsvr.localdomain.com
      Component                Type         Up Status    In Sync Status
      ================================================================
  1   HTTP_Server              HTTP_Server  Up           True
  2   OC4J_Demos               OC4J         Up           True
  3   OC4J_Portal              OC4J         Up           True
  4   OC4J_Testing             OC4J         Up           True
  5   OC4J_Wireless            OC4J         Up           True
  6   home                     OC4J         Up           True
```

The dcmctl utility starts the instance and then provides a list of the current state. To stop the instance, you have two options, the stop command or the shutdown command. The shutdown command is used to stop the instance and OPMN/DCM, and is used to shut everything down before restarting or shutting down the server. The restart command will start an already down system, or shut down and restart a running system. Last, the getstate command returns the state of the instance/component.

```
$ dcmctl stop -co OC4J_Testing
Current State for Instance:porta904.appsvr.localdomain.com
      Component                Type         Up Status    In Sync Status
      ================================================================
  1   OC4J_Testing             OC4J         Down         True
```

Here, we stop the OC4J_Testing container using dcmctl. One dcmctl command has already been introduced a number of times in previous chapters and at the beginning of this chapter. If you manually change a configuration file, you must update the repository using the updateConfig command:

```
$dcmctl updateConfig
```

This command reads the configuration files and updates the repository data. You can specify the container as OHS or OC4J with the -co option. The default is both.

The dcmctl utility has a number of useful commands that allow you to maintain components inside the application server instances. To list the component types contained in an instance, use the listcomponenttypes command. Remember, we have already defined the ORACLE_HOME environment variable.

```
$ dcmctl listcomponenttypes
OC4J
Portal
Wireless
HTTP_Server
WebCache
```

You can also request the component type by using the getcomponenttype with a -co option to define the component. You can create a component using dcmctl, such as creating an OC4J container in the next example.

```
$ dcmctl createcomponent -ct OC4J -co OC4J_New
1   HTTP_Server:HTTP_Server
2   OC4J:OC4J_Demos
3   OC4J:OC4J_New
4   OC4J:OC4J_Portal
5   OC4J:OC4J_Testing
6   OC4J:OC4J_Wireless
7   OC4J:home
8   WebCache:WebCacheAdmin
9   WebCache:WebCache
```

Once created, dcmctl can remove a component. Note that if you remove an OC4J container that contains web components and EJBs, those components will also be removed. There is no verification notice to warn you that the container you are removing is not empty. To remove a component, pass in the component name option:

```
$ dcmctl removecomponent -co OC4J_New
```

Now that you can add and remove components, let's look at how to deploy applications to a component. First, after restarting the OC4J_Testing container, list the currently installed applications:

```
$ dcmctl listapplications -co OC4J_Testing
1   petstore
```

The OC4J_Testing container has one application installed, called petstore. It is contained in an EAR file. Chapter 6 demonstrated deploying an EAR file using Enterprise Manager. Now let's deploy the same application, using dcmctl, into the OC4J_New container just created:

```
dcmctl deployapplication -file petstore.ear -a petstore -co OC4J_New

$ dcmctl listapplications -co OC4J_New
1  petstore
```

A script for deploying an application to all containers in a cluster was provided in Chapter 1.

Before leaving the dcmctl utility, there is another useful function that allows you to back up and restore your instances. It is useful to back up an instance before making changes in case there is a problem. The saveInstance command will save the instance configuration and any application contained in the instance, including clustering information. After making changes, you can restore the instance using the restoreInstance command. This command restores the instance to the state it was saved in. If you do not specify a directory where the saved state is located, dcmctl will restore the instance to the original installed state. If the instance is part of a cluster, it will remove it from the cluster when it is restored, so you will need to add it back to the cluster. You can create a script that saves the state of your instance before you start making changes:

```
# Customize ORACLE_HOME and ORACLE_SID for this Instance
export ORACLE_HOME=/home/oracle/oraportal904
export PATH=$PATH:$ORACLE_HOME/bin:$ORACLE_HOME/dcm/bin: \
          $ORACLE_HOME/webcache/bin:$ORACLE_HOME/opmn/bin
export ORACLE_SID=iasdb
export LD_LIBRARY_PATH=$LD_LIBRARY_PATH:$ORACLE_HOME/lib
dcmctl saveInstance -dir /home/oracle/saveDir
ls -l /home/oracle/saveDir
```

The file listing command at the end of the script produces the following output:

```
total 44
drwxrwx---   4 oracle   oracle      4096 Aug 19 11:20 dcm
-rw-rw----   1 oracle   oracle        37 Aug 19 11:19 inst_id
-rw-rw----   1 oracle   oracle     20952 Aug 19 11:20 opmn.xml
-rw-rw----   1 oracle   oracle     11377 Aug 19 11:20 sysmgmtProperties.xml
```

As you have just seen, the dcmctl utility provides a powerful command-line capability to configure and maintain an instance and its internal components. Using scripts, you can automate functions that apply to instances across multiple servers within the clustered application server environment. However, the recommended method to manage instances and components is with Enterprise Manger.

Managing OC4J Using Enterprise Manager

Oracle recommends that you manage all instances and component parameters using Enterprise Manager (EM). Once you log onto EM, select the link for the instance you are working on to go to the instance status page.

OC4J—Instance or Container

As shown in Figure 7-1, the Application Server 10*g* is composed of multiple instances. The midtier contains an OHS instance and multiple OC4J instances, while the infrastructure adds a database instance. Most database administrators who are used to dealing with only the database instance can become confused about which application server instance is being discussed. For this reason, we will refer to the container when referring to a particular OC4J instance, and refer to the instance as the Application Server instance to try and avoid some confusion. Thus, an Application Server 10*g* instance contains many OC4J containers, rather than many OC4J instances.

Under System Components in Figure 7-2 is a list of components installed for that instance, including a number of OC4J containers. To look at the status page for a component, simply select the name link in the component list. Before leaving this page however, we want to create an OC4J container for our test application.

Creating an OC4J Container

Simply click the Create OC4J Instance button in the upper right of the System Components listing. This starts the Create OC4J Instance Wizard, which asks you for a name for this container (Figure 7-3). Enter the name for this OC4J container and select Create. The Create OC4J Instance Wizard creates the container (Figure 7-4) and notifies you when it is completed.

Once the wizard is finished, select OK to return to the instance status page. The newly created OC4J container is now listed in the System Components section.

Deleting an OC4J Container

Deleting an OC4J container is just as easy. Select the radio button for the OC4J container to delete, and then select the Delete OC4J Instance button in the upper right of the System Components area. EM will display a verification page; selecting OK will delete the OC4J

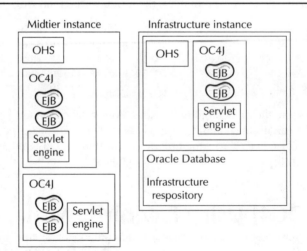

FIGURE 7-1. *Application Server 10g instance*

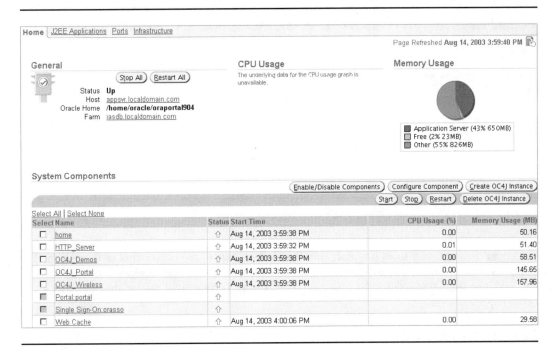

FIGURE 7-2. *Enterprise Manager instance status page*

container. Note that if you have components deployed in this container, they are removed along with the container. Don't accidentally delete the wrong container!

Starting an OC4J Container

Notice that the container we just created is currently not running. This is indicated by the red down-arrow in the Status column, shown in Figure 7-5. Before using the container, you must start it.

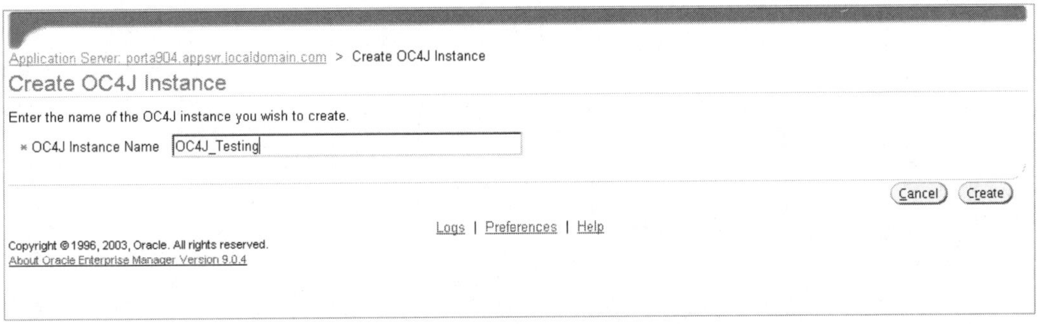

FIGURE 7-3. *Create OC4J Instance Wizard*

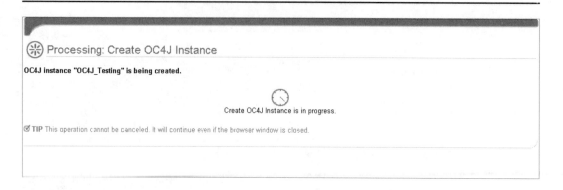

FIGURE 7-4. *Creating an OC4J container using the wizard*

Select the container's radio button, and then select Start in the upper right of the System Components area. This is a relatively quick operation because we have not deployed our application yet. Selecting the name link for the new container "OC4J_Testing" will display the container's home page.

OC4J Home Page

Selecting the name link for an OC4J container will display the container's home page (Figure 7-6). The home page for our new OC4J container does not have much information to display because

General

Stop All | Restart All | Start All

Status	**Partially Up**
Host	appsvr.localdomain.com
Oracle Home	**/home/oracle/oraportal904**
Farm	iasdb.localdomain.com

CPU Usage

The underlying data for the CPU usage graph is unavailable.

Memory Usage

■ Application Server (44% 659MB)
□ Free (2% 29MB)
■ Other (54% 811MB)

System Components

Enable/Disable Components | Configure Component | Create OC4J Instance

Start | Stop | Restart | Delete OC4J Instance

Select All | Select None

Select	Name	Status	Start Time	CPU Usage (%)	Memory Usage (MB)
☐	home	⇧	Aug 14, 2003 4:19:24 PM	Unavailable	50.50
☐	HTTP_Server	⇧	Aug 14, 2003 4:19:21 PM	Unavailable	57.07
☐	OC4J_Demos	⇧	Aug 14, 2003 4:19:24 PM	Unavailable	59.02
☐	OC4J_Portal	⇧	Aug 14, 2003 4:19:24 PM	Unavailable	146.33
☐	OC4J_Testing	⇩			
☐	OC4J_Wireless	⇧	Aug 14, 2003 4:19:24 PM	Unavailable	158.25
☐	Portal:portal	⇧			
☐	Single Sign-On:orasso	⇧			

FIGURE 7-5. *Application Server instance status page*

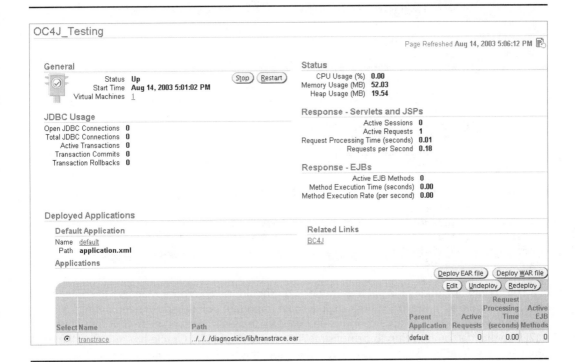

FIGURE 7-6. *OC4J home page*

we just started it and there are no components deployed, except for transtrace. Transtrace is an EJB that interfaces with opmn to provide status and performance statistics. It is deployed in every OC4J container and is preconfigured.

As you scroll down to the bottom of the OC4J home page, you find the Administration section. Like the instance status page, the Administration section allows you to configure the OC4J container. The sections map back to the server files that were introduced at the beginning of this chapter. In the Administration section of the OC4J home page, select Server Properties. This section tracks with the server.xml file, among others.

```
server.xml
<?xml version="1.0"?>
<!DOCTYPE application-server PUBLIC "-//Evermind//DTD Orion Application
server//EN" "http://xmlns.oracle.com/ias/dtds/application-server.dtd">

<application-server localhostIsAdmin="true"
 application-directory="../applications"
 deployment-directory="../application-deployments"
 connector-directory="../connectors"
>
  <rmi-config path="./rmi.xml" />
  <sep-config path="./internal-settings.xml" />
  <jms-config path="./jms.xml" />
```

```
<javacache-config path="../../../javacache/admin/javacache.xml" />
<log>
  <file path="../log/server.log" />
</log>
<transaction-config timeout="30000" />
<java-compiler name="javac"
  in-process="false"
  extdirs="/home/oracle/oraportal904/jdk/jre/lib/ext" />
<global-application name="default" path="application.xml" />
<application name="transtrace"
    path="../../../diagnostics/lib/transtrace.ear"
    auto-start="true" />
<application name="petstore"
    path="../applications/petstore.ear"
    auto-start="true" />
<global-web-app-config path="global-web-application.xml" />
<web-site default="true" path="./default-web-site.xml" />
<cluster  id="-1402673903" />
</application-server>
```

You should not modify the flat files; rather, you should use Enterprise Manager to configure OC4J. But before jumping to EM, let's look at some important points in the server.xml file. In Chapter 6, we deployed an application called petstore that was archived in an EAR file. This is a J2EE application built by Sun to demonstrate the concepts of J2EE. Oracle has modified the original application to connect to an Oracle database. It is available on Oracle Technology Network at otn.oracle.com. Notice that one of the things that happened when we deployed the EAR file was that a number of files were updated. In the server.xml file you find

```
<application name="petstore"
    path="../applications/petstore.ear"
    auto-start="true" />
```

This tells OC4J the application name and where to find it. Manually deploying a J2EE component is complicated because of the different configuration files that need to be updated to support the application. Always use some automated tool (dcmctl, Enterprise Manager, JDeveloper, and so on) to deploy WAR and EAR files into OC4J containers.

Like the instance status page, the OC4J home page has an Administration section (Figure 7-7). This is an area where you will find almost all the OC4J configuration parameters. This section is divided into two areas, one related to the OC4J container and the other to the applications running

FIGURE 7-7. *OC4J home page Administration section*

inside the container. Using the OC4J container created earlier, OC4J_Testing, let's look at how this container is configured.

Server Properties Page

Selecting the Server Properties link takes you to the properties page in Figure 7-8.

At the top is the Server Root, which is the location for all the configuration files for this OC4J container. Here is a listing of the configuration files located in the Server Root directory that support the OC4J_Testing container and the applications running in it:

```
application.xml
data-sources.xml.smibak
default-web-site.xml
global-web-application.xml
http-web-site.xml
internal-settings.xml
java2.policy
jazn-data.xml
jazn-data.xml.smibak
jazn.xml
jms.xml
mime.types
oc4j-connectors.xml
oc4j.properties
principals.xml
rmi.xml
server.xml
```

When you make a change in EM, the change is updated to the flat file; so if you examine the server.xml file, it will match the data in the EM repository for the OC4J_Testing container. As discussed earlier in this chapter, if you edit the flat file, the change does not get propagated into the repository and could cause corruption in the repository. Some of these files are the same as the deployment files in the EAR file, such as application.xml. These files provide default configuration information to the OC4J container that the file in the EAR will overwrite. The Default Application Name is "default." All applications deployed into this OC4J container will be subclasses of the default application.

Next is the Default Web Module Properties file, here defined as global-web-application.xml. This file is located in the Server Root. To modify the parameters defined in this file, return to the OC4J home page and select the Website Properties and/or Advanced Properties links. We will discuss Website Properties later; for now, let's continue looking at the container page. Further down, you will find the Application directory and the Deployment directory, both off the ./OC4J_Testing directory. The Application directory is where you can find the actual components that make up the application (the EAR components), while the Deployment directory contains all the deployment descriptor files that have had default values added to them. Both follow the subdirectory structure of the EAR file.Next is the Multiple VM Configuration section, which is part of Oracle's Application Server clustering. This will be discussed in detail in Chapter 9. There are two parameters listed under Islands, the Island ID and the Number of Processes. The Island ID is the instance of the clustered OC4J container. In this case, we are not using Oracle clustering, so there is only one island, the default_island. There is also only one process for the default island.

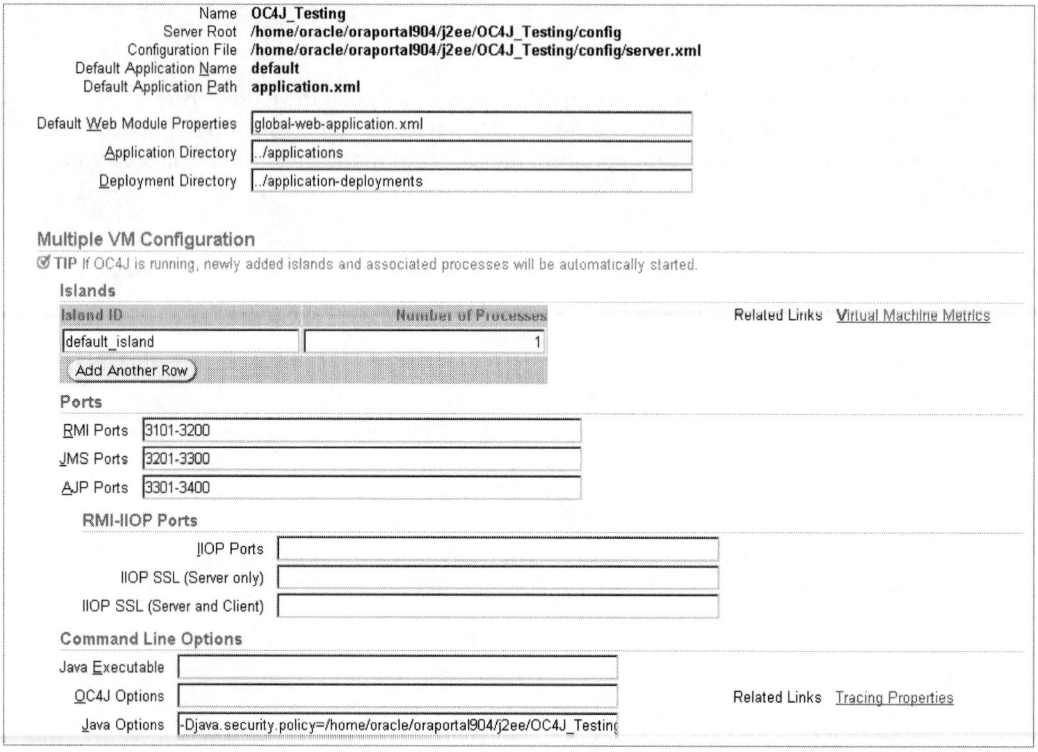

```
                      Name  OC4J_Testing
               Server Root  /home/oracle/oraportal904/j2ee/OC4J_Testing/config
          Configuration File  /home/oracle/oraportal904/j2ee/OC4J_Testing/config/server.xml
    Default Application Name  default
    Default Application Path  application.xml
```

Default Web Module Properties `global-web-application.xml`

Application Directory `../applications`

Deployment Directory `../application-deployments`

Multiple VM Configuration

☑ TIP If OC4J is running, newly added islands and associated processes will be automatically started.

Islands

Island ID	Number of Processes		Related Links Virtual Machine Metrics
default_island	1		

(Add Another Row)

Ports

RMI Ports `3101-3200`

JMS Ports `3201-3300`

AJP Ports `3301-3400`

RMI-IIOP Ports

IIOP Ports

IIOP SSL (Server only)

IIOP SSL (Server and Client)

Command Line Options

Java Executable

OC4J Options   Related Links   Tracing Properties

Java Options `-Djava.security.policy=/home/oracle/oraportal904/j2ee/OC4J_Testing`

FIGURE 7-8. *OC4J Server Properties page*

You can increase the number of processes to add fault tolerance to the OC4J container. If you define more than one process and that process fails, the container will continue to support the application with the other processes. To change the number of processes, simply enter a different setting and click on the Apply button at the bottom of the screen. The remaining parameters were set when the instance was created and should work without being changed. The Ports section defines a range of ports to use for Remote Method Invocation (RMI), the Java Messaging Service (JMS), the Apache JSP/servlet communication API (AJP), and the RMI-IIOP. RMI-IIOP allows interoperability between Java programs and programs written in other languages, like C++. Each of these parameters has a range of ports defined for them. We will discuss ports later in this chapter.

The Command Line Options area allows you to define arguments for starting Java for the OC4J container. The most commonly used command-line option for the JVM is to change the JVM heap size. If your application is memory intensive, additional memory will improve performance. You should set the minimum heap size equal to the maximum heap size using the following command:

```
-Xms128m -Xms128m
```

This will set the min and max heap size to 128MB. If required, the heap size can be set much larger; however, you must balance the memory allocated to the JVM with the available memory on the server. Remember, forcing the server to page memory will have a dramatic, negative impact on overall performance.

The final entry allows you to specify an environmental variable for use within the container. Examples of environmental variables can be displayed by typing **env** at the command line in UNIX/Linux and **set** in a Windows DOS box. ORACLE_SID or ORACLE_HOME are good examples of environmental variables. If your application had logging capabilities, you could use an environmental variable to tell the program what level to log, such as PET_LOG=debug, during development or troubleshooting. Once you make configuration changes, click the Apply button to make them permanent. If the container needs to be restarted, EM will automatically take care of that.

Website Properties Page

The Website Properties page contains parameters found in the default-web-site.xml and the global-web-application.xml files:

```
<?xml version="1.0"?>
<!DOCTYPE web-site PUBLIC "Orion Web-site" "http://xmlns.oracle.com/ias/dtds/
web-site.dtd">

<web-site port="3302" protocol="ajp13"
     display-name="Default Oracle9iAS Containers for J2EE Web Site">
<default-web-app application="default" name="defaultWebApp" root="/j2ee" />
<default-web-app application="default" name="defaultWebApp" root="/j2ee" />
<web-app application="transtrace" name="transtrace" root="/transtrace" />
<web-app application="default" name="dms" root="/dmsoc4j" />
<web-app application="petstore" name="petstore"
    load-on-startup="true" root="/estore" />
<access-log path="../log/OC4J_Testing_default_island_1/
    default-web-access.log" />
</web-site>
```

This file correlates directly to the application/URL mapping in the Website Properties page for this container, shown in Figure 7-9. Here, you'll find the current URL mappings supporting this container.

If you select the application name link, you are taken to the Web Module page (Figure 7-10) for the petstore application. Here, you will find some performance statistics and a list of the JSPs and servlets that support the application, along with some performance statistics. You can select one of the JSPs or servlets to get additional details about that particular item. At the bottom of the page is the Administration section for configuring the Web Module, including adding filters, environmental variables, or editing the orion-web.xml file.

JSP Configuration Page

Next is the JSP Configuration page. Returning to the OC4J home page (Figure 7-7), select JSP Container Properties in the Administration section to move to the JSP Container Properties page, as shown in Figure 7-11. These parameters apply to all JSPs executed in this container. All of these parameters are in the global-web-application.xml file and were discussed in detail in Chapter 6.

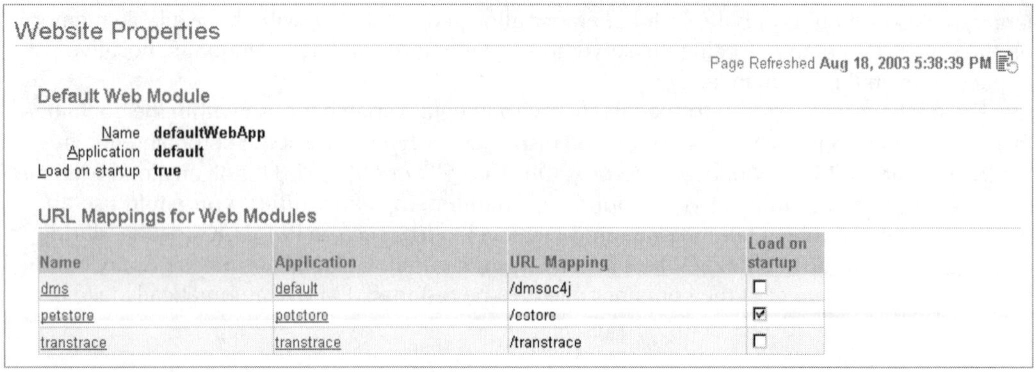

Website Properties

Page Refreshed **Aug 18, 2003 5:38:39 PM**

Default Web Module

Name **defaultWebApp**
Application **default**
Load on startup **true**

URL Mappings for Web Modules

Name	Application	URL Mapping	Load on startup
dms	default	/dmsoc4j	☐
petstore	potctoro	/ootoro	☑
transtrace	transtrace	/transtrace	☐

FIGURE 7-9. *OC4J Website Properties page*

Web Module: petstore

Page Refreshed **Aug 18, 2003 5:51:39 PM**

General

Status **Loaded**
URL Mapping **/estore**
Referenced EJBs **6**

Response and Load

Active Sessions **3**
Active Requests **0**
Request Client Time (seconds) **0.05**
Request Load Time (seconds) **0.0004**
Requests per Second **0.10**
Requests Processed **114**

Servlets/JSPs

⊗ Previous 10 | 11-20 of 21 ▾ | Next 1 ⊗

Name ▵	Status	Type	Source	Active Requests	Request Client Time (seconds)	Requests per Second	Startup Priority
jsp	Loaded	Servlet		0	0.03	0.31	
editaccount.jsp	Loaded	JSP		0	0	0	
productcategory.jsp	Loaded	JSP		0	0.11	0.02	
index.jsp	Loaded	JSP		0	0	0.01	
banner.jsp	Loaded	JSP		0	3.0E-4	0.03	
product.jsp	Loaded	JSP		0	0	0	
petfooter.jsp	Loaded	JSP		0	0	0.01	
signin.jsp	Loaded	JSP		0	0	0	
template.jsp	Loaded	JSP		0	0.07	0.03	
confirmshippingdata.jsp	Loaded	JSP		0	0	0	

⊗ Previous 10 | 11-20 of 21 ▾ | Next 1 ⊗

Administration

Properties	Security
General	General

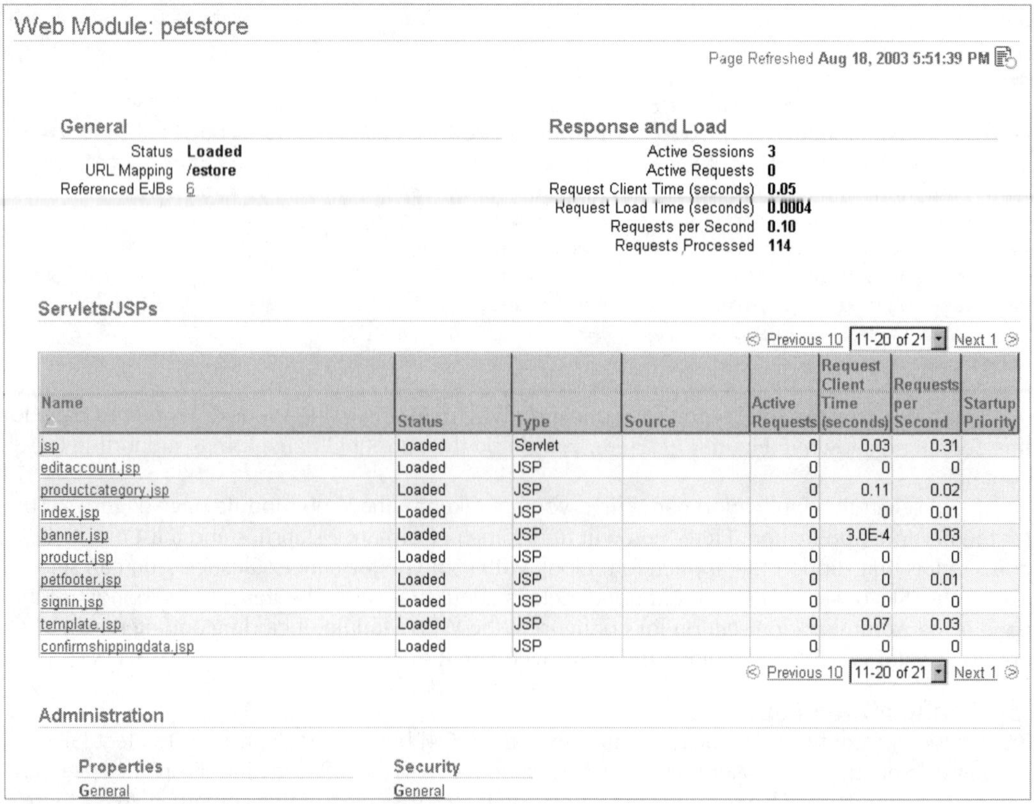

FIGURE 7-10. *Application Web Module page*

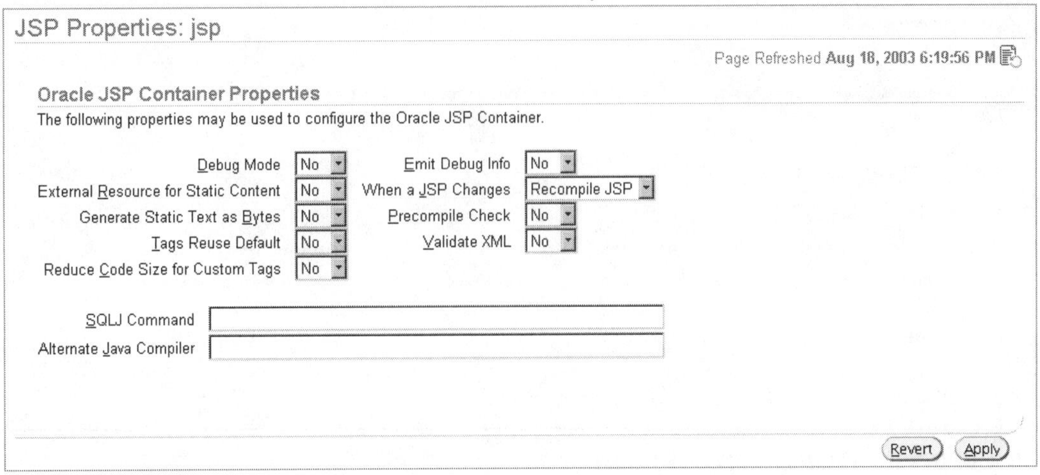

JSP Properties: jsp

Page Refreshed **Aug 18, 2003 6:19:56 PM**

Oracle JSP Container Properties

The following properties may be used to configure the Oracle JSP Container.

_D_ebug Mode	No	_E_mit Debug Info	No
External _R_esource for Static Content	No	When a _J_SP Changes	Recompile JSP
Generate Static Text as _B_ytes	No	_P_recompile Check	No
_T_ags Reuse Default	No	_V_alidate XML	No
Reduce _C_ode Size for Custom Tags	No		

_S_QLJ Command

Alternate _J_ava Compiler

_R_evert   _A_pply

FIGURE 7-11.   _OC4J JSP Container Properties page_

Advanced Properties

Selecting Advanced Server Options brings you to a page that allows direct editing of the configuration files within EM. Once you apply the changes to the file, it will automatically update the repository with the changes. All of the files are actually located in the Server Root directory. They include

```
global-web-application.xml
jms.xml
server.xml
rmi.xml
defautl-web-site.xml
```

Use this method of updating these files only if you cannot include or modify a parameter in another part of the Administration section. If you directly edit the file and make an error in format or structure, the application server may not be able to restart after applying the changes.

Data Sources

Data sources are normally connections to a database; however, they can be connections to any type of persistent storage. Data sources are registered with the Java Naming and Directory Interface (JNDI), where components can find the sources when needed. A data source can be defined at the application level to support a specific application or at the container level, available to any application running in that container. Normally, the EAR file contains a data-source.xml file that defines the required data sources. Data sources are listed in the Data Sources page, shown in Figure 7-12 (off the OC4J home page—Figure 7-7) and are available to any application running inside the container. If you select the application name link, you will be taken to the application page, where you will find another Data Sources page relating only to that specific application.

Data Sources

This table contains all the data sources configured for this application. Each data source is bound to the specified JNDI location.

Create

Select a Data Source and...   Edit   Create Like   Delete

Select	Name	JNDI Location	Class	JDBC Driver	Monitor Performance
⦿	EstoreDB	jdbc/EstoreDataSource	com.evermind.sql.ConnectionDataSource	oracle.jdbc.driver.OracleDriver	
○	InventoryDB	jdbc/InventoryDataSource	com.evermind.sql.ConnectionDataSource	oracle.jdbc.driver.OracleDriver	
○	OracleDS	jdbc/OracleCoreDS	com.evermind.sql.DriverManagerDataSource	oracle.jdbc.driver.OracleDriver	
○	SignOnDB	jdbc/SignOnDataSource	com.evermind.sql.ConnectionDataSource	oracle.jdbc.driver.OracleDriver	

FIGURE 7-12. *OC4J Data Sources page*

Although data sources are normally defined within an Enterprise Application Archive (EAR), you can also define a new data source from this page by selecting the Create button or by selecting the radio button of an already-defined data source and selecting the Create Like button. Creating a new data source within the schema of an already-defined data source using the Create Like button opens the Create Data Source page, with many of the data fields already filled in, including the data source class file, JDBC driver, URL, and the username and password. You must enter a unique name for the data source. In an Oracle database, a user has a schema, so you can skip the entry for schema and just use the username. The only remaining required field is the JNDI Location field. The location must be identified so that the container can bind the class instance to the JNDI name space. We will discuss JNDI in greater detail in Chapter 8.

Security
The Security link takes you to the container Security page. OC4J defines security through Users, Groups, and Roles. These will be discussed in greater detail in Chapter 12. Security parameters are defined in the jazn-xml file, located in the Server Root directory along with the jazn-data.xml file.

JMS Providers
The JMS Provider page allows you to define or remove a Java Message Service provider. As discussed in the previous chapter, JMS allows for asynchronous execution of messages by message EJBs. Oracle uses the advance queuing capabilities of the Oracle Database to support the JMS API. You can also implement third-party JMS support from this page. We will leave the implementation of JMS to the developers; just note that this is the page where you can define JMS providers.

Global Web Module
The last Administration link is the Global Web Module page shown in Figure 7-13. Here, you define and configure parameters that apply to all web applications. These parameters define how the web component will handle certain types of files and are located in the global-web-application.xml and orion-web.xml files. You can modify or define mappings, filtering, environmental, and security parameters from this page.

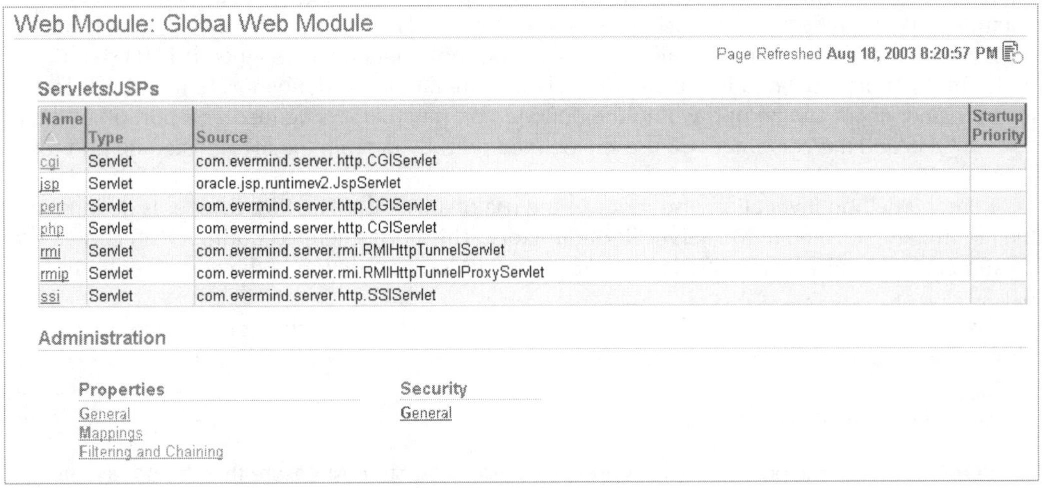

Web Module: Global Web Module

Page Refreshed **Aug 18, 2003 8:20:57 PM**

Servlets/JSPs

Name △	Type	Source	Startup Priority
cgi	Servlet	com.evermind.server.http.CGIServlet	
jsp	Servlet	oracle.jsp.runtimev2.JspServlet	
perl	Servlet	com.evermind.server.http.CGIServlet	
php	Servlet	com.evermind.server.http.CGIServlet	
rmi	Servlet	com.evermind.server.rmi.RMIHttpTunnelServlet	
rmip	Servlet	com.evermind.server.rmi.RMIHttpTunnelProxyServlet	
ssi	Servlet	com.evermind.server.http.SSIServlet	

Administration

Properties	Security
General	General
Mappings	
Filtering and Chaining	

FIGURE 7-13.   *Global Web Module page*

This completes the tour of the OC4J home page. When using OC4J standalone containers, you must configure the container using the XML files. In Application Server 10g, you should always configure OC4J using Enterprise Manager to ensure that the repository and the flat XML file are in synch. Many of the OC4J parameters can be set for both the container and for individual applications. To configure container parameters, select the Administration pages from the OC4J home page. To configure parameters for a specific application, select the application link from the OC4J home page, and then select the appropriate configuration page in the application's Administration section.

OC4J Listeners

To allow access to an OC4J instance, the container maintains a number of listeners that listen on a port for a request and then pass that request to the container. On the OC4J Server Properties page (Figure 7-8), a range of ports was defined for three methods of access.

Most web applications connect to the Oracle HTTP Server (OHS) and communicate through the Apache Java API (AJP). Another method uses a Java program to directly call a method belonging to an EJB in the container. This is referred to as a Remote Method Invocation (RMI). An RMI connection bypasses the OHS and communicates directly with the OC4J container. Finally, the container can be passed Java messages using JMS.

OC4J containers normally maintain listeners for each of these connection strategies. When the Application Server 10g instance is installed, it is configured to listen for HTTP requests on port 7777. If that port is in use, the configuration program will increment the port number by one until it finds an unused port. The configuration utility configures the HTTP port in the file default-web-site.xml. OHS will listen for HTTP requests on that port. If you remember the Server Properties page (Figure 7-8), there was a range of ports defined for AJP. When OHS starts up, it negotiates with the OC4J container for an available port within the defined range. Because OHS cannot communicate with the container using AJP and receive an HTTP request on the same port, you must ensure that the port range available for AJP does not contain the assigned HTTP listening port. The AJP port is defined in the default-web-site.xml file. If it is defined as 0, then OHS and the container negotiate the port within the defined port range. If it is defined as a port other than 0, then OHS and the container will use the defined port. By default, the HTTP listening port for OHS is 7778.

Remote Method Invocation also requires the use of a listener. The RMI listener is defined in the file rmi.xml, located in the Server Root directory. This port is defined during OC4J container creation and can only be modified in the Advanced Properties section of the container home page.

The Java Message Service API also uses a listener that is defined initially at container creation. This port is located in the jms.xml file:

```
<jms-server port="9127">
```

Remember that one port can only support one listener. You must ensure that the ports defined at the creation of the instance are not included in the available ports for negotiated listener ports.

Summary

The OC4J container is the heart of the application server, supporting web components and EJBs with communications, security, and reliability. Future chapters will build on the capabilities discussed in this chapter, as we tie all the parts together that make up Application Server 10*g*. The main points in this chapter are as follows:

■ The OC4J container should be maintained using the Enterprise Manager web site. This includes creating the container and updating the container configuration. Errors made while directly editing the OC4J configuration files could result in the container not restarting.

■ The OC4J container must have a mapping for the application in the Website Properties page in order for a user to connect through the Oracle HTTP Server (OHS) to the application running in the OC4J container.

■ Data sources are normally defined within the Enterprise Archive (EAR) file, but they can also be defined within the OC4J container that will support the application.

Now that you can configure your container and deploy an application into it, you need to connect that application to a persistent storage or database. This chapter discussed how to locate and edit the data source defined in an OC4J container. In the next chapter, we will discuss the details of how an application implements a database connection to include using JDBC, TopLink, and Entity Enterprise JavaBeans.

CHAPTER
8

Database
Connections
and TopLink

atabase connectivity is a key element of an enterprise Java application, and we'll consider it in this chapter. The J2EE specification provides several methods to directly or indirectly connect an application to a database. Many Java programs use JDBC (Java Database Connectivity) connections and directly read, write, or update data stored in a database. J2EE has an additional layer of abstraction that can hide the mechanics of database access with the entity Enterprise JavaBean (EJB).

As you learned in Chapter 6, entity EJBs can manage the database interactions using JDBC (bean managed persistence), or they can allow the container to manage the database interactions (container managed persistence). The entity EJB can hide the actual database interactions while supporting advanced capabilities, such as transactions. Another advantage of the entity EJB is that it survives application and container crashes.

However, you are not required to use entity EJBs to interact with a database. A JDBC connection is returned as a Java object, so any method may define and execute a SQL statement that has access to the connection object. This type of database access is normally executed by a servlet or client application.

This chapter also discusses Oracle Application Server TopLink 10*g*, which helps map application objects to data in a relational or object database. As with other chapters, we introduce the concepts and show you how and where they exist in Oracle Application Server 10*g*. You can obtain additional information about actually programming these concepts in *Oracle9iAS Building J2EE Applications* by Morisseau-Leroy (McGraw-Hill/Osborne, 2002) or *Oracle9i JDBC Programming* by Price (McGraw-Hill/Osborne, 2002).

Before getting into the mechanics of connecting to a database, we need to talk about persistent data and the problems of mapping objects into a relational database.

Persistence

All applications are based on some type of information, or data. The heart of most J2EE applications consists of entity EJBs maintaining some type of data. So what is persistent data? The basic answer is that it is data whose state remains the same after the application stops running. Persistent data could be stored in a database or stored on disk as a file, such as an XML configuration file. For an enterprise application, that includes maintaining the current state, even if the container or application server crashes.

Disk files are convenient for storing data that is read once and rarely changed. You have already seen that most of the Application Server 10*g* configuration files are stored as XML files. Most of that data is also stored in the infrastructure's repository database. For business data, we are talking about storing data in a database. All major enterprise-level databases have JDBC drivers to support J2EE connectivity, and Oracle Application Server 10*g* can connect to any database that supports J2EE connections.

For this discussion, however, we will confine ourselves to connecting to an Oracle database. Oracle introduced object-oriented features starting with Oracle8, but most applications use Oracle as a relational database, while implementing some object-oriented features, such as abstract data types. This conversion from the object model to the relational model is one of the difficulties in implementing persistent data.

The problems encountered when mapping an object-oriented language, such as Java, to a declarative language like SQL are called *impedance mismatch*. When attempting to reconcile the object-oriented Java program with the relational database, it is important to recognize that the Java program deals with data at a much higher level than the relational database. The database deals with data as columns and rows; Java deals with data as objects that can consist of many collections of data items. One Java object, such as a customer order, may map data to multiple databases, such as the customer database and the inventory database.

How this is managed internally by the entity EJB is beyond the scope of this book. However, as mentioned earlier, we are going to introduce you to TopLink, which can be used to create and manage the mapping of object data and relational data. To accomplish all this, you need to connect to the database, and for that you use Java Database Connectivity.

Java Database Connectivity (JDBC)

The JDBC specification defines a means of connecting to a database and retrieving and storing data. The specification is independent of the database, but each major database comes with JDBC drivers. The provided JDBC drivers implement the specification for that particular database program.

Oracle provides a set of Java class files for implementing the JDBC specification with almost all their products, including the Database, the Application Server, and JDeveloper. The Oracle drivers connect to the database either through a local Oracle client or directly through the database listener (Oracle Net). Oracle's drivers include support for advanced data types, such as BLOB, CLOB, abstract data types, collections, and some inheritance in abstract data types. The drivers can also use a data source to locate a database, which we will cover later in this chapter. Newer versions of Oracle's JDBC driver employ advanced capabilities, such as connection pooling and transaction failover. For a Java application to use these drivers, they must be packaged with the application or available in the CLASSPATH. On the database server and the application server, they are located in the $ORACLE_HOME/jdbc/lib directory.

To enable the driver in JDeveloper, you must open the project setting and select Libraries from the settings tree. Select the ORACLE JDBC from the Available Libraries for the Selected Libraries and click OK.

Oracle provides three JDBC drivers for accessing an Oracle database:

- Thin driver
- OCI driver
- Server-side/internal driver

Programs running within Application Server 10g will normally use the thin driver to access an Oracle Database.

Thin Driver

The thin driver is a small, 100 percent pure Java driver that can connect to an Oracle database without installing the Oracle client. It connects either locally, or across the network to the database server's Oracle Net listener, and requires TCP/IP. This driver can be used with applets downloaded from the Internet to connect back to the database; in fact, this driver can be used with any Java program, including OC4J.

OCI Driver

The OCI driver uses the Oracle client to connect to the database and cannot be used in all situations, such as with a program downloaded across the Internet. The OCI driver allows you to take advantage of the additional capabilities available with the Oracle client. However, the latest thin client is capable of many advanced features, such as connection pooling, and we recommend that you use the thin driver unless there is some requirement to use the OCI driver.

Server-Side Driver

There are actually two server-side drivers, and they are used to connect Java programs running on the database server or in the database itself. These drivers allow access not only to the local database but also to remote databases. They only run in the database's Oracle JVM and are written in 100 percent pure Java.

Now that we have introduced the JDBC drivers, let's look at how they are used to interact with the Oracle Database. Again, the programmatic details are beyond the scope of this book. For additional information, please refer to the sources mentioned at the beginning of this chapter.

Dynamic SQL

Once you have a connection using a JDBC driver, you can create and execute a SQL statement. This statement can be defined in the program or built at run time prior to execution. First, create the SQL statement as a Java string. Use the connection to execute the string, and a result set is returned that contains your requested data.

```
// con is the JDBC Connection Object
Statement stat = con.createStatement();
// create the Query statement
String query =
  "select distinct company from job_list order by company"
// execute the query
ResultSet rs = stat.executeQuery(query);
```

In this example, a statement object is created using the connection createStatement method. A string, called query, is then created, and the SQL statement is defined. Finally, the statement object executes the query and places the returned data in the result set rs.

You can create a very complicated method to generate the query string, and if the database accepts it, you will get your response. Methods include using Data Definition Language (DDL) and Data Manipulation Language (DML) commands, in addition to calling PL/SQL procedures and functions. The JDBC also supports performance features like Prepared Statements with bind variables and bulk INSERTS. This method is fine when you need to create the query at run time; alternatively, you can embed SQL directly into Java using SQLJ.

SQLJ

SQLJ is a Java specification for embedding SQL into a Java program. Originally, it was supported only for static SQL; Oracle9*i* introduced dynamic SQLJ support. Oracle is deprecating support for SQLJ and may not support it in future releases. For a detailed explanation of SQLJ, refer to the Oracle Press book, *Oracle9i SQLJ Programming*, by Morisseau-Leroy, Solomon, and Momplaisir (McGraw-Hill/Osborne Media, 2001).

The following example uses SQLJ to insert data into the Expense table:

```
#sql {INSERT INTO EXPENSE VALUES ( :jobNo, :expDate
                                  ,:expType,:expName
                                  ,:expVendor,:expCost)
};
```

Note that the # character is not a comment in Java.

So far, we have briefly discussed database connectivity with Java. It is important that you have an understanding of what the applications you are supporting are doing. From here on, we introduce topics that will help you administer the application server, such as creating a data source. But first, we'll cover how the application locates a database from within the application server. The application does this by looking up the data in the Java Naming and Directory Interface (JNDI).

Java Naming and Directory Interface (JNDI)

The Java Naming and Directory Interface is an API that provides a method of defining parameters and allows other elements to find and use them. It is part of the J2EE specification and is used by the EJB to locate other EJBs or data sources. JNDI can be used to find users, computers on a network, objects (local and remote), and services.

When using JNDI to connect to a database, you must search for a data source. A *data source* is a JNDI context that defines the information needed to connect to a database. An application need only know the name of the data source to retrieve the information and connect to the database. The real advantage of using a data source to connect to a database is that it uncouples the application code from the database connection. If the customer database is moved, all you need to do is update the data source information in JNDI, and any application using the database will automatically connect using the new connection data. If the connection data is placed into the application source code, a change requires recompiling the code and redeploying it to the application server.

When an OC4J container starts up, it creates a JNDI context (data) for each application deployed in it by reading configuration files (or from the repository). The context is stored in memory, so anything that is dynamically loaded into the JNDI context will be lost when the container restarts. Once the application is started, it can look up other components using the container's JNDI context to locate other objects.

Data Sources and OC4J

At this point, we are most concerned with finding a way to connect to our customer database. This is done by finding a data source in the JNDI context. A *data source* is a method to connect to a database. It contains all the information needed to locate and connect to the database. An application may use multiple data sources during execution to access different information. There are three ways to create a data source: using an OracleDataSource object, adding the definition to the data-source.xml file, and using the Enterprise Manager web site.

The programmatic method of creating a data source creates an OracleDataSource object and binds it to a JNDI context object; however, the data-source.xml file or the Enterprise Manager method are preferred with Application Server 10g. Using the Enterprise Manager web site is the easiest method of defining a new data source, but the developer should define the data source so that when the application is deployed, the initial data source is deployed with it.

As an example, we will look at the data sources defined for the Pet Store application deployed in Chapter 7. Start with the data-sources.xml file, located in the instance's $ORACLE_HOME/j2ee /<OC4J_Name>/config subdirectory. Since we deployed the application into the OC4J_Testing container, its location on our system expands to

/home/oracle/oraportal904/j2ee/OC4J_Testing/config/data-sources.xml

Here is part of the data-source.xml file deployed with the Pet Store application:

```
<data-source
class="com.evermind.sql.ConnectionDataSource"
name="InventoryDB"
location="jdbc/InventoryDataSource"
xa-location="jdbc/xa/InventoryXADS"
ejb-location="jdbc/InventoryDB"
url="jdbc:oracle:thin:@192.168.1.105:1521:navdb"
connection-driver="oracle.jdbc.driver.OracleDriver"
username="estoreuser"
password="estore"
inactivity-timeout="30"
/>
    <data-source
    class="com.evermind.sql.ConnectionDataSource"
    name="EstoreDB"
    location="jdbc/EstoreDataSource"
    xa-location="jdbc/xa/EstoreXADS"
    ejb-location="jdbc/EstoreDB"
    url="jdbc:oracle:thin:@192.168.1.105:1521:navdb"
    connection-driver="oracle.jdbc.driver.OracleDriver"
    username="estoreuser"
    password="estore"
    inactivity-timeout="30"
/>
    <data-source
    class="com.evermind.sql.ConnectionDataSource"
    name="SignOnDB"
    location="jdbc/SignOnDataSource"
    xa-location="jdbc/xa/EstoreXADS"
    ejb-location="jdbc/EstoreDB"
    url="jdbc:oracle:thin:@192.168.1.105:1521:navdb"
    connection-driver="oracle.jdbc.driver.OracleDriver"
    username="estoreuser"
    password="estore"
    inactivity-timeout="30"
/>
```

The preceding partial listing of the data-sources.xml file contains three separate data sources, as well as the information to locate the data store and the referenced database. This can also be found on the Enterprise Manager web site by opening the OC4J_Testing page and selecting the Data Sources link under Application Defaults (Figure 8-1).

To see the details of the InventoryDB data source, select the radio button for InventoryDB and select the Edit button. You will see a page like the one shown (in two parts) in Figure 8-2.

Using either the data-source.xml file or the Enterprise Manager web site, you can see the details of the InventoryDB data source. The Class attribute is the class that handles the data source. The JDBC URL attribute defines the database and type of driver used for the connection. In this case, the application is connecting to the database using the Oracle thin driver at 192.168.1.105 on port 1521 with an ORACLE_SID of navdb.

The JDBC Driver parameter defines the classes where the thin driver can be found—oracle .jdbc.driver.OracleDriver. These classes must be available to the JVM or included in the application. Last, the database username and password are provided. With the database information complete, you need to identify how this data source will be found in the JNDI. The location, xa-location, and ejb-location all identify this data source within the JNDI. This is referred to as binding the data source to a name. To locate this data source, the application would look up the ejb-location within the JNDI context.

```
DataSource ds = (DataSource)context.lookup("jdbc/InventoryDB");
```

The object context is a JNDI Context object. Once the application has the data source, it can connect to the database. So how do you create a new data source?

Creating a Data Source

Normally, you will not manually create a data source. The data-source.xml file should be deployed with the application when it is deployed into the OC4J container as part of the EAR file. So you usually change a current data source, rather than create a new one on the application server.

The easiest way to do either is by using the Enterprise Manager web site. Navigate to the OC4J container web page for the container that contains or will contain the data source, and select the data source link. If you wish to change a data source, select the radio button for the data source, and then click the Edit button. From this page, you can update the data for that data source. If you wish to create a new data source, select the Create Like button. This will take you to the Create Like Data Source page with the Drivers and URL fields already populated (Figure 8-3). To create the

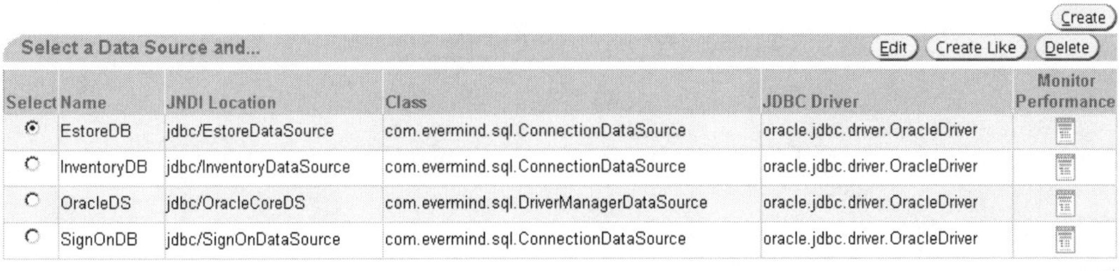

Select	Name	JNDI Location	Class	JDBC Driver	Monitor Performance
●	EstoreDB	jdbc/EstoreDataSource	com.evermind.sql.ConnectionDataSource	oracle.jdbc.driver.OracleDriver	
○	InventoryDB	jdbc/InventoryDataSource	com.evermind.sql.ConnectionDataSource	oracle.jdbc.driver.OracleDriver	
○	OracleDS	jdbc/OracleCoreDS	com.evermind.sql.DriverManagerDataSource	oracle.jdbc.driver.OracleDriver	
○	SignOnDB	jdbc/SignOnDataSource	com.evermind.sql.ConnectionDataSource	oracle.jdbc.driver.OracleDriver	

Select a Data Source and...   Edit   Create Like   Delete   Create

FIGURE 8-1. *OC4J_Testing data sources*

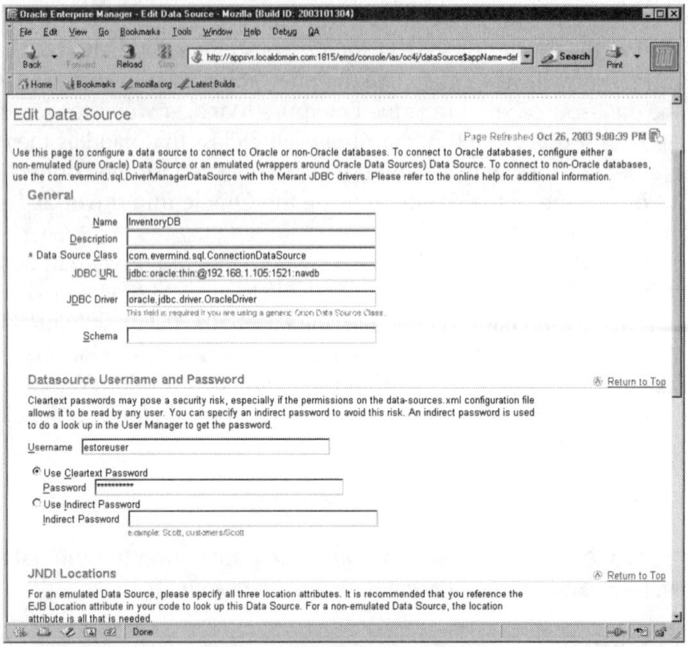

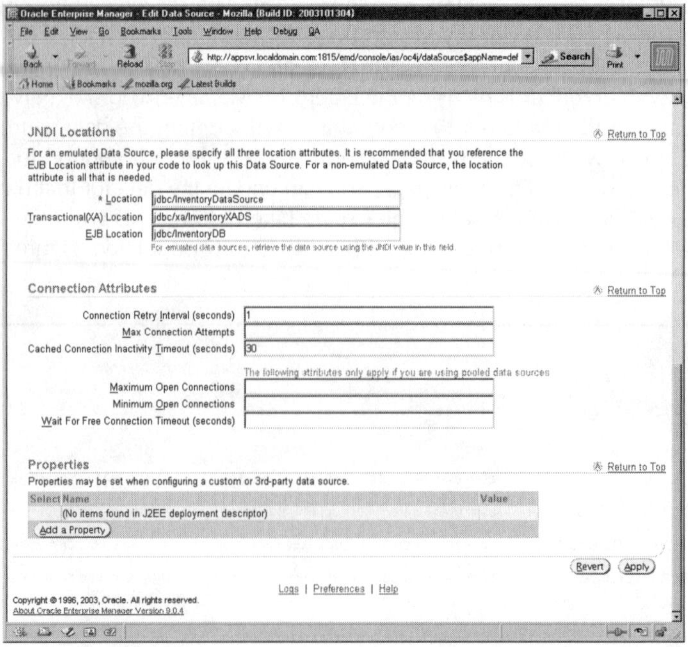

FIGURE 8-2. *Details of the InventoryDB Edit Data Source page*

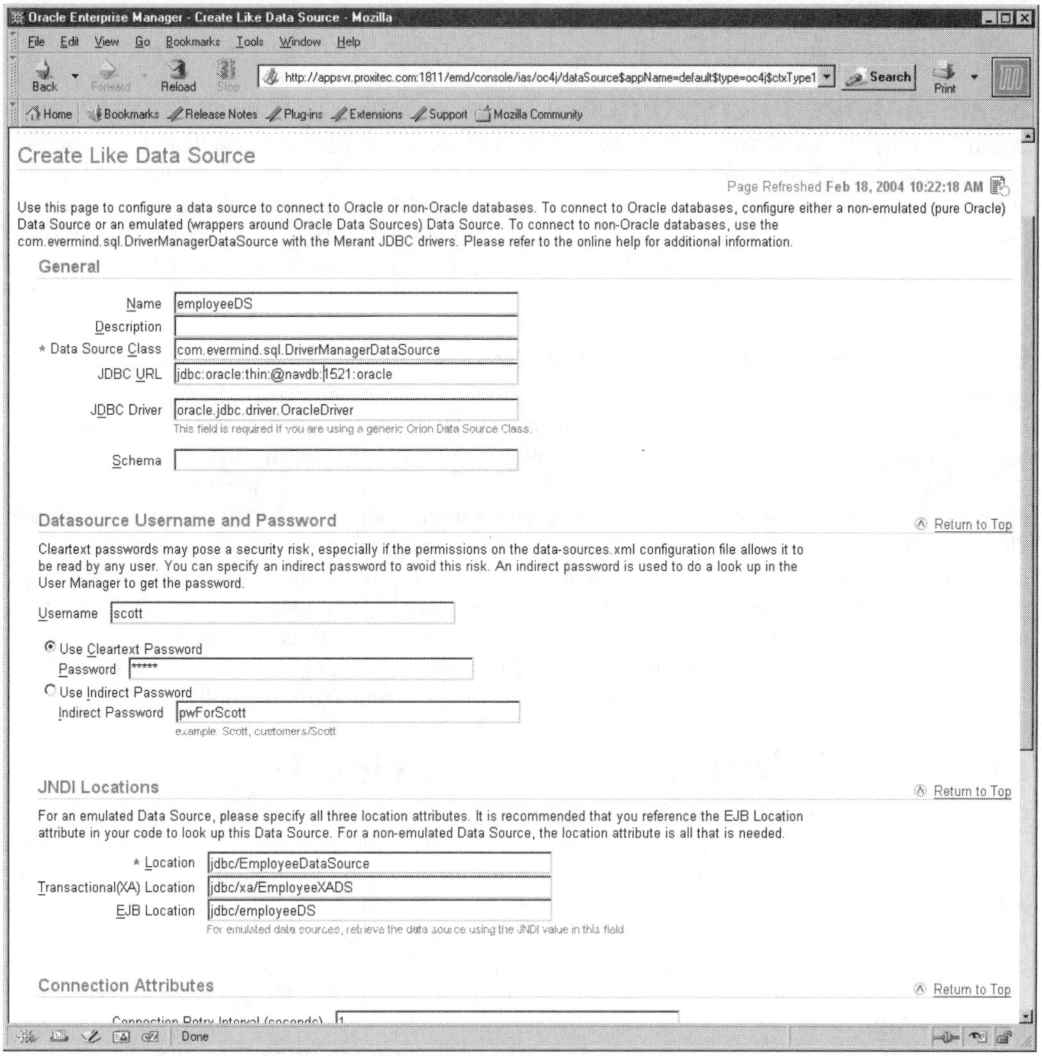

FIGURE 8-3.   *Creating a new data source in Enterprise Manager*

employeeDS data source that accesses the SCOTT schema of the navdb database, enter the name and update the Username and Password to scott and tiger. Now assign the JNDI locations as follows:

```
Location="jdbc/EmployeeDataSource"xa-location="jdbc/xa/EmployeeXADS"
ejb-location="jdbc/employeeDS"
```

Select the Create button to create the data source. After restarting the container, any application deployed in this OC4J container will be able to access and use the new data source.

Entity EJBs can connect to the database directly or through the container. If the entity EJB uses the OC4J container to manage the database connection, it is called container managed persistence (CMP). If the entity EJB does not use the container, it is called bean managed persistence (BMP).

Bean Managed Persistence

When an entity EJB uses BMP, the EJB uses a JDBC connection to connect directly to the database. The EJB must contain all the code to create and execute queries. The EJB can generate dynamic SQL or SQLJ to interact with the database and is responsible for ensuring that the database is updated. If data is updated in the entity EJB but not in the database, and the container or server crashes, the update will be lost. Using BMP means that the developer of the entity EJB is responsible for all facets of database interaction.

Container Managed Persistence

An entity EJB using CMP allows the container to handle all database access. The OC4J container manages the storage and retrieval of data from the database. The container also maintains relationships with the entity FJB, including relationships with other entity EJBs.

With CMP, the application developer does not code the actual SQL needed to interact with the database; instead, the container generates the required code when the EJB is deployed into it. This not only relieves the developer of the task of developing the database access code, but also provides portability to the application, because the container will generate the code to access the database identified by the data source. If the database is changed from Oracle to DB2, the container will generate code needed to access the DB2 database when the EJB is deployed.

The actual coding of an entity EJB is beyond the scope of this book. If you would like additional information, please refer to the excellent books identified at the beginning of this chapter.

Oracle Application Server TopLink 10*g*

Oracle added TopLink to its family of products in 2002 and has integrated it into Oracle Application Server and JDeveloper. TopLink's current release is Oracle Application Server TopLink 10*g* (10.0.3). TopLink allows you to quickly generate the relationship between the relational data in a database and a Java object. Using TopLink to construct your J2EE application simplifies many of the persistence issues discussed in this chapter and also provides advanced capabilities related to performance and ease of development that are lacking in the hand-coded solution. TopLink offers great flexibility in the choice of persistent architecture, supporting Java objects and EJB entity beans with both BMP and CMP.

This release has introduced some powerful new features such as using TopLink with container managed persistence (CMP), query optimization, object caching, and password encryption. It works with any JDBC-accessible data source and any J2EE application server. TopLink is made up of the TopLink Foundation Library and the TopLink Mapping Workbench. You can implement TopLink's function programmatically within your Java code, or you can use the TopLink Mapping Workbench to create the mapping graphically and have TopLink generate the necessary mapping code. We recommend using the Mapping Workbench, as it greatly reduces the amount of code required and the complexity of mapping and maintaining this persistence metadata.

You can use TopLink to handle complex mapping problems to existing database objects. TopLink is a persistence framework that allows you to work at a higher level than the JDBC connection and produce high-performance queries, while still being able to customize its behavior at a fine-grain level.

TopLink Mapping Workbench 10*g*

The Mapping Workbench is the graphical interface to the capabilities of TopLink. With it you can connect to the database, create or update the schema, or generate the schema DDL for later use. The Mapping Workbench can also inspect your code to determine object information. TopLink can automatically generate an object model from the database schema, a database schema from the object model, or a mapping from a current object model to a current database schema. Of course it also allows you to manually create the object-to-schema mappings for the popular and flexible meet-in-the-middle approach required of most complex applications.

For this simple example, we are going to create two Java objects that map to the Products and Inventory tables in the database used by the Pet Store application introduced earlier.

To start the Mapping Workbench on Windows, select Start and navigate through TopLink to the Mapping Workbench shortcut. If TopLink was not installed in the Start menu, use

```
<ORACLE_HOME>\toplink\bin\workbench.cmd
```

On UNIX/Linux, execute the following script:

```
$ORACLE_HOME/toplink/workbench/workbench.sh
```

When you start the Mapping Workbench, it opens with no data. Create a new project by selecting File | New Project to open the Create New Project window, shown in Figure 8-4.

The new project defaults to a relational database using Oracle. If you select the Browse button, you will see that TopLink is capable of connecting to almost any database. After selecting the OK button, you will be asked to save the project file. For this example, we named the file Expense. The next step is to connect to the database. Once the project file is saved, it appears in the Navigator pane. Expand Expense, select Oracle, and the database information is displayed in the Editor pane (Figure 8-5).

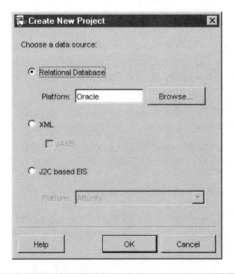

FIGURE 8-4. *TopLink Mapping Workbench, Create New Project*

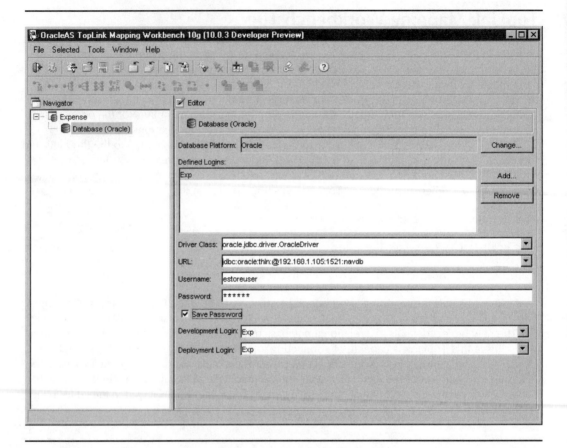

FIGURE 8-5. *TopLink Mapping Workbench, database configuration*

To define the database connection information, select the Add button to add a login. We named the login Exp. Next, select the Exp login, and the connection data fields become active. Use the drop-down box to select the Oracle driver and the URL for the thin driver.

```
oracle.jdbc.driver.OracleDriver
jdbc:oracle:thin:@
```

Add the *"server name:port:SID"* after the @ sign, and enter the username and password. Our URL became

```
jdbc:oracle:thin:@192.168.1.105:1521:navdb
```

Save the connection data by clicking the Floppy Disk icon, and then click the Key icon with the *x* flag to connect to the database. The Database icon in the Navigator pane will have a check on it to indicate that you are connected. Right-click on the Database icon in the Navigator pane, and select Add or Update Existing Tables. This will bring up a window where you select which schema tables you are going to work with.

In the Schema Pattern combo box, select the estoreuser schema and click the Get Table Names button. A list of the tables used in the Pet Store application appears in the Available Tables pane. For this simple example, we are going to map an object to the Product and Inventory tables. Select both tables and use the right arrow to move them to the Selected Tables pane, as shown in Figure 8-6. Select OK to import the tables into the Mapping Workbench.

The Product and Inventory tables now appear under the Database icon in the Navigator pane, as shown in Figure 8-7. Select the Product table in the Navigator pane, and its definition information appears in the Editor pane. From here you can modify the table if you need to; however, for this example, we are going to create a Java object based on the two tables.

Right-click on the Product table, select Generate Classes and Descriptors, and then select Selected Tables. If your project has not been saved, you will be prompted to save it. Then you need

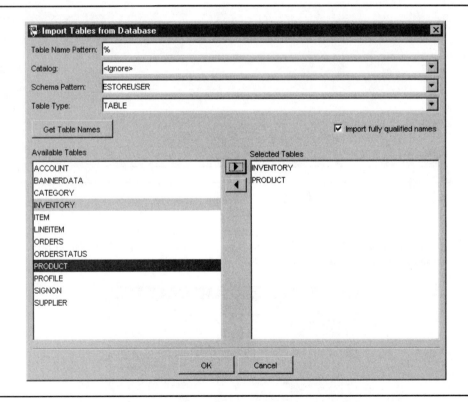

FIGURE 8-6.   *TopLink Mapping Workbench, Import Tables from Database*

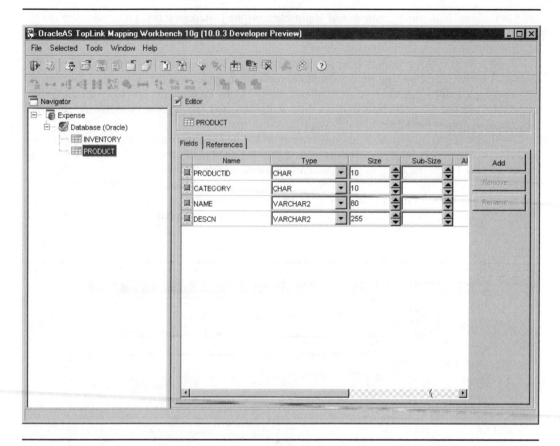

FIGURE 8-7. *TopLink Mapping Workbench, product table definition*

to define the package name that the objects will be placed in. Package names are normally your domain name backward, so we used com.estore, as shown here:

Repeat the process for the Inventory table using the same package name. Notice that under the Expense project, the package now has an icon and contains two objects (Figure 8-8). Also notice that there is an exclamation mark on the project icon, the package, and the Inventory object. If you look at the status area at the bottom of the Mapping Workbench, you see the message that the Inventory table does not have a primary key. This is part of the problem discussed at the beginning of this chapter about mapping a relational database to an object. A database has no problem having multiple rows in a table with the same data, but each row must be uniquely identifiable either by using a single primary key or a compound primary key. The same requirement is true for plain Java objects or EJBs that are mapped to a database table. To address this issue, we define the ItemId field as the primary key.

At this point, we have generated objects that we can integrate into our application. However, to be useful, some of the objects' attributes may need to be modified. By selecting the Product object and then Class Info from the Editor pane, you will see how TopLink defined the Product object and how it can modify many of the methods and attributes.

The last step in this process is to generate the actual Java code. Right-click on the Product object and select Export Model Java Source (Figure 8-9). You will be asked for a directory to save the files to, and, when completed, a dialog box will tell you it is completed. When you look in

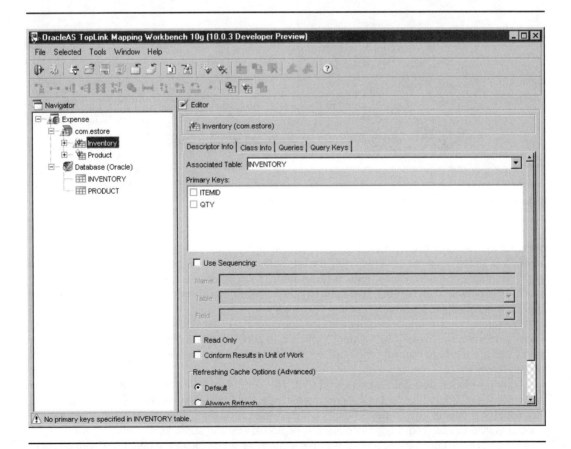

FIGURE 8-8. *TopLink Mapping Workbench, primary key missing from inventory*

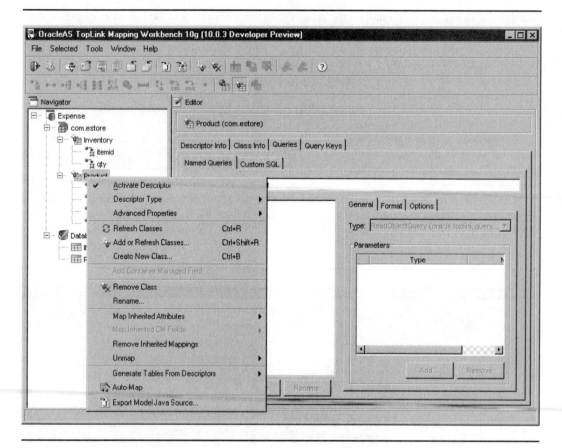

FIGURE 8-9. *TopLink Mapping Workbench, generating code*

the directory you specified, you will find the Java source code. Note that the code generated consists of simple Java objects containing the attributes that will be mapped to the database and the get/set methods, but no business logic is generated. The developer is responsible for writing the business logic and also the code (typically in other classes) that is required to actually instantiate and then persist these objects.

The last step is to produce deployment descriptors for the classes. Select the com.estore package name, and select the Export Deployment XML icon to generate the deployment descriptors. At this point you are ready to compile the code with your application and deploy it to the application server.

For a developer, TopLink is a powerful tool. This simple demonstration used the standalone Mapping Workbench, but TopLink is completely integrated into JDeveloper 10*g*.

TopLink produces any requested code, which is integrated into the application, so there are no special administration requirements once it is deployed into the application server. The TopLink code is part of the application, and runs in the same JVM as the OC4J container and requires no special attention to function.

Summary

Database connectivity and persistent data are at the heart of any business application. In this chapter, we have introduced the different ways to connect the application to the database and discussed some of the problems associated with mapping relational databases to application objects. We discussed the capabilities of the Entity EJB both with bean managed persistence and with container managed persistence. After introducing you to finding a data source with JNDI, we covered administration of data sources in the application server. Last, we went through a quick introduction to TopLink and its ability to automatically create the object to relational mapping. The main points are as follows:

- The most common method for connecting a Java application to a database is through a JDBC connection. Oracle provides three JDBC connectors—thin, thick, and server-side.

- EJBs can use a JDBC connection or rely on the container to maintain the connection to the database. The JDBC connection is the most flexible, but it places on the programmer the responsibility for ensuring that data is updated in the database.

- Applications can use a data source to retrieve database connection information. Data sources can be stored in an OS file or in the Oracle Internet Directory. Centralizing connection data in a data source reduces management over having the connection data hard-coded in the application.

- Differences in data representation between an object-oriented application and a relational database introduces significant programmatic problems in data storage and retrieval. Many tools are available to help solve this problem, such as Oracle Application Server TopLink 10*g*.

At this point, we have introduced the basic components of Application Server 10*g*. From here on, we focus on its features and capabilities in the areas of high availability, performance, and security.

CHAPTER
9

High Availability

I n a nutshell, *high availability* means that all Oracle Application Server 10*g* components are readily available to the end-user community. However, keep in mind that high availability is a relative term, and there is a direct trade-off between computing resources and availability.

If your system must have continuous availability, even in the face of a disaster, then expensive (more resource intensive) failover mechanisms must be implemented in your application, and additional failover servers are required. If your system can tolerate an occasional downtime, then less aggressive failover techniques can be used.

There is also a trade-off between recovery time and expense. Since Oracle introduced recovery products 12 years ago, their technologies have evolved significantly. The options range from recovery that can take hours to true continuous availability. At the database level, these techniques range from traditional database recovery, to standby databases, all the way to Real Application Clusters. As discussed in Chapter 2, the infrastructure repository database can be created in an existing Oracle 9*i* database (and once certified, 10*g* database) to include one using RAC to provide that continuous availability.

In this chapter, we will focus on the high availability features of Application Server 10*g*. For information on high availability options for Oracle back-end databases, refer to the books *Oracle Database 10*g* DBA Handbook* by Loney and Bryla (McGraw-Hill/Osborne, 2004) and *Oracle Database 10*g* High Availability with RAC, Flashback, and Data Guard* by Hart and Jesse (McGraw-Hill/Osborne, 2004).

We will start the discussion with the application server overall and then work down to the high availability features of the separate components.

Why Are Systems Unavailable?

First, what is considered system availability? A system is available if it accepts and processes end-user requests. Basically, if an end user cannot get on the system, it is unavailable. Systems become unavailable for three main reasons: application failure, hardware failure, or maintenance. Hardware failure is less and less the reason for systems being unavailable. Most large multiprocessor UNIX computers, for example, are fault tolerant and will bypass bad memory or a failed CPU until it is repaired. Disk drives have become very reliable, and disk arrays can be configured to tolerate multiple drives that do fail. A disk array that is striped and triple mirrored has a mean time between failures measured in decades. However, Oracle's Application Server 10*g* does not require large computers and is designed to run on low-cost commodity servers. Computers that are not fault tolerant must be protected with redundancy. Since the computer cannot detect errors and work around them, it is up to the software to determine that a computer has failed and take the necessary actions to complete the user transaction.

Application failure occurs when a request causes the application to fail. This failure includes anything from human errors that crash a system, to program exceptions that crash the application (or the OC4J container). Oracle Corporation data shows that 75 percent of Oracle outages are the result of human error. In this case, the application server must be able to detect components that have failed and restart them.

Last, there is maintenance downtime. This one is tricky. Failure to properly back up the application server to include the Metadata Repository database repository is to risk losing the entire system and having to reinstall the application server and your application. Included in maintenance downtime is the requirement to update your application or the application server itself. However, with a properly configured application server, you will be able to maintain 24/7 availability to your end users while taking the necessary precautions to safeguard your system.

Fortunately, one of the real fortes for Application Server 10*g* is its ability to eliminate downtime. In this chapter, we will start with clustering application server instances to eliminate single points of failure and then dig down to the abilities of the individual components, like OC4J's ability to upgrade or deploy your application while it is running.

Eliminating Single Points of Failure

Since Application Server 10*g* achieves high performance on low-cost commodity servers, you do not need to invest in large, expense hardware with built-in fault tolerance. At much lower cost, you can add low-cost servers to create a clustered architecture.

The diagram in Figure 9-1 shows a basic architecture that contains complete redundancy from the Internet and back to the database using Real Application Clusters.

One important note: you must also create a redundant network infrastructure within the Application Server 10*g* infrastructure to eliminate all single points of failure. If all the network connections between the midtiers and the back-end database connect through one switch, that switch is a single point of failure that can bring down the entire infrastructure.

Let's start at the Internet/intranet connection and work toward the back-end database.

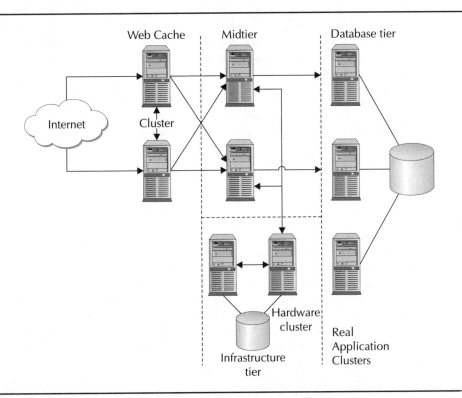

FIGURE 9-1. *Application server architecture with complete redundancy*

Web Cache Tier

Redundancy begins with multiple connections to the Internet (or intranet) attached to a pair of clustered Web Cache servers. As we discussed in Chapter 5, multiple Web Cache instances can be clustered so that they not only share cached content, but also provide failover and load balancing to multiple midtier application server instances. The Web Cache also has the ability to respond to a request for content that is contained in its cache, even if the midtier application servers are temporarily unavailable. As you learned in Chapter 5, the Web Cache pings each of the OHS servers to ensure that it does not send a request to an OHS instance that is down. If you do not have multiple connections to the network, a single Web Cache instance can support and load-balance multiple midtier instances. However, in this case, you will have two single points of failure—the Web Cache server and the router/switch in front of the Web Cache server.

Midtier

At the midtier, there normally are multiple instances of the application server, each implementing Oracle's HTTP Server (OHS) and possibly multiple OC4J containers running multiple copies of the application. As we discussed in Chapter 4, each OHS server implements multiple processes to handle requests, the loss of one having little or no effect on the server. OHS also has the ability to restart without shutting down. As each process completes its request, OHS will kill it and restart it with the new configuration. Thus OHS is available even while reconfiguring itself. Additionally, OHS will use mod_oc4j to load-balance to the OC4J containers, providing redundancy within the midtier instance. The mod_oc4j module ensures that the OC4J container is running before sending it a request. Because OC4J containers clustered in an island replicate their state to all containers within the island, mod_oc4j can reroute a request to another container within the island if a container is no longer running and still maintain the session's state.

The midtier instances are clustered using the infrastructure tier for configuration, Oracle Internet Directory (OID) and Single Sign-On (SSO). A *cluster* is a group of midtier instances that share a common configuration and work together to distribute the load across multiple servers. A cluster is created using the Enterprise Manager Application Server Control or the DCM utility. All instances in each cluster have the same configuration, and changes to one instance will be propagated to all the other instances in the cluster. If you deploy your application onto an instance that belongs to a cluster, it is propagated to all other instances in the cluster. To create a cluster using the Enterprise Manager web site, you need at least two instances associated with an infrastructure. Figure 9-2 shows an infrastructure with two instances. For this example, both midtier instances are installed on one server; normally, they would be installed on separate servers.

Select the Create Cluster button (Figure 9-3) to create a new cluster. Enter the name for this cluster (I used TestCluster1), and select Create. This creates an empty cluster.

Now we need to add the two midtier instances to the cluster. Select the midtier instance to add to TestCluster1 and select the Join Cluster button. You will get a list of available clusters and a warning that unless the cluster is empty, the OC4J instances will be invalidated because they will be reconfigured to match the other instances in the cluster. For this example, I created two midtier instances, midtier_1 and midtier_2. I deployed the Pet Store application into midtier_1 and then added it to TestCluster1. Next I added the midtier_2 instance to the TestCluster1 cluster. From the Enterprise Manager Farm page, select the TestCluster1 link to list the instances and their status, as shown in Figure 9-4, which make up the cluster.

You can now view the status page for each of the instances in the cluster by selecting their link. The clustered instances share a common configuration. Applications deployed into one

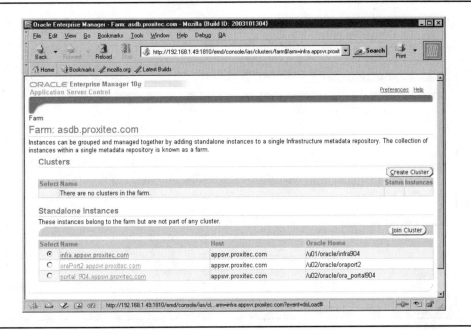

FIGURE 9-2. *Enterprise Manager Farm asdb.proxitec.com*

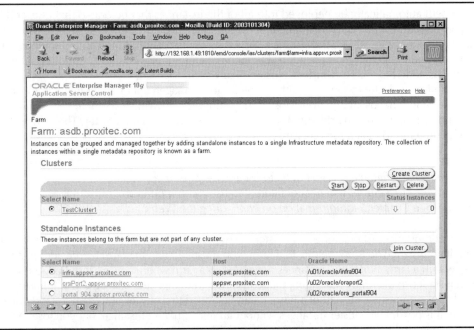

FIGURE 9-3. *Enterprise Manager Farm with TestCluster1*

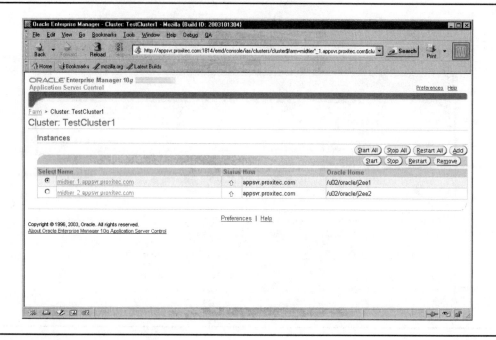

FIGURE 9-4. *Enterprise Manager TestCluster1 status page*

instance will automatically be deployed into all of the Instances that belong to that cluster. In this example, I deployed the Pet Store application into midtier_1 before adding it to the cluster. Since it was the first instance added, the cluster assumed its configuration. I then added midtier_2 to the cluster, and the Pet Store application was automatically deployed into the midtier_2 instance when it was added to the TestCluster1 cluster (Figure 9-5).

This ability to cluster instances greatly simplifies the management of multiple midtier instances. When the midtier needs an additional instance to support a growing workload, you can install a basic midtier instance on an additional server and simply add it to the cluster. The new instance will be configured to match the other instances in the cluster.

NOTE
You must reconfigure the Web Cache to use the new instance. Adding the instance to a cluster will not configure it to use a common Web Cache. See Chapter 5 for information on configuring the Web Cache.

Mid_tier instances (standalone and clusters) associated with a single infrastructure make up a farm. If an instance does not belong to a farm, you must add it to the farm before adding it to a cluster within a farm. Normally, instances are added to a farm when they are installed, but you can add an instance to a farm by navigating to the instance web page and using the Use Infrastructure Wizard. Once an instance is part of a farm, it can be added to a cluster or remain a standalone instance. It is possible to cluster instances without an infrastructure instance, but you lose the cluster manageability because you are now responsible for ensuring that configuration changes are propagated to each instance.

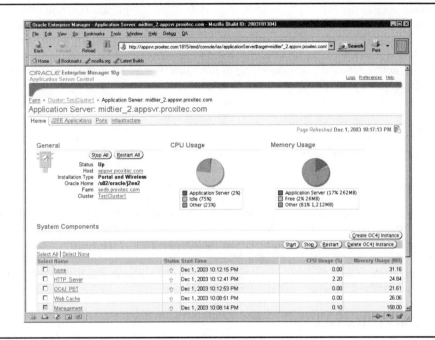

FIGURE 9-5.   *Enterprise Manager midtier_2 status page*

Infrastructure Tier

The infrastructure tier not only contains the infrastructure instance but also the repository database. The diagram in Figure 9-1 shows the infrastructure tier configured within a Cold Failover Cluster. Unlike the midtier clusters that are all active, in a Cold Failover Cluster, only one server is active, while the other is standing by in case the first fails. This configuration requires an OS-supported clustering system such as Sun Cluster. When the active node fails, the clustering software restarts the failed programs on the cold node. An exciting new feature in Application Server 10*g* is the ability to create the repository database in an existing database. This allows the repository database to take advantage of an already existing high-available back-end database that may implement RAC or be hosted on a large, highly available server. This provides availability for the repository database but not for the infrastructure instance. Oracle will soon provide a capability to cluster and load-balance multiple infrastructure instances so that you can create a redundant infrastructure without using a cold server on standby.

Back-End Database

Behind the application servers is some type of continuous availability database using RAC, Data Guard, or replication, as shown in Figure 9-6. Oracle Real Application Clusters, or RAC, creates multiple database instances of the same database and allows for very fast recovery from an instance failure. Data Guard implements a standby database that is constantly updated from the active database. If the active database fails, the administrator will convert the standby database into an active database, reconfigure the network to point to the new active database, and resume processing. Replication implements multiple active databases that exchange changes between them so that they are consistent (with a small time delay). With replication, if one of the databases fails, processing continues on the remaining databases. Normally, the back-end database will implement RAC, which is why the ability to implement the infrastructure's repository database in the back-end RAC database greatly improves reliability. Implementing Real Application Clusters is outside the scope of this book. For additional information on implementing RAC, refer to the book *Oracle9i RAC: Oracle Real Application Clusters Configuration and Internals* by Ault and Tumma (Rampant TechPress, 2003).

Disaster Recovery

With an implementation such as the one depicted in Figure 9-1, you have a completely redundant system, capable of continuous availability, even with the loss of a server in each tier. Before digging deeper into the high availability capabilities of the individual components, we need to discuss recovering from a disaster, say an earthquake or a fire. You need the ability to recover if you lose your data center. Oracle Application Server Disaster Recovery is the solution to provide off-site replication of the application server. The administrator periodically executes scripts that update the configuration of the standby site to match the active site. If the active site is lost, the standby site is activated, and the DNS is changed to address the new location. The standby site must match the active site. The standby back-end database must also be configured to stay current with the active database, possibly using Oracle Data Guard.

Backup and Recovery

Sometimes it is easier to recover a failed component than to spend time trying to repair it. Application Server 10*g* comes with a new Backup and Recovery component that allows you to create a

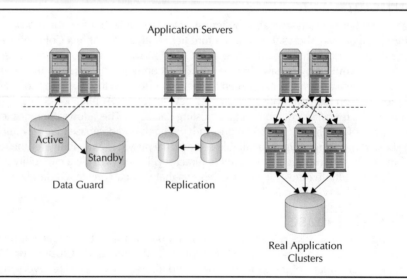

FIGURE 9-6. *Highly available database solutions*

checkpoint of the system and, if need be, quickly recover to that checkpoint. This capability is instrumental in implementing Disaster Recovery, discussed in the previous section. For additional information, refer to Chapter 11.

At this point, we need to discuss how the individual components implement high availability.

Rolling Upgrades

One of the requirements that creates downtime is maintenance. Part of maintenance is upgrading the application server itself. Application Server 10g has the ability to upgrade from Oracle9iAS Release 2 (9.0.2) with minimal downtime. In fact, if you have implemented a completely redundant system like Figure 9-1, you can upgrade a component (such as the OHS/OC4J behind the Web Cache) and test it while the other components are still supporting your application. As each upgraded component is accepted, you can bring it online and upgrade the next component. In this way, you could completely upgrade the application server with no downtime while implementing a rigorous testing and verification routine.

Oracle plans to implement the rolling upgrade in all future releases of the Oracle Application Server. For more details on planning and executing a minimal downtime upgrade from Oracle9iAS (9.0.2) to Oracle Application Server 10g, refer to the *Oracle Application Server Upgrading to 10g* documentation.

OC4J High Availability Features

The Application Server 10g OC4J container was discussed in detail in Chapter 7. The OC4J container has a number of its own high availability features. These include the ability to deploy components into a running container, to use multiple JVMs, and to replicate state across containers and instances.

Hot Deployments and Redeployments

Rolling upgrades are available not only for the application server, but also for your application running on the application server. This is referred to as a *hot deployment* or a *redeployment*. During a hot deployment, the OC4J container deploys the new Enterprise JavaBean (EJB)/web components while continuing to support the present components. This can cause a temporary performance impact as the deployment occurs.

During a redeployment, updates to existing application components are deployed. Redeployments of a currently running application require additional planning and testing to ensure success. The problem with redeploying a live application is that the current session's state may not exist upon completion of the new application components. A stateful EJB will be upgraded, but there is no way to ensure that the new EJB assumes the state of the previous version of the EJB. One way around this problem is to always store the component's state in the back-end database; however, there are trade-offs with this solution that must be considered during development. A redeployment that fails may leave the OC4J container in an inoperable state, which may require you to restore the OC4Jcontainer using DCM (see Chapter 7).

OC4J Islands

Islands are multiple containers working together to ensure availability. OC4J containers start in a default island that contains one process. You can increase the processes in the default island to ensure that the container continues to run after a process fails. Multiple OC4J containers, in a single island, will replicate state information so that if one container fails, the other will continue to support the active sessions. This can be expanded to multiple OC4J containers on different servers so that the application continues to support active sessions, even with the complete loss of a server. When planning for and creating islands of containers, ensure that the island spans multiple servers. Also, state replication among the containers in an island requires some overhead. Creating multiple islands reduces the overhead of propagating state information to other containers in the island while maintaining the ability to recover from the loss of a server or container.

In Figure 9-7, four applications are deployed into six OC4J containers on two separate midtier instances. Application 1 is deployed into OC4J-APP1, which maintains state across the two tiers because they are part of island App1. Application 2 is deployed into island App2 and also maintains state across the two tiers. Applications 3 and 4 are not deployed into containers within an island, and their state is not maintained across the two midtier instances.

It is the job of mod_oc4j to map sessions to OC4J islands. If a server fails and the OC4J island spans multiple servers, mod_oc4j will route the transaction to an available container within the original island. If there are no OC4J containers remaining in the island, the session state is lost. For more information on OC4J islands, refer to Chapter 7.

Transparent Application Failover

Transparent Application Failover (TAF) is available on the connection from the application server to the back-end database. To use TAF, the database connections must use the thick JDBC client, and the back-end database must be running Real Application Clusters. When the application server sends a request to the back-end database, it gets assigned to an instance in the RAC cluster. That database instance will execute the request and return the response. If the assigned database instance fails (even in the middle of executing the request), TAF will detect this and automatically route the request to another instance in the database cluster.

TAF uses Oracle Net connection, and thus your application must use the thick Oracle JDBC client to connect to the database. TAF is not something that you can just turn on and walk away.

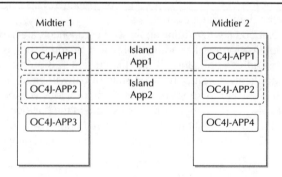

FIGURE 9-7. *Distribution of islands across multiple servers*

Your application must understand how TAF works and respond accordingly. TAF supports the following functions:

- **Active transactions**   Uncommitted inserts, updates, and deletes are automatically rolled back if the instance fails. TAF will return an error to the application until a rollback command is submitted.

- **Database connections**   TAF will automatically reconnect to another database instance if the current instance fails.

- **Select failover**   If your application is retrieving data using a Select statement (open cursors) and is in the process of fetching rows when the database instance fails, TAF will reconnect and reexecute the cursor select statement, discard the already returned rows, and allow you to fetch the remaining rows. For example, if your application is processing 1 million rows and the instance fails after you have fetched 200 rows, TAF will automatically reconnect, reexecute the cursor, discard the already fetched rows, and allow the application to continue fetching the remaining rows. To the application, it appears that the database stops for a few seconds and then continues.

TAF is not fail proof. When the connected database instance fails, the nonpersistent session data is not automatically restored. Also, any server-side program variables or PL/SQL package state is also lost.

TAF can also be configured to create two connections, each to a separate database instance, to reduce the time required to recover from an instance failure.

TAF is a powerful feature that requires additional planning to implement in your application. For more information, refer to the Oracle documentation or to the Oracle9*i* RAC book mentioned earlier.

High Availability of Applications

Each component of Application Server 10*g* has the ability to create redundancy. However, you must ensure that your application is implemented in a way to take advantage of this capability. Ensure that your applications replicate stateless components to multiple servers and that stateful components are contained in islands that span multiple servers. Complete redundancy in the application server will be of little use if the back-end database is not available. Creating a high-available infrastructure will also remove that critical single point of failure.

Depending on your application, using the Web Cache to continue to respond to user requests will allow you some time to switch systems, but will eventually result in failed requests or serving stale content. The bottom line is that you must plan the infrastructure needed to ensure that all components of your application are using the high availability features built into Application Server 10*g* and the Real Application Clusters Database 10*g*.

Summary

In this chapter, we have discussed the high availability features of Oracle Application Server 10*g* and how they are implemented. Since the application server does not require the use of expensive hardware, high availability is achieved by providing redundancy of every component, from the network/Internet connection through the back-end database.

The key points of this chapter are as follows:

- High availability requires careful planning up front. To have a truly high available solution, you must eliminate all single points of failure.

- When designing your infrastructure, ensure that you consider single points of failure outside of the application server, such as power supplies and network configurations.

- Once you have ensured that there is redundancy at each tier of the application server, you must next ensure that, if needed, there is redundancy within each tier, such as implementing OC4J islands on components that must maintain state, and implementing a TAF connection to the back-end database.

Now that we have the application server configured for high availability, we need to address performance. Performance-tuning Application Server 10*g* can be difficult and frustrating because of the interrelation of multiple components. However, the Oracle Enterprise web site provides a multitude of statistics to help you locate bottlenecks and performance problems. The next chapter details methods to help you tune Application Server 10*g*.

CHAPTER
10

Performance Tuning

his chapter deals with the most important areas of Oracle Application Server 10*g* administration, optimization, and high availability. Even if you have done a superb job in installing and configuring Application Server 10*g*, if the system is not always available or if performance is poor, you have not succeeded in your job. This chapter starts with an overview of performance tuning and then discusses how to set up your monitoring environment. We'll discuss the concepts and tools you need for the following tasks:

■ Monitoring and load balancing the Oracle HTTP Server

■ Tuning the Web Cache

■ Load balancing your servers and other components

Proactive Tuning: An Overview

Being complex, an Application Server 10*g* environment has a huge amount of tuning opportunities. For example, the Oracle database back end has more than 250 initialization parameters, each Application Server 10*g* component has many interrelated parameter and configuration settings, and each server has dozens of tuning options. Tuning any one of the components is challenging by itself, but when you consider the complex interactions between them, there can be an overwhelming amount of tuning activity.

We must start by noting that every system has a bottleneck. Even a well-tuned system will have some resource that comprises the majority of the response time. The best approach is to identify the component that is the bottleneck and then drill-down and identify the component resource that is responsible for the latency. The bottleneck may be hardware related (CPU, RAM, disk I/O, or network shortages), or software related (locks, latches, or contention).

There are two approaches to Application Server 10*g* tuning—reactive and proactive. In the reactive approach, you receive a response time complaint from the end-user community, and you use tools such as OEM to ascertain the cause of the performance problem. In the proactive tuning approach, you collect detailed statistics from all Application Server 10*g* components, analyze the data, and develop predictive models that can predict those conditions that will impede performance.

Let's start by examining the tuning "knobs." By altering a knob, you adjust the configuration and resources for the Application Server 10*g* farm and change the processing characteristics. Common knobs for Application Server 10*g* include three areas—physical server (hardware-level) tuning, parameter tuning, and RAM cache tuning.

Server tuning offers the following opportunities for improving performance:

■ **Hardware configuration** Adding RAM or CPU resources to existing servers will improve the throughput.

■ **Hardware load balancing** Adding new servers to the Application Server 10*g* farm and relocating components onto the servers will allow for scalability during times of peak usage. Spare servers can be configured with both Web Cache and Application Server 10*g*, and the appropriate components can be started as needed.

■ **Server parameter tuning**   Adjusting the parameters on your server can have a huge impact on the performance of the components running on that server.

Tuning your Application Server 10*g* and database parameters can also help performance:

■ **Application Server 10*g* parameters**   Adjusting the configuration parameters for each component has influence on performance and throughput.

■ **Database parameters**   Because most Application Server 10*g* systems are disk I/O intensive, adjusting the Oracle database parameters for the infrastructure database (iasdb) and the back-end database can heavily influence performance.

Finally, RAM cache tuning will improve throughput:

■ **Data buffer tuning**   Adding RAM to the database db_cache_size on the Oracle infrastructure and back-end database can greatly reduce disk I/O and improve throughput.

■ **Web Cache tuning**   Adding RAM to the Web Cache can improve the delivery rates of HTML and XML through the Oracle HTTP Server.

Proactive tuning is the best approach for the tuning of Application Server 10*g* because you can analyze historical database information, observe trends, and identify performance thresholds. In order to do proactive monitoring, you must develop data collection mechanisms for the servers and each component.

Setting Up the Monitoring Environment

In order to develop a coherent picture of overall performance of Application Server 10*g*, you must collect data from a variety of sources, including the following:

■ **Resource usage monitoring**   Assuming that each component is optimally tuned, any hardware-related overload must be addressed by adding more hardware. The solutions may be to add a new application server, add RAM or CPU to existing servers, or install faster disks. In UNIX or Linux, you can monitor your servers with the vmstat utility, top, glance, or iostat, and store the data in Oracle tables for time-based resource analysis. In a Windows environment you can use the Windows performance monitor to measure hardware usage. We will explore hardware monitoring and tuning later in this chapter.

■ **Response time monitoring**   Several components within Oracle Application Server 10*g* allow you to track overall response time and the components of response time. For example, web applications using the Forms Server can use the Forms Server log to generate detailed response time reports. We will address this in greater detail later in this chapter.

■ **Wait event monitoring**   Performing a wait event analysis on each component can provide insights into the main source of latency. For example, in the Oracle database, a STATSPACK report will show the top five database wait events. The following listing gives an example:

```
Top 5 Timed Events
~~~~~~~~~~~~~~~~~~                              % Total
```

```
Event                          Waits  Time (s)  Ela Time
------------------------------ -----  --------  --------
CPU time                                  30      91.43
direct path read                95        1       3.53
control file sequential read    54        1       2.33
log file parallel write         62        0        .95
db file parallel write          20        0        .68
```

Because the bulk of Oracle Application Server 10*g* systems run in a UNIX environment, this section will focus on establishing a server-monitoring environment in UNIX. We will begin by describing how to establish a standard server environment and then look at capturing server performance data.

Establishing a Standard User Environment

Because your enterprise may consist of dozens of servers, it is important to establish a common environment for the *oracle* user on each server. The *oracle* user is the owner of all of the Application Server 10*g* software and has full privileges to all command-line utilities. When each server has a common prompt, common aliases, and common shell and editing settings, management is greatly simplified.

In UNIX, the environment is established by the login file. The /etc/passwd file contains the location of the login file and the default shell for the user. The default location for the login file is the default directory for the *oracle* user. The name of the login file depends on the shell specified in the /etc/passwd file. If the default shell is the Korn shell (ksh), the login file is called .profile. If you specify the C shell (csh), your login file is called .cshrc.

The columns in /etc/passwd are separated with a colon (:) and include

- **Username**   In our case, we are interested in the *oracle* user.

- **Password**   This is an encrypted value and is often stored in a shadow file in /etc/shadow.

- **User number**   This is a distinct number for each UNIX user.

- **User group**   The *oracle* user is kept in the dba group.

- **Name**   This is the name of the user.

- **Home directory**   This is the home directory for the *oracle* user, and you will be placed into this directory at login time.

- **Default shell**   This is the shell that will determine the name of your login file.

Here is a sample /etc/passwd file:

```
root> cat /etc/passwd|grep oracle

oracle:KChstVXg:110:20:Oracle9ias software owner:/u01/app/oracle:/bin/ksh
```

Here, the *oracle* user is user ID 110, and the dba group is group 20. The home directory is /u01/app/oracle, and the shell is Korn shell (ksh), indicating that the login file is /u01/app/oracle/.profile. Now that we know the name of the login file, let's examine a standard login file for the *oracle* user.

A Standard Login File for Oracle Users

Here is a sample login file for Korn shell Application Server 10*g* systems. Note that this login file sets all of the PATH and ORACLE_HOME locations, sets default editor and display values, and sets handy alias names.

.profile.ksh

```ksh
#!/bin/ksh
#************************************************************
#  DO NOT customize this .profile script.
#  The directive below will allow to you add customizations
#  to the .kshrc file.  All host-specific profile customizations
#  should be placed in the .kshrc file.
#************************************************************
umask 022

DBABRV=ora; export DBABRV

ORACLE_TERM=vt100; export ORACLE_TERM

TERM=vt100; export TERM

wout=`who am i`

#DISPLAY=`expr "$wout" : ".*(\([0-9]*\.[0-9]*\.[0-9]*\.[0-9]*\))"`
DISPLAY="${DISPLAY}:0"; export DISPLAY

ORAENV_ASK=NO; export ORAENV_ASK

export EDITOR=vi

NLS_LANG='english_united kingdom.we8iso8859p1'; export NLS_LANG

ORA_NLS33=$ORACLE_HOME/ocommon/nls/admin/data; export ORA_NLS33

JAVA_HOME=/usr/local/jre; export JAVA_HOME

ORACLE_HOME=/u01/app/oracle/product/9.2.0; export ORACLE_HOME

PATH=.:$PATH:.;$ORACLE_HOME/dcm/bin/:$ORACLE_HOME/j2ee/home/:$ORACLE_HOME/
ldap/bin/:$ORACLE_HOME/ldap/odi/admin/:$ORACLE_HOME/oca/bin/:$ORACLE_HOME/
opmn/bin/:$ORACLE_HOME/portal/admin/plsql/sso/:$ORACLE_HOME/sso/lib/:$ORACLE_
HOME/uddi/lib/:$ORACLE_HOME/upgrade/:$ORACLE_HOME/wireless/bin/
#************************************************************
# Keyboard
#************************************************************
stty erase ^?
set -o vi


#************************************************************
```

```
# Standard UNIX Prompt
#*******************************************************************
ORACLE_SID=iasdb; export ORACLE_SID
PS1="
`hostname`*\${ORACLE_SID}-\${PWD}
>"
export PS1


#*******************************************************************
# Aliases
#*******************************************************************

# Oracle database aliases
alias alert='tail -100 $DBA/$ORACLE_SID/bdump/alert_$ORACLE_SID.log|more'
alias arch='cd $DBA/$ORACLE_SID/arch'
alias bdump='cd $DBA/$ORACLE_SID/bdump'
alias cdump='cd $DBA/$ORACLE_SID/cdump'
alias pfile-'cd $DBA/$ORACLE_SID/pfile'
alias udump='cd $DBA/$ORACLE_SID/udump'
alias rm='rm -i'
alias sid='env|grep -i sid'
alias admin='cd $DBA/admin'
alias logbook='/u01/app/oracle/admin/$ORACLE_SID/logbook'
# Oracle9iAS aliases
alias dcmlib='$ORACLE_HOME/dcm/bin/'
alias j2eelib='$ORACLE_HOME/j2ee/home/'
alias ldaplib='$ORACLE_HOME/ldap/bin/'
alias odilib='$ORACLE_HOME/ldap/odi/admin/'
alias ocalib='$ORACLE_HOME/oca/bin/'
alias opmnlib='$ORACLE_HOME/opmn/bin/'
alias ssolib='$ORACLE_HOME/portal/admin/plsql/sso/:$ORACLE_HOME/sso/lib/'
alias uddilib='$ORACLE_HOME/uddi/lib/'
alias upgradelib='$ORACLE_HOME/upgrade/'
alias wirelesslib='$ORACLE_HOME/wireless/bin/'
```

Note that the UNIX PS1 variable determines the UNIX prompt. Let's take a closer look.

A Uniform UNIX Prompt
Placing the following code snippet in your *oracle* user login file will give you a standard UNIX prompt that identifies your current server name, the database name your environment is set for (that is, the value of your $ORACLE_SID UNIX variable), and your current working directory. This standard prompt makes it very easy to know where you are when navigating UNIX, and it also ensures that you know where you are located at all times.

unix_prompt.ksh

```
#*******************************************************************
# Standard UNIX Prompt
#*******************************************************************
PS1="
```

```
`hostname`*\${ORACLE_SID}-\${PWD}
>"
```

The best feature of the standard command prompt is that it also places the command prompt on the next line so you can have a full 80 characters to type UNIX commands:

```
cheops*CCPRO-/home/oracle
>pwd

/home/oracle

cheops*CCPRO-/home/oracle
>cd /u01/oradata/CPRO

cheops*CCPRO-/u01/oaradata/CPRO
>
```

Forms Server Monitoring

Oracle has two methods for retrieving Forms Server response time metrics:

- **Forms Server 6*i*** Extract data from OS flat file.
- **Forms Server 9*i*** Extract data from Oracle performance tables.

Oracle Forms Server 6*i* provides a flat file log that contains all of the information required to measure end-to-end Oracle response time. This response time monitoring mechanism can be used for end-user applications using SQL*Forms (Forms Server 6*i*) and Application Server 10*g*. This approach works with any application that uses the Forms Server, including SQL*Forms or web applications.

Using a scripting language, such as Javascript, you can extract details from the Forms Server logs and get a complete breakdown of Oracle response time, including client response time, network response time, database response time, and Forms Server response time (Figure 10-1).

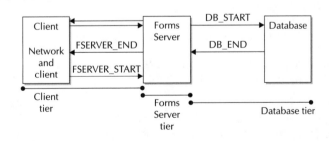

FIGURE 10-1. *Components of Oracle Forms Server response time*

The Forms Server log is a flat file that contains details for all transactions. A sample is shown in the following listing. Note that the statistics are displayed on separate lines, requiring a program to read and summarize the performance data.

```
Forms Runtime Performance Collection Log
File Name: perf_392
Process ID: 392
Client IP: 172.16.1.76:1789
Forms 6.0 (Forms Runtime) Version 6.0.8.14.1 (Production)
PL/SQL Version 8.0.6.3.0 (Production)
Oracle Virtual Graphics System Version 6.0.5.37.0 (Production)
Oracle Multimedia Version 6.0.5.34.0 (Production)
Oracle Tools Integration Version 6.0.8.13.0 (Production)
Oracle Tools Common Area Version 6.0.5.32.1
Oracle CORE Version 4.0.6.0.0 - Production

TSE Startup Time : 43574343
TSE Handshake Duration  : 43574343
##### CTIME STARTS HERE
# C
WINDOW NONAME START START

Opened file: d:\hri1\forms\F_main.fmx

TSE FSERVER_START 0 0 43574828
TSE DBLOGON_START 0 0 43574828
TSE DBLOGON_END 0 0  43575093
Opened file: d:\hri1\forms\F_LOGIN.fmx

TSE FSERVER_END -1  0 43576343
IXPROP_VIEW_OUTERSIZE
IXPROP_VIEW_OUTERSIZE
# 1 - F_LOGIN:DISCLAIMER.DISAGREE_BTN.43577156
WINDOW F_LOGIN DISCLAIMER_WINDOW ACTIVATE 3

TSE FSERVER_START -1 1953 43577156
TSE FSERVER_END -1  0 43577156
##### CTIME STARTS HERE
TSE FSERVER_START -1 1182 43578359
TSE FSERVER_END -1  0 43578359
# 2 - F_LOGIN:DISCLAIMER.DISAGREE_BTN.43578500
CLICK F_LOGIN DISCLAIMER AGREE_BTN 1 MOUSE

IXPROP_VIEW_OUTERSIZE
# 3 - F_LOGIN:CNTL.USER_LOGIN.43578515
WINDOW F_LOGIN DISCLAIMER_WINDOW DEACTIVATE 3

# 4 - F_LOGIN:CNTL.USER_LOGIN.43578515
WINDOW F_LOGIN LOGWINDOW ACTIVATE 3
```

```
TSE FSERVER_START -1 140 43578500
TSE FSERVER_END -1 0 43578515
##### CTIME STARTS HERE
TSE FSERVER_START -1 390 43578921
TSE FSERVER_END -1  0 43578921
TSE FSERVER_START -1 591 43579531
TSE FSERVER_END -1  0 43579531
TSE FSERVER_START -1 1362 43580890
TSE FSERVER_END -1  0 43580890
# 5 - F_LOGIN:CNTL.USER_LOGIN.43582031
VALUE F_LOGIN CNTL USER_LOGIN 1 PLK

# 6 - F_LOGIN:CNTL.USER_LOGIN.43582031
KEY Next_item

##### CTIME STARTS HERE
TSE FSERVER_START -1 1112 43582031
TSE FSERVER_END -1  0 43582031
TSE FSERVER_START -1 981 43583031
TSE FSERVER_END -1  0 43583031
##### CTIME STARTS HERE
TSE FSERVER_START -1 6750 43589796
TSE FSERVER_END -1  0 43589796
# 7 - F_LOGIN:CNTL.USER_PASSWORD.43589890
VALUE F_LOGIN CNTL USER_PASSWORD 1 BLESSED

# 8 - F_LOGIN:CNTL.USER_PASSWORD.43589890
CLICK F_LOGIN CNTL PB_LOGIN 1 MOUSE

Opened file: d:\hri1\forms\F_DIARY.fmx

TSE FSERVER_START -1 80 43589890
TSE DB_START 0 0 43589968
TSE DB_END 0 0  43589968
TSE DB_START 0 0 43590046
TSE DB_END 0 0  43590250
TSE FSERVER_END -1  0 43591031
```

As you can see, the Forms Server log produces transaction-level response time details for all transactions. The Forms Server creates a log for each connection and logs timing marks as the transaction enters and exits the Forms Server. Hence, this log file can get very large on highly active systems. Once your program gathers the data and stores the summaries into an Oracle table, you may want to delete the log to keep the disk from becoming full. While the programmatic details are beyond the scope of this text, you can write a summarization program using C, Perl, or Java.

Oracle Forms Server 6*i* contains a Perl script to analyze a single performance log, which is very useful during development; however, it does not scale to provide performance statistics for a production system. By automating the analysis for the entire performance log over an extended period, you can produce extensive statistics of actual system performance.

The Forms Server tier metric measures the time spent inside the Forms Server itself, and the database tier is the time spent in the database. All times are recorded as the program transits to and from the Forms Server, so network latency is included in the database tier time for the connection to the database, and is included in the network/client tier's time for the connection between the client and the Forms Server. The program should store the sums as each event occurs and with the transition between different forms. Other statistics can also be collected, such as number of database calls per form or event. You can use these to determine which forms and which events within each form are causing performance problems and thus focus your performance tuning efforts.

NOTE
Writing custom log analysis programs is a critical part of tuning because the format of Application Server 10g logs does not lend itself to easy time-based analysis.

Once you write a simple program to read the information provided by Forms Server, you can collect the response time in the database, Forms Server client, and network.

Summarizing Forms Server Log Information

The collected data is stored in an Oracle table with the code shown in the following listing. This is the same approach that you will use to capture and analyze other Application Server 10*g* logs, so the principles in this section will apply to all areas of performance collection.

```
create table FormStats (
        FORM_ID             VARCHAR2(120),
        EVENT               VARCHAR2(120),
        FSERVER_TIME        NUMBER,
        DBASE_TIME          NUMBER,
        NWORK_TIME          NUMBER,
        CLIENT_TIME         NUMBER,
        DATE                DATE)
;
```

The FormStats table contains the following columns, which can be easily populated by a procedural program:

- **A unique form ID**   This is unique to each transaction and corresponds to the form's name in the Forms Server. Unfortunately, you cannot capture the exact form name and track response time by it.

- **The event**   This is a response process on the form. These are named events (for example, Add New Item) and correspond to buttons on the form.

- **Forms Server response time**   You can monitor the response time within the Forms Server.

- **Database response time**   You can monitor the total time the transaction spent inside the Oracle database.

■ **Network response time**   You can monitor the time in the network and in the client processing information, but not the time spent interacting with the user.

■ **Client response time**   You can monitor the response time within the client layer.

■ **Date**   This is the exact date that the transaction was invoked.

You can populate the file with a program snippet (usually written in Perl or Java) to process the Forms Server log, one line at a time; extract the event and form name; and store the data in your table. The pseudocode in the following listing shows the basic form of the code snippet.

```
while (((str = in.readLine()) != null)
  if (str.startsWith("TSE")) { Add time to appropriate tier}
 if (str.startsWith("# "))
    { Extract Event and Form Name;
      Load record into database;
      Clear times;
    }
}
```

This task is normally scheduled via dbms_job or cron to run daily and then reinitialize the Forms Server log file. Once collected, you can use SQL to do easy reporting from your FormStats table. For example, the following code finds the number of events with database access time greater than four seconds:

```
SELECT
    COUNT(*)
FROM FormStats
  WHERE ((DBASE_TIME)/1000) > 4
  AND DATE >= SYSDATE-1
  AND DATE <= SYSDATE
;
```

You can also use the data in the FormStats table to locate those forms with the greatest total response time. The next example finds the form with the greatest time in the Forms Server:

```
SELECT
    form_id,
    fserver_time
FROM
    FormStats
Where
    fserver = (SELECT MAX(fserver) FROM FormStat)
;
```

Once extracted and summarized, this response time data can be easily pasted into a spreadsheet and plotted to produce valuable trend reports. Figure 10-2 shows a report produced by using the Excel Chart Wizard. For details on these techniques, see *Oracle9i High-Performance Tuning with STATSPACK* by Burleson (McGraw-Hill/Osborne, 2002).

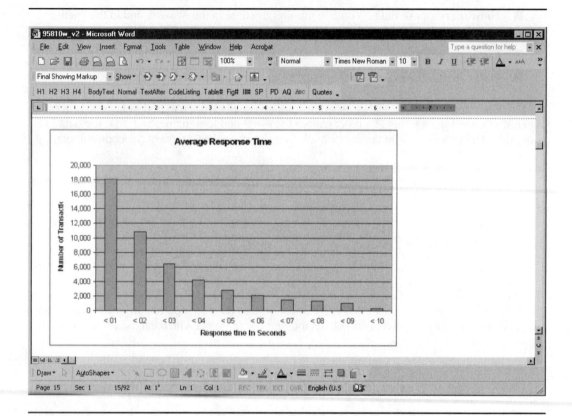

FIGURE 10-2. *Forms Server aggregation of total application response time*

You can also use this data to show average total response time and the components of total response time for the Forms application (Figure 10-3). As you can see, the Forms Server data can be aggregated to provide specific response time information. This is useful for shops that have Service Level Agreements guaranteeing satisfactory response time for all transactions.

Transaction-Level Response Time Monitoring

The data in the Forms Server file can also be used to get the average response time for all Forms Server transactions. In Figure 10-4, we have produced a top-ten report showing the slowest transactions in the system.

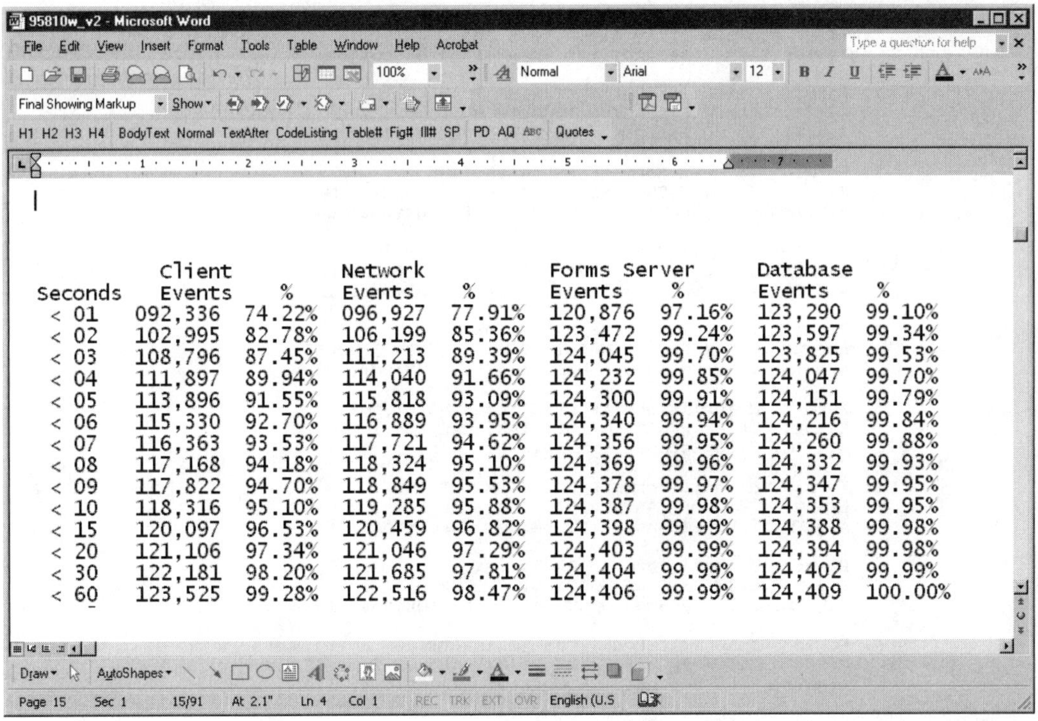

```
95810w_v2 - Microsoft Word                                                          _□×
File  Edit  View  Insert  Format  Tools  Table  Window  Help  Acrobat        Type a question for help  ▾ ×
□ ☞ ☐  ☐ ☐ ☐ ☐  ▪ ▾ ◦ ▾  ▦ ☐ ☐  100%  ▾  »  ⏷ Normal  ▾ Arial  ▾ 12 ▾  B I U 堇 堇 A ▾ ᴬᴬ  »
Final Showing Markup  ▾ Show ▾  ⏷ ⏷ ⏷ ▾ ⏷ ▾  ☐ ▾ ☐ ☐ .              ☑ ☑ .
H1 H2 H3 H4  BodyText Normal TextAfter CodeListing Table# Fig# Ill# SP  PD AQ Abc  Quotes
```

	Client		Network		Forms Server		Database	
Seconds	Events	%	Events	%	Events	%	Events	%
< 01	092,336	74.22%	096,927	77.91%	120,876	97.16%	123,290	99.10%
< 02	102,995	82.78%	106,199	85.36%	123,472	99.24%	123,597	99.34%
< 03	108,796	87.45%	111,213	89.39%	124,045	99.70%	123,825	99.53%
< 04	111,897	89.94%	114,040	91.66%	124,232	99.85%	124,047	99.70%
< 05	113,896	91.55%	115,818	93.09%	124,300	99.91%	124,151	99.79%
< 06	115,330	92.70%	116,889	93.95%	124,340	99.94%	124,216	99.84%
< 07	116,363	93.53%	117,721	94.62%	124,356	99.95%	124,260	99.88%
< 08	117,168	94.18%	118,324	95.10%	124,369	99.96%	124,332	99.93%
< 09	117,822	94.70%	118,849	95.53%	124,378	99.97%	124,347	99.95%
< 10	118,316	95.10%	119,285	95.88%	124,387	99.98%	124,353	99.95%
< 15	120,097	96.53%	120,459	96.82%	124,398	99.99%	124,388	99.98%
< 20	121,106	97.34%	121,046	97.29%	124,403	99.99%	124,394	99.98%
< 30	122,181	98.20%	121,685	97.81%	124,404	99.99%	124,402	99.99%
< 60	123,525	99.28%	122,516	98.47%	124,406	99.99%	124,409	100.00%

```
Draw ▾ ⏷  AutoShapes ▾ \ ↘ □ ○ ☐ ◢ ⌖ ☐ ☐ ◇ ▾ ◢ ▾ A ▾ ≡ ≡ ⇄ ☐ ☐ .
Page 15  Sec 1      15/91    At 2.1"   Ln 4   Col 1    REC TRK EXT OVR  English (U.S  ☐☑
```

FIGURE 10-3. *Breakdown of response time components*

Component Response Time Breakdown

The Forms Server data also provides details about the amount of time spent in the Forms Server and the amount of time spent in the back-end Oracle database (Figure 10-5). This information can provide critical clues about the best place to start tuning Forms Server transactions.

While the complete coding details are beyond the scope of this text, this gives you a basic understanding of the concepts involved in extracting the raw data from the Forms Server log file and providing accurate response time reports.

```
Top 10 Forms and Events that use the most Average Database Time
  with a minimum of 10 executions and
  greater than 2 seconds for an average execution.

1. Form:    d:\hri1\forms\F_STAGING_TO_OLTP.fmx
   Event:   CLICK F_STAGING_TO_OLTP BUTTONS SEARCH 1 MOUSE
   Avg Tm: 13.00 Seconds.  Number of Executions: 28

2. Form:    d:\hri1\forms\F_END_USER.fmx
   Event:   CLICK F_END_USER BUTTONS STD_QUERY 1 MOUSE
   Avg Tm: 4.00 Seconds.  Number of Executions: 14

3. Form:    d:\hri1\forms\F_STAGING_TO_OLTP.fmx
   Event:   SCROLL F_STAGING_TO_OLTP STAGE_EVENT UP ONE
   Avg Tm: 4.00 Seconds.  Number of Executions: 13

4. Form:    d:\hri1\forms\F_PARTY.fmx
   Event:   CLICK F_CASE_MAINT DIARY CAL_LOV 1 MOUSE
   Avg Tm: 3.00 Seconds.  Number of Executions: 68

5. Form:    d:\hri1\forms\F_EVENT_CASE_MAINT.fmx
   Event:   CLICK F_CASE_MAINT DIARY CAL_LOV 1 MOUSE
   Avg Tm: 3.00 Seconds.  Number of Executions: 13

6. Form:    d:\hri1\forms\F_DOCACT_MAINT.fmx
   Event:   CLICK F_CASE_MAINT DIARY CAL_LOV 1 MOUSE
   Avg Tm: 2.00 Seconds.  Number of Executions: 58

7. Form:    d:\hri1\forms\F_PARTY.fmx
   Event:   CLICK F_CASE_MAINT DIARY DUE_DATE 1
   Avg Tm: 2.00 Seconds.  Number of Executions: 10

8. Form:    d:\hri1\forms\f_case_maint.fmx
   Event:   CLICK F_CASE_MAINT DIARY CAL_LOV 1 MOUSE
   Avg Tm: 2.00 Seconds.  Number of Executions: 150

9. Form:    d:\hri1\forms\F_PARTY.fmx
   Event:   CLICK F_PARTY BUTTONS SAVE_EXIT 1 MOUSE
   Avg Tm: 2.00 Seconds.  Number of Executions: 280

10. Form:   d:\hri1\forms\f_case_maint.fmx
   Event:   ALERT xNo
   Avg Tm: 2.00 Seconds.  Number of Executions: 11
```

FIGURE 10-4. *Oracle Forms Server top-ten report*

Monitoring and Load-Balancing the Oracle HTTP Server(OHS)

The HTTP Server is an important part of the Application Server 10g architecture because a delay at this level will delay initial connection to your system and also cause delays in the generation and dispatch of outgoing HTML and XML documents. As noted in Chapter 1, connection to OHS requires several round-trips while establishing connectivity (Figure 10-6).

Because OHS is used at least twice during every web transaction, you must be able to identify the components of processing and find a way to track each component process. The next sections examine the common tools to help you do this.

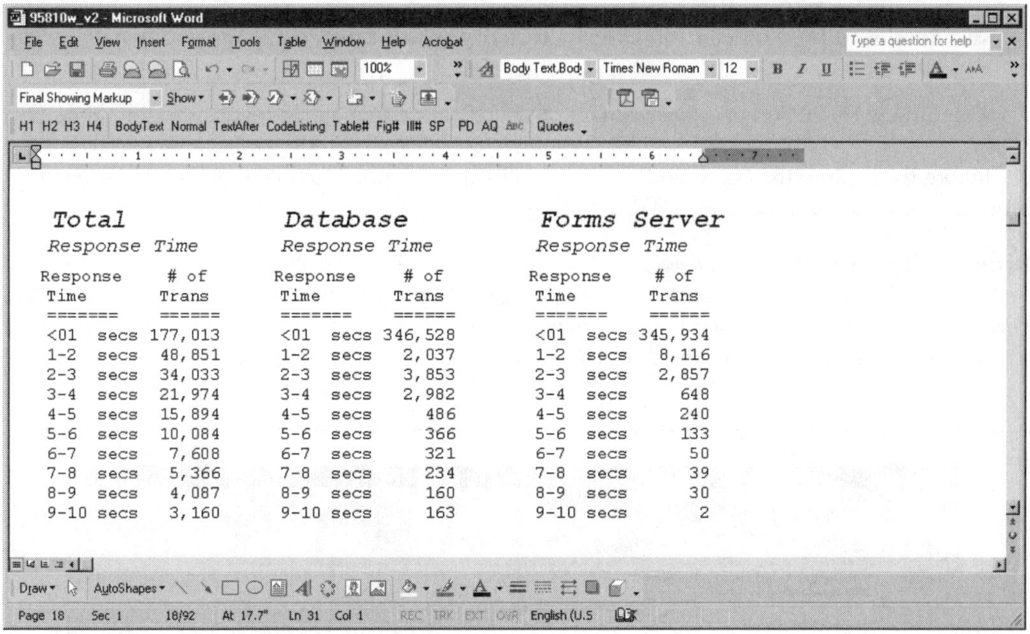

```
95810w_v2 - Microsoft Word                                                    _ □ ×
File   Edit   View   Insert   Format   Tools   Table   Window   Help   Acrobat          Type a question for help   ▾ ×
□ ☞ ◉  ◉ ◈ ◉ ◘  ◔ ▾ ◌ ▾  ▣ ▭ ▦  100%  ▾    �  Body Text,Bod ▾  Times New Roman ▾  12  ▾   B  I  U  ▤ ▦ ◈  ▲ ▾ ᴬᴬᴬ  »
Final Showing Markup  ▾ Show ▾  ◈ ◈ ◿ ▾ ◈ ▾  ◻ ▾  ◈ ◉ ▾               ▣ ▣ ▾
H1 H2 H3 H4  BodyText Normal TextAfter CodeListing Table# Fig# Ill# SP  PD AQ Aᵇᶜ  Quotes ▾
```

	Total Response Time			Database Response Time			Forms Server Response Time	
Response Time		# of Trans	Response Time		# of Trans	Response Time		# of Trans
=======		======	=======		======	=======		======
<01	secs	177,013	<01	secs	346,528	<01	secs	345,934
1-2	secs	48,851	1-2	secs	2,037	1-2	secs	8,116
2-3	secs	34,033	2-3	secs	3,853	2-3	secs	2,857
3-4	secs	21,974	3-4	secs	2,982	3-4	secs	648
4-5	secs	15,894	4-5	secs	486	4-5	secs	240
5-6	secs	10,084	5-6	secs	366	5-6	secs	133
6-7	secs	7,608	6-7	secs	321	6-7	secs	50
7-8	secs	5,366	7-8	secs	234	7-8	secs	39
8-9	secs	4,087	8-9	secs	160	8-9	secs	30
9-10	secs	3,160	9-10	secs	163	9-10	secs	2

```
Draw ▾  ⌖  AutoShapes ▾  ╲  ╲ □ ○ ▨ ◢ ⬙ ◙ ◙ ◙  ◇ ▾ ◢ ▾ ▲ ▾ ▦ ▥ ▤ ◼ ☐ .
Page 18   Sec 1      18/92    At 17.7"   Ln 31  Col 1     REC TRK EXT OVR  English (U.S  ◻⌖
```

FIGURE 10-5. *Forms Server details report*

Using dmstool

The Dynamic Monitoring Service (DMS) utility provides a command-line program, dmstool, that is used to display elapsed-time performance metrics. You use dmstool to view metrics on several Application Server 10*g* components:

■ **OC4J**   dmstool can measure the time required to parse incoming requests and the total free RAM in the JVM.

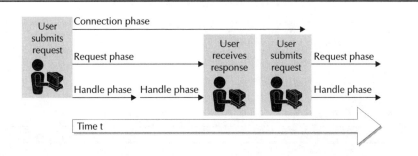

FIGURE 10-6. *OHS entry procedure*

- **Portal** Important Portal metrics can be easily displayed.
- **Servlet code** You can add DMS metrics of any Java code to capture additional statistics.
- **Oracle HTTP Server** dmstool can measure the current active requests in the OHS.

Before we explore the command syntax for dmstool, we need to note that you can use your browser to quickly look at detailed DMS statistics.

Browser-Based Statistics Viewing

You can see the raw dmstool statistics by reviewing the httpd.conf file and finding the URL for the DMS dump file. Invoking the URL will display the raw DMS data in your browser. In Figure 10-7 we issued the http://appsvr.localdomain.com:7778/dms0 URL to see the DMS data.

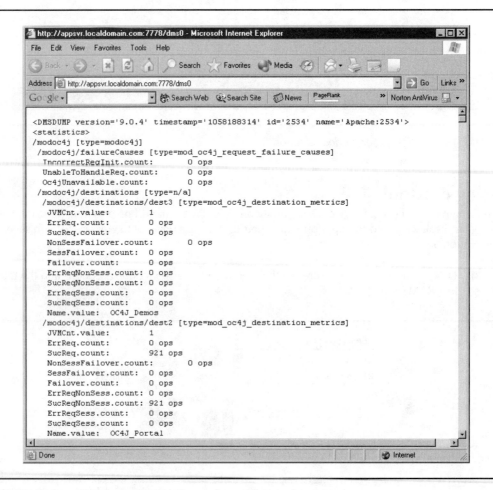

FIGURE 10-7. *Displaying the DMS raw data with your browser*

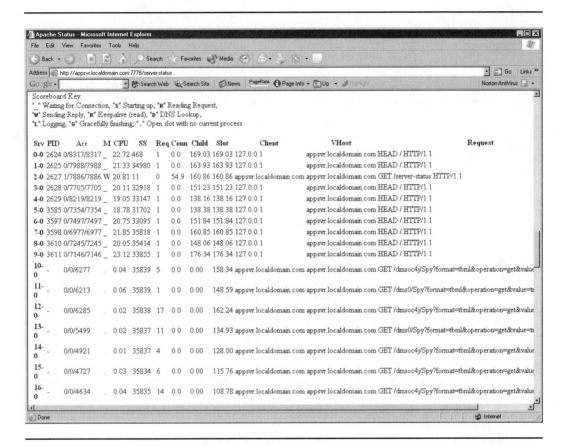

FIGURE 10-8. *Displaying the DMS raw data about the Apache server*

You can also use URL-based queries to locate server performance data. In Figure 10-8 we invoked the http://appsvr.localdomain.com:7778/server-status URL to see details on the Apache server status.

Extending DMS for Java Code

As we have noted, you can capture your own DMS diagnostics. Let's look at how you can add these metrics to a servlet. First, in the following listing, we print "This is a test."

```java
import java.io.*;
import javax.servlet.*;
import javax.servlet.http.*;

public class  Test  extends HttpServlet
{
  public void doGet(HttpServletRequest request,   HttpServletResponse response
)
    throws ServletException, IOException
```

```
      {
        response.getWriter().println("This is a Test. " );
      }
    }
```

Now we take this code and add a DMS metric by importing the Oracle DMS instrument library and adding a display message each time the servlet is executed, as shown in the following listing:

```
import java.io.*;
import javax.servlet.*;
import javax.servlet.http.*;
import oracle.dms.instrument.*;

public class  TestA  extends HttpServlet
{
  public void doGet(HttpServletRequest request,   HttpServletResponse response
)
    throws ServletException, IOException
    {
        Event  beginAccess  = Event.create("/ oracle / TestA / dms ",
                            " TestA Write Succeded");
res.getWriter().println(" This is a test of Test. ");
    begin Access.occurred();
    }
}
```

Now let's take a close look at issuing native dmstool commands to extract Application Server 10*g* performance data.

Using dmstool Commands

When using the dmstool list option (-l), you will generate a list of over 300 monitoring metrics for Application Server 10*g*. In the next example, we constrain the dmstool output to only those lines that contain the "completed" string:

```
#!/bin/ksh

PATH=$PATH:/home/oracle/oraportal904/bin
export PATH

dmstool -l |grep completed
```

The output of this script (shown in the following listing) shows all of the available metrics containing the word "completed." We will use this list as input to a more detailed dmstool command in the next step.

```
/appsvr.lcldm.com/OC4J:3303:6004/oc4j/default/WEBs/parseRequest.completed
/appsvr.lcldm.com/OC4J:3303:6004/oc4j/default/WEBs/processRequest.completed
/appsvr.lcldm.com/OC4J:3303:6004/oc4j/default/WEBs/resolveContext.completed
/appsvr.lcldm.com/OC4J:3303:6004/oc4j/portal/WEBs/parseRequest.completed
/appsvr.lcldm.com/OC4J:3303:6004/oc4j/portal/WEBs/processRequest.completed
/appsvr.lcldm.com/OC4J:3303:6004/oc4j/portal/WEBs/resolveContext.completed
/appsvr.lcldm.com/OC4J:3303:6004/oc4j/syndserver/WEBs/parseRequest.completed
```

```
/appsvr.lcldm.com/OC4J:3303:6004/oc4j/syndserver/WEBs/processRequest.completed
/appsvr.lcldm.com/OC4J:3303:6004/oc4j/syndserver/WEBs/resolveContext.completed
```

NOTE
*The Application Server 10g parameters are generally specified in
"camel" notation. In this convention, the words are concatenated,
and all words after the first are capitalized, creating the "humps" that
give the notation its name.*

We can use this listing of completed operations to get counts of the total operations over
a specific period. Let's use this list as input parameters for more advanced dmstool commands.

Summarizing dmstool Data by Time Intervals

You can use the dmstool with the interval option (-i) and the collection option (-c). The dmstool
command here specifies the collection of 100 sets of data at 60-second intervals:

```
#!/bin/ksh
PATH=$PATH:/home/oracle/oraportal904/bin
export PATH

dmstool -i 60 -c 100 \
/appsvr.localdomain.com/Apache:2534:6004/Apache/handle.completed    \
/appsvr.localdomain.com/Apache:2534:6004/Apache/request.completed   \
/appsvr.localdomain.com/Apache:2534:6004/Apache/handle.completed    \
/appsvr.localdomain.com/Apache:2534:6004/Apache/request.completed  > t1.lst
```

The output from this script is shown in the following listing. You see the cumulative number
of operations, displayed every minute, for each handle, request, and completion operation.

```
Sun Jul 13 20:19:43 MDT 2003

/appsvr.localdomain.com/Apache:2534:6004/Apache/handle.completed     240320 ops
/appsvr.localdomain.com/Apache:2534:6004/Apache/request.completed    146504 ops
/appsvr.localdomain.com/Apache:2534:6004/Apache/connection.completed 56908 ops

Sun Jul 13 20:20:43 MDT 2003

/appsvr.localdomain.com/Apache:2534:6004/Apache/handle.completed     240474 ops
/appsvr.localdomain.com/Apache:2534:6004/Apache/request.completed    146598 ops
/appsvr.localdomain.com/Apache:2534:6004/Apache/connection.completed 56948 ops

Sun Jul 13 20:21:43 MDT 2003

/appsvr.localdomain.com/Apache:2534:6004/Apache/handle.completed     240668 ops
/appsvr.localdomain.com/Apache:2534:6004/Apache/request.completed    146732 ops
/appsvr.localdomain.com/Apache:2534:6004/Apache/connection.completed 56978 ops
```

```
Sun Jul 13 20:22:43 MDT 2003

/appsvr.localdomain.com/Apache:2534:6004/Apache/handle.completed      240825 ops
/appsvr.localdomain.com/Apache:2534:6004/Apache/request.completed     146829 ops
/appsvr.localdomain.com/Apache:2534:6004/Apache/connection.completed 57028 ops
```

By itself, this output does not show the marginal changes between time periods, but you can either write a program or paste the output into an Excel spreadsheet and use the Chart Wizard to plot the changes. Figure 10-9 shows a sample of the time-based changes to the three HTTP Server operation counts.

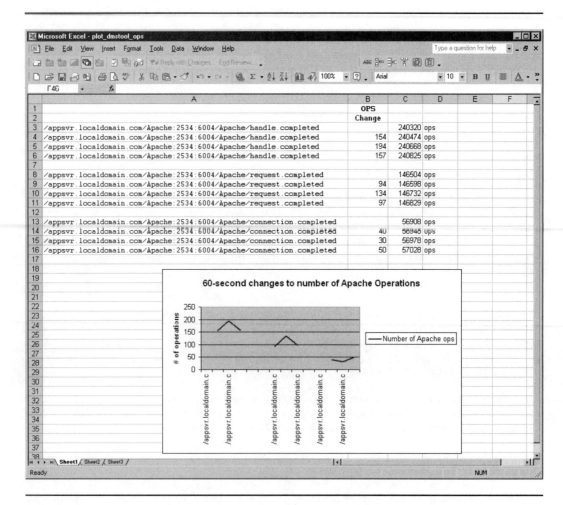

FIGURE 10-9. *Plotting dmstool output with Excel*

Getting Dump Details from dmstool

By using the -dump option of dmstool, you can collect all metrics from an Application Server 10*g* instance. Most administrators use a small shell script like the one shown here and schedule it to run every hour:

```ksh
#!/bin/ksh

PATH=$PATH:/home/oracle/oraportal904/bin
export PATH

dmstool -dump >> dumparch.lst
```

You can use the -dump option to store dmstool performance metrics for later analysis, as shown in the following listing. However, note that the -dump option does not display the metrics in an easy-to-summarize format, and a code snippet is required to gather the information and place it inside a metadata table.

```
   /DMS-Internal/Measurement [type=n/a]
   createNoun.count:      136        ops
   createSensor.count:    591        ops
   destroyNoun.count:     4          ops
   destroySensor.count: 25           ops
   lastTreeNodeID.value:             0
   sampleMetric.count:    5531850 ops
   sensorWeight.value:    5
   treeNodes.maxValue:    1635.0
   treeNodes.value:       1635
/JDBC/OracleConnectionCacheImpl [type=JDBC_ConnectionSource]
   CacheFreeSize.count: 18           ops
   CacheFreeSize.maxValue:      5.0         connections
   CacheFreeSize.minValue:      0.0         connections
   CacheFreeSize.value: 2       connections
   CacheGetConnection.active:   0          threads
   CacheGetConnection.avg:      0.42857142857142855        msecs
   CacheGetConnection.completed:        7          ops
   CacheGetConnection.maxTime: 1          msecs
   CacheGetConnection.minTime: 0          msecs
   CacheGetConnection.time:     3          msecs
   CacheHit.count:        7          ops
   CacheMiss.count:       2          ops
   CacheSize.count:       3          ops
   CacheSize.maxValue:    5.0        connections
   CacheSize.minValue:    1.0        connections
   CacheSize.value:       1          connections
```

While this listing may be cumbersome, it is a trivial matter to write a program to parse and summarize this output, storing the metrics inside special iasdb tables. For details on this technique, see the earlier discussion on Forms Server performance analysis.

Next let's look at using dmstool to gather load-balancing performance information on your Oracle HTTP Servers.

Using dmstool to Monitor and Load-Balance Oracle HTTP Servers

You can use the dmstool command with the -table ohs_server option to gather detailed information about the performance of all the components of OHS. Table 10-1 shows the most important metrics. Note that "usecs" represents microseconds (millionths of a second).

Most administrators automate this collection task by placing the dmstool command inside a shell script and directing the output to a flat file for later analysis. For example:

```
#!/bin/ksh

PATH=$PATH:/home/oracle/oraportal904/bin
export PATH

dmstool -table ohs_server >> ohs.1st
```

Metric	Description	Unit
handle.maxTime	Maximum time spent in module handler	usecs
handle.minTime	Minimum time spent in module handler	usecs
handle.avg	Average time spent in module handler	usecs
handle.active	Child servers currently in the handle processing phase	threads
handle.time	Total time spent in module handler	usecs
handle.completed	Number of times the handle processing phase has completed	ops
request.maxTime	Maximum time required to service an HTTP request	usecs
request.minTime	Minimum time required to service an HTTP request	usecs
request.avg	Average time required to service an HTTP request	usecs
request.active	Child servers currently in the request processing phase	threads
request.time	Total time required to service HTTP requests	usecs
request.completed	Number of HTTP requests completed	ops
connection.maxTime	Maximum time spent servicing any HTTP connection	usecs
connection.minTime	Minimum time spent servicing any HTTP connection	usecs
connection.avg	Average time spent servicing HTTP connections	usecs
connection.active	Number of connections currently open	threads
connection.time	Total time spent servicing HTTP connections	usecs

TABLE 10-1. *Metrics from the dmstool ohs_server Command*

The following listing shows a small sample of the output from this script. The output is voluminous because it performs a snapshot of the values every ten seconds and provides details on the number of operations (ops) and timing information on all OHS components.

```
Sun Jul 13 21:01:45 MDT 2003


----------
ohs_server
----------
busyChildren.value:         16
childFinish.count:          24703     ops
childStart.count:           24748     ops
connection.active:          24        threads
connection.avg: 116999118             usecs
connection.completed:       58559     ops
connection.maxTime:         120275397680      usecs
connection.minTime:         1437      usecs
connection.time:            6851351400020     usecs
error.count:      138       ops
get.count:        150940    ops
handle.active:    1         threads
handle.avg:       8620      usecs
handle.completed:           247278    ops
handle.maxTime: 32791802              usecs
handle.minTime: 2         usecs
handle.time:      2131602896          usecs
internalRedirect.count: 7650          ops
lastConfigChange.value: 1057965990
numChildren.value:          44
numMods.value:    0
post.count:       2         ops
readyChildren.value:        27
request.active: 1           threads
request.avg:      15321     usecs
request.completed:          150942    ops
request.maxTime:            32792567          usecs
request.minTime:            533       usecs
request.time:     2312728152          usecs
responseSize.value:         1622607150
Host:     appsvr
Name:     Apache
Parent: /
Process:          Apache:2534:6004
```

The details on OHS child server processes are the most useful part of the ohs_server listing. The values for the child servers are specified in the httpd.conf file by the MaxSpareServers and MinSpareServers parameters, and OHS will create and destroy child server processes based on the volume of incoming requests. It is valuable to know the number of child servers in use and the number of child servers that are processing HTTP requests.

Referring to the bold lines of the preceding listing, notice that numChildren.value is 43, indicating that there are 43 child servers active. Of these 43 servers, busyChildren.value is 16, indicating that there are currently 27 child servers ready to accept work, as verified by the readyChildren.value metric. Notice also that the childStart.count is 24,748, showing the number of invocations of child processes since startup. The most important of these metrics is request.avg, which shows that the average time spent in the HTTP Server is 15,321 milliseconds, or about one-tenth of a second for connection.active = 24 transactions. Taken together, these metrics give you a good idea about the volume of transactions experienced on each HTTP Server.

Remember, when the demand on the HTTP Server exceeds the number of child servers defined in the httpd.conf parameter file, OHS will spawn more child processes, but it is a good idea to determine the peak load for each server and perform load balancing from the Web Cache to ensure that no single server becomes overloaded.

Now that you see the concept, let's expand on it and write a short script to filter the voluminous statistics and extract information on active requests and the status of the child processes.

extract_ohs_time_series.ksh

```
#!/bin/ksh

PATH=$PATH:/home/oracle/oraportal904/bin
export PATH

dmstool -table ohs_server > ohs.lst

cat ohs.lst|grep connection.active     > con_active.lst
cat ohs.lst|grep request.active        > req_active.lst
cat ohs.lst|grep busyChildren.value    > busy_child.lst
cat ohs.lst|grep readyChildren.value   > readyChild.lst
cat ohs.lst|grep numChildren.value     > det.lst
```

From extracting and plotting the data in these files (Excel's Chart Wizard works great), you should carefully monitor the volume of transactions (connection.active) and the average response time (request.avg) to determine the threshold where performance drops. In the example in Figure 10-10, the server becomes overwhelmed (usually due to a RAM shortage and the resulting paging), and performance declines sharply, after 50 active connections. Once this threshold is identified, you can create enough new HTTP Servers to ensure that no server exceeds this threshold.

NOTE
Charts like the one shown in Figure 10-10 are critical to OHS load balancing. Recall from previous chapters, the Web Cache performs automatic load balancing between the active HTTP Servers. However, as an administrator, you can keep a pool of servers on standby with Web Cache and OHS installed on them and add them to the architecture as needed.

Again, most administrators will collect this information on a scheduled basis and write programs to gather summary information to store in iasdb extension tables. This builds the

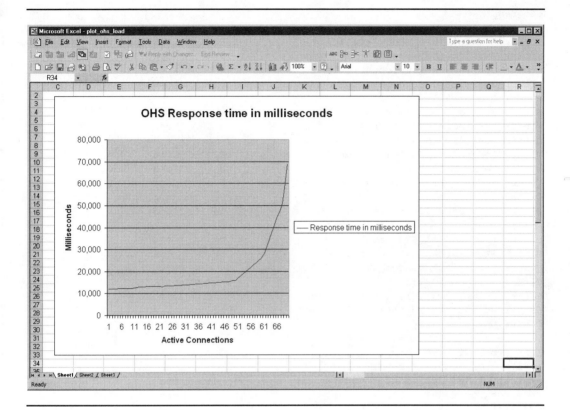

FIGURE 10-10.   *Transaction levels and OHS average response time*

framework for time-series analysis of this important performance data. Next let's look at using dmstool to show statistics for active requests.

Tracking Errors with dmstool

The dmstool utility is also useful for tracking important internal errors within OHS. In the following example, we use dmstool with the ohs_responses argument to see detailed error information.

```ksh
#!/bin/ksh

PATH=$PATH:/home/oracle/oraportal904/bin
export PATH

dmstool -table ohs_responses > resp.lst
```

The following listing shows sample output of all OHS errors, reported in ten-minute intervals.

```
Mon Jul 14 14:56:22 MDT 2003

-------------
```

```
ohs_responses
-------------
CltErr_Authorization_Required_401.count:          0         ops
CltErr_BadRange_416.count:                        0         ops
CltErr_Bad_Request_400.count:                     0         ops
CltErr_Conflict_409.count:                        0         ops
CltErr_ExpectFailed_417.count:                    0         ops
CltErr_Failed_Dependency_424.count:               0         ops
CltErr_Forbidden_403.count:                       0         ops
CltErr_Gone_410.count:                            0         ops
CltErr_LengthRequired_411.count:                  0         ops
CltErr_Locked_423.count:                          0         ops
CltErr_Method_Not_Allowed_405.count:              0         ops
CltErr_Not_Acceptable_406.count:                  0         ops
CltErr_Not_Found_404.count:                      14         ops
CltErr_Payment_Required_402.count:                0         ops
CltErr_PreCondFail_412.count:                     0         ops
CltErr_ProxyAuthReq_407.count:                    0         ops
CltErr_ReqEntityTooLarge_413.count:               0         ops
CltErr_Timeout_408.count:                         0         ops
CltErr_URITooLarge_414.count:                     0         ops
CltErr_Unprocessable_Entity_422.count:            0         ops
CltErr_UnsuppMediaType_415.count:                 0         ops
Info_Continue_100.count:                          0         ops
Info_Processing_102.count:                        0         ops
Info_ProtoSwitch_101.count:                       0         ops
Redirect_Found_302.count:                      1046         ops
Redirect_Moved_301.count:                         0         ops
Redirect_MultiChoice_300.count:                   0         ops
Redirect_NotModified_304.count:                   0         ops
Redirect_SeeOther_303.count:                      0         ops
Redirect_Temporary_307.count:                     0         ops
Redirect_UseProxy_305.count:                      0         ops
Success_Accepted_202.count:                       0         ops
Success_Created_201.count:                        0         ops
Success_Multi-Status_207.count:                   0         ops
Success_NoContent_204.count:                      0         ops
Success_NonAuthInfo_203.count:                    0         ops
Success_OK_200.count:                        173910         ops
Success_PartialContent_206.count:                 0         ops
Success_ResetContent_205.count:                   0         ops
SvrErr_BadGateway_502.count:                      0         ops
SvrErr_GtwyTimeout_504.count:                     0         ops
SvrErr_Insufficient_Storage_507.count:            0         ops
SvrErr_InternalError_500.count:                 155         ops
SvrErr_NotImplemented_501.count:                  0         ops
SvrErr_Not_Extended_510.count:                    0         ops
SvrErr_SvcUnavail_503.count:                      0         ops
SvrErr_Variant_Also_Negotiates_506.count:         0         ops
SvrErr_VersionNotSupp_505.count:                  0         ops
```

```
Host:    appsvr
Name:    Responses
Parent: /Apache
Process:        Apache:2534:6004
ohs_server:     Apache
```

The most common error is the "404 Not Found" message when an invalid URL is encountered. Most administrators write automated scripts to review these logs and report on the important internal errors such as the SvrErr_InternalError_500.count error line. For example:

```ksh
#!/bin/ksh

PATH=$PATH:/home/oracle/oraportal904/bin
export PATH

dmstool -table ohs_responses|grep SvrErr_InternalError_500.count|cut -d' ' -f1
```

Here you can get the numerical lists of the internal errors at ten-minute intervals. When you see a large number of internal errors, you will want to check the OHS error_log file to see the URL that is causing the internal error. This output can be easily charted and graphed for time-series analysis. An example is shown here:

```
34
1
1
5
61
77
12
3
```

Capturing Detailed Module Performance Data in OHS

The dmstool interface also allows you to gather drill-down details for all modules within OHS. The default OHS installation includes the modules listed in Table 10-2, and you can get detailed performance values on each of these components.

While each of these modules serves important functions, there are some that are especially noteworthy, namely, http_core.c and mod_oc4j.c. We will take a close look at these in just a minute.

Here is a small script to generate the performance details for each module:

```ksh
#!/bin/ksh

PATH=$PATH:/home/oracle/oraportal904/bin
export PATH

dmstool -table ohs_module -c 1
```

http_core.c	mod_access.c	mod_actions.c	mod_alias.c
mod_asis.c	mod_auth.c	mod_auth_anon.c	mod_auth_dbm.c
mod_autoindex.c	mod_cern_meta.c	mod_cgi.c	mod_dav.c
mod_define.c	mod_digest.c	mod_dir.c	mod_dms.c
mod_env.c	mod_example.c	mod_expires.c	mod_fastcgi.c
mod_headers.c	mod_imap.c	mod_include.c	mod_info.c
mod_log_agent.c	mod_log_config.c	mod_log_referer.c	mod_mime.c
mod_mime_magic.c	mod_mmap_static.c	mod_negotiation.c	**mod_oc4j.c**
mod_onsint.c	mod_ossl.c	mod_osso.c	mod_perl.c
mod_plsql.c	mod_proxy.c	mod_rewrite.c	mod_setenvif.c
mod_so.c	mod_speling.c	mod_status.c	mod_unique_id.c
mod_userdir.c	mod_usertrack.c	mod_vhost_alias.c	mod_wchandshake.c

TABLE 10-2. *Default Modules Within the Oracle HTTP Server*

This gives you a huge listing showing a verbose record of detailed performance metrics for all OHS processes. In the following listing, you see the details for the http_core.c and the mod_oc4j.c OHS processes.

```
Name: mod_oc4jc
Parent: /Apache/Modules
Process:       Apache:2534:6004
ohs_server:    Apache

decline.count:    13487    ops
handle.active:    0        threads
handle.avg:       3        usecs
handle.completed: 13487    ops
handle.maxTime: 8          usecs
handle.minTime: 2          usecs
handle.time:    43710      usecs

Host:    appsvr
Name:    http_core.c
Parent: /Apache/Modules
Process:       Apache:2534:6004
ohs_server:    Apache

decline.count:    0        ops
handle.active:    0        threads
handle.avg:       0        usecs
handle.completed: 0        ops
```

```
handle.maxTime:  0         usecs
handle.minTime:  0         usecs
handle.time:     0         usecs
  . . .
```

This listing shows execution time details for the mod_oc4j.c and http_core.c modules, including the number of executions (handle.completed), the max time, min time, and average time for execution in milliseconds. The most important metric is the handle.avg statistic because it shows the average time for execution. Let's see why these are important modules:

- **http_core.c**   This module handles every request for static pages in OHS and warrants special attention. Monitoring http_core.c is critical because the Web Cache layer should be preventing static pages from reaching the HTTP Server. Hence, the processing values for http_core.c usually indicate a problem at the Web Cache level. In the preceding listing, http_core.c shows very little activity, indicating a properly configured Web Cache.

- **mod_oc4j.c**   This module processes all J2EE requests (OC4J) and will be one of the most important modules in OHS. This value gives you a good idea about the number of transactions that have been forwarded to OC4J.

Now let's take a close look at this data and see how to compute the real response time for an OHS module.

Computing Real Response Time for OHS Modules

One problem with the OHS statistics is that the one-time operations will skew the overall averages in the ohs_response listings. To remove these factors, Oracle recommends computing the real response time as follows:

$$real\_average = \frac{(time - min - max)}{(completed - 2)}$$

Using the data from the mod_oc4j.c listing shown in the preceding section, we can compute the real response time:

$$real\_average = \frac{(43,710 - 2 - 8)}{(13,487 - 2)}$$

$$real\_average = \frac{(43,700)}{(13,485)} = 3.24 \text{ milliseconds}$$

Next, let's take a quick look at the aggrespy online interface. The aggrespy utility provides a summary of useful performance information.

Monitoring with aggrespy

The aggrespy utility is a Java servlet that is used with standalone OC4J instances. The aggrespy utility can be used to display metrics for many Application Server 10*g* processes, including

- HTTP Server processes

- OC4J processes

- OPMN processes

Unlike the dmstool utility, which provides statistics in time intervals, the aggrespy web pages only provide a real-time summary of overall performance.

NOTE
Many beginners misinterpret the aggrespy output, attempting to use it to diagnose a current performance problem. Remember, aggrespy contains roll-up information since startup and is not useful for spotting current performance bottlenecks. For acute performance troubleshooting, you should use the dmstool utility to get time-slice summaries.

You can access aggrespy by invoking this URL: http://myhost:myport/dmsoc4j/AggreSpy. In our system, we invoke http://appsvr.localdomain.com:7778/dmsoc4j/AggreSpy, and we see the aggrespy main screen shown in Figure 10-11.

The main window of this screen allows you to drill-down into increasing levels of detail. For example, clicking the ohs_module link from the right-hand pane shows the same details as the command dmstool -table ohs_module -c 1. In Figure 10-12, you can quickly see that the http_core.c module has processed 57,972 requests with an average response time of 247 milliseconds.

The aggrespy utility is a fast way to examine specific real-time performance metrics within your Application Server 10*g* architecture, but for time-series analysis most administrators use the dmstool utility to capture time-based data for trend analysis.

Monitoring the Oracle Database Instances

Because the infrastructure and Oracle back-end database are critical components of Application Server 10*g*, special care should be taken to ensure their optimal performance. The concept of instance tuning is one of the most misunderstood areas of Oracle tuning. In practice, an overstressed Oracle System Global Area (SGA) can cause serious performance problems, but once tuned, the Oracle SGA really needs little attention.

Tuning the Oracle instance involves checking all of the initialization parameters for the Oracle database—a huge topic and far beyond the scope of this book. As most Oracle professionals know, the init.ora parameters are getting more complex as the Oracle database becomes more sophisticated. Of the hundreds of initialization parameters, there are only a handful that are very important for Oracle tuning. We give you a glimpse of them here; for in-depth details on Oracle

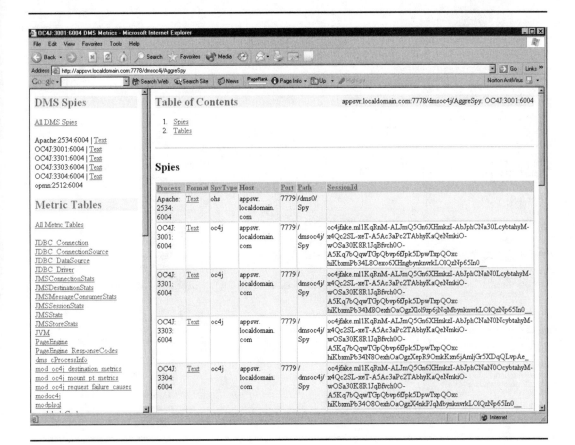

FIGURE 10-11.   *The aggrespy main screen*

database tuning, see *Oracle9i High-Performance Tuning with STATSPACK* by Burleson (McGraw-Hill/Osborne, 2003).

- **buffer_pool_keep**   This data buffer pool is used to store small tables that perform full table scans.

- **buffer_pool_recycle**   This pool is reserved for table blocks from very large tables that perform full table scans.

- **db_cache_size**   This parameter determines the number of database block buffers in the Oracle SGA and represents the single most important parameter to Oracle memory.

- **db_block_size**   The size of the database blocks can make a huge improvement in performance. While the default value may be as small as 2048 bytes, data warehouses and applications that have large tables with full table scans will see a tremendous improvement in performance by increasing db_block_size to a larger value. As a general

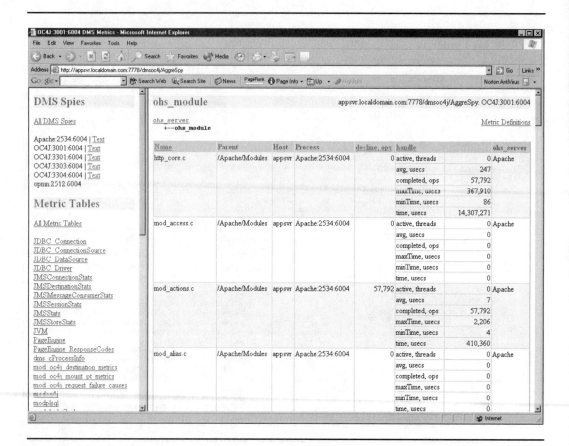

FIGURE 10-12. *Using aggrespy to view performance details for the OHS modules*

rule, the larger the block size, the less physical I/O, and the faster the overall performance.

■ **db_file_multiblock_read_count** This parameter is used for multiblock reads when performing full table scans or large-range scans.

■ **large_pool_size** This is a special area of the shared pool that is reserved for SGA usage when using the multithreaded server. The large pool is also used for parallel query and RMAN processing.

■ **log_buffer** This parameter determines the amount of memory to allocate for Oracle's redo log buffers. If there is a high amount of update activity, the log_buffer should be allocated more space.

■ **shared_pool_size** This parameter defines the pool that is shared by all users in the system, including SQL areas and data dictionary caching. As you will learn later in this chapter, a large shared_pool_size is not always better than a smaller shared pool. If your application contains nonreusable SQL, you may get better performance with a smaller shared pool.

- **pga_aggregate_target**   This parameter determines the memory region that is allocated for in-memory sorting. When the stats$sysstat value sorts (disk) becomes excessive, you may want to allocate additional memory.

Web Cache Tuning

The Oracle Web Cache is one of the most important areas of Application Server 10*g* tuning because of its role in reducing cross-layer traffic. Because the Web Cache can keep HTML pages in RAM, administrators can define sophisticated rules to govern the amount of RAM storage and cacheability, and to control Web Cache invalidations. Oracle-sponsored studies have shown that a beefy Web Cache can reduce load on the back-end database by as much as 95 percent, reducing repetitive queries for common information. Most Application Server 10*g* installations use inexpensive hardware (Intel-based servers) and add more servers as system load increases.

Oracle provides detailed instructions for the configuration of the Web Cache parameters and components, but the overall tuning is relatively simple, involving adding new Web Cache servers and adjusting the size of the data buffers, cacheability rules, and parameters for each Web Cache instance.

Cacheability Rules

The Web Cache allows you to specify cacheability rules for both static and dynamic page content. It also allows you to specify multiversion HTML, where the same page format is used but with slightly different text content. In addition, you can specify personalization rules whereby standard HTML pages are cached but dynamically modified to include custom messages, depending on the user ID of the invoking URL.

For web content that is segmented into included components (such as header, footer, and table of contents), the Web Cache allows you to specify cacheability rules for each component. This is similar to the FrontPage concept of "include pages," whereby pages are dynamically assembled at invocation by including separate HTML files. This allows for highly dynamic content and the effective reuse of components. For example, if you need to change your web page header, you can change the HTML, and the Web Cache will invalidate the old copy, immediately reloading it into the Web Cache and quickly including the new content in all outgoing requests.

Monitoring the Web Cache

The main screen for the Web Cache allows you to start and stop the Cache (often required for parameter changes) and displays summary statistics on Web Cache usage (Figure 10-13). From this screen, you can click the Activity link, under Performance, and see Web Cache details (Figure 10-14).

This screen gives you important information about the effectiveness of the Web Cache:

- **Requests**   This shows the current, average, and max transactions per second, which provides a high-level gauge of the throughput of the Web Cache. The backlog section is especially important, as any value here usually indicates that the Web Cache is overwhelmed with requests and another Web Cache server should be started.

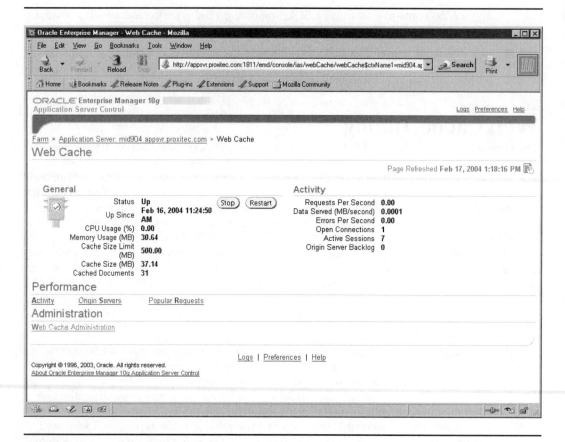

FIGURE 10-13. *Web Cache main screen*

- **Errors** This summarizes the network, site busy, and particle-page errors for the Web Cache. Many administrators write automated alerts to notify them about excessive numbers of errors.

- **Misses** This section shows cacheable and noncacheable misses along with the number of refreshes for the Web Cache. Remember, an incoming HTTP request will be a "hit" if the components exist in the Web Cache, a "miss" if the contents must be loaded from the database, and "refreshed" if the dynamic HTML content has changed.

- **Compression** The compression sections show the total amount of RAM saved by compression and provide a gauge of the effectiveness of the Web Cache.

You can define the Web Cache to service multiple HTTP Servers, providing both load balancing and failover. Please see the later section "Load Balancing Oracle Application Server 10*g*" for details. Web Cache tuning is generally performed by adding data buffers to the cache and adjusting the Web Cache parameters using the OEM Web Cache manager.

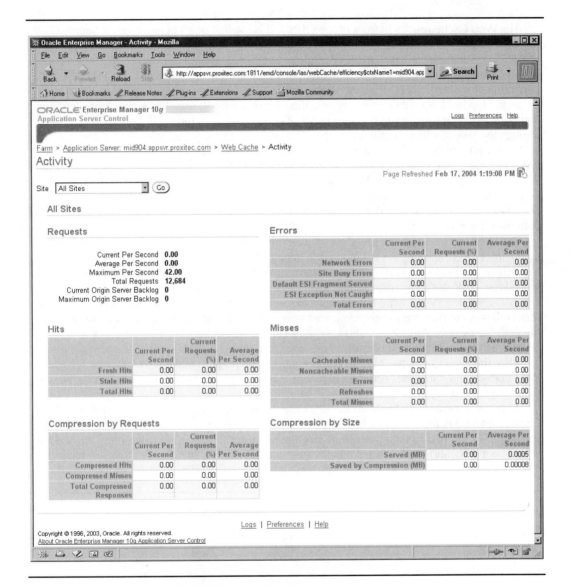

FIGURE 10-14.   *Details of Web Cache activity*

Oracle HTTP Server and Web Cache

The Web Cache and OHS work together to allow implementation of web-based interactive applications that work closely with the Oracle database. At first glance, the architecture of the Web Cache and OHS may seem confusing. Since the OHS is a powerful product, there is a plethora of ways to configure and implement Web Cache and OHS.

The Web Cache resides in front of the OHS and is the first point of entry for incoming requests. Each Web Cache can be made to automatically load-balance with up to 100 Oracle HTTP Servers (Figure 10-15). The HTTP requests are then passed to the Oracle HTTP Servers, where OHS may access the Oracle database back end. On the outgoing side, the HTTP Server communicates outgoing HTML to the Web Cache.

At the top level, the OHS listener runs at the web server level (sometimes on a separate server) and polls its port for incoming HTTP requests. As each request is received, the OHS directs it through the layers, where Application Server 10g extracts the required information from the HTTP request, creates and executes an Oracle database query, prepares an outgoing HTML or XML document, and passes the result set back to OHS for transmission to the requesting client.

At the top end, you see the Web Cache and its association with the OHS. During initial configuration, the OHS components are generally configured first and are assigned a specific port. Next, you configure the Web Cache and assign it to a port and configure it to communicate with the OHS on port 81.

The Web Cache is used to speed the delivery of static and dynamic web pages to users over the Internet. By employing RAM storage, the Web Cache can keep important web page data instantly available. In the real world, the Web Cache stores images (GIFs and JPEGs) that are embedded in the outgoing page immediately before transmission.

In a sense, the Web Cache is analogous to the Oracle database's data buffer cache because they both serve to store frequently referenced information. However, unlike the data buffer cache, the Web Cache only stores information about its current transactions. Hence it must be in constant communication with OHS to create and destroy cached objects as transactions are processed.

Also, the Web Cache has built-in compression technology to make the most effective use of RAM storage, and it includes Apache extensions that allow you to perform load balancing between the HTTP Servers.

As already mentioned, the Web Cache content is usually images that are included inside the HTML content (via the IMG tag). Initially, these images may be stored inside the Oracle database using the BFILE or BLOB data types, but once fetched from Oracle, they will remain cached for subsequent invocations. This initial latency is why many Application Server 10g users report that

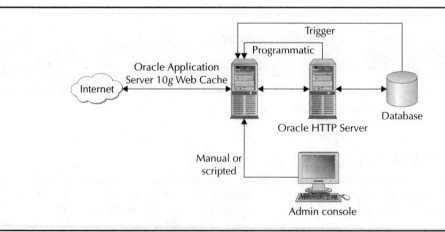

FIGURE 10-15.   *Web Cache architecture*

the initial loads of their pages are far slower than subsequent transactions. It is important to note that these cached images are shared between instances of the OHS. In other words, once an OHS has loaded the page header and footer images, they remain in the cache where they can be used by transactions inside other OHS instances. This sharing of the Web Cache is a vital tuning area for the administrator.

The association between the Web Cache and OHS instances can have a dramatic effect on system performance, and you should pay careful attention to the Web Cache monitoring statistics and make appropriate adjustments. There are pros and cons to each association:

- **Many OHS instances per Web Cache** This is the typical configuration for small and medium-sized systems. The benefit of sharing a Web Cache is the sharing of common items (such as page header JPEGs), while the downside is the lack of control over the RAM allocations for a specific OHS and introduction of a single point of failure. Small and medium-sized shops will run all of the Web Cache instances and the Web Cache on a single server.

- **One Web Cache per OHS** This isolates the Web Cache to the specific OHS. The upside is more granular management of the RAM cache, and the downside is the nonsharing of Web Cache between OHS instances. Many large Application Server 10*g* sites give each OHS its own Web Cache, both on a separate server from the other OHS instances.

As mentioned before, the Web Cache performs automatic load balancing between the active HTTP Servers. However, administrators can keep a pool of servers in standby mode with Web Cache and OHS installed on them. Depending on need, you can add them to the Application Server 10*g* architecture as an HTTP Server or a Web Cache server.

Load Balancing Oracle Application Server 10*g*

Application Server 10*g* has several points where load balancing occurs. Figure 10-16 illustrates the typical three-tiered architecture with the Web Cache layer, the application server layer, and the database layer. Within this architecture, you have the following areas of load balancing:

- **Web Cache to HTTP Server** The Web Cache interrogates HTTP Server statistics and routes transactions to the least-loaded HTTP Server.

- **HTTP Server to database listener** The HTTP Server load-balances transactions to multiple database listeners.

- **Database listener to MTS dispatcher** When using the Oracle multithreaded server (MTS), numerous dispatcher processes funnel transactions to the database. The listener will route an incoming database transaction to the least-loaded dispatcher.

- **MTS dispatcher to database instance** When using Oracle Real Application Clusters (RAC), the dispatcher can route a database transaction to the least-loaded Oracle instance. Each instance in the RAC accesses the same back-end database files.

In addition, you can perform hardware load balancing by defining a pool of spare servers and starting either a Web Cache or an application server on these servers. This allows you to reallocate processing resources depending on the nature of the system load.

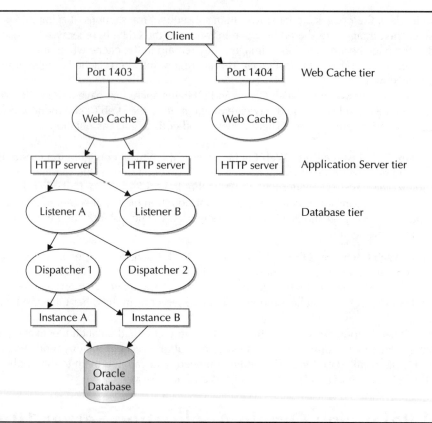

FIGURE 10-16. *Load-balancing points within Application Server 10*g

Oracle Application Server 10*g* Monitoring

Measuring server stress (RAM and CPU) is a critical part of tuning. Most administrators use the vmstat utility to monitor server stress because it is common to all dialects of UNIX and easy to invoke and interpret.

When capturing server metrics, be aware that server-level resource contention is transient and fleeting, and it is often very easy to miss a bottleneck unless you are constantly vigilant. For this reason, you can create an Oracle table that will accept vmstat data from all of your servers and collect all data relating to resource contention. The concept behind this collection is to execute the vmstat utility and capture the performance information within an Oracle table called stats$vmstat. This technique not only works well for monitoring the Oracle database server, but these operating system statistics can also be used to monitor all of the servers in your farm.

If you want to monitor vmstat data on your Oracle database or infrastructure server, it is quite easy to write a vmstat script that will collect elapsed-time vmstat information and store it inside the Oracle Database.

NOTE
*You must install the Oracle*Net client software on all of the servers,
with a tnsnames.ora file pointing to the infrastructure database (iasdb).
This establishes connectivity for the vmstat scripts to place entries into
your centralized Application Server 10g repository.*

Capturing vmstat Information for All Servers

It is a simple matter to create an Oracle table on the infrastructure database server to store the
vmstat server statistics from each server in the enterprise. Creating the automated vmstat monitor
begins by creating an Oracle table to contain the vmstat output from each server.

cr_vmstat_tab.sql

```
connect perfstat/perfstat;

drop table stats$vmstat;
create table stats$vmstat
(
        start_date              date,
        duration                number,
        server_name             varchar2(20),
        runque_waits            number,
        page_in                 number,
        page_out                number,
        user_cpu                number,
        system_cpu              number,
        idle_cpu                number,
        wait_cpu                number
)
tablespace perfstat
storage (initial    10m
         next          1m
         pctincrease 0)
;
```

Now that we have defined an Oracle table to capture the vmstat information, we need to
write a UNIX script that will execute vmstat, capture the vmstat output, and place it into the
Oracle table.

The main script to collect the vmstat information is a Korn shell script called get_vmstat.ksh.
As noted earlier, each dialect of UNIX displays vmstat information in different columns, so you
need slightly different scripts for each type of UNIX.

The idea is to write a script that continually runs the vmstat utility on every application server
and then directs the results into your Oracle table on the infrastructure database (iasdb), as shown
in Figure 10-17.

The script shown here (get_vmstat.ksh) gives the vmstat capture utility for the Linux operating
system. The Oracle Press web site contains complete code for vmstat scripts in all major UNIX
dialects. Go to http://shop.osborne.com/cgi-bin/oraclepress/downloads.html to get the code
samples.

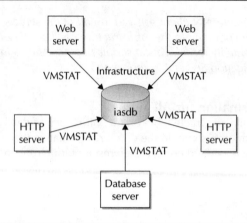

FIGURE 10-17. *Capturing vmstat output into the infrastructure table*

Note that you must change this script in several places to make it work for you:

- You must set ORACLE_HOME to your directory:

  ```
  ORACLE_HOME=/usr/app/oracle/admin/product/8/1/6
  ```

- You must set your ORACLE_SID in the sqlplus command:

  ```
  $ORACLE_HOME/bin/sqlplus -s perfstat/perfstat@iasdb<<EOF
  ```

- You can change the duration of samples by resetting SAMPLE_TIME UNIX variable:

  ```
  SAMPLE_TIME=300
  ```

The script shown next (get_vmstat.ksh) will capture Linux vmstat information for any server in your implementation.

get_vmstat.ksh (Linux Version)

```
#!/bin/ksh

# This is the Linux version

ORACLE_HOME=/usr/app/oracle/admin/product/8/1/6
export ORACLE_HOME

PATH=$ORACLE_HOME/bin:$PATH
export PATH
SERVER_NAME=`uname -a|awk '{print $2}'`
typeset -u SERVER_NAME
export SERVER_NAME
```

```
# sample every five minutes (300 seconds) . . . .
SAMPLE_TIME=300

while true
do
    vmstat ${SAMPLE_TIME} 2 > /tmp/msg$$


# run vmstat and direct the output into the Oracle table . . .
cat /tmp/msg$$|sed 1,3d | awk  '{ printf("%s %s %s %s %s %s\n", $1, $8, $9,
14, $15, $16) }' | while read RUNQUE PAGE_IN PAGE_OUT USER_CPU SYSTEM_CPU
DLE_CPU
    do

        $ORACLE_HOME/bin/sqlplus -s perfstat/perfstat@iasdb<<EOF
        insert into perfstat.stats\$vmstat
                        values (
                            sysdate,
                            $SAMPLE_TIME,
                            '$SERVER_NAME',
                            $RUNQUE,
                            $PAGE_IN,
                            $PAGE_OUT,
                            $USER_CPU,
                            $SYSTEM_CPU,
                            $IDLE_CPU,
                            0
                                );
        EXIT
EOF
    done
done

rm /tmp/msg$$
```

Because of the differences in implementations of vmstat, the first task is to identify the columns of the vmstat output that contain the information you want to capture. Once you know the columns that you want to capture, you can add them to the script to put the output in your table. In Application Server 10g, it is common to have multiple types of servers, and Linux servers are very popular as HTTP Servers, while the database back-end may be Sun or HP/UX.

Using Table 10-3, you can adjust the capture script according to your operating system. You customize the script by changing the line in the script that reads the vmstat output and places it into the stats$vmstat table. The UNIX dialect changes to this line are given in the following sections.

HP/UX vmstat Columns

```
cat /tmp/msg$$|sed 1,3d |\
   awk  '{ printf("%s %s %s %s %s %s\n", $1, $8, $9, $16, $17, $18) }' |\
   while read RUNQUE PAGE_IN PAGE_OUT USER_CPU SYSTEM_CPU IDLE_CPU
```

Dialect	Run Queue Column	Page-In Column	Page-Out Column	User Column	System Column	Idle Column	Wait Column
HP/UX	1	8	9	16	17	18	NA
AIX	1	6	7	14	15	16	17
Solaris	1	8	9	20	21	22	NA
Linux	1	8	9	14	15	16	NA

TABLE 10-3.   *vmstat Columns for Application Server 10g Server Types*

IBM AIX vmstat Columns

```
cat /tmp/msg$$|sed 1,3d |\
   awk '{ printf("%s %s %s %s %s %s\n", $1, $6, $7, $14, $15, $16, $17) }' |\
   while read RUNQUE PAGE_IN PAGE_OUT USER_CPU SYSTEM_CPU IDLE_CPU WAIT_CPU
```

Sun Solaris vmstat Columns

```
cat /tmp/msg$$|sed 1,3d |\
   awk '{ printf("%s %s %s %s %s %s\n", $1, $8, $9, $20, $21, $22) }' |\
   while read RUNQUE PAGE_IN PAGE_OUT USER_CPU SYSTEM_CPU IDLE_CPU
```

Linux vmstat cColumns

```
cat /tmp/msg$$|sed 1,3d |\
   awk '{ printf("%s %s %s %s %s %s\n", $1, $8, $9, $14, $15, $16) }' |\
   while read RUNQUE PAGE_IN PAGE_OUT USER_CPU SYSTEM_CPU IDLE_CPU
```

Internals of the vmstat Capture Script

To be sure you understand how the get_vmstat.ksh script functions, let's examine the steps in this script:

1. It executes the vmstat utility for the specified elapsed-time interval (SAMPLE_TIME=300).

2. The output is directed to the /tmp directory.

3. The output is then parsed using the awk utility, and the values are inserted into the mon_vmstats table.

Once started, the get_vmstat.ksh script will run continually and capture the vmstats into your stats$vmstat table. This script is an example of a UNIX daemon process, and it will run continually to sample the server status. However, the script may be terminated if your server is rebooted, so it is a good idea to place a crontab entry to make sure that the get_vmstat.ksh script is always running. The script shown next, called run_vmstat.ksh, will ensure that the vmstat utility is always running on your server.

Note that you must make the following changes to this script:

- Set the file location variable vmstat to the directory that contains your get_vmstat.ksh script:

```
vmstat=`echo ~oracle/vmstat`
```

- Create a small file in your UNIX file directory ($vmstat) called mysid. This file will contain one line and specify the name of your ORACLE_SID:

```
ORACLE_SID=`cat ${vmstat}/mysid`
```

The following script (run_vmstat.ksh) is used to submit the get_vmstat.ksh script to start the server polling.

run_vmstat.ksh

```
#!/bin/ksh

# First, we must set the environment . . . .
vmstat=`echo ~oracle/vmstat`
export vmstat
ORACLE_SID=`cat ${vmstat}/mysid`
export ORACLE_SID

ORACLE_HOME=`cat /etc/oratab|grep $ORACLE_SID:|cut -f2 -d':'`
export ORACLE_HOME
PATH=$ORACLE_HOME/bin:$PATH
export PATH

#----------------------------------------
# If it is not running, then start it . . .
#----------------------------------------
check_stat=`ps -ef|grep get_vmstat|grep -v grep|wc -l`;
oracle_num=`expr $check_stat`
if [ $oracle_num -le 0 ]
 then nohup $vmstat/get_vmstat_linux.ksh > /dev/null 2>&1 &
fi
```

The run_vmstat.ksh script can be scheduled to run hourly on the server. As you can see by examining the code, this script checks to see if the get_vmstat.ksh script is executing. If it is not, the script resubmits it for execution. In practice, the get_vmstat.ksh script will not abort, but if the server is shut down and restarted, the script will need to be restarted.

Here is an example of the UNIX crontab file. For those not familiar with cron, it is a UNIX scheduling facility that allows tasks to be submitted at specific times. Note that it schedules the run_vmstat.ksh script every hour, and runs a vmstat exception report every day at 7:00 A.M.

```
00 * * * * /home/vmstat/run_vmstat.ksh > /home/vmstat/r.lst

00 7 * * * /home/vmstat/run_vmstat_alert.ksh prodb1 > /home/vmstat/v.lst
```

Now that you have an understanding of server monitoring, let's drill-down and see how OEM can be used to monitor Oracle Application Server 10*g* components.

Monitoring and Load-Balancing the UNIX Server

Tracking the performance of the UNIX server is critical because no amount of tuning is going to solve a server-related performance problem. Of course, Application Server 10*g* parameter changes may reduce server load, but you always need to pay careful attention to the performance of every server in your enterprise.

When tuning a UNIX server, always remember the goal of fully loading the CPUs and RAM on the server. Unused processing and RAM power can never be reclaimed, and with the significant depreciation of the value of most servers, maximizing the utilization is a noble goal. On any server that is dedicated to an Oracle Application Server 10*g* component, you want to dedicate as much hardware resources to Oracle as possible without causing a server-related slowdown.

This section covers the following topics:

■ **UNIX monitoring goals** We examine the goals of UNIX server tuning and show tools for displaying UNIX performance metrics.

■ **Extension of vmstat to capture server statistics** Here we will review a method for capturing vmstat data inside tables on the infrastructure (iasdb) database.

■ **Reports on server statistics** We will look at some handy scripts that alert you to server exceptions, and we'll show you how to create trend and usage reports for your server.

Let's begin with a brief review of the goals of UNIX server monitoring.

UNIX Monitoring Goals

The monitoring of Oracle Application Server 10*g* servers involves tracking your disk, RAM, CPU, and network components. CPU consumption on an Oracle server is a simple matter because the server manages all CPU transactions automatically. All servers are configured to use CPU cycles on an as-needed basis, and all Oracle Application Server 10*g* components will use CPU resources freely. The internal machine code will manage the assignment of processors to active tasks and ensure that the maximum amount of processing power is applied to each task.

CPU shortages are evidenced in cases where the CPU run queue is greater than the number of CPUs. In these cases, you can either increase the number of CPUs on the processor or reduce the CPU demands on the server, mainly by changing configuration parameters or adding another application server. You can also decrease CPU demands on the Oracle Database and infrastructure by turning off Oracle Parallel Query, replacing the standard Oracle listener with the multithreaded server (MTS), and performing other actions that would reduce the processing demands on the hardware.

Tasks are serviced in UNIX according to their internal dispatching priority. Important tasks such as the UNIX operating system tasks will always have a more favorable dispatching priority because the UNIX system tasks drive the operating system.

CPU overload is usually evidenced by high values in the vmstat runqueue column. Whenever the runqueue value exceeds the number of CPUs of the server, some task may be waiting for service. When you see a CPU overload, you have several alternatives:

- ■ **Add CPUs**   This is usually the best solution, because a server that is overloading the CPU will always run faster with additional processors.

- ■ **Reduce server load/add servers**   If the CPU overload is not constant, task load balancing may be the solution. For example, it is not uncommon to see a server overloaded during peak work hours and then return to 80 percent idle in the evenings. In these cases, batch tasks can be rescheduled to execute when more idle CPU resources are available.

- ■ **Alter task dispatching priorities**   Almost all UNIX operating systems allow the root user to change the dispatching priority for tasks. As a general rule, the online database background tasks are given more priority (a smaller priority value), while less critical batch processes are placed with less priority (a higher priority value). However, altering the default dispatching priorities is not a good long-term solution, and it should only be undertaken in emergency situations.

Upgrading an Entire Server

On mission-critical databases where speed is a primary concern, adding processors may not be the best solution. Oracle tuning professionals will sometimes recommend upgrading to faster server architecture. For example, many of the new 64-bit CPUs will handle Oracle Application Server 10*g* transactions an order of magnitude faster than their 32-bit predecessors. For example, in the IBM AIX environment, the IBM SP2 processors run on 32 bits. IBM's next generation of processors utilize a 64-bit technology, and these systems can process information far faster than their 32-bit ancestors.

When making recommendations for upgrades of entire servers, many tuning professionals use the analogy of the performance of a 16-bit PC compared to the performance of a 32-bit PC. In general, moving to faster CPU architecture can greatly improve the speed of Oracle applications, and many vendors such as IBM will allow you to load your production system onto one of the new processors for speed benchmarks before purchasing the new servers.

Adding CPU Processors

Most symmetric multiprocessor (SMP) architectures for Oracle Application Server 10*g* servers are expandable, and additional processors can be added at any time. Once added, the processor architecture will immediately make the new CPUs available to the Oracle Database.

The problem with adding processors is the high cost that can often outweigh the cost of a whole new server. Adding processors to an existing server can commonly cost over $100,000, and most managers require a detailed cost-benefit analysis when making the decision to buy more CPUs. Essentially, the cost-benefit analysis compares the lost productivity of the end users (due to the response time latency) with the additional costs of the processors.

Another problem with justifying additional processors is the sporadic nature of CPU overloads. Oracle Application Server 10*g* servers often experience "transient" overloads, and there will be times when the processors are heavily burdened and other times when the processors are not at full utilization. Before recommending a processor upgrade, most administrators will perform a load-balancing analysis to ensure that any batch-oriented tasks are presented to the server at nonpeak hours.

Next, let's look at some of the tools that you can use to monitor server usage.

Overview of the vmstat Utility

The vmstat utility is the most common UNIX monitoring utility, and it is found in the majority of UNIX dialects. (Note that vmstat is called osview in the IRIX dialect of UNIX.) The vmstat utility displays various server values over a given time interval. It is invoked from the UNIX prompt and has several numeric parameters. The first numeric argument to vmstat represents the time interval (expressed in seconds) between server samples. The second argument specifies the number of samples to be reported. In the example that follows, vmstat is executed to take five samples at two-second intervals:

```
root> vmstat 2 5
```

Almost all UNIX servers have some version of vmstat. Before we look at the details of this powerful utility, let's explore the differences that you are likely to see.

Dialect Differences in vmstat

Because each hardware vendor writes their own vmstat utility, there are significant differences in vmstat output. The output differs depending on the dialect of UNIX, but each dialect contains the important server metrics. It can be useful to consult the online UNIX documentation to see the display differences. In UNIX, you can see your documentation by invoking the man pages. ("Man" is short for "manual.") You can see the documentation for your particular implementation of vmstat by entering **man vmstat** from your UNIX prompt.

Samples of vmstat output for the four most popular dialects of UNIX follow. In each example, the important metrics appear in bold.

vmstat for Solaris In the Sun Solaris operating environment, the output from vmstat will look like this:

```
root> vmstat 2 5
```

procs			memory			page			disk			faults			cpu		
r	b	w	swap	free	re	mf	**pi**	po	…	s6	--	--	in	sy	cs	**us**	**sy**	**id**
0	0	0	2949744	988800	0	4	**0**	0	…	0	0	0	148	200	41	**0**	**0**	**99**
0	0	0	2874808	938960	27	247	**0**	1	…	0	0	0	196	434	64	**1**	**2**	**98**
0	0	0	2874808	938960	0	0	**0**	0	…	0	0	0	134	55	32	**0**	**0**	**100**
0	0	0	2874808	938960	0	0	**0**	0	…	0	0	0	143	114	39	**0**	**0**	**100**
0	0	0	2874808	938960	0	0	**0**	0	…	0	0	0	151	86	38	**0**	**0**	**100**

vmstat for Linux In the Linux operating environment, the output from vmstat will look like this:

```
root> vmstat 2 5
```

procs						memory	swap		io		system			cpu		
r	b	w	swpd	free	buff	cache	**si**	…	bi	bo	in	cs	**us**	**sy**	**id**
1	0	0	140	90372	726988	26228	**0**	…	0	0	14	7	**0**	**0**	**4**
0	0	0	140	90372	726988	26228	**0**	…	0	2	103	11	**0**	**0**	**100**
0	0	0	140	90372	726988	26228	**0**	…	0	5	106	10	**0**	**0**	**100**

| 0 | 0 | 0 | 140 | 90372 | 726988 | 26228 | 0 | … | 0 | 0 | 101 | 11 | 0 | 0 100 |
| 0 | 0 | 0 | 140 | 90372 | 726988 | 26228 | 0 | … | 0 | 0 | 102 | 11 | 0 | 0 100 |

vmstat for AIX   In the IBM AIX operating environment, the output from vmstat will look like this:

```
root> vmstat 2 5
```

kthr		memory		page					faults			cpu			
r	b	avm	fre	re	**pi**	po	fr	sr	cy	in	sy	cs	**us**	**sy id wa**	
7	5	220214	141	0	0	0	42	53	0	1724	12381	2206	**19**	**46 28**	7
9	5	220933	195	0	0	1	216	290	0	1952	46118	2712	**27**	**55 13**	5
13	5	220646	452	0	0	1	33	54	0	2130	86185	3014	**30**	**59 8**	3
6	5	220228	672	0	0	0	0	0	0	1929	25068	2485	**25**	**49 16**	10

vmstat for HP/UX   In the Hewlett-Packard HP/UX operating environment, the output from vmstat will look like this:

```
root> vmstat 25
```

r	b	w	avm	free	re	at	**pi**	po	…	in	**sy**	**cs**	**us**	**sy id**	
1	0	0	70635	472855	10	5	2	0	…	2024	**2859**	**398**	**4**	**1 96**	
1	0	0	74985	472819	9	0	1	0	…	1864	**1820**	**322**	**0**	**0 100**	
0	0	0	83056	472819	2	0	0	0	…	1846	**1684**	**302**	**0**	**0 100**	
0	0	0	81390	472819	0	0	0	0	…	1847	**1571**	**288**	**0**	**0 100**	
0	0	0	78788	472819	0	0	0	0	…	1852	**1608**	**291**	**0**	**0 100**	

Now that you have seen the different display options for each dialect of vmstat, let's take a look at the data items in vmstat and understand the common values that can be captured in STATSPACK tables.

What to Look for in vmstat Output

As you can see, each dialect of vmstat reports different information about the current status of the server. Despite these dialect differences, only a small number of metrics are important for server monitoring. These metrics include

- **r (runqueue)**   The runqueue value shows the number of tasks executing and waiting for CPU resources. As stated earlier, when this number exceeds the number of CPUs on the server, a CPU bottleneck exists, and some tasks are waiting for execution.

- **pi (page-in)**   A page-in operation occurs when the server is experiencing a shortage of RAM. While all virtual memory servers will page out to the swap disk, page-in operations show that the server has exceeded the available RAM storage. Any nonzero value for pi indicates excessive activity as RAM memory contents are read in from the swap disk.

- **us (user CPU)**   This is the amount of CPU that is servicing user tasks.

- **sy (system CPU)**   This is the percentage of CPU being used to service system tasks.

- **id (idle)**   This is the percentage of CPU that is idle.

- **wa (wait—IBM-AIX only)**   This shows the percentage of CPU that is waiting on external operations such as disk I/O.

Note that all of the CPU metrics are expressed as percentages. Hence, all of the CPU values (us + sy + id + wa) will always sum to 100. Now let's look into some methods for using vmstat to identify server problems.

Identifying CPU Bottlenecks with vmstat

Waiting CPU resources can be shown in UNIX vmstat command output as the second column under the kthr (kernel thread state change) heading. Tasks may be placed in the wait queue (b) if they are waiting on a resource, while other tasks appear in the run queue (r) column.

In short, the server is experiencing a CPU bottleneck when r is greater than the number of CPUs on the server. To see the number of CPUs on the server, you can use one of the following UNIX commands.

Remember that you need to know the number of CPUs on your server because the vmstat runqueue value must never exceed the number of CPUs. A runqueue value of 32 is perfectly acceptable for a 36-CPU server, while a value of 32 would be a serious problem for a 24-CPU server.

In the following example, we run the vmstat utility. For our purposes, we are interested in the first two columns: the runqueue r and the kthr wait b column. In the listing you will see that there are an average of about eight new tasks entering the run queue every five seconds (the r column), while there are five other tasks that are waiting on resources (the b column). Also, a nonzero value in the b column may indicate a bottleneck.

```
root> vmstat 5 5
```

kthr		memory			page						faults			cpu			
r	b	avm	fre	re	pi	po	fr	sr	cy	in	sy	cs	us	sy	id	wa
7	5	220214	141	0	0	0	42	53	0	1724	12381	2206	19	46	28	7
9	5	220933	195	0	0	1	216	290	0	1952	46118	2712	27	55	13	5
13	5	220646	452	0	0	1	33	54	0	2130	86185	3014	30	59	8	3
6	5	220228	672	0	0	0	0	0	0	1929	25068	2485	25	49	16	10

The rule for identifying a server with CPU resource problems is quite simple. Whenever the value of the r column exceeds the number of CPUs on the server, tasks are forced to wait for execution. There are several solutions to managing CPU overload, and these alternatives are presented in their order of desirability:

1. Add more processors (CPUs) to the server.

2. Load-balance the system tasks by rescheduling large batch tasks to execute during off-peak hours.

3. Adjust the dispatching priorities (nice values) of existing tasks.

To understand how dispatching priorities work, remember that incoming tasks are placed in the execution queue according to their nice value. Tasks with a low nice value are scheduled for execution above those tasks with a higher nice value.

Let's look into vmstat further and see how you can tell when the CPUs are running at full capacity.

Identifying High CPU Usage with vmstat

You can also easily detect when you are experiencing a busy CPU on the Oracle database server. Whenever the times in the us (user) column plus the sy (system) column approach 100 percent, the CPUs are operating at full capacity.

Please note that it is not uncommon to see the CPU approach 100 percent even when the server is not overwhelmed with work. This is because the UNIX internal dispatchers will always attempt to keep the CPUs as busy as possible. This maximizes task throughput, but it can be misleading for a neophyte.

Remember, it is not a cause for concern when the user + system CPU values approach 100 percent. This just means that the CPUs are working to their full potential. The only metric that identifies a CPU bottleneck is when the runqueue value exceeds the number of CPUs on the server.

```
root> vmstat 5 1
```

kthr		memory		page						faults			cpu			
r	b	avm	fre	re	pi	po	fr	sr	cy	in	sy	cs	**us**	**sy**	id	wa
0	0	217485	386	0	0	0	4	14	0	202	300	210	**20**	**75**	3	2

The approach of capturing server information along with Oracle information provides you with a complete picture of the operation of the system.

Monitoring RAM Consumption

In the UNIX environment, RAM is automatically managed by the operating system. In systems with "virtual" memory, a special disk called "swap" is used to hold chunks of RAM that cannot fit within the available RAM on the server. In this way, a virtual memory server can allow tasks to allocate memory above the RAM capacity on the server. As the server is used, the operating system will move some memory pages out to the swap disk in case the server exceeds its physical capacity. This is called a page-out operation. Remember, page-out operations occur even when the database server has not exceeded the RAM capacity.

RAM shortages are evidenced by page-in operations. Page-in operations cause slowdowns because tasks must wait until their memory region is moved back into RAM from the swap disk. There are several remedies for overloaded RAM:

- Add RAM to the server.
- Reduce the size of the RAM regions by adjusting the parameters for each Oracle Application Server 10*g* component.

Generating Reports on UNIX Server Overload

Once data is captured in the stats$vmstat table, there is a wealth of reports that can be generated. Because all of the server statistics exist inside a single Oracle table, it is quite easy to write SQL*Plus queries to extract the data.

The vmstat data can be used to generate all types of interesting reports, which fall into four classes:

- **Exception reports** These show the time period where predefined thresholds are exceeded.

■ **Daily trend reports** These are often run and used with Excel spreadsheets to produce trending graphs.

■ **Hourly trend reports** These show the average utilization, by the hour of the day. They are useful for showing peak usage periods in a production environment.

■ **Long-term predictive reports** These generate a long-term trend line for performance. The data from these reports is often used with a linear regression to predict when additional RAM or CPU power is required for the server.

Next we'll examine the script that can be used to generate these server reports and see how this information can help you tune your Oracle Database.

Server Exception Reports

The SQL script vmstat_alert.sql can quickly give a complete exception report on all of the servers in your Oracle environment. This report displays times when the CPU and RAM exceed your predefined thresholds:

```
set lines 80;
set pages 999;
set feedback off;
set verify off;

column my_date heading 'date          hour' format a20
column c2       heading runq   format 999
column c3       heading pg_in  format 999
column c4       heading pg_ot  format 999
column c5       heading usr    format 999
column c6       heading sys    format 999
column c7       heading idl    format 999
column c8       heading wt     format 999


ttitle 'run queue > 2|May indicate an overloaded CPU|When runqueue exceeds
the number of CPUs| on the server, tasks are waiting for service.';


select
 server_name,
 to_char(start_date,'YY/MM/DD    HH24') my_date,
 avg(runque_waits)       c2,
 avg(page_in)            c3,
 avg(page_out)           c4,
 avg(user_cpu)           c5,
 avg(system_cpu)         c6,
 avg(idle_cpu)           c7
from
perfstat.stats$vmstat
WHERE
runque_waits > 2
```

```
and start_date > sysdate-&&1
group by
 server_name,
 to_char(start_date,'YY/MM/DD    HH24')
ORDER BY
 server_name,
 to_char(start_date,'YY/MM/DD    HH24')
;

ttitle 'page_in > 1|May indicate overloaded memory|Whenever Unix performs a
page-in, the RAM memory | on the server has been exhausted and swap pages are
being used.';


select
 server_name,
 to_char(start_date,'YY/MM/DD    HH24') my_date,
 avg(runque_waits)        c2,
 avg(page_in)             c3,
 avg(page_out)            c4,
 avg(user_cpu)            c5,
 avg(system_cpu)          c6,
 avg(idle_cpu)            c7
from
perfstat.stats$vmstat
WHERE
page_in > 1
and start_date > sysdate-&&1
group by
 server_name,
 to_char(start_date,'YY/MM/DD    HH24')
ORDER BY
 server_name,
 to_char(start_date,'YY/MM/DD    HH24')
;

ttitle 'user+system CPU > 70%|Indicates periods with a fully-loaded CPU
subsystem.|Periods of 100% utilization are only a | concern when runqueue
values exceed the number of CPUs on the server.';


select
 server_name,
 to_char(start_date,'YY/MM/DD    HH24') my_date,
 avg(runque_waits)        c2,
 avg(page_in)             c3,
 avg(page_out)            c4,
 avg(user_cpu)            c5,
 avg(system_cpu)          c6,
 avg(idle_cpu)            c7
```

```
from
perfstat.stats$vmstat
WHERE
(user_cpu + system_cpu) > 70
and start_date > sysdate-&&1
group by
 server_name,
 to_char(start_date,'YY/MM/DD    HH24')
ORDER BY
 server_name,
 to_char(start_date,'YY/MM/DD    HH24')
;
```

The standard vmstat alert report is used to alert the Oracle Application Server 10*g* administrator and systems administrator to out-of-bounds conditions on each Oracle server. These conditions include

- **CPU waits > 40% (AIX version only)** This may indicate I/O-based contention. The solution is to spread files across more disks or add buffer memory.

- **Runqueue > *xxx* (where *xxx* is the number of CPUs on the server, 2 in this example)** This indicates an overloaded CPU. The solution is to add processors to the server.

- **Page_in > 2** Page-in operations indicate overloaded memory. The solution is to reduce the size of the Oracle SGA, PGA, or add RAM to the server.

- **User CPU + System CPU > 90%** This indicates periods where the CPU is highly utilized.

While the SQL here is self-explanatory, let's look at a sample report and see how it will help monitor the server's behavior:

```
SQL> @vmstat_alert 7

Wed Dec 20                                                          page    1
                              run queue > 2
                        May indicate an overloaded CPU.
                  When runqueue exceeds the number of CPUs
                 on the server, tasks are waiting for service.


SERVER_NAME     date        hour       runq pg_in pg_ot  usr  sys  idl
--------------- ----------------- ---- ----- ----- ---- ---- ----
AD-01           00/12/13    17          3     0     0   87    5    8

Wed Dec 20                                                          page    1
                              page_in > 1
                        May indicate overloaded memory.
                 Whenever Unix performs a page-in, the RAM memory
              on the server has been exhausted and swap pages are being used.


SERVER_NAME       date        hour       runq pg_in pg_ot  usr  sys  idl
--------------- ----------------- ---- ----- ----- ---- ---- ----
```

AD-01	00/12/13	16	0	5	0	1	1	98
AD-01	00/12/14	09	0	5	0	10	2	88
AD-01	00/12/15	16	0	6	0	0	0	100
AD-01	00/12/19	20	0	29	2	1	2	98
PROD1DB	00/12/13	14	0	3	43	4	4	93
PROD1DB	00/12/19	07	0	2	0	1	3	96
PROD1DB	00/12/19	11	0	3	0	1	3	96
PROD1DB	00/12/19	12	0	6	0	1	3	96
PROD1DB	00/12/19	16	0	3	0	1	3	96
PROD1DB	00/12/19	17	0	47	68	5	5	91

```
Wed Dec 20                                                      page    1
                            user+system > 70%

              Indicates periods with a fully-loaded CPU subsystem.
                    Periods of 100% utilization are only a
            concern when runqueue values exceed the number of CPUs on the server.
```

SERVER_NAME	date	hour	runq	pg_in	pg_ot	usr	sys	idl
AD-01	00/12/13	14	0	0	2	75	2	22
AD-01	00/12/13	17	3	0	0	87	5	8
AD-01	00/12/15	15	0	0	0	50	29	22
AD-01	00/12/15	16	0	0	0	48	33	20
AD-01	00/12/19	07	0	0	0	77	4	19
AD-01	00/12/19	10	0	0	0	70	5	24
AD-01	00/12/19	11	1	0	0	60	17	24
PROD1	00/12/19	12	0	0	1	52	30	18
PROD1	00/12/19	13	0	0	0	39	59	2
PROD1	00/12/19	14	0	0	0	39	55	6
PROD1	00/12/19	15	1	0	0	57	23	20

You may notice that this exception report gives the hourly average for the vmstat information. If you look at the get_vmstat.ksh script, you will see that the data is captured in intervals of every 300 elapsed seconds (five-minute intervals). Hence, if you see an hour where your server is undergoing stress, you can modify your script to show the vmstat changes every five minutes. You can also run this report in conjunction with other Oracle Application Server 10*g* monitoring reports to identify what tasks may have precipitated the server problem.

Daily vmstat Trend Reports

One job of the Oracle Application Server 10*g* administrator is to monitor the database and the server for regular trends. This is not just an exercise in searching for trends, because every database will exhibit regular patterns of CPU and memory consumption.

Using the stats$vmstat table, it is easy to write a query that will aggregate the CPU and memory. Here is a sample SQL script that aggregates server values:

```
connect perfstat/perfstat;
set pages 9999;

set feedback off;
set verify off;
```

```
column my_date heading 'date' format a20
column c2       heading runq    format 999
column c3       heading pg_in   format 999
column c4       heading pg_ot   format 999
column c5       heading usr     format 999
column c6       heading sys     format 999
column c7       heading idl     format 999
column c8       heading wt      format 999


select
 to_char(start_date,'day') my_date,
-- avg(runque_waits)        c2
-- avg(page_in)             c3,
-- avg(page_out)            c4,
avg(user_cpu + system_cpu)                c5,
-- avg(system_cpu)          c6,
-- avg(idle_cpu)            c7,
avg(wait_cpu)              c8
from
   stats$vmstat
group  BY
 to_char(start_date,'day')
order by
 to_char(start_date,'day')
 ;
```

Here you can see that you can easily get any of the vmstat values aggregated by day. In the output shown next, you see the average user and wait CPU times for each day of the week:

```
SQL@rpt_vmstat_dy
Connected.


date                   usr   wt
-------------------- ---- ----
friday                  8   0
monday                 10   0
saturday                1   0
sunday                  1   0
thursday                6   0
tuesday                15   0
wednesday              11   0
```

This data can be extracted into Excel and quickly plotted for graphical reference, as shown in Figure 10-18. Please note that the book *Oracle High Performance Tuning with STATSPACK* by Burleson (McGraw-Hill/Osborne, 2002) covers a method of plotting STATSPACK data in Excel.

Hourly vmstat Trend Reports

You can use the same techniques to average vmstat information by the hour of the day. An average by hour of the day can provide valuable information regarding times when the server is experiencing stress.

```
connect perfstat/perfstat;
set pages 9999;

set feedback off;
set verify off;

column my_date heading 'date' format a20
column c2        heading runq    format 999
column c3        heading pg_in   format 999
column c4        heading pg_ot   format 999
column c5        heading cpu     format 999
column c6        heading sys     format 999
column c7        heading idl     format 999
column c8        heading wt      format 999


select
 to_char(start_date,'day') my_date,
-- avg(runque_waits)        c2
-- avg(page_in)             c3,
-- avg(page_out)            c4,
avg(user_cpu + system_cpu)            c5,
-- avg(system_cpu)          c6,
-- avg(idle_cpu)            c7,
avg(wait_cpu)            c8
from
   stats$vmstat
group  BY
 to_char(start_date,'day')
order by
 to_char(start_date,'day')
;
```

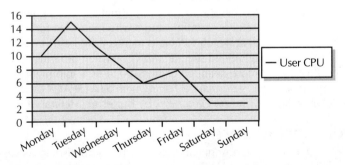

FIGURE 10-18.   *Plotting Application Server stress averages by hour of the day*

Next, you see the output from this script and get the average runqueue and user + system CPU values and wait CPU values, aggregated by hour of the day:

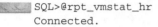

```
SQL>@rpt_vmstat_hr
Connected.
```

date	runq	cpu	wt
00	0	4	0
01	0	5	0
02	0	3	0
03	0	1	0
04	0	1	0
05	0	1	0
06	0	1	0
07	0	1	0
08	0	1	0
09	0	1	0
10	0	1	0
11	0	1	0
12	0	11	0
13	0	21	0
14	0	23	0
15	0	20	0
16	0	15	0
17	0	20	0
18	0	12	0
19	0	10	0
20	0	5	0
21	0	1	0
22	0	1	0
23	0	1	0

This hourly information can also be extracted into Excel for graphical plotting charts to show trends that may not be evident from raw observation.

Long-Term Server Analysis and Trending

You can also use the data from stats$vmstat to gather information for long-term trend analysis. This long-term trend analysis is useful for administrators who must plan for additional application server resources. Knowing the rate at which CPU and memory are being consumed on the server is critical, since there is often a lag time of several weeks between ordering and installing new hardware resources. If you want more detail on using STATSPACK information for management planning, please see *Oracle High Performance Tuning with STATSPACK* by Burleson, mentioned earlier, or *Oracle9i UNIX Administration Handbook* by Burleson (McGraw-Hill/Osborne, 2002).

Daily Server Alert Report

It goes without saying that the Oracle Application Server 10g administrator is very interested in monitoring conditions on the Oracle Database servers, application servers, and Oracle HTTP Servers. This script is generally run daily to report on exceptional conditions within any server in the Oracle environment. The data is collected in five-minute intervals and reported with hourly averages. When you find an out-of-bounds server condition, you can run detailed reports that display the data in five-minute intervals. These two scripts from http://shop.osborne.com/cgi-bin/ oraclepress/downloads.htm will produce the vmstat reports on all servers:

- **run_vmstat.ksh**   This is the driver script that submits the vmstat alert report and e-mails the output to the appropriate staff members.

- **vmstat_alert.sql**   This report provides information on the server conditions that may contribute to poor performance.

CPU Overload Report with runqueue Waits

When the runqueue exceeds the number of CPUs, the server is experiencing CPU bottlenecks:

```
Fri Dec 29                                                     page     1
                           run queue > 2
                    May indicate an overloaded CPU

SERVER_NAME         date          hour       runq pg_in pg_ot  usr  sys  idl
----------------    --------------------     ---- ----- -----  ---- ---- ----
BAD-01              00/12/22      13            6     0     0   62    7   32
BAD-01              00/12/22      15            3     0     0   82   18    0
BAD-01              00/12/22      17            3     0     0   76   16    8
BAD-01              00/12/27      11            3     0     0   77    5   20
```

RAM Overload Report with Swapping

When page-in operations exist, the maximum RAM capacity of the server has been exceeded. Most server administrators rely on the pi column in vmstat to signal when the server is swapping RAM. However, there is more to the story.

There are times when the pi column will be nonzero, even though there is no real RAM swapping. To illustrate this, let's take a simple example. Suppose we invoke a 20MB Oracle executable program, such as a Pro*C program. We don't need to load all 20MB of the executable into RAM at once. Rather, we just want to load those pieces of the executable code that require immediate execution. Hence, UNIX will use memory frames as necessary later and rely on the principle of spatial locality to minimize the amount of pages in the RAM working set.

To manage the memory segments, the UNIX kernel builds a memory map of the entire program when it starts. Included in this map is a note on whether the storage is "in memory" or "on swap disk." As the program starts, it begins accessing some of its pages that have never been loaded into RAM. Hence, you may see vmstat page-ins when a large number of programs are starting and allocating their RAM.

During normal operation, you may see various points in time when paging in happens a lot, and this is not always cause for concern. Remember, a UNIX process may page-in when the UNIX program is starting or is accessing parts of its code that it had not used before.

Paging out (the po column in vmstat) happens frequently as UNIX prepares for the possibility of a page-in. With UNIX virtual memory, you are always anticipating running out of RAM, and a page-out is a method for being ready for a subsequent page-in. Also, as UNIX processes end, they call the free() system call to free the RAM pages so they can be used by new processes.

Internals of RAM Paging   So if RAM paging in (pi) may be acceptable and paging out (po) may be acceptable, how do you tell when the RAM on a server is overstressed and swapping? One answer is to correlate the UNIX scan rate with page-in operations. When an Oracle server begins to run low on RAM, the page stealing daemon process awakens and UNIX begins to treat the RAM as a sharable resource, moving memory frames to the swap disk with paging operations.

The page stealing daemon operates in two modes. When RAM shortages are not critical, the daemon will steal small chunks of least-recently-used RAM from a program. As RAM resource demands continue to increase, the page stealing daemon escalates and begins to page-out entire programs in the RAM regions. In short, you cannot always tell if the page-in operations that you see are normal housekeeping or a serious memory shortage unless you correlate the activity of the page stealing daemon with the page-in output.

To aid in this, the vmstat utility provides the sr column to designate the memory page scan rate. If you see the scan rate rising steadily, you will have hit the page stealing daemon's first threshold, indicating that entire programs in RAM regions are being paged out to the swap disk. Then you will begin to see high page-in numbers as the entire process is paged back into RAM.

Carefully review the following list from vmstat. The scan rate is the far-right column, and here you see the value of sr rising steadily as the page stealing daemon prepares for a page-in. As the sr value peaks, you see the page-in operation (pi) as the real RAM on the Oracle server is exceeded.

```
root> vmstat 2
        procs            memory              page
    r   b   w      avm    free   re  at   pi   po   fr   de   sr
    3   0   0   144020   12778   17   9    0   14   29    0    3
    3   0   0   144020   12737   15   0    1   34    4    0    8
    3   0   0   144020   12360    9   0    1   46    2    0   13
    1   0   0   142084   12360    5   0    3   17    0    0   21
    1   0   0   142084   12360    3   0    8    0    0    0    8
    1   0   0   140900   12360    1   0   10    0    0    0    0
    1   0   0   140900   12360    0   0    9    0    0    0    0
    1   0   0   140900   12204    0   0    3    0    0    0    0
    1   0   0   137654   12204    0   0    0    0    0    0    0
```

High CPU Usage Report

As an administrator, you will often be interested in times when the database CPU utilization is greater than 95 percent.

```
Fri Dec 29                                                       page    1
                        user+system > 70%
                    Indicates an overloaded CPU

SERVER_NAME       date        hour     runq pg_in pg_ot  usr  sys  idl
----------------  ----------  ------   ---- ----- -----  ---- ---- ----
AD-01             00/12/22    08          2     0     0   69    3   28
AD-01             00/12/22    13         12     0     0   89   11    1
AD-01             00/12/22    15          0     0     0   63   29    8
AD-01             00/12/22    17          1     0     0   53   27   20
AD-01             00/12/26    12          1     0     0   77    4   19
AD-01             00/12/27    11          3     0     0   86    6    9
```

Summary

Oracle Application Server 10*g* is an extremely complex combination of interrelated servers, programs, and databases, and successful administrators will automate much of their monitoring and tuning tasks. The main points of this chapter are as follows:

- Most Oracle applications administrators use OS-level monitoring tools to manage the resources on each server.

- The dmstool utility provides a great way to capture elapsed-time metrics for detailed performance analysis.

- Application Server 10*g* has several GUI-based tools to view performance metrics (aggrespy, Web Cache administrator, and so on), but these tools are not useful for long-term trend analysis.

- Hardware resources (server) load balancing is critical to a properly scalable environment. The savvy administrator will carefully watch system load and add Web Cache or HTTP Servers as demand changes.

- The standard UNIX vmstat utility is an easy way to monitor the overall stress on each server, and simple shell scripts can be used to capture these metrics into Oracle tables for long-term analysis.

- You can easily monitor the CPU, RAM, and network demands on all of your servers and store the details in iasdb extension tables. This allows you to analyze past usage patterns and predict future processing needs.

- Most Application Server 10*g* administration in a UNIX environment will use a third-party server monitoring suite, or you can write custom vmstat scripts to capture server performance for Web Cache servers, HTTP Servers, infrastructure servers, and the back-end database servers.

CHAPTER
11

Backup and Recovery

hether you are working on a development system or a production system, you need to take precautions to protect your valuable work from external problems such as power outages or server crashes. In the case of a production system, a company in many cases has bet its continued existence on Oracle software. The Oracle Database has built its reputation as a powerful data management system that can safely maintain the data entrusted to it. Oracle Application Server 10*g* continues in that vein with a robust capability to recover from external or internal problems. Chapter 9 discussed high availability solutions that can reduce or eliminate application server downtime. In this chapter, we discuss methods to back up the application server and if necessary restore from a backup.

Why You Need a Backup Plan

Before discussing methods of backing up and restoring the application server, we need to discuss the types of problems that the system could encounter and how they affect the application server. We have divided these problems into two types, internal and external. An external problem happens outside the application server or within the application server code itself. Internal problems happen within the user application running in the application server.

External Problems

Most system crashes are the result of human error. An operator makes a change, and the effect cascades to the point of crashing the entire system. The second most common cause of system crashes is equipment failures.

Equipment Failures

In the not too distant past, one of the basic tasks of a DBA was to recover data files from disk failures. With the rapid adoption of RAID systems, many DBAs have never had to perform this task. As discussed in Chapter 9, you can create an array of application servers so that any equipment-related failure would not stop the application server from servicing user requests. This is the basis for using multiple inexpensive commodity servers to produce fault-tolerant systems. Still, even though the application server is still running, an operator must recover the failed node and place it back into operation.

Server Crashes

A crash is the sudden failure of a system. It may be caused by loss of power, equipment failure, or a software problem such as a memory leak. The primary problem with a system crash is that data in memory is lost before it can be saved. Oracle Application Server 10*g* and the Oracle Database (including the metadata repository database) can normally self-recover from a server crash, but the user application may not.

User Error

The most common problem that administrators must deal with, and many times the hardest to recover from, is user error. Consider this scenario: The development team spends the last three days working late at night to prepare the application upgrade for deployment into the production system. A tired developer accidentally deletes a critical application file. If (as commonly happens) the team has not backed up the development system, they may not be able to recover that critical file. In many companies, the development system will require daily backups, while the production system may need only occasional backups. It all depends on when the system changes.

Another common error is deleting the wrong data. This can be a user error and the failure of some type of automation such as a nightly script. For example:

```
SQL> delete from transactions where tans_date > SYSDATE -7;
```

Here, if the user was trying to delete all transactions older than seven days, he just made a mistake. Instead he deleted all transactions younger than seven days. If he realizes his mistake before committing, the database can roll back the delete. If the user commits or logs off (implicit commit), the deleted data must be recovered.

Another form of user error is incomplete automation of a task. A company implements a nightly script that processes the daily transactions and then truncates the transaction table. The process fails (maybe for something simple like a database link being unavailable), and the second part kicks in and truncates the table, causing the loss of that day's receipts.

Site Disaster

To protect against total loss of the system site, from earthquake or fire, for example, backups and/or failover systems must be maintained off site at a location that will not be affected by the disaster that strikes the main site. Failover systems are discussed in Chapter 9.

Internal Problems

Internal problems happen within the user application and involve programming practices that ensure persistent data is properly maintained and updated to reflect the application data in memory. This was discussed briefly in Chapter 7, but is beyond the scope of this book. Application Server 10*g* has several features that assist with internal problems, such as OC4J islands that maintain state across instances; but these features (Chapter 9) are designed to support the loss of an application server instance, not to compensate for poor programming of the user applications.

Between external and internal problems, there will come a time when you will need to recover the application server or database. Oracle provides a robust set of tools to ensure data protection, but you have to use them. We are always amazed when we visit a new client and find that they have no backup strategy and in many cases are not running their database in archivelog mode. Our philosophy is that if your data is worth being in an Oracle product, then implementing the tools to protect it is worth the time and effort.

Backing Up Application Server 10*g*

Begin by defining your backup strategy and implementing it. You must also periodically review your strategy to ensure that it still meets your business needs. A backup strategy defines when you need to back up each server and how you will recover if a server goes down. Part of this discussion must also address downtime cost. If a system has a high per-minute downtime cost (thousands of dollars per minute), you need to implement a high availability solution, even if system availability requirements are only 10 hours per workday. Most companies start by stating that their system must be available 24 hours a day, 7 days a week. If this is the case for you, refer to Chapter 9. Faced with the expense of these solutions, many companies more realistically define their availability needs based on user/customer requirements. Your backup strategy must support your business needs.

The system availability requirements will determine whether you can perform cold or hot backups. A *cold backup* requires that you shut down the application server, including the metadata repository. A cold backup is consistent across the application server components because they are not running when the backup is taken. Cold backups are the easiest to execute and maintain. *Hot backups* are required when the application server must remain available to respond to users during the backup process. A hot backup of the middle tier instances is a relatively easy process but is much more complicated for the metadata repository database and the back-end database. Finally, there are solutions external to the Oracle software to automate backups, such as products from Veritas. (For information on such products, refer to the vendor.) For this discussion, we will focus on the application server and the metadata repository database.

What to Back Up

On each server within the application server topography, there are four types of files that need different levels of protection. This is true for both the application server and the Oracle9i database containing the metadata repository. Your backup strategy needs to address each category of file.

First are the operating system files, which make up the OS. You need to refer to the OS reference to determine which files need protection. Normally, these files do not change over time unless you change the configuration or apply patches. A full backup, taken after updates, will usually suffice.

The second set of files that need protection are the Oracle product files. These files are located in the instance $ORACLE_HOME and the oraInventory directories. They include the product binary files. Like the OS, these files do not change once installed unless additional components or patches are installed. Again, a full backup after changes in configuration or patches will suffice. Be sure to include any environment configuration files that may also be configured to support Oracle products. These include the .bashrc, .bash_profile, and oratab files.

The third set of files are the data, configuration, and application files that change during the normal course of operation. These include files maintained by the user application, Oracle Internet Directory, and the metadata repository database data files, control files, and archive log files. It is these files for which backup protection must be routinely maintained.

The final set of files are the log files. Unless you have an audit, SLA, or other reason to ensure that these files are protected, their loss will have little impact and they can be excluded from a backup routine. Note, this does not include database archive log files that are critical to the database recovery mechanism.

The easiest protection strategy is to execute a full backup of all servers each night. While easy, there are drawbacks. First, the backup will be large and time consuming. It will also be time consuming if you are required to restore one file, which must be located within the full backup. Second, this strategy wastes resources because, for the most part, you are constantly backing up unchanged data. A more useful strategy would be to execute a full backup on the weekend and do nightly backups of the third set of files.

A final word of advice: know your system. You may only need to back up the middle tier once, with nightly backups of the infrastructure tier. If the files on the middle tier are static, they only need to be backed up when changed.

Application Server Protection

For the most part, the files that make up the application server do not change over time. Static web pages and configuration files will not change unless you update the user application or deploy additional applications. For example, if the Web Cache is placed in front of a cluster of application servers, it only needs to be backed up when the configuration changes. It is a waste of resources to back up the Web Cache server nightly, since the only data that has changed is in the cache itself, and you don't want a backup of the cache data. On the other hand, the infrastructure instance contains OID, which normally is regularly updated by the user application and the application server.

Backing Up Application Server Instances

Developing a backup strategy for a middle tier instance requires knowledge of the user application running on it. For instance, if the user application maintains local data or state information in a local file, routine backup of that file may be critical. If all persistent data is maintained in a back-end database, there may be no requirement to back up a middle tier instance every night. Normally, a nightly backup of the instance $ORACLE_HOME will suffice.

You can also take incremental backups of only changed files; however, this could lead to problems while attempting to find a file that needs to be restored. Since it was only backed up when changed, you will first have to identify which backup contains the file before beginning the restore process. To completely restore the instance, you would need to restore the last full backup and all later incremental backups to ensure that you have restored the latest version of each file. For that reason, we recommend that you take a full backup of the instance $ORACLE_ HOME for each routine backup. This can be accomplished using the tar utility or your backup utility.

```
[oracle@appsvr oracle]$ . ./midenv
[oracle@appsvr oracle]$ cd $ORACLE_HOME
[oracle@appsvr oracle]$ tar cvzf /u03/oracle/backup/mid_back.tz .
```

The commands shown here will source the midtier environment, change to the midtier's $ORACLE_HOME directory, and then back up that entire directory to the backup location. You can then back up mid_back.tz to tape in the background if needed. This command can be used while the instance is running.

In the case of the infrastructure instance, the metadata repository database is an Oracle9*i* database and must be maintained accordingly (see the section "Metadata Repository Database Protection," a little later in the chapter). You still want to back up the database files with the instance, but you will also have to execute a database backup (hot or cold).

Finally, do not forget to back up the oraInventory directory whenever you take any action that requires starting the Oracle Universal Installer. This is where Oracle saves information about what is installed on the server, including patch information. If you have to rebuild the server, you will need to restore the oraInventory directory in order to apply patches/upgrades in the future. When you back up the oraInventory directory, include the oraInst.loc and oratab files.

Once you have a backup, we hope you will never use it. But if you need it, you need to know how to use it to recover an application server instance.

Recovering the Application Server

Recovery of the application server is required if the server will not restart. If the application server instance fails but will restart, recovery is not required. The first step in the recovery will be to rebuild the server. Typically, the UNIX administrator has had to make specific changes to prep the machine for installation. Although the install doc and readme list these changes, it's a good practice to make a list of all the changes or deviations from the normal install. That way if you have to do a restore or rebuild from scratch, you can just look at the cookbook and quickly make the changes instead of perusing the Oracle documentation. In addition, the administrator should have a CD with patches, rpms, changed files, and so on. When time is tight during a restore/install, you don't have to hunt for the files.

If you have a recent full (complete) backup, recovery may require no more than a full restore and restart. If you can use a backup to restore the server, use the recent instance backup to overwrite the $ORACLE_HOME files with valid files, and that may be all you need to recover the instance to the last backup. If you must reinstall the OS or move the instance to a new server, take the following steps to ensure a successful restore of the application server instance.

Restoring a Middle Tier Instance

If you lose a middle tier instance that belongs to a cluster, you may just want to rebuild the server (or use a new server), reinstall the middle tier instance using the Oracle Universal Installer, and then join the original cluster. This will reconfigure the new instance to the configuration of the cluster. Do not forget to add the new instance to the load-balancing Web Cache.

If you must reinstall the server OS, be sure that you reinstall the same OS (versions and patches) and follow the OS setup requirements. Follow these steps to restore the application server instance:

1. Ensure that the /etc/hosts file matches the original file from the failed installation.

2. Create the same user and groups to own the Oracle files.

3. Restore the oraInst.loc and oratab files to the appropriate directories (depending on your OS).

4. Create the instance $ORACLE_HOME directory (empty) using the same mount point and path (ensure that it is owned by the user that owns the Oracle files).

5. Create and restore the oraInventory directory from the backup.

6. Restore the $ORACLE_HOME directory from backup. You need a full restore of the $ORACLE_HOME. Ensure that you execute the restore as the user that owns the Oracle files.

7. Set the file permissions by running $ORACLE_HOME/root.sh as the root user.

8. If the new host server has a different host name and/or IP address, you must refer to Chapter 9 of the *Oracle Application Server 10*g *Administrator's Guide* (9.0.4).

9. Start the instance as you normally would.

10. Apply any changes applied to the instance since the backup was taken.

If you are required to restore the middle tier to the same host without having to reinstall the OS, follow these steps:

1. Stop the instance if running.

2. Restore the $ORACLE_HOME, overwriting all files with the files in the most recent backup.

3. Start the instance in the normal way.

4. Apply any changes made to the instance since the backup was taken.

Restoring an Infrastructure Instance

Restoring an infrastructure instance follows the same steps as restoring a middle tier instance except that you must restore the metadata repository database before restarting the instance (discussed in the next section).

If you installed OID in a separate $ORACLE_HOME, you must restore the OID ORACLE_HOME before restoring the metadata repository database.

Metadata Repository Database Protection

The infrastructure metadata repository is maintained in an Orcale9*i* database. Normally, this is a standalone database, installed with the infrastructure and specifically tuned for the repository. This special-purpose implementation should not be used for other persistent storage. However, this database does require that you protect its data from loss. Protecting the metadata repository is the same as protecting any other Oracle9*i* database.

> **NOTE**
> *This is an introduction to backup and recovery of Oracle9i databases. You will need to refer to the Oracle Database documentation or obtain a book that covers Oracle Database backup and recovery thoroughly, such as the* Oracle9i DBA Handbook *by Loney and Theriault (McGraw-Hill/ Osborne, 2001) or* Oracle Backup & Recovery 101 *by Smith and Haisley (McGraw-Hill/Osborne, 2002).*

The metadata repository is stored in a precisely tuned Oracle9*i* database that implements all of the data protection inherent in all Oracle databases. We recommend that you implement a separate back-end database to provide application persistent object storage.

Undo Logs

The Oracle9*i* database implements safeguards to ensure data integrity and consistency. In this section, we discuss the major features used by Oracle to protect data. The Oracle9*i* database implements a transaction log that records most changes to the database. The database uses this log to recover data if necessary. Some changes are not logged and so are not recoverable, such as truncating a table. Here is a simplified example of a logged change: A user inserts a row into the employee table. The information about the change is recorded in the undo logs. The user issues a commit to make the change permanent, and the undo log is updated to show that the change is committed. If the user instead issued a rollback command, the database would use the data in the undo log to remove the change to the employee table.

Let's go back to the user issuing the commit. The actual change to the employee table is in memory. On commit, the database updates the undo logs but may not write the change to disk for speed reasons. The data on disk does not match the data in memory, but that is OK since the undo log has a record of the change. The database writer (DBW) process will write changes in memory to disk in the background at certain intervals. Once the database no longer needs to keep the change information, it writes the change to a *redo log file group*. The redo files are lists of changes that the database no longer needs. The metadata repository is created with three redo log file groups. They are filled with changes in a round-robin method. Once the last one is used, the database will begin overwriting the first one (see Figure 11-1).

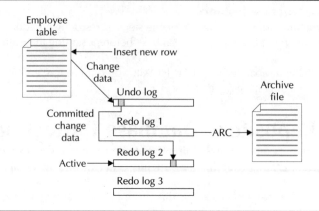

FIGURE 11-1. *Database transaction log files*

But let's say that our database crashes before the DBW writes the change to the employee table to disk. When we restart the database after the crash, Oracle will verify that each data file is consistent using a system change number (SCN). If it finds that the data file does not contain the SCN that it expects, the database will go to the undo/redo logs and recover the data file, updating it with all the missing changes. This is referred to as *rolling forward*. Once all missing transactions are added, the database then uses the undo logs to roll back the uncommitted transaction. At this point, the data file has been recovered and is up-to-date. Once all data files are up-to-date, the database will open and resume work. Hence the undo logs allow the database to roll back uncommitted changes, and the redo and undo logs allow the database to roll data files forward.

Archive Logs

The archive logs are files created by the archive (ARC) process from the redo logs. Once a redo log is full, the database performs a log switch and begins overwriting the next redo log. The ARC process starts copying the changes from the full redo log to an archive log file. By default, the archive log files are located in the infrastructure's $ORACLE_HOME/dbs/arch directory. The ARC process creates one file for each redo log it copies (Figure 11-1). The archive log files are the mechanism that Oracle uses to recover the database from a backup.

Let's say that we took a backup of the metadata repository on Monday, and on Tuesday an operator deleted one of the database's data files. We shut down the database, restore the one missing data file, and restart the database. Oracle will see that the SCN for the restored data files is incorrect and will determine which archive log file has the first change it needs to apply. It will then begin rolling the data file forward, applying each change recorded in the archive logs. The database will continue until the data file is current. When the ARC process is copying changes to archive logs, the database is in *archivelog* mode. When the installer creates the metadata repository database, it is created in *noarchivelog* mode, which means that to recover the database from a backup, you must first place it into archivelog mode. To place the database in archivelog mode using the default log file locations, you must shut it down, partially restart it, switch to archivelog mode, and, finally, open the database.

```
[oracle@appsvr oracle]$ $ORACLE_HOME/bin/sqlplus "/ as sysdba"
# Change the log_archive_start=true
SQL> alter database set log_archive_start=true scope both;
SQL> shutdown immediate
SQL> startup mount
SQL> alter database archivelog;
SQL> alter database open;
```

NOTE
The metadata repository database is created in noarchivelog mode. You must change it to archivelog mode to be able to recover and roll forward the database. If the database is in noarchivelog mode, you can only restore the backup file, and all changes made since that time will be lost.

Now that you are in archivelog mode, how long do you keep the archive logs? The answer is, as long as you maintain a backup. If you rotate backup tapes and maintain a week's worth of tapes, you need to maintain a week's worth of archive logs. If you no longer have the backup, the archive logs for that backup are of no value. Likewise, if you have the backup but have deleted the archive logs, the backup can only be used to restore to the backup's point in time. The database cannot roll forward without the archive logs. Also, the database cannot skip a missing archive log. The database will roll forward until it needs the missing archive log and no further.

Now that you have a basic understanding of how Oracle maintains transaction logs, we will discuss the methods of backing up the database. The key to having a valid backup is that each file is consistent and did not change during the backup.

Control Files

The database control file maintains information about the physical structure of the database. The control file is critical to recovering a data file because it maintains the system change number (SCN) for each data file. On startup, the database checks the control file to ensure that all the data files are available and that they are current. When you replace a data file with one from a backup, the database will determine that the restored data file requires recovery using the control file and will require that the recovery be performed before opening the database. If the database loses all copies of the control file, it cannot open. For this reason, the database will maintain multiple copies of the control file and update them together. The database needs access to only one of the copies to function.

The database is created with three copies of the control file in one location. DBAs will normally spread these copies to different locations so that the loss of one control file will not affect the other control files. In the days before RAID arrays, a DBA would ensure that each control file was on a different drive. To locate the control files for the metadata repository, sign on as SYSDBA and issue the following command (results are edited for readability):

```
SQL> show parameter control_files

NAME                  VALUE
-----------------     -----------------------------
control_files         /u01/oracle/infra904/oradata/asdb/control01.ctl,
                      /u01/oracle/infra904/oradata/asdb/control02.ctl,
                      /u01/oracle/infra904/oradata/asdb/control03.ctl
```

To look at the internals of the control file you can create a trace file:

```
SQL> ALTER DATABASE BACKUP CONTROLFILE TO TRACE;
```

This will produce a trace file in the user dump directory $ORACLE_HOME/admin/asdb/udump. Here is a partial listing of the trace file:

```
STARTUP NOMOUNT
CREATE CONTROLFILE REUSE DATABASE "ASDB" NORESETLOGS ARCHIVELOG
    MAXLOGFILES 50
    MAXLOGMEMBERS 5
    MAXDATAFILES 100
    MAXINSTANCES 1
    MAXLOGHISTORY 226
LOGFILE
  GROUP 1 '/u01/oracle/infra904/oradata/asdb/redo01.log'  SIZE 50M,
  GROUP 2 '/u01/oracle/infra904/oradata/asdb/redo02.log'  SIZE 50M,
  GROUP 3 '/u01/oracle/infra904/oradata/asdb/redo03.log'  SIZE 50M
# STANDBY LOGFILE
DATAFILE
  '/u01/oracle/infra904/oradata/asdb/system01.dbf',
  '/u01/oracle/infra904/oradata/asdb/undotbs01.dbf',
  '/u01/oracle/infra904/oradata/asdb/drsys01.dbf',
  '/u01/oracle/infra904/oradata/asdb/dcm.dbf',
  '/u01/oracle/infra904/oradata/asdb/portal.dbf',
  .
  .
  .
  '/u01/oracle/infra904/oradata/asdb/battrs1_oid.dbf',
  '/u01/oracle/infra904/oradata/asdb/gcats1_oid.dbf',
  '/u01/oracle/infra904/oradata/asdb/gdefault1_oid.dbf',
  '/u01/oracle/infra904/oradata/asdb/svrmg1_oid.dbf',
  '/u01/oracle/infra904/oradata/asdb/ias_meta01.dbf'
CHARACTER SET WE8MSWIN1252;
```

The trace file can be used to re-create the control file if necessary, so it is created as a series of commands.

Now that we have described the mechanisms Oracle uses to protect data in the database, let's see how those features are used in backup and recovery.

Cold Backup

As mentioned earlier, a cold, or closed, backup is taken when the database is closed, using a shutdown normal or a shutdown immediate command. A shutdown abort is an inconsistent shutdown and requires recovery. Once the database is "down normal" (or immediate), all necessary files are up-to-date. All open transactions are closed (committed or rolled back) when the database shuts down, and the data files' SCN matches the SCN in the control files.

A cold backup is the easiest and simplest method of backing up the database. Close the database, copy the files to the backup medium, and restart the database. You do not need to back up the undo tablespaces, as there are no open transactions. The drawback of a cold backup is that the database is not available, and in the case of the application server, that requires that the application server also be unavailable. If the application server requires constant availability, you must use a hot backup.

Hot Backup

A hot, or open, backup is taken while the database is open and servicing user requests. Because data is changing while the backup is in progress, steps must be taken to ensure that the backup is valid. Because transactions are taking place while the backup is in operation, the database *must* be in archivelog mode. The backup will not be consistent—meaning that each data file may be backed up at a different transactional point in time. This is OK because as long as the database has access to the archive log files, the Oracle recovery mechanism will be able to recover the data files to a consistent point.

Executing a hot backup is more complicated and stressful to the database. It is not recommended that you create hot backups during high transaction periods. The basis of a hot backup is Oracle's ability to place a tablespace in backup mode. If you remember, changes to data are logged in the transaction logs and are written to disk in the background by the DBW process. When you place a tablespace in backup mode, DBW will not update the data file until it is taken out of backup mode. So the steps to executing a hot backup of the metadata repository are as follows:

1. Get a list of data files that support each tablespace.

2. Place a tablespace in backup mode.

3. Copy the data files to another location or to a backup medium.

4. Take the tablespace out of backup mode.

5. Repeat steps 2, 3, and 4 for all remaining tablespaces.

6. Back up all the archive log files since the last backup.

7. Back up the control file.

8. Back up necessary support files.

To get a list of data files and tablespaces use the following command:

```
SQL> set pages 999 line 90
SQL> column c1 heading 'File Name' format a52;
SQL> column c2 heading Tablespace|Name format a16;
SQL> select file_name c1, tablespace_name c2 from dba_data_files
  2  order by c2;

                                                     Tablespace
File Name                                            Name
---------------------------------------------------- ----------------
/u01/oracle/infra904/oradata/asdb/dcm.dbf            DCM
/u01/oracle/infra904/oradata/asdb/discopltc1.dbf     DISCO_PTM5_CACHE
/u01/oracle/infra904/oradata/asdb/discopltm1.dbf     DISCO_PTM5_META
```

```
/u01/oracle/infra904/oradata/asdb/drsys01.dbf          DRSYS
/u01/oracle/infra904/oradata/asdb/oss_sys01.dbf        DSGATEWAY_TAB
/u01/oracle/infra904/oradata/asdb/ias_meta01.dbf       IAS_META
/u01/oracle/infra904/oradata/asdb/ip_dt.dbf            IP_DT
/u01/oracle/infra904/oradata/asdb/ip_idx.dbf           IP_IDX
/u01/oracle/infra904/oradata/asdb/ip_lob.dbf           IP_LOB
/u01/oracle/infra904/oradata/asdb/ip_rt.dbf            IP_RT
/u01/oracle/infra904/oradata/asdb/oca.dbf              OCATS
/u01/oracle/infra904/oradata/asdb/attrs1_oid.dbf       OLTS_ATTRSTORE
/u01/oracle/infra904/oradata/asdb/battrs1_oid.dbf      OLTS_BATTRSTORE
/u01/oracle/infra904/oradata/asdb/gcats1_oid.dbf       OLTS_CT_STORE
/u01/oracle/infra904/oradata/asdb/gdefault1_oid.dbf    OLTS_DEFAULT
/u01/oracle/infra904/oradata/asdb/svrmg1_oid.dbf       OLTS_SVRMGSTORE
/u01/oracle/infra904/oradata/asdb/portal.dbf           PORTAL
/u01/oracle/infra904/oradata/asdb/ptldoc.dbf           PORTAL_DOC
/u01/oracle/infra904/oradata/asdb/ptlidx.dbf           PORTAL_IDX
/u01/oracle/infra904/oradata/asdb/ptllog.dbf           PORTAL_LOG
/u01/oracle/intra904/oradata/asdb/system01.dbf         SYSTEM
/u01/oracle/infra904/oradata/asdb/uddisys01.dbf        UDDISYS_TS
/u01/oracle/infra904/oradata/asdb/undotbs01.dbf        UNDOTBS
/u01/oracle/infra904/oradata/asdb/wcrsys01.dbf         WCRSYS_TS
```

To place a tablespace in and out of backup mode, use the command

```
ALTER TABLESPACE tablespace_name BEGIN BACKUP;
ALTER TABLESPACE tablespace_name END BACKUP;
```

To back up the database control file, use the following command:

```
ALTER DATABASE BACKUP CONTROL FILE TO 'location' REUSE;
```

where "location" is a directory where you are placing the backup files.

The final step is to back up other necessary files such as the init.ora/SPFILE, tnsname.ora, and so on. These files do not normally change, so they may not be backed up every time. To execute a hot backup, you create a script that executes each step. The following script will create a hot backup for the metadata repository database as configured during installation. Remember, the database must be in archivelog mode.

```
Hot Backup Script
- Run as SYSDBA

ALTER TABLESPACE DCM BEGIN BACKUP;
HOST cp /u01/oracle/infra904/oradata/asdb/dcm.dbf /u03/oracle/backup/.
ALTER TABLESPACE DCM END BACKUP;

ALTER TABLESPACE DISCO_PTM5_CACHE BEGIN BACKUP;
HOST cp /u01/oracle/infra904/oradata/asdb/discopltc1.dbf
        /u03/oracle/backup/.
ALTER TABLESPACE DISCO_PTM5_CACHE END BACKUP;

ALTER TABLESPACE DISCO_PTM5_META BEGIN BACKUP;
HOST cp /u01/oracle/infra904/oradata/asdb/discopltm1.dbf
        /u03/oracle/backup/.
```

```
ALTER TABLESPACE DISCO_PTM5_META END BACKUP;

ALTER TABLESPACE DRSYS BEGIN BACKUP;
HOST cp /u01/oracle/infra904/oradata/asdb/drsys01.dbf /u03/oracle/backup/.
ALTER TABLESPACE DRSYS END BACKUP;

ALTER TABLESPACE DSGATEWAY_TAB BEGIN BACKUP;
HOST cp /u01/oracle/infra904/oradata/asdb/oss_sys01.dbf /u03/oracle/backup/.
ALTER TABLESPACE DSGATEWAY_TAB END BACKUP;

ALTER TABLESPACE IAS_META BEGIN BACKUP;
HOST cp /u01/oracle/infra904/oradata/asdb/ias_meta01.dbf
        /u03/oracle/backup/.
ALTER TABLESPACE IAS_META END BACKUP;

ALTER TABLESPACE IP_DT BEGIN BACKUP;
HOST cp /u01/oracle/infra904/oradata/asdb/ip_dt.dbf /u03/oracle/backup/.
ALTER TABLESPACE IP_DT END BACKUP;

ALTER TABLESPACE IP_IDX BEGIN BACKUP;
HOST cp /u01/oracle/infra904/oradata/asdb/ip_idx.dbf /u03/oracle/backup/.
ALTER TABLESPACE IP_IDX END BACKUP;

ALTER TABLESPACE IP_LOB BEGIN BACKUP;
HOST cp /u01/oracle/infra904/oradata/asdb/ip_lob.dbf /u03/oracle/backup/.
ALTER TABLESPACE IP_LOB END BACKUP;

ALTER TABLESPACE IP_RT BEGIN BACKUP;
HOST cp /u01/oracle/infra904/oradata/asdb/ip_rt.dbf /u03/oracle/backup/.
ALTER TABLESPACE IP_RT END BACKUP;

ALTER TABLESPACE OCATS BEGIN BACKUP;
HOST cp /u01/oracle/infra904/oradata/asdb/oca.dbf /u03/oracle/backup/.
ALTER TABLESPACE OCATS END BACKUP;

ALTER TABLESPACE OLTS_ATTRSTORE BEGIN BACKUP;
HOST cp /u01/oracle/infra904/oradata/asdb/attrs1_oid.dbf
        /u03/oracle/backup/.
ALTER TABLESPACE OLTS_ATTRSTORE END BACKUP;

ALTER TABLESPACE OLTS_BATTRSTORE BEGIN BACKUP;
HOST cp /u01/oracle/infra904/oradata/asdb/battrs1_oid.dbf
        /u03/oracle/backup/.
ALTER TABLESPACE OLTS_BATTRSTORE END BACKUP;

ALTER TABLESPACE OLTS_CT_STORE BEGIN BACKUP;
HOST cp /u01/oracle/infra904/oradata/asdb/gcats1_oid.dbf
        /u03/oracle/backup/.
ALTER TABLESPACE OLTS_CT_STORE END BACKUP;

ALTER TABLESPACE OLTS_DEFAULT BEGIN BACKUP;
```

```
HOST cp /u01/oracle/infra904/oradata/asdb/gdefault1_oid.dbf
         /u03/oracle/backup/.
ALTER TABLESPACE OLTS_DEFAULT END BACKUP;

ALTER TABLESPACE OLTS_SVRMGSTORE BEGIN BACKUP;
HOST cp /u01/oracle/infra904/oradata/asdb/svrmg1_oid.dbf
         /u03/oracle/backup/.
ALTER TABLESPACE OLTS_SVRMGSTORE END BACKUP;

ALTER TABLESPACE PORTAL BEGIN BACKUP;
HOST cp /u01/oracle/infra904/oradata/asdb/portal.dbf /u03/oracle/backup/.
ALTER TABLESPACE PORTAL END BACKUP;

ALTER TABLESPACE PORTAL_DOC BEGIN BACKUP;
HOST cp /u01/oracle/infra904/oradata/asdb/ptldoc.dbf /u03/oracle/backup/.
ALTER TABLESPACE PORTAL_DOC END BACKUP;

ALTER TABLESPACE PORTAL_IDX BEGIN BACKUP;
HOST cp /u01/oracle/infra904/oradata/asdb/ptlidx.dbf  /u03/oracle/backup/.
ALTER TABLESPACE PORTAL_IDX END BACKUP;

ALTER TABLESPACE PORTAL_LOG BEGIN BACKUP;
HOST cp /u01/oracle/infra904/oradata/asdb/ptllog.dbf  /u03/oracle/backup/.
ALTER TABLESPACE PORTAL_LOG END BACKUP;

ALTER TABLESPACE SYSTEM BEGIN BACKUP;
HOST cp /u01/oracle/infra904/oradata/asdb/system01.dbf  /u03/oracle/backup/.
ALTER TABLESPACE SYSTEM END BACKUP;

ALTER TABLESPACE UDDISYS_TS BEGIN BACKUP;
HOST cp /u01/oracle/infra904/oradata/asdb/uddisys01.dbf /u03/oracle/backup/.
ALTER TABLESPACE UDDISYS_TS END BACKUP;

ALTER TABLESPACE UNDOTBS BEGIN BACKUP;
HOST cp /u01/oracle/infra904/oradata/asdb/undotbs01.dbf /u03/oracle/backup/.
ALTER TABLESPACE UNDOTBS END BACKUP;

ALTER TABLESPACE WCRSYS_TS BEGIN BACKUP;
HOST cp /u01/oracle/infra904/oradata/asdb/wcrsys01.dbf /u03/oracle/backup/.
ALTER TABLESPACE WCRSYS_TS END BACKUP;

- Backup the Control File
ALTER DATABASE BACKUP CONTROLFILE TO '/u03/oracle/backup/' REUSE;

- Create a text version of the Control File
ALTER DATABASE BACKUP CONTROLFILE TO TRACE;

- Backup the Archive logs  First Switch log files
ALTER SYSTEM SWITCH LOGFILE
- Stop Logging
```

```
ALTER SYSTEM ARCHIVE LOG STOP;
HOST cp /u01/oracle/infra904/dbs/arch/*.dbf /u03/oracle/backup/.
ALTER SYSTEM ARCHIVE LOG START;

- Backup init.ora and SPFILE
HOST cp /u01/oracle/infra904/dbs/initasdb.ora /u03/oracle/backup/.
HOST cp /u01/oracle/infra904/dbs/spfileasdb.ora /u03/oracle/backup/.
```

This file is very basic and is used to illustrate the method of creating a hot backup. There is no error checking of logging. Notice that if we add an additional data file to a tablespace, we have to manually add it to the backup script. A production hot backup script should obtain current information on data files and tablespaces from the database at execution time. Likewise, it should create a log file of the actions performed so that the administrator can be sure that the backup was error free.

Creating a hot backup is more complicated than a cold backup, but recovery is pretty much the same. Recover the missing or corrupted data file and start the database. The database will determine what archive logs need to be applied and will roll the database forward until the data file is recovered, provided the archive logs are available.

Recovery Manager (RMAN)

A server-managed backup and recovery strategy uses a tool called Recovery Manager (RMAN) to handle both the backup and recovery. RMAN will create the backup, execute the restore, and perform the recovery. One significant advantage of using RMAN is that it normally works at the data block level rather than the file level. RMAN backs up the data blocks to a remote location and if needed uses the data in those blocks to rebuild and recover blocks in the database. RMAN uses a catalog (created in a separate database) to maintain backup information such as what backups are available and where they are located.

You can configure RMAN to maintain your backup strategy, and RMAN will create the backups and purge old backups automatically. When you need to restore a file, RMAN will use the catalog to locate the backup, restore the file (or data blocks), and recover the database. RMAN is intelligent enough to determine what needs to be restored and recovered and execute the appropriate actions. RMAN excels in environments with multiple Oracle databases and can maintain backup and recovery for both your metadata repository databases and your back-end databases. For additional information on Recovery Manager, refer to the Oracle Database documentation or a book on Oracle databases like the ones mentioned earlier in this chapter.

Database Recovery

You should never have to recover your database; the Oracle9*i* database will automatically recover itself from most common problems. If an instance fails or the operator issues a shutdown abort command, the database will recover itself on startup without intervention. However, the Oracle 9*i* database has all the required mechanisms to allow user recovery from serious failures.

NOTE
We recommend that you attempt to recover a database only once, and if it fails, contact Oracle Support. If the first attempt fails, repeated attempts might cause additional damage and leave the database in a state where only partial recovery is possible. When in doubt, contact Oracle Support.

The first step, if you do have to recover your database, is determining what needs recovery. If the metadata repository does not open on startup, it will manifest itself in the failure of other components to start. If you can start middle tier components, such as the OC4J instances, check the infrastructure tier to ensure that OID is running. If OID will not start, look to the metadata repository database. If you find that the database is the problem, the first place to check is the database alert log. The alert log is located in the infrastructure's $ORACLE_HOME/admin/asdb/ bdump directory and is called alertasdb.log. Substitute your SID if you did not install the database with the SID set to asdb. This log file will tell you why the database did not open. It may also lead you to other trace files with more detailed information.

Because of the way the Oracle9i database stores changes in the transaction logs, recovery is a two-step process: roll the database forward until all changes are applied, and then roll back any uncommitted (open) transactions. At the end of this two-step operation, the database is recovered to a consistent state with no data loss.

The Oracle9i database has two main types of recovery—complete and incomplete. A complete recovery uses the transaction logs to recover all committed data. An incomplete recovery uses whatever logs are available to recover as much data as possible and then stops. There is always some type of data loss in an incomplete recovery. Incomplete recovery is required if the database is not in archivelog mode or if necessary archive log files are no longer available. Generally, the steps to execute a recovery are

1. Fix the problem (replace faulty equipment, drives, and so on).

2. Restore the affected files.

3. Locate (or restore) the archive log files.

4. Start the database.

5. Recover the database.

6. Open the database.

If a disk crash caused the problem, you must replace the drive or place the restored file in another location. Restore the most recent backup of the damaged files. The older the backup, the longer it will take to roll the file forward. Locate or restore the archive log files that cover transactions back to the date of the backup. If restored to the archive log directory, the Oracle Database will know where to find them. If you restore the logs to another location, the database will ask you where they are. Now start the database. If the database can automatically recover, the database will end up in an open, ready-to-use state. If not, the database will start up to the mount point and issue an error stating that the data file needs recovery. Issue the command

```
SQL> RECOVER DATABASE;
```

Oracle will tell you the name of the first archive log file needed for the recovery. If you placed all the archive logs in the original directory, press ENTER to apply that log. Enter **auto** to have Oracle automatically apply all necessary logs without asking. Finally, if you did not replace the log files in the original directory, enter the new location where Oracle can find the files. Upon completion, Oracle will respond with

```
Media Recovery Complete
```

Open the database and check the alert log for any other problems.

Complete Database Recovery

A complete database recovery is required when you are recovering an infrastructure instance from backup and are restoring all of the files in the $ORACLE_HOME/oradata directory, including all control files. If you restored all files (including the archive log files) for that backup, the database should self-recover on startup. If the backup was created using a hot (open) backup, media recovery may be required. Ensure that you restore the archive log files that were copied with the hot backup.

Database Recovery Issues

We have discussed basic file recovery on a database that is not open. For additional information, refer to the sources already mentioned. If in doubt, get help; call Oracle Support. Here are some points to remember when faced with a database recovery:

- Use the current control file. The control file contains the information that defines the current status of each file. If one of the control files needs to be restored, copy it over from one of the other current control files. Never use a restored copy of a control file unless all copies of the current control file are lost.

- Any time you open the database with the RESETLOGS clause, there is data loss. Always contact Oracle Support before using RESETLOGS. Once used, it cannot be undone.

- When restoring files, only restore files that are damaged or lost. This will reduce the roll forward time.

Now that you have a basic understanding of the mechanisms involved in backing up and restoring, we will introduce you to a tool that will automate most of these tasks.

Application Server 10*g* Backup and Recovery Tool

The Oracle Application Server 10*g* Backup and Recovery tool is a Perl script that will not only handle your backup needs, but will automatically handle a restore. This tool handles the instance configuration files to include the metadata repository database data files (the third group of files described earlier). Since these are the files that change often, you can build your backup strategy around this tool. You can now take a full backup of the instance's $ORACLE_HOME and then use the Backup and Recovery tool to back up the "group three" files nightly. To restore the instance, follow the same steps as presented in the earlier section "Recovering the Application Server," except after restoring the $ORACLE_HOME directory, run the Backup and Recovery tool to restore the latest configuration files.

The Backup and Recovery tool is located on the OracleAS RepCA and Utilities CD-ROM in the utilities/backup directory. The file name is backup_restore.tar. You must install and run the tool on each server. Once it is installed and configured, it will copy all the instance configuration files to the user-defined backup directory. If run against an infrastructure instance, the script will also use RMAN to create a backup of the metadata repository database. If the user application maintains local files, the Backup and Recovery tool can be configured to back up those files as well.

For additional information on the Oracle Application Server 10*g* Backup and Recovery tool, refer to Chapter 12 of the *Oracle Application Server 10g Administrator's Guide* (9.0.4).

Summary

This chapter has been an introduction to the backup and recovery capabilities of Oracle Application Server 10g. We stress that this is an introduction, as there are lengthy books written about backup and recovery of the Oracle9i database alone, and the documentation runs in the thousands of pages. The main points are as follows:

- Ensure that your backups are complete. They must include the instance $ORACLE_HOME, the oraInventory directory, the oraInst.loc and oratab files, and if it is an infrastructure instance, a consistent backup (hot or cold) of the metadata repository database.

- You can only restore an instance from backup onto the same OS (including patch level), configured with the $ORACLE_HOME and oraInventory directories located on the same mount point and path as the original installation.

- Create a backup and recovery plan and test it. Ensure that you can recover from all levels of failure—from instance failure to a server failure. Reduce recovery time by having backups of the properly configured operating system.

- The Oracle9i database that supports the metadata repository is installed in the default noarchivelog mode. You must change the database to archivelog mode to support recovery.

- Don't be afraid to get help, especially with recovering the database. If the first attempt does not succeed, call Oracle Support.

We hope you will never need the restore portion of this chapter, but you should immediately implement a backup strategy that fits your resources and requirements if you do not have one. Without a complete backup, there is no chance to restore. And the only way to verify that your backup is sufficient is to execute a restore. Don't wait until you need it to find out that your backup plan is not complete.

CHAPTER
12

Oracle Application
Server 10g Security

ecurity is a major concern when deploying an application to the Internet or on an intranet. The application has to ensure that only authorized users gain access and that the application only returns information that the user has privileges to see. Likewise, the application server needs to secure the authentication information from unauthorized disclosure. Oracle Application Server 10*g* implements security features in each component, from the Web Cache to the back-end database.

When a user requests content (such as an employee's pay records), the application must ensure that the user is allowed to access this information, possibly by verifying a user password. When the content is returned, the application needs to provide some method to re-identify the user. The application can constantly ask for the user's password or return a cookie/URL parameter that is returned with each request to verify a user's identity. If the company has a suite of applications, the user must be validated by each application before gaining access. Again, each application can request the user's password (causing him to constantly reenter his password), or the first application can return an identity object (cookie, for example) that is validated once. Then as the user moves from application to application, the cookie acts as his identity. This is the basis of Oracle's Single Sign-On. A user signs on once and is automatically validated as he moves from application to application within the system. Of course, this capability requires that some secure directory knows the user and verifies his privileges. This is the job of the Oracle Internet Directory. Before going further, we should point out that a user might not be a person, such as a customer or employee, it could be another application or system.

Component Security Features

We will start by discussing the separate application server components and their security features. Each component integrates its security features into the security of the application server as a whole. Except for Web Cache, most components are tied to Oracle Internet Directory (OID) for directory services, so we devote most of the chapter to OID) and its partner Single Sign-On (SSO).

Web Cache

As discussed in detail in Chapter 5, the Oracle Web Cache uses caching rules and content invalidation to ensure that it serves the correct content to the correct user. However, it is up to the application to correctly implement these rules. When the application server serves a page containing personal content, Web Cache stores the content and the cookie/URL parameter with the content and will only re-serve that content to a request that returns the cookie/URL parameter. If the user's browser does not accept or return the cookie, Web Cache will submit the request to the origin server because it can't identify the requester. The initial authentication of the user is the responsibility of the origin server.

Oracle HTTP Server

The Oracle HTTP Server (OHS), discussed in Chapter 4, is built on the industry standard Apache web server. OHS is responsible for accepting a request and either sending the requested information or passing the request to the application (via mod_oc4j) for processing. Since OHS's main function is to serve static content, it performs basic rule-based authentication to determine what content to serve. These rules are defined in the Directory Container sections of the httpd.conf file or the

.htaccess files. OHS uses the HTTP header information sent with the request to determine whether the requester has access to the static information, and either serves the content or returns an error message. In this way, OHS implements security based on the identity of the user's IP address or host name. If the request is for dynamic content, OHS passes the request to one of its modules for processing. In Application Server 10*g*, this module will be mod_oc4j if the request is a JSP, servlet, or a J2EE application. Mod_oc4j will pass the request to an Oracle Container for Java (OC4J) instance for processing.

Later in this chapter, we will introduce mod_osso, which is used by OHS to interface with Oracle's Single Sign-On application.

OHS ensures the security of exchanged data through its implementation of Secure Sockets Layer (SSL) and Public Key Infrastructure (PKI). When Application Server 10*g* is installed, a Secure Sockets Layer virtual host connection is installed in OHS. To use the secure connection, log onto the server using the SSL port (identified in the ports list of the tier's Enterprise Manager web page) using the https:// URL identifier, for example:

```
https://appsvr.proxitec.com/4446
```

The SSL implementation in the user's browser interacts with SSL in OHS to provide a secure connection. The two SSL implementations negotiate the encryption scheme used to encrypt the connection. OHS implements an Oracle module called mod_ossl to provide the SSL features. Mod_ossl is a plug-in to Oracle HTTP Server that enables the server to use SSL. It is very similar to the OpenSSL module, mod_ssl. However, in contrast to the OpenSSL module, mod_ossl is based on the Oracle implementation of SSL, which supports SSL version 3 and is based on Certicom and RSA Security technology.

One of the most common encryption suites that SSL implements is PKI. In short, the PKI methodology is to create two keys, public and private. The public key is used to encrypt data; the private is required to decrypt data encrypted by the public key. Even though the data is encrypted using the public key, it cannot be decrypted using the public key. To see how this works, consider that a user's browser provides a public key to one party that it uses both to encrypt data and send it back. The private key (retained by the sender) is the only key that can decrypt data encrypted with the public key. To exchange information both ways, each party must have two keys, a private key and a public key. They must exchange public keys. Each party encrypts data with the other party's public key and decrypts data with their own private key. In this way, all data exchanged is encrypted and secure. However, because there is significant overhead to using a two-key system, most SSL implementations use PKI to securely exchange a single encryption key and then encrypt/ decrypt all data using the single key. These keys are only valid for a session, and each session generates different keys. Since the keys are constantly changing, any given key will have changed long before someone could break the encryption.

In earlier versions of Oracle Application Server, the SSL virtual host was configured in the httpd.conf file. In Application Server 10*g*, it is configured in an included file called ssl.conf. The ssl.conf file contains the directives to create the virtual host and all the default directives for any other virtual host that implements SSL.

For developers, OHS's implementation of SSL is important because it removes the requirement that you implement some type of encryption to ensure secure communication. Once you ensure that the user is accessing the application server using SSL (https:\\), you can send data through OHS, and it will ensure that the data is encrypted.

Oracle Container for Java

OC4J supports the operation of Java Server Pages (JSPs), servlets, and J2EE applications. As such, most of the authentication work takes place here. Oracle's implementation of the Java Authentication and Authorization Service (JAAS) standard, known as "JAZN," adds PAM-based pluggable authentication and subject-based, fine-grained authorization to the Java2 platform. OC4J implements the J2EE JAAS API to facilitate security within the J2EE application.

The two JAAS implementations provided by OC4J are JAZN-LDAP and JAZN-XML. JAZN-LDAP is an implementation of the JAAS API that retrieves user and authorization information securely from Oracle Internet Directory (OID). JAZN-LDAP is particularly useful for applications that have a large user community, for which scalability is a strong requirement. JAZN-XML is a fast, lightweight implementation of the JAAS API that is based on XML as an encoding mechanism. JAZN-XML allows Java developers to retrieve user and role information securely from operating system files rather than retrieving information from Oracle Internet Directory (as is the case with JAZN-LDAP). JAZN_XML supports lightweight deployments of Application Server 10*g* and provides a more secure alternative to principals.xml. JAZN_XML will usually use the file JAZN-DATA.xml to store and retrieve user data. To get additional information on using JAAS within your application, go to otn.oracle.com and search on JAAS.

Authentication

Authentication establishes a network entity's identity. An entity could be users or another application. Entities that access an application are asked for a password, which the application verifies against a user directory. The user directory can be a file, LDAP directory, or Oracle Internet Directory. The user directory's job is to store users' credentials. External applications may also need to be authenticated and could either provide passwords or use a digital certificate. A developer can create a login module that supports whatever authentication method is required.

Authorization

Authorization means granting privileges to an authenticated entity. Roles are defined within the J2EE application that determine access rights to different objects. Application Server 10*g* supports a fully declarative implementation of the J2EE security, which means you can secure your Java application without writing code. Once an entity, such as a user, is authenticated, it is granted a role or roles that allow it to access the necessary parts of the application. These authorizations can be centrally managed in the Oracle Internet Directory or in XML files. Placing the authorizations in OID allows for centralized management of privileges within an organization. JAAS and OID also allow you to relate a section of code to a user so that users can execute that part of the code without being authorized to execute all the code.

Delegation

With delegation, an EJB runs with the privileges of a certain user. This allows a user with limited privileges to execute an EJB, which will execute with a higher authorization to perform some task. This supports the idea of assigning a user the lowest privilege level necessary to accomplish a task.

Oracle Identity Management

One benefit of using the Application Server 10*g* infrastructure is the integration of Oracle Identity Management, which provides a single location for the complete management of users and network entities. This can greatly reduce the cost of managing large groups of users. As new users are added to the system, Oracle Identity Management provides a single location for modifying application and system privileges to include account creation and suspension, privilege modification, and attribute management. Users can be company employees, customers, or anyone that requires access to your applications, servers, or network devices.

Identity Management in Application Server 10*g* consists of several components, but the primary ones are the Oracle Internet Directory and Single Sign-On. OID is Oracle's implementation of LDAP version 3, and Single Sign-On uses OID to authenticate users. A third essential component is Delegated Administration Services, which provides application server components with secure access to OID. Certificate Authority issues and manages X.509v3-compliant certificates to secure e-mail and network connections. Directory Integration allows integration with other directories (for example, ADS, SunONE). And, finally, provisioning integration provides automatic provisioning of users in the Oracle environment.

Oracle Internet Directory

OID is an integral part of Application Server 10*g*'s security as the repository for usernames and passwords. However, OID is a complete directory service based on the Lightweight Directory Access Protocol (LDAP). OID combines the capabilities of a directory service with the power and security of the infrastructure repository Oracle9*i* database.

LDAP was first used as a method of looking up e-mail information on the Internet, but its use has quickly expanded as an efficient method of storing and retrieving all types of lookup data, even PKI keys. It is normally used to ask for information from a directory, but in the case of OID, it includes the actual directory. This simple capability has become the basis for looking up resources on the Internet, such as web services and devices. In Application Server 10*g*, the Oracle Internet Directory can contain application configuration information that can be delegated to different levels of administrators for maintenance.

The Application Server 10*g* infrastructure instance contains an instance of an OID application, which listens for directory requests. The OID application handles the security requirements, while the repository database handles the information storage. OID uses SSL to ensure that data is not modified or intercepted during transmission. An example of an Oracle product that can use OID is Oracle Net. Most DBAs only use tnsnames.ora files to maintain their database connection data. If your organization grows to a point where multiple application servers are accessing multiple back-end databases, the tnsnames.ora file can become problematic to maintain. In this case, you can implement an LDAP directory to centralize the location data. Oracle Net services can access OID to resolve database services. The client connection strings will contain connection identifiers, which are resolved by OID. If a database is moved, only OID must be updated.

Oracle Directory Manager

OID is maintained using a Java-based GUI called oidadmin, located in the infrastructure's $ORACLE_ HOME/bin directory. In Windows, go to the Start menu and navigate to the Oracle Directory Manager program. When Oracle Directory Manager starts, it will ask you to connect to a server. Use the OID information entered when installing the midtier instance. You will next see the logon screen (Figure 12-1).

The username is orcladmin, and the password is the ias_admin password you selected during the infrastructure installation. Once you have connected, the Oracle Directory Manager opens as seen in Figure 12-2.

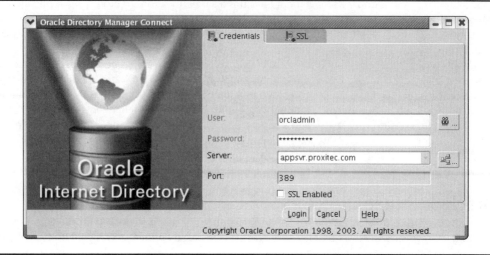

FIGURE 12-1. *Oracle Directory Manager logon screen*

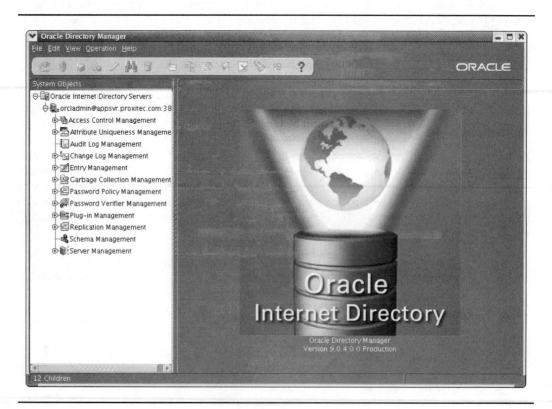

FIGURE 12-2. *Oracle Directory Manager opening screen*

The Oracle Directory Manager, like OID, is built on a tree structure. We have created a Portal user called Sam Spade and used Oracle Directory Manager to locate the entry. We executed a search in the Entry Management branch for entries beginning with "sam" and got the results shown in Figure 12-3.

Looking around the Oracle Directory Manager, you will find data pertaining to users, application configuration, database connectors, and security profiles. For detailed explanations of the capabilities of the Oracle Directory Manager, refer to the Oracle OID documentation.

Delegated Administration Services

Delegated Administration Services (known as DAS) provides application server components with secure access to OID. DAS is actually a set of utilities that act as intermediaries to the information in OID. Each application server component will actually request directory information from DAS, which will then retrieve the information from OID. An example of a DAS service is the password

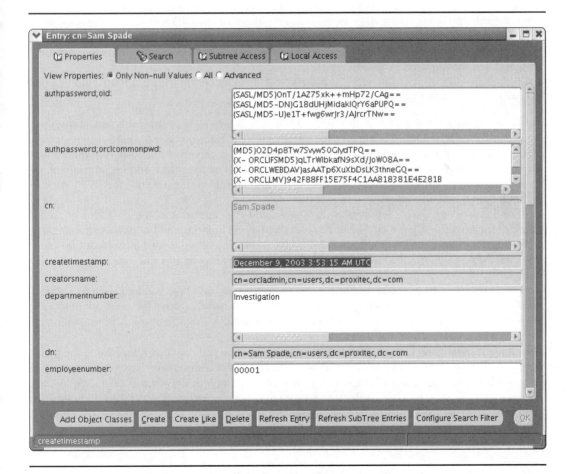

FIGURE 12-3.   *Oracle Directory Manager: entry data*

verifier. An application will pass the authentication information to the password verifier, which will validate the information. In this way, the application does not have to be granted privileges to OID since it does not directly access it.

DAS establishes a tree structure to manage administration of OID. The *global administrator* is at the top of the tree. Below the global administrator are sets of *realms*, each of which has a *realm administrator*. Below the realm administrator are the users that belong to that realm. Users that have common privileges and roles can be placed in a *group*.

One advantage of using DAS is increased security for access to OID. In Application Server 10*g*, the user accesses a servlet or application to get a result. If the servlet or application needs information from OID, it will send the request to DAS, which will in turn retrieve the required information from OID and return it. This adds a layer to the process, but it ensures that a malicious user never accesses OID directly.

One of the useful tools provided by DAS is the Self Service Console.

Oracle Internet Directory Self Service Console

Although the Oracle Directory Manager is a powerful tool, as the application server administrator, you will probably prefer to use the web-based tool oiddas, or the OID Self Service Console. The OID Self Service Console (SSC) is part of the Delegated Administration Services and is much easier to use when managing a user. To access SSC, open your browser, point to the infrastructure OHS port, and add the oiddas directory to the URL:

```
http://appsvr.proxitec.com:7777/oiddas/
```

This will bring up the Oracle Internet Directory Self Service Console web site, shown in Figure 12-4, which is installed along with the infrastructure. This screen allows you to view your own profile or create another user (if you have that privilege). You can enter the basic user information (names, passwords, roles, and so on) and allow the user to fill in other data (address, and so on). Depending on their assigned privileges, both users and administrators can use the SSC to update and maintain user information.

The Self Service Console integrates with Single Sign-On to authenticate a user. To log on, select a link or the Login link. (The administrator username is orcladmin, and the password is the ias_ admin password from the infrastructure install.) After login, you return to the Self Service Console. From the home page, you can select My Profile to review your own account information, as seen in Figure 12-5.

Selecting the Edit My Profile button (or the My Profile tab) will take you to a page that allows you to edit your account information or upload a photo. Across the top of the page are links to allow you to change your password and perform other tasks.

User Page   Select the Directory tab to view the page where you can search for other users in the directory. The example in Figure 12-6 shows a list of all users whose name begins with "sam." As the orcladmin user, you can create a new user or edit a current user. To edit a current user, locate the user with the Search feature, select the user's radio button, and then select the Edit button. To simply see the user's information, select the username link directly. If you wanted to list all users, you would select the Go button with a blank Search field, and all users would be listed.

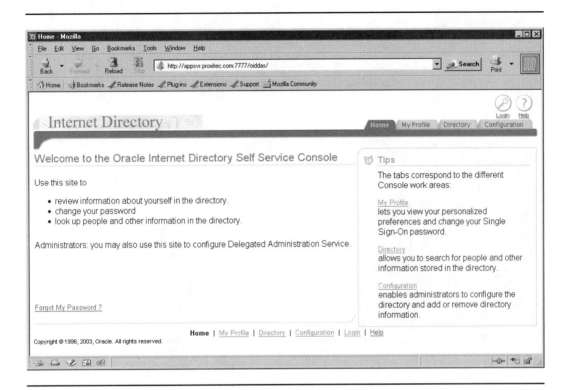

FIGURE 12-4. *Oracle Internet Directory Self Service Console (OID SSC)*

Group Page   A group can be private (only visible to the members) or public (visible to all users). Its creator and whoever is added to the owner list own a group. Another group can own a group. Group membership includes users and other groups. If a group is created as a privileged group, you can assign privileges to the group. We have created an employee group called EMP in Figure 12-7. We added Sam Hearts (the human resource clerk) as the owner and all the example users as members.

After returning to the Group page, you can list all current groups by selecting Go with an empty Search field. As seen in Figure 12-7, the Company Employee group is listed. To view the group information, select the Company Employee link. Because we did not make the EMP group a privileged group, we cannot assign privileges to it. However, you can make the group a privileged group by selecting the group radio button and selecting Edit. Now you can select the check box to make EMP a privileged group. You can assign privileges to a group by selecting the group's radio button and then selecting the Assign Privileges button. Figure 12-8 demonstrates granting the members of the EMP group privileges that allow them to create, edit, and delete users.

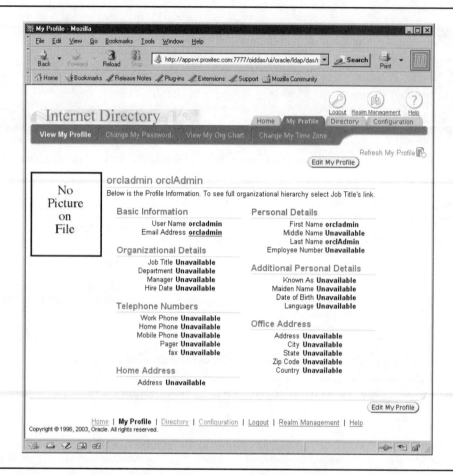

FIGURE 12-5. *OID SSC: My Profile page*

Service Page   A service is one or more applications that provide some capability. It can perform the task for all users or groups of specific users/groups. The Self Service Console is an example of a service.

Account Page   On the Account page, you can unlock, enable, or disable an account. Select the function you want to perform, and then search for the user account. Select the account and perform the function.

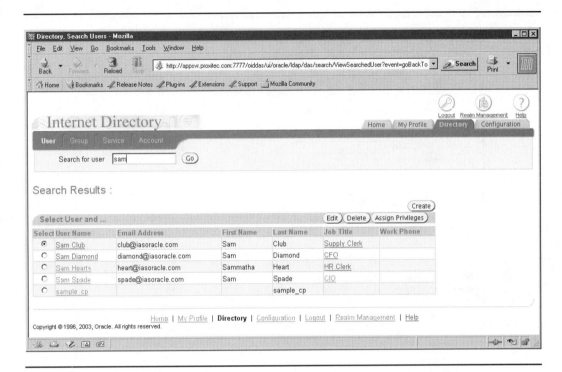

FIGURE 12-6. *OID SSC: Directory tab, User page*

Identity Realms

As previously discussed, DAS divides users/groups into realms, and each realm has a realm administrator. When installed, there is only one realm, called DEFAULT COMPANY. If you log in as the global administrator (installed as orcladmin), you can create additional realms. Select the Realm Management link at the top of the Internet Directory screen. Empty the text box (if necessary), and click Go to see a listing of all current realms. Select the Create button to move to the Create Identity Management Realms page, as shown in Figure 12-9. Enter a name, contact information, and a description of the new realm. If you want to display a logo for the realm or a product logo, select the check box and browse to the file. Select Submit, and SSC will create the new realm.

At this point, you have a basic understanding of the Oracle Internet Directory and the Delegated Administration Services. For additional information on OID and DAS, to include bulk loading of user information into OID, refer to the *Oracle Internet Directory Administration Guide 10*g.

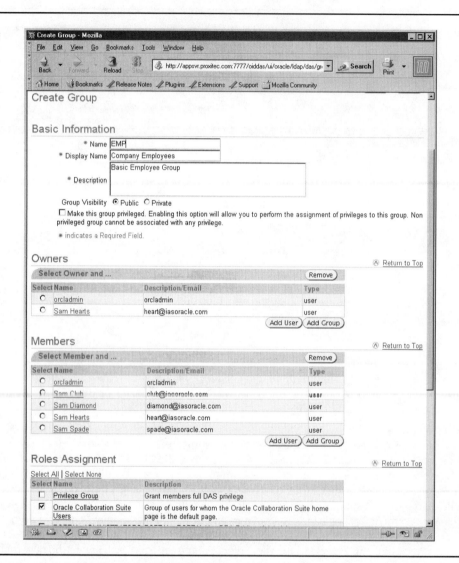

FIGURE 12-7. *OID SSC: Create Group page*

Single Sign-On

As described at the beginning of the chapter, Single Sign-On allows users to provide their credentials once and then automatically authenticates them as they switch between applications. The first time users enter their username/password (or other credentials), SSO creates an encrypted cookie that contains the identity information. When users change applications, the new application uses the cookie to authenticate the user and retrieve the authorizations. This way, users not only move

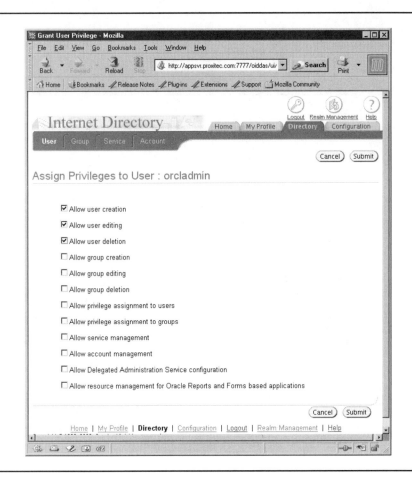

FIGURE 12-8.   *OID SSC: Assign Group Privileges*

from application to application without having to reenter their username and password, but when they are finished, they can log out of SSO and it will log them out of all SSO partner applications.

We have already seen this when we logged out of the OID Self Service Console. Figure 12-10 shows SSO logging us out after we selected the Logout option in SSC.

If you spend some time looking around the Self Service Console, you may run into another feature of SSO—time limits. The encrypted cookie that SSO creates when you log in has a timestamp and is only valid during that time. If a user logs off without logging out of SSO, when she returns, the cookie will be invalid, and she will be required to re-log in before she is authenticated.

Since SSO uses encrypted cookies to identify a user after she logs in, Oracle HTTP Server is a key component. OHS uses a module called mod_osso to handle SSO actions. Mod_osso is used to integrate SSO transparently into an application, accepting requests for authentication and providing the appropriate header parameters. SSO support is also built into OC4J using the SSO software

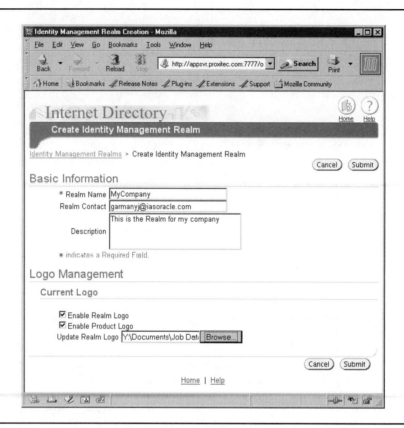

FIGURE 12-9. *OID SSC: Create Identity Management Realms*

development kit (SDK). Note, however, this is for backward compatibility with earlier versions of Oracle Application Server and is deprecated in Application Server 10*g*. SSO itself is an application that runs in the infrastructure tier, handling authentication for both partner and external applications.

Partner Applications
A partner application runs in Application Server 10*g* and implements SSO to authenticate a user through mod_osso or the SSO SDK. The application must identify the user's privileges within the application but must also integrate with SSO. Portal is an example of a partner application. To access a partner application, the user logs onto the application and is redirected to the SSO server. The SSO server requests the user's credentials, and, verifies them against the data stored in OID, and if valid, sets an encrypted cookie and redirects the user back to the application. On subsequent requests to the application, mod_osso verifies the cookie information and either allows access to the application or redirects the user back to the SSO server if invalid.

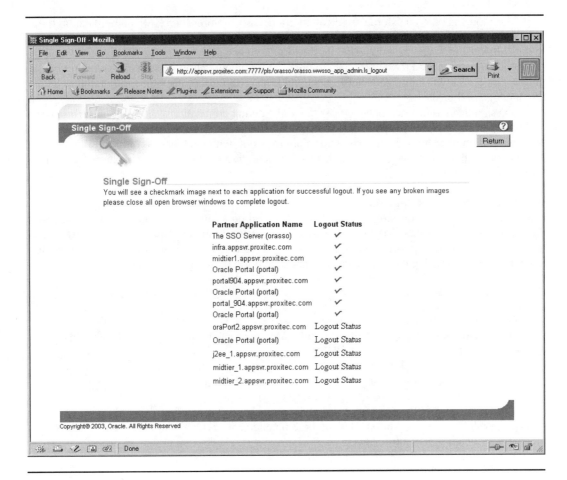

FIGURE 12-10. *Single Sign-Off page*

External Applications

External applications do not implement SSO for user authentication and in fact may not even run on the application server. If the external application uses an HTML login form, SSO can provide the login credentials for the application. An example of an external application is a web mail program. When the SSO user attempts to access the web mail program, SSO will retrieve the user's name and password and automatically respond to the HTML authentication form, logging the user into the program. SSO in Application Server 10*g* has added to this feature so that an SSO user can automatically log into a Windows server using a Kerberos ticket. SSO also allows the use of x.509 certificates for authentication.

When logging onto an external application, mod_osso captures the HTML authentication form and looks in SSO for credentials. If you have not yet logged into SSO, you will be asked to log in. If this is the first time you have logged onto this site, SSO will prompt you for your site credentials. SSO will then return the HTML form data to the site for authentication. Upon subsequent returns to the site, mod_osso will capture the authentication form and automatically return your authentication credentials for that site.

One significant difference between partner and external applications is logging off. When you log off a partner application, you log out of SSO and must log back in to continue to access them. External programs that do not reverify your authentication with each access (almost all of them) will not know that you logged out of SSO. The user is required to log off of each external program to ensure against unauthorized access.

Administering Single Sign-On

You begin by assigning privileges to the users that will be administering SSO. Use the Oracle Directory Manager application discussed earlier to add users to the iASAdmin group in OID. Those users in the iASAdmin group have the privileges needed to administer SSO. Start the Oracle Directory Manager using the following command, and log on as cn=orcladmin.

```
$INFRA_ORACLE_HOME/bin/oidadmin
```

Note that the user cn=orcladmin is not the same user as orcladmin. You must log in using the userid cn=orcladmin. Navigate through Entry Management, OracleContext, and Groups to the iASAdmin group, as shown in Figure 12-11.

Scroll to the bottom of the Properties tab, and add the administration users to the uniquemember text box. Select Apply to set your changes. If you attempt to add a user who does not currently have an account in OID, you will receive an exception error.

When a member of the iASAdmin group connects to SSO using the following command, the SSO page will contain an additional link at the top called SSO Server Administration. This link will take you to the administration page.

```
$Infra_ORACLE_HOME/pls/orasso
```

The SSO Server Administration page contains three links: Edit SSO Server Configuration, Administer Partner Applications, and Administer External Programs.

Edit SSO Server Configuration   This link lets you set the Single Sign-On session duration in hours. This determines how long users can be signed on before their authentication is reverified by SSO. It also allows you to force the SSO server to verify that the IP of the browser is the same as the IP of the verification request. This added step is used to stop IP spoofing.

For sensitive applications Oracle provides a Global User Inactivity Timeout that by default is not set. If you need this feature, refer to the *Oracle Application Server Single Sign-On Administration Guide.*

Administer Partner Applications   This link allows you to add, delete, or edit partner applications. As shown in Figure 12-12, to add a partner application, select the Add Partner Application link.

Enter the application name (this is the name used by SSO) and the home URL. When users access the application's home, they are redirected to the SSO server for validation. The Success

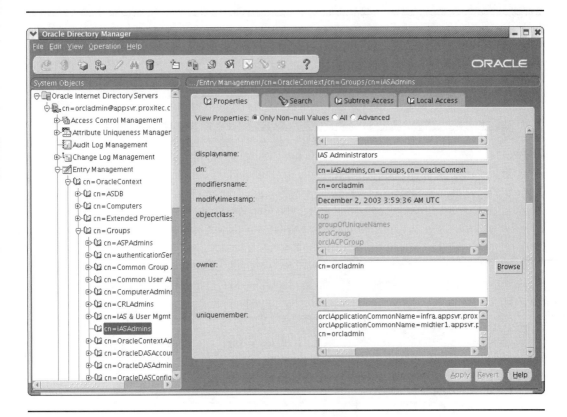

FIGURE 12-11. *Oracle Directory Manager: iASAdmin group*

URL is the location where the SSO server redirects users after successfully authenticating them. Normally, the Success URL is the same as the Home URL. The Logout URL is where SSO redirects users when they log out of SSO. This allows the application to interact with the user on logout. When users log out of SSO they are passed to each of the logout URLs for the applications they used.

Setting the start and end dates allows you to limit access to the partner application. The Application Administrator data is also available if required but is not shown to users.

Administer External Programs This link allows you to add, delete, and edit the validation method for external programs. Select the Add External Program link to move to the Create External Application page shown in Figure 12-13. Enter the application name and URL. Again, mod_osso will intercept the HTML validation form, retrieve the authentication data from OID, and submit it back to the application.

The User Name/ID and Password fields are the names of the fields in the HTML source for the authentication form. You find these values by looking at the HTML source, normally by selecting View | Page Source in your browser. While viewing the HTML source, determine how the browser is expected to return the user credentials. Normally, these are performed by a POST or GET statement.

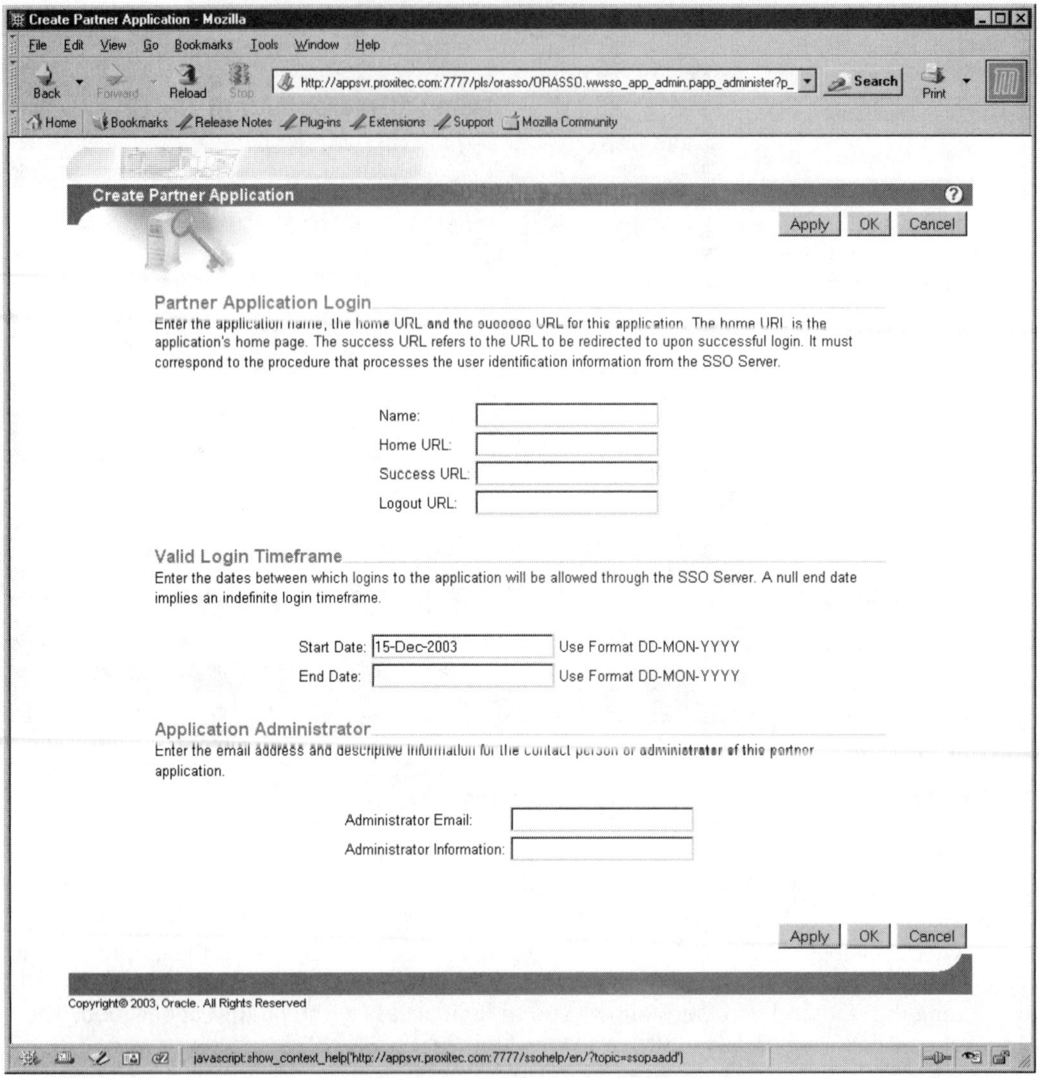

FIGURE 12-12. *ORASSO Administer: Create Partner Application page*

The data in Additional Fields is used to return information other than the username and password that the application may be expecting, such as a company name. Again, these requirements are found in the HTML source for the authentication form. The Field Name is the name of the item in the HTML source, and the Field Value is the value returned by SSO for that field. If you select the Show User check box, the additional fields will be shown to users when they sign into the SSO server.

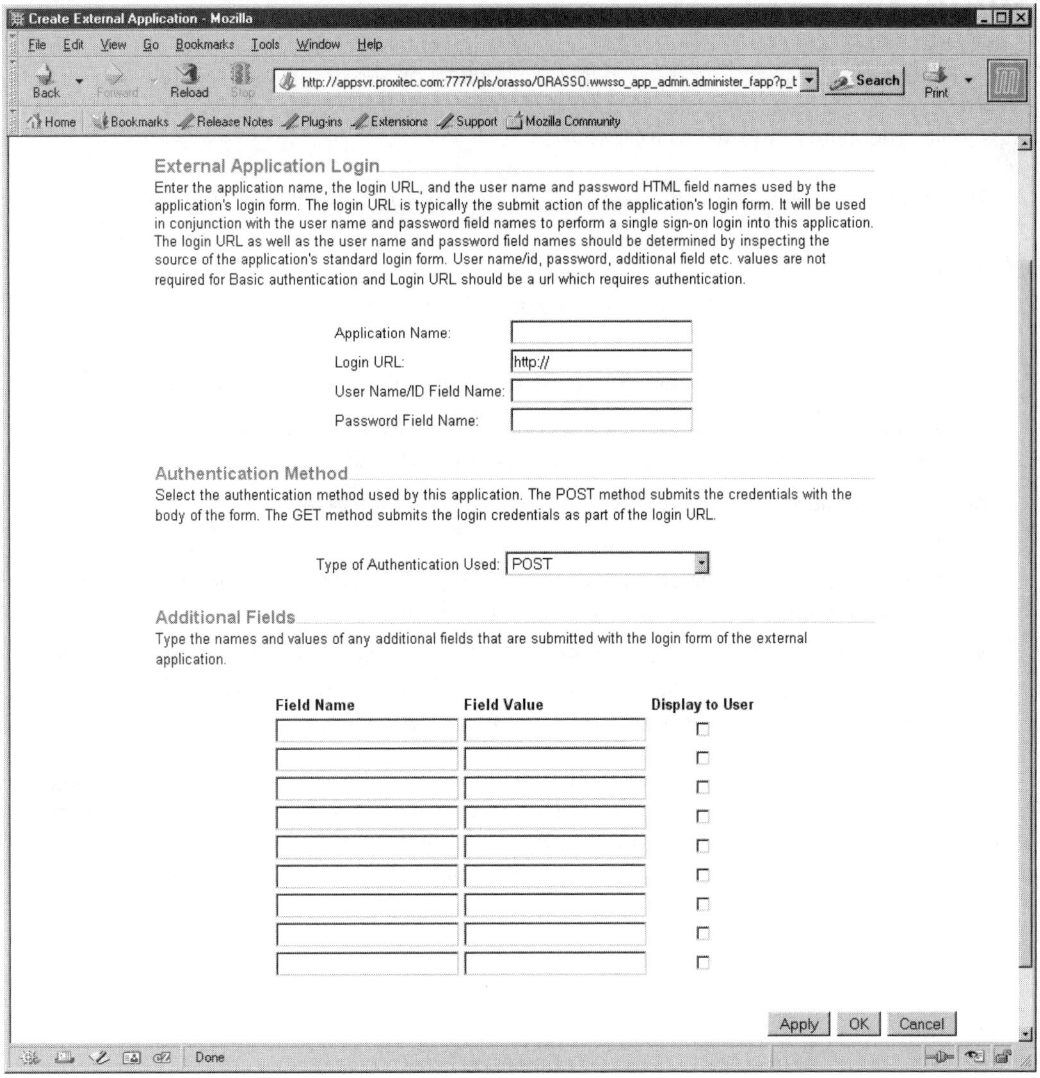

FIGURE 12-13.   *ORASSO Administer: Create External Application Login page*

This has been an introduction to the capabilities of Oracle Single Sign-On. For additional information on the numerous features, including language capabilities, refer to the *Oracle Application Server Single Sign-On Administration Guide.*

Summary

In this chapter, we have looked at the different security features of Oracle Application Server 10g. Oracle has made a concerted effort to see that the application server operates securely right out of the box. Each component integrates its security features into the security of the application server as a whole. The main points are as follows:

- Except for Web Cache, most components are tied to Oracle Internet Directory for directory services.

- Oracle HTTP Server (OHS) implements a Secure Sockets Layer (SSL) with Public Key Infrastructure to ensure that communication between the user's browser and OHS is not intercepted or modified.

- OC4J container implements JAAS to facilitate security within a J2EE application.

- Oracle identity management consists of a set of tools used to authenticate and authorize users. At the root is the Oracle Internet Directory, an LDAP version 3–compatible directory.

- Basic user administration is accomplished using the Oracle Internet Directory Self Service Console.

- Oracle's Single Sign-On application is used to allow authenticated access to multiple partner and external applications using one user authentication.

- OHS loads a module called mod_osso that is the primary interface with the Single Sign-On application. The SSO software development kit is included for compatibility with older Application Server versions and is deprecated in Application Server 10g.

We have not discussed security related to the back-end database. If the application connects to the back-end database using Oracle Net (JDBC thick connections), all of the Oracle advanced security features are available to secure the connection between the application server and the database. Please refer to the database documentation related to the database version you are using for additional information.

Index

INTERNATIONAL CONTACT INFORMATION

AUSTRALIA
McGraw-Hill Book Company
Australia Pty. Ltd.
TEL +61-2-9900-1800
FAX +61-2-9878-8881
http://www.mcgraw-hill.com.au
books-it_sydney@mcgraw-hill.com

CANADA
McGraw-Hill Ryerson Ltd.
TEL +905-430-5000
FAX +905-430-5020
http://www.mcgraw-hill.ca

GREECE, MIDDLE EAST, & AFRICA (Excluding South Africa)
McGraw-Hill Hellas
TEL +30-210-6560-990
TEL +30-210-6560-993
TEL +30-210-6560-994
FAX +30-210-6545-525

MEXICO (Also serving Latin America)
McGraw-Hill Interamericana Editores
S.A. de C.V.
TEL +525-1500-5108
FAX +525-117-1589
http://www.mcgraw-hill.com.mx
carlos_ruiz@mcgraw-hill.com

SINGAPORE (Serving Asia)
McGraw-Hill Book Company
TEL +65-6863-1580
FAX +65-6862-3354
http://www.mcgraw-hill.com.sg
mghasia@mcgraw-hill.com

SOUTH AFRICA
McGraw-Hill South Africa
TEL +27-11-622-7512
FAX +27-11-622-9045
robyn_swanepoel@mcgraw-hill.com

SPAIN
McGraw-Hill/
Interamericana de España, S.A.U.
TEL +34-91-180-3000
FAX +34-91-372-8513
http://www.mcgraw-hill.es
professional@mcgraw-hill.es

UNITED KINGDOM, NORTHERN, EASTERN, & CENTRAL EUROPE
McGraw-Hill Education Europe
TEL +44-1-628-502500
FAX +44-1-628-770224
http://www.mcgraw-hill.co.uk
emea_queries@mcgraw-hill.com

ALL OTHER INQUIRIES Contact:
McGraw-Hill/Osborne
TEL +1-510-420-7700
FAX +1-510-420-7703
http://www.osborne.com
omg_international@mcgraw-hill.com

Sound Off!

Visit us at **www.osborne.com/bookregistration** and let us know what you thought of this book. While you're online you'll have the opportunity to register for newsletters and special offers from McGraw-Hill/Osborne.

We want to hear from you!

Sneak Peek

Visit us today at **www.betabooks.com** and see what's coming from McGraw-Hill/Osborne tomorrow!

Based on the successful software paradigm, Bet@Books™ allows computing professionals to view partial and sometimes complete text versions of selected titles online. Bet@Books™ viewing is free, invites comments and feedback, and allows you to "test drive" books in progress on the subjects that interest you the most.

ET FREE SUBSCRIPTION
OUR
TO ORACLE MAGAZINE

racle Magazine is essential gear for today's information technology ofessionals. Stay informed and increase your productivity with every issue *Oracle Magazine*. Inside each free bimonthly issue you'll get:

- Up-to-date information on Oracle Database, Oracle Application Server, Web development, enterprise grid computing, database technology, and business trends
- Third-party vendor news and announcements
- Technical articles on Oracle and partner products, technologies, and operating environments
- Development and administration tips
- Real-world customer stories

THERE ARE OTHER ORACLE USERS YOUR LOCATION WHO WOULD E TO RECEIVE THEIR OWN SUB- RIPTION TO ORACLE MAGAZINE, ASE PHOTOCOPY THIS FORM AND SS IT ALONG.

Three easy ways to subscribe:

① Web
Visit our Web site at otn.oracle.com/oraclemagazine. You'll find a subscription form there, plus much more!

② Fax
Complete the questionnaire on the back of this card and fax the questionnaire side only to +1.847.763.9638.

③ Mail
Complete the questionnaire on the back of this card and mail it to P.O. Box 1263, Skokie, IL 60076-8263

FREE SUBSCRIPTION

○ **Yes, please send me a FREE subscription to *Oracle Magazine*.**
To receive a free subscription to *Oracle Magazine*, you must fill out the entire card, sign it, and date it (incomplete cards cannot be processed or acknowledged). You can also fax your application to +1.847.763.963⬛
Or subscribe at our Web site at otn.oracle.com/oraclemagazine

○ N

○ From time to time, Oracle Publishing allows our partners exclusive access to our e-mail addresses for special promotions and announcements. To be included in this program, please check this circle.

signature (required)		date
X		

○ Oracle Publishing allows sharing of our mailing list with selected third parties. If you prefer your mailing address not to be included in this program, please check here. If at any time you would like to be removed from this mailing list, please contact Customer Service at +1.847.647.9630 or send an e-mail to oracle@halldata.com.

name	title
company	e-mail address
street/p.o. box	
city/state/zip or postal code	telephone
country	fax

YOU MUST ANSWER ALL TEN QUESTIONS BELOW.

① WHAT IS THE PRIMARY BUSINESS ACTIVITY OF YOUR FIRM AT THIS LOCATION? (check one only)
- ☐ 01 Aerospace and Defense Manufacturing
- ☐ 02 Application Service Provider
- ☐ 03 Automotive Manufacturing
- ☐ 04 Chemicals, Oil and Gas
- ☐ 05 Communications and Media
- ☐ 06 Construction/Engineering
- ☐ 07 Consumer Sector/Consumer Packaged Goods
- ☐ 08 Education
- ☐ 09 Financial Services/Insurance
- ☐ 10 Government (civil)
- ☐ 11 Government (military)
- ☐ 12 Healthcare
- ☐ 13 High Technology Manufacturing, OEM
- ☐ 14 Integrated Software Vendor
- ☐ 15 Life Sciences (Biotech, Pharmaceutical)
- ☐ 16 Mining
- ☐ 17 Retail/Wholesale/Distribution
- ☐ 18 Systems Integrator, VAR/VAD
- ☐ 19 Telecommunications
- ☐ 20 Travel and Transportation
- ☐ 21 Utilities (electric, gas, sanitation, water)
- ☐ 98 Other Business and Services

② WHICH OF THE FOLLOWING BEST DESCRIBES YOUR PRIMARY JOB FUNCTION? (check one only)
Corporate Management/Staff
- ☐ 01 Executive Management (President, Chair, CEO, CFO, Owner, Partner, Principal)
- ☐ 02 Finance/Administrative Management (VP/Director/ Manager/Controller, Purchasing, Administration)
- ☐ 03 Sales/Marketing Management (VP/Director/Manager)
- ☐ 04 Computer Systems/Operations Management (CIO/VP/Director/ Manager MIS, Operations)
IS/IT Staff
- ☐ 05 Systems Development/ Programming Management
- ☐ 06 Systems Development/ Programming Staff
- ☐ 07 Consulting
- ☐ 08 DBA/Systems Administrator
- ☐ 09 Education/Training
- ☐ 10 Technical Support Director/Manager
- ☐ 11 Other Technical Management/Staff
- ☐ 98 Other

③ WHAT IS YOUR CURRENT PRIMARY OPERATING PLATFORM? (select all that apply)
- ☐ 01 Digital Equipment UNIX
- ☐ 02 Digital Equipment VAX VMS
- ☐ 03 HP UNIX
- ☐ 04 IBM AIX
- ☐ 05 IBM UNIX
- ☐ 06 Java
- ☐ 07 Linux
- ☐ 08 Macintosh
- ☐ 09 MS-DOS
- ☐ 10 MVS
- ☐ 11 NetWare
- ☐ 12 Network Computing
- ☐ 13 OpenVMS
- ☐ 14 SCO UNIX
- ☐ 15 Sequent DYNIX/ptx
- ☐ 16 Sun Solaris/SunOS
- ☐ 17 SVR4
- ☐ 18 UnixWare
- ☐ 19 Windows
- ☐ 20 Windows NT
- ☐ 21 Other UNIX
- ☐ 98 Other
- 99 ☐ None of the above

④ DO YOU EVALUATE, SPECIFY, RECOMMEND, OR AUTHORIZE THE PURCHASE OF ANY OF THE FOLLOWING? (check all that apply)
- ☐ 01 Hardware
- ☐ 02 Software
- ☐ 03 Application Development Tools
- ☐ 04 Database Products
- ☐ 05 Internet or Intranet Products
- 99 ☐ None of the above

⑤ IN YOUR JOB, DO YOU USE OR PLAN TO PURCHASE ANY OF THE FOLLOWING PRODUCTS? (check all that apply)
Software
- ☐ 01 Business Graphics
- ☐ 02 CAD/CAE/CAM
- ☐ 03 CASE
- ☐ 04 Communications
- ☐ 05 Database Management
- ☐ 06 File Management
- ☐ 07 Finance
- ☐ 08 Java
- ☐ 09 Materials Resource Planning
- ☐ 10 Multimedia Authoring
- ☐ 11 Networking
- ☐ 12 Office Automation
- ☐ 13 Order Entry/Inventory Control
- ☐ 14 Programming
- ☐ 15 Project Management
- ☐ 16 Scientific and Engineering
- ☐ 17 Spreadsheets
- ☐ 18 Systems Management
- ☐ 19 Workflow

Hardware
- ☐ 20 Macintosh
- ☐ 21 Mainframe
- ☐ 22 Massively Parallel Processing
- ☐ 23 Minicomputer
- ☐ 24 PC
- ☐ 25 Network Computer
- ☐ 26 Symmetric Multiprocessing
- ☐ 27 Workstation
Peripherals
- ☐ 28 Bridges/Routers/Hubs/Gateways
- ☐ 29 CD-ROM Drives
- ☐ 30 Disk Drives/Subsystems
- ☐ 31 Modems
- ☐ 32 Tape Drives/Subsystems
- ☐ 33 Video Boards/Multimedia
Services
- ☐ 34 Application Service Provider
- ☐ 35 Consulting
- ☐ 36 Education/Training
- ☐ 37 Maintenance
- ☐ 38 Online Database Services
- ☐ 39 Support
- ☐ 40 Technology-Based Training
- ☐ 98 Other
- 99 ☐ None of the above

⑥ WHAT ORACLE PRODUCTS ARE IN USE AT YOUR SITE? (check all that apply)
Oracle E-Business Suite
- ☐ 01 Oracle Marketing
- ☐ 02 Oracle Sales
- ☐ 03 Oracle Order Fulfillment
- ☐ 04 Oracle Supply Chain Management
- ☐ 05 Oracle Procurement
- ☐ 06 Oracle Manufacturing
- ☐ 07 Oracle Maintenance Management
- ☐ 08 Oracle Service
- ☐ 09 Oracle Contracts
- ☐ 10 Oracle Projects
- ☐ 11 Oracle Financials
- ☐ 12 Oracle Human Resources
- ☐ 13 Oracle Interaction Center
- ☐ 14 Oracle Communications/Utilities (modules)
- ☐ 15 Oracle Public Sector/University (modules)
- ☐ 16 Oracle Financial Services (modules)
Server/Software
- ☐ 17 Oracle9*i*
- ☐ 18 Oracle9*i* Lite
- ☐ 19 Oracle8*i*
- ☐ 20 Other Oracle database
- ☐ 21 Oracle9*i* Application Server
- ☐ 22 Oracle9*i* Application Server Wireless
- ☐ 23 Oracle Small Business Suite

Tools
- ☐ 24 Oracle Developer Suite
- ☐ 25 Oracle Discoverer
- ☐ 26 Oracle JDeveloper
- ☐ 27 Oracle Migration Workbench
- ☐ 28 Oracle9/ AS Portal
- ☐ 29 Oracle Warehouse Builder
Oracle Services
- ☐ 30 Oracle Outsourcing
- ☐ 31 Oracle Consulting
- ☐ 32 Oracle Education
- ☐ 33 Oracle Support
- ☐ 98 Other
- 99 ☐ None of the above

⑦ WHAT OTHER DATABASE PRODUCTS AR IN USE AT YOUR SITE? (check all that apply)
- ☐ 01 Access
- ☐ 02 Baan
- ☐ 03 dBase
- ☐ 04 Gupta
- ☐ 05 IBM DB2
- ☐ 06 Informix
- ☐ 07 Ingres
- ☐ 08 Microsoft Access
- ☐ 09 Microsoft SQL Serv
- ☐ 10 PeopleSoft
- ☐ 11 Progress
- ☐ 12 SAP
- ☐ 13 Sybase
- ☐ 14 VSAM
- ☐ 98 Other
- 99 ☐ None of the above

⑧ WHAT OTHER APPLICATION SERVER PRODUCTS ARE IN USE AT YOUR SITE? (check all that apply)
- ☐ 01 BEA
- ☐ 02 IBM
- ☐ 03 Sybase
- ☐ 04 Sun
- ☐ 05 Other

⑨ DURING THE NEXT 12 MONTHS, HOW MUCH DO YOU ANTICIPATE YOUR ORGANIZATION WILL SPEND ON COMPUTER HARDWARE, SOFTWARE, PERIPHERALS, AND SERVICES FOR YOUR LOCATION? (check only one)
- ☐ 01 Less than $10,000
- ☐ 02 $10,000 to $49,999
- ☐ 03 $50,000 to $99,999
- ☐ 04 $100,000 to $499,999
- ☐ 05 $500,000 to $999,999
- ☐ 06 $1,000,000 and over

⑩ WHAT IS YOUR COMPANY'S YEARLY SALES REVENUE? (please choose one)
- ☐ 01 $500, 000, 000 and above
- ☐ 02 $100, 000, 000 to $500, 000, 000
- ☐ 03 $50, 000, 000 to $100, 000, 000
- ☐ 04 $5, 000, 000 to $50, 000, 000
- ☐ 05 $1, 000, 000 to $5, 000, 000

1001